For Thy Truth's Sake

Not unto us, O LORD not unto us,
but unto thy name give glory,
for thy mercy and for thy truth's sake.
—Psalm 115:1

For Thy Truth's Sake

A Doctrinal History
of the
Protestant Reformed Churches

by **Herman Hanko**

REFORMED
FREE PUBLISHING
ASSOCIATION
Jenison, Michigan

Book design by Jeff Steenholdt

Reformed Free Publishing Association
1894 Georgetown Center Dr.
Jenison, MI 49428
www.rfpa.org
mail@rfpa.org
616-457-5970

ISBN: 0-916206-61-0
ISBN: 978-1-944555-61-0 (hardcover)
ISBN: 978-1-944555-62-7 (ebook)
LCCN: 99-80028

Dedicated to
the memory of

Rev. Herman Hoeksema,
the spiritual father of the
Protestant Reformed Churches,
who, with Paul, could say:

*"My little children,
of whom I travail in birth again
until Christ be formed in you."*
(Galatians 4:19)

Contents

Editors' Foreword

With a great deal of excitement and enthusiasm we welcome this new book on the doctrinal history of the Protestant Reformed Churches in America (PRC). Commissioned for the seventy-fifth anniversary of these churches, to be observed in June 2000, it is a work that records and celebrates the mighty work of our faithful covenant God in giving, preserving, developing, and proclaiming the truth of His absolute sovereignty and particular grace in Jesus Christ. Throughout, the theme is sounded, "God alone is worthy to be thanked and praised for all that the PRC are and have!" Such is a fitting note for such a book and for such an anniversary.

This is a significant book. It covers the seventy-five years of Protestant Reformed history. It treats the major controversies in the history of the churches, the first of which led to their origin, the second to their further distinctiveness in the Reformed church world. It lays out the major doctrines inherited and developed by the PRC as God used them to contribute to the enriching and strengthening of the Reformed faith. Along the way the joys and the sorrows, the temptations and the triumphs, the struggles and the sins, are revealed with simple forthrightness. Yet this is no provincial work. In recording this history the book also pays tribute to the work of God through His church in the past. All who love the truth will delight in the account of this heritage.

In many areas the book breaks new ground. This is especially true of Part Three. It brings together material, such as the doctrine of the antithesis, that was previously scattered throughout other Protestant Reformed sources. It introduces doctrines heretofore not treated systematically (the doctrine of miracles and the organic conception in Protestant Reformed doctrine). Besides, the book goes into historical detail not found elsewhere in Protestant Reformed literature.

The author is well-qualified to write such a doctrinal history of the PRC. Not only has Professor Hanko taught the history of dogma in the Theological School of the PRC, but he has also lived through and been a part of much of Protestant Reformed history. He was born and raised in the denomination. He was catechized in the truths of which he writes. He lived through the controversy of 1953. He has seen the churches develop in the truth of God's Word. He has taught these doctrines in the seminary and preached them in the churches. He has personally defended the truths of sovereign grace. These truths have been the air he has breathed and the food he has digested. The faith once for all delivered to the saints that he presents is *his* faith.

This also means the author is "biased" in favor of the history and doctrines of which he writes. He writes with a sympathetic pen. That will be evident to any reader. Yet that is not stating the matter strongly enough. Professor Hanko writes with genuine love for the PRC and with fervor for the doctrines they hold dear. He believes these truths with all his heart and has zeal for their defense and preservation. It is his conviction that the history of the PRC is part of the great history of God's truth throughout the ages. Clearly portrayed is the author's passion to see these truths acknowledged and accepted by *all* who read the book. We are glad to see this emphasis.

The reader is urged to give *For Thy Truth's Sake* his careful attention. It is not an "easy read" as books go today. You will have to put your thinking cap on, as Herman Hoeksema used to say. But if you read it in humble faith, desiring to be reminded of God's amazing grace and covenant faithfulness and longing to grow in the knowledge of church history and of the truth, you will be richly rewarded. Let Protestant Reformed members read it and grow in appreciation for their denomination and her doctrines. Let other readers give this book a fair hearing, evaluating it in the light of the history, and, of course, Scripture and the confessions.

May the Lord of the church be pleased to use this writing for the humble and thankful celebration of the PRC. And may He be pleased to bless it for the continued maintenance, development, and promotion of His sovereign, particular grace!

Rev. Charles J. Terpstra
Don Doezema

$\mathcal{P}$reface

The 1997 synod of the Protestant Reformed Churches, in making plans for the commemoration of the denomination's seventy-fifth anniversary, authorized the writing of a book on the doctrinal history of those churches. Emphasis was put on the word "doctrinal." Herman Hoeksema's long-out-of-print *Protestant Reformed Churches in America* dealt with the history of the common grace controversy in 1924–1925. Gertrude Hoeksema's *A Watered Garden* brought the history of the PRC up to date. *Ready to Give an Answer*, a recent publication of the Reformed Free Publishing Association, gives, in addition to a brief background-history of the controversies in 1924–1925 and 1953, a question-and-answer treatment of the doctrinal issues involved. But that treatment was brief and was restricted to the issues directly related to those controversies. Something more in the area of the doctrine of the PRC was needed.

More particularly, something was needed which answers this question: What is the PRC's *raison d'etre* (reason for existence) as a separate denomination among the proliferation of denominations in America today? What are the doctrinal distinctives that set them apart from other churches—also those in the Reformed tradition? And—a question not to be treated lightly—what effect did the controversies of the 1920s and 1950s have on the life and calling of the PRC?

The watchword in today's ecclesiastical scene is "tolerance," and ecumenism has considerable influence on the thinking and actions of countless churches. Those who hold membership in the PRC ought to be very clear on why the denomination insists on maintaining its own identity, and why membership in this denomination is important. This is especially true as the PRC celebrate their seventy-fifth anniversary.

While the book, written for an anniversary celebration, is intended primarily for those of the PRC, we hope and

pray that others may be curious enough and /or sufficiently
interested to want to read what we stand for as churches.
Perhaps they will wonder about that small denomination
which insists on doctrinal integrity as one of its chief virtues.
Perhaps there will be those who are curious as to what the
PRC have been doing all these seventy-five years. And if
others read the book, it is our hope and prayer that they
will also see that in it God's glory is the one important truth
than which there is none greater. And, God willing, the book
might show them that this is what the PRC desire above all
else.

I consider it to be a distinct honor to be asked to write
the book. While the writing of it weighed like a great burden
on my soul for the two years since synod commissioned the
work, it was in most respects a joyous pilgrimage, a delightful
task, and an enterprise that gave me a fresh appreciation for
the heritage which God has entrusted to us. If some sense
of this thankfulness wells up in the hearts of those who read
it, the work in preparing it will not have been in vain. If a
renewed commitment to this precious faith "once for all
delivered to the saints" is the result of reading this book, God
will be praised and the churches will be able to look with
confidence to the years remaining before the Lord comes
back.

It is, when one stops to think about it, quite a remarkable
blessing of God that the very same truths which were
emphasized by our spiritual fathers in the heat of controversy
are still taught from all the pulpits of Protestant Reformed
churches and from the classroom podiums of the seminary.
This fact alone ought to create in us a sense of humility and
awe at God's great goodness over the decades. Faithfulness
to the truth for such a long time has not happened often in
history.

The scope of the book ought to be clearly understood.
I have not taken a "doctrinal history" to mean that all the

doctrines of the faith as confessed and believed by the PRC are to be treated in this book. Herman Hoeksema, by anyone's standards an outstanding Reformed theologian, has written in his *Reformed Dogmatics* the sum of the Reformed faith as it is maintained within the denomination. Those interested in the teachings of the PRC on doctrines other than those which were at stake in our history should consult Hoeksema's magnum opus.

Anyone who has a passing acquaintance with the history of the Reformed faith will recognize that *Reformed Dogmatics* is in the tradition of Dutch Reformed theology. The PRC are Calvinistic, unashamedly and unabashedly so. But the PRC also take seriously the fact that the Canons of Dordt is one of their confessions. The PRC hold to the doctrines of grace as developed by the great synod of Dordt against the errors of Arminianism. The five doctrines of TULIP are total depravity, unconditional election, limited atonement, irresistible grace, and preservation of the saints.

However, in addition to the Calvinism of John Calvin and Dordt, to which the PRC are committed, the churches also stand in the tradition of the Reformed faith as developed in the Netherlands, from the Dordt pronouncements to the establishment of Reformed churches on American soil. The emphasis in this line of development falls upon what has become known as federal theology, or covenantal theology. It was, after all, not very long after Dordt when the heirs of Dordt turned their attention to God's covenant of grace. We do not exaggerate when we say that no single doctrine was more dominant in Reformed thought in the Lowlands than the doctrine of the covenant.

In fact, the most outstanding feature of PRC thought is its doctrine of the covenant. If anyone would like to know what makes the PRC distinct from other denominations, or what gives the PRC its right of existence, the answer is: the truth of God's sovereign, particular, and unconditional covenant of grace.

The book is not intended to deal with such doctrines as the Trinity, providence, the creation of the worlds and man, the fall, the deity of our Lord Jesus Christ, etc. If one wants to know where the PRC stand on all these doctrines, the answer in general is: the historic Christian faith. Specific answers are not in this book.

To ignore ninety percent of the historic Reformed and Christian faith is not, however, to discredit it or even to suggest that it is unimportant. Exactly the opposite is true. That for which the PRC stand is, surely, the "faith of our fathers," albeit a *development* of that faith. The church develops the truth of the sacred Scriptures, though always under the guidance (and sometimes under the prodding) of the Holy Spirit, who is the Spirit of Truth. Its development is not like the building of a wall around a city, where individual blocks of stone are put into place as the walls rise higher. Doctrine develops like an oak tree develops from an acorn. The acorn contains the whole oak, no matter how large the mature tree may be. And even when the oak tree is a sapling, the whole tree is present. But its continual growth reveals that which is in principle in the acorn and sapling. So with the truth of God. It grows. If today the truth has become a mighty oak, that is only because the larger tree of the truth has grown from a smaller plant.

One who consciously engages in the gloriously rewarding work of developing the truth does so in the full consciousness of the faith of the past. It is increasingly popular today to ignore, if not ridicule, the confessions of Nicea, Chalcedon, Dordt, Westminster, and the "faith of our fathers" expressed in them. But such cavalier treatment of the faith of past years is a slap in the face of the Holy Spirit and an act of ecclesiastical suicide.

And so the doctrinal history of the PRC is a history of one branch of the mighty oak that began to grow at Pentecost. We are going to be talking about, not the whole tree, but only about the PRC's part in it. We are going to talk about the growth of one of the branches. That one branch is an important part of the tree. It has something to contribute to the whole. Of that we shall speak.

HERMAN HANKO

$\mathcal{A}$cknowledgements

The help which Mr. Don Doezema and Rev. Charles Terpstra gave me in the writing of this book is so extensive that I am embarrassed not to have their names appear with mine on the cover as its authors. To enumerate all the ways in which they helped would mean an additional chapter, but their most important contributions should not go unmentioned. They read the manuscript carefully and gave meticulous attention to every part of the writing. They corrected bad grammar and punctuation; they improved word order where mine went astray; they gave suggestions in many rhetorical and syntactical constructions within the manuscript; they checked the history for accuracy; but, most importantly, they weighed the doctrinal statements with care, questioned my theology at key points, curbed my exuberance where it needed to be curbed, reined in my excesses, and brought my writing down to earth when that was necessary. I am grateful for the hours of painstaking labor they spent to help the book along the way of publication.

Many judgments concerning theological matters were necessary in writing the book. My colleague, Professor David Engelsma, was always willing to permit me to test my conclusions and judgments against his considerable theological acumen and deep commitment to the truths of Scripture and Protestant Reformed theology. His help was of decisive importance.

Two of my daughters, Marcia and Sharon, contributed greatly to the book. They both did a large amount of research for me, going through almost all the volumes of the *Standard Bearer* from about 1940 on and cataloguing pertinent material. If I had had to do this work, the book would not have been finished in the time allotted me. Sharon added to the work of research the burden of reading the entire manuscript. She checked all the footnotes for accuracy (except those referring to Dutch sources) and read the manuscript for the flow of the thought. When she was still home she was known as our resident grammar whiz. She has not lost her abilities.

One other person must be mentioned who did invaluable work in the area of research. I refer to Mr. Marvin Kamps, who saved me quantities of time by reading the Dutch sources on which the first chapter of this book is based. If that were not enough, he was gracious in reading the entire manuscript and making important suggestions which have enhanced its value and significance.

I cannot overlook the contribution of my wife, who was patient beyond the call of duty through the whole time this book was in the making. She bore with my preoccupation, frustration, and absorption in the work—to the point of having to forego vacations. Around the house the project became known as "that book." Together we looked eagerly to the day of its completion. Her patience with me meant a great deal more to me than I have told her. I hope she reads this acknowledgment.

$\mathcal{A}$bbreviations

Art(s).	Article(s), as in church confessions, church orders, and *Acts of Synod*
comp.	compiled or compiler
CR	Christian Reformed
CRC	Christian Reformed Church (in North America)
D.K.O.	Church Order
Dordt	synod of Dordrecht in the Netherlands or the Canons of Dordt formulated by the synod
ed.	editor, edition, edited, or edited by
GKN	Gereformeerde Kerk in Nederland (the Reformed Church in the Netherlands)
LC	Gereformeerde Kerken in Nederland Onderhouding Artikel 31 (Reformed Churches in the Netherlands Maintaining Article 31 of the Church Order of Dordt), commonly called the Liberated Churches
L.D.	Lord's Day (in Heidelberg Catechism)
PR	Protestant Reformed
PRC	Protestant Reformed Churches (in America)
RCA	Reformed Church in America
RCUS	Reformed Church in the United States
SB	The *Standard Bearer*
tr.	translated

Illustrations

The author and publisher thank the following sources for permission to reproduce the illustrations listed.

Source Symbols

‡ Alphenaar, Ken

* Calvin College, Archives

° Engelsma, Dena

< Grand Rapids Public Library

¶ Kalamazoo Public Library

† Kregel, Lois from Hoeksema collection

§ Ophoff, Edward

+ Ophoff, Herman

** PRC, Archives

Private collections

± Slager, John and Tressa

> Steenholdt, Jeff

^ Theological School of the Protestant Reformed Churches

Illustration Numbers

1. DeCock, Hendrik *
2. Reformed Church at Ulrum *
3. VanVelzen, Simon *
4. VanRaalte, Albertus *
5. Graafschap CRC, 1849 (replica of original) *
6. Scholte, Hendrik *
7. Brummelkamp, Anthony *
8. Kuyper, Abraham *
9. *DeHeraut* *
10. Bavinck, Herman *
11. DeCock, Helenius *
12. *Religion and Culture* *
13. *Witness* *
14. *Banner* *

49. First PR Church †
50. Schilder, Klaas ^
51. PRC theological conference ^
52. Hoeksema, Rev. and Mrs. with Schilder in Wash., DC †
53. DeJong, John ^
54. Kok, Bernard ^
55. DeJong trip to the Netherlands #
56. Cammenga, Andrew ^
57. Petter, Andrew ^
58. *Concordia* **
59. *Reformed Guardian* **
60. Hoeksema, Herman ^
61. Ophoff, George ^
62. DeWolf, Hubert ^
63. Hanko, Cornelius ^
64. *Yearbook*, 1953 **
65. *Yearbook*, 1954 **
66. PR ministers, collage of photos >

PART 1:
The Roots of the Denomination

CHAPTER 1

Roots in the Netherlands

[The Reformers] did not think that reformation meant leaving the Church of their ancestors. They had no wish to make a new Church, still less to create a new religion. The religion they professed was the religion of the Old Testament and of the New, the religion of the saints of God from the days of Pentecost downwards. The Church to which they belonged after their severance from Rome was the Church of the Apostles, and of the Martyrs, and of the Church Fathers. It was the Church in which God had been adored, and Christ trusted, and the presence of the Holy Spirit felt from the times of Christ's Apostles down to their own day.

—T. M. Lindsay, *The Reformation*[1]

Introduction

History is an ever-flowing stream, its beginning at creation and its end at the return of our Lord Jesus Christ. Because history is continuous, the present always lies in the past, the recent past in the more distant past, and the future in the present.

So it is with the church of Christ. The church is a part of history. It has its beginning in the first Paradise, and has its perfect end in the second Paradise. It too has a past, a present, and a future. In it also the present flows out of the past while containing in it the seeds of the future.

---

1. (Edinburgh: T. & T. Clark, 1882), 181.

The church is one. "I believe an holy catholic church"; that is the confession of the Apostles' Creed. But the oneness of the church is the oneness of its faith, for the church is one in Christ its Head; and Christ is the full revelation of God in all His truth and infinite perfection. And so the truth which the church confesses, at any given time in its history, is a truth rooted in the past, enriched during the present, and containing in it the seeds of the future confession of the saints.

A story is told of a small church building in the province of Groningen, the Netherlands. It belonged to the Secessionists who followed Hendrik De Cock out of the apostate state church into a new denomination. On the left side of the entrance was an inscription on a stone slab which read "Man Nothing"; and on a piece of granite on the right side were engraved the words "Christ Everything." Those two inscriptions, so the story goes, made the entrance too narrow for many people in the village, and they chose to worship in the "Large Church" where the worship and the preaching fitted their broader outlook on life.[2]

Those two inscriptions, offensive as they were to many, captured the one central theme that runs like a golden thread through all the history of the church of Christ. The battles which the church has been called to fight have been in defense of those two inscriptions. And the confession of the church which, more than any other, has united the saints from every age, is the confession that man is nothing, but Christ is everything.

---

2. The story is told in Henry Danhof and Herman Hoeksema, *Van Zonde en Genade* (Concerning Sin and Grace) (n.p.: by the authors, [1923]), 13. Kuyper apparently makes a reference to the same story in *Abraham Kuyper: A Centennial Reader*, ed. by James D. Bratt (Grand Rapids: Wm. B. Eerdmans Publishing Co., 1998), 490. In his speech on "Sphere Sovereignty," Kuyper speaks of the fact that the Calvinistic credo has always been: "To esteem God as *everything* and man as *nothing*."

When, however, the church confesses that man is nothing, but Christ everything, the saints have something much more specific in mind than the mere statement. When the inscriptions quoted above were on either side of the door of a small church of the Secession, the reference was very specifically to God's work of salvation through Christ. And even more specifically, the inscriptions meant to convey to all who entered that salvation was the sovereign work of God through Christ and in no sense the work of man.

The issue of salvation by sovereign grace has always been the one real issue in the history of the church when the church was called to fight against false doctrine.

This was already the issue in the apostolic era when Paul, in his battles against the Judaizers in Galatia and Rome, fought tenaciously against any kind of salvation by works.

Sovereign grace was the issue at Nicea in A.D. 325 when the truth of the divinity of Christ was given creedal formulation. Athanasius, the great defender of the truth, made that clear when he argued passionately for Christ's divinity on the ground that if Christ were not "very God of very God" we could not be saved. Salvation, he said, is of God alone.

Sovereign grace was the issue when Augustine waged battle with the Pelagian and Semi-Pelagian heresies brought into the church in the fifth century. Augustine not only defended salvation by sovereign grace, but insisted that sovereign grace could be maintained only on the basis of sovereign predestination, that is, on the basis of sovereign election and sovereign reprobation. Yet, Semi-Pelagianism became the official teaching of Rome. That Rome adopted Semi-Pelagianism is not surprising, for Rome was intent on preserving the doctrine of human merit, and sovereign grace destroys human merit.

Though the truths of sovereign grace were hidden beneath the many layers of Rome's errors concerning the merit of good works, God restored His truth to the church through the work of the Reformers. Luther insisted that "justification by faith alone without works" was the hinge on which the whole church turned. And that doctrine, written in large letters, was the theme of the entire reformatory work of the sixteenth century.

This was the issue at Dordrecht (Dordt) when Arminianism went down in defeat at the greatest assembly of Reformed theologians in post-Reformation times.

And this is the issue in the history of the Protestant Reformed Churches (PRC). Sovereign grace. Nothing else.

But for us to go back to Pentecost to find our roots is to make this book longer than it ought to be. So I shall trace the roots of the history of our own churches back to the Netherlands and the church reformations of the nineteenth century. There too the issues were those of sovereign grace.

The Secession

The Lord brought reformation to His church in the Netherlands in 1834 when Hendrik De Cock and his consistory signed an "Act of Secession" (see Appendix A) by which they broke with the state church[3] and established an independent congregation.

The "Act of Secession" urged all who agreed with the Seceders and believed that the state church had become the false church to join with them in the cause of Christ. This plea was heard by thousands, and the churches of the Secession grew rapidly.

De Cock was not the only pastor involved in the Secession movement. With him were several others: H. P. Scholte, who later moved with his congregation to Pella, Iowa; A. Van Raalte, who emigrated with a number of people to Holland,

---

3. This state church was called De Hervormde Kerk, and it still exists in the Netherlands.

Michigan; S. Van Velzen, who really was the theologian of
the movement; and A. Brummelkamp.[4]

De Cock had not been a staunch and unwavering defender
of sovereign grace when he began his ministry. He was a
product of the schools operated by the state church, and he
was, in effect, a modernist. But God providentially brought
various influences to bear on him. He was influenced by the
"Scholte Club" while in university; he was moved by some
colleagues to read Calvin's *Institutes of the Christian Religion*
and the Canons of Dordt;[5] he was troubled by a remark from
one of his uneducated but godly parishioners: "Reverend,
if I had to contribute so much as one sigh to my salvation, I
would be forever lost." By these means God led him to the
truths of sovereign grace.

The issue was very clearly sovereign grace.[6] That this
is true became evident in controversies over issues which
troubled the churches in the Netherlands from nearly the
beginning of the Secession until the early 1940s. These
controversies had to do with the doctrine of the covenant,
with common grace, and with the well-meant offer of the
gospel, all of which were to play a major role in the history of
the PRC.

---

4. G. F. Gezelle-Meerburg was also one of the leaders, but he died very shortly
after the movement began.

5. It is a commentary on the state of the churches at the time of the Secession
that a minister could graduate from school in a Reformed church without having
read either the *Institutes* or the Canons of Dordt. See John Calvin, *Institutes of the
Christian Religion*, 2 vols., tr. by Ford Lewis Battles and ed. by John T. McNeill in
vols. 20 and 21 of the Library of Christian Classics (Philadelphia: The Westminster
Press, 1960).

6. The immediate issues tended to obscure the fact that the sovereignty of
grace was the real occasion for the Secession. De Cock was disciplined by the
state church for, among other things, baptizing children of parents who were
not members of his congregation, for openly criticizing the state church for its
failure to use the prescribed psalm book in singing and the adopted forms for the
administration of the sacraments, and for attacking his fellow ministers in the state
church for being unfaithful in their calling.

The Well-meant Offer
among the Secessionists

The issue of the well-meant offer of the gospel really came
into Dutch theology prior to the Secession.[7] There is reason
to believe that it came to the Netherlands from Scotland
during the time of the Later Reformation.[8] The "Marrow
Men," who held firmly to a well-meant offer (and were, in
fact, condemned by the Presbyterian Church of Scotland
for holding to this), were widely read in the Netherlands.
Especially Thomas Boston and the two Erskine brothers,
Ebenezer and Ralph, were esteemed in the conventicles as
some of the best writers of devotional material.

Close contact between the Netherlands churches and the
Scottish churches made mutual influence inevitable. Students
from both countries were exchanged; ministers from each
preached in the churches of the other country. One such
Scottish minister in the Netherlands was Alexander Comrie,
who often expressed himself as being in agreement with the
"Marrow Men," and who spoke freely of the well-meant offer.[9]

---

7. By the term "well-meant offer" I mean that view which teaches that in the
preaching of the gospel God offers salvation to all who hear. God's offer to all
expresses His desire to save all.

8. Arie Vergunst, "The Sincere Offer of Christ and the Covenant Benefits in the
Gospel," *Banner of Truth* 63 (September 1997): 230.

The "Later Reformation" was a movement within the state church in the
Netherlands from nearly the end of the seventeenth century till the time of the
Afscheiding (Secession). It served a dual purpose: it was a silent protest against
apostasy in the state church, and it was a means to cultivate piety among those
who wished to remain faithful to the Word of God. Many, dissatisfied with the
preaching in their own congregations, met in private homes for purposes of
studying Scripture, prayer, reading of the "old fathers" whose writings were
considered orthodox, and mutual edification. These meetings were called
"conventicles." At times the conventicles became extremely mystical gatherings,
as people examined each other's conversions to determine the legitimacy of them.
Although the "Later Reformation" had a profound effect upon the Secession, the
movement never separated from the state church. The name "Later Reformation"
is really a translation of the Dutch name *Nadere Reformatie*, sometimes translated,
perhaps a bit more accurately, "Further Reformation."

9. Ibid.

Although many Dutch theologians held to the idea of an offer, some repudiated it. In fact, in their writings they went out of their way to combat this error. One outstanding example is A. Francken, whose influence continued for two centuries among Dutch Reformed people. He writes, for example,

Q. Does God then intend the salvation of all whom He calls externally?
A. By no means, God intends only the salvation of the elect.
Q. Prove that God does not intend to save all through the external preaching.
A. That would be in conflict with God's eternal decree of reprobation, in which He has determined to condemn some in their sins. He cannot intend to save those through the preaching of the gospel whom He has appointed as vessels of wrath.[10]

The disagreement over the offer which characterized Dutch theology prior to the Secession of 1834 was also to be found among the ministers of the Secession, and, in fact, this disagreement became a source of friction among them.[11]

---

10. Aegidius Francken, *Kern der Christelijke Leer* (Kernel of Christian Doctrine) (Groningen, Netherlands: R. Boerma, 1893), 246. The translation in the text is mine. This quote is taken from a section in which Francken discusses the calling. This section is important, for Francken also connects the calling of the gospel with the promise of the covenant in baptism. See also quotations from Peter Nahuys, Herman Witsius, and Wilhelmus à Brakel in my syllabus, "The History of the Free Offer" (Grandville, Mich.: Theological School of the Protestant Reformed Churches, 1989), 143–57.

11. De Cock and Van Velzen, while willing to speak of an offer of the gospel in the sense of "presentation or setting forth" the gospel, rejected the view that God expresses in the gospel a willingness and desire to save everyone. Brummelkamp and Van Raalte, on the other hand, held to such a view. See, for example, H. Algra, *Het Wonder van de Negentiende Eeuw* (The Wonder of the Nineteenth Century) (Kampen, Netherlands: J. H. Kok, 1965). See also Lubbertus Oostendorp, *H. P. Scholte: Leader of the Secession of 1834 and Founder of Pella* (Franeker, Netherlands: T. Wever, 1964), 123, 124, especially footnote 16.

The Covenant and Baptism

From a certain point of view, however, the differences among the men of the Secession over baptism and the covenant were greater and more important.

Because the issue of baptism and the covenant plays such a large role in the history of the PRC, we do well to examine carefully what precisely the issues were.

It is clear, first of all, that some of the best theologians from the "Later Reformation" emphasized strongly God's sovereign grace as it applied to the doctrine of the covenant. They held to the close relation between election and the covenant, teaching that God's covenant was established only with the elect. They maintained that, because the covenant was a covenant of grace, it was a unilateral (one-sided) covenant, that is, established and maintained by God alone without any conditions that man must fulfill. And they insisted that the demands of faith and conversion in the covenant were not conditions, but gracious promises.[12]

The men of the Secession followed their lead. They too were convinced that God's covenant was established with the elect only; and, in fact, they maintained strongly that God included in His covenant only the elect children of believers and granted to them in their infancy the blessings of the covenant.[13]

---

12. E. Smilde, *Een Eeuw van Strijd over Verbond en Doop* (A Century of Struggle over the Covenant and Baptism) (Kampen, Netherlands: J. H. Kok, 1946), 29, 30. Francken, to whom I referred in footnote 10, is quoted in Smilde as follows: "The covenant of grace really has no conditions of faith and conversion, which God demands of men, because (1) The elect receive everything for nothing (Isa. 55:1; Rev. 21:6); and (2) In the representation of the covenant of grace, faith and conversion emerge as pure promise (Jer. 31:33). With the demand of faith and conversion, God presents only the order between the mentioned blessings, and the way to the possession of them, and not the right to it. Faith and conversion are gifts which God grants to the sinner . . ."

13. Ibid., 32. Smilde writes of Van Velzen: ". . . he wanted nothing of the idea which, in connection with the phrase 'sanctified in Christ' in the first question of the Baptism Form, thinks of an external separation of the children of believers

But the "Later Reformation" was also characterized by a very strong subjectivism. It reacted against the superficial faith and false assurance which characterized so many within the state church. After all, in a state church all the citizens of the commonwealth are more or less members. And thousands, while technically members of the church, lived worldly and carnal lives, but nevertheless claimed heaven as their reward because they were baptized and married within the church.

The Pietism of the "Later Reformation," finding the "easy religion of the state church revolting, emphasized much soul-searching and engaged in a great deal of discussion about the wiles of Satan, who filled people with false assurances of heaven while leading them to hell." The people of the conventicles spoke of a "hopeful hopelessness," "a long, tortuous way of doubts and tears which only rarely led to a certainty for the 'chosen few.'"[14]

This Pietism was also to be found in De Cock. It became evident in his differences with Scholte over the baptism of children born in the church. Many members of De Cock's church had not made public confession of faith because they had no assurance of salvation. But when they were married and had children, the question arose concerning the baptism of these children. De Cock freely baptized them. Scholte refused because baptism was for *believers* and their seed. Scholte took the position he did because he emphatically maintained that the elect children of believers were saved as children.

In an important letter to De Cock, Scholte wrote:

---

from those of unbelievers ..." The first question at the time of baptism which is asked of parents reads: "Whether you acknowledge, that ... our children ... are sanctified in Christ." Some, who did not want to teach that the work of sanctification actually takes place in the hearts of children of believers in infancy, gave to sanctification the meaning of "external separation." De Cock and Brummelkamp agreed with the position of Van Velzen.

14. Lubbertus Oostendorp, *H. P. Scholte: Leader of the Secession of 1834*, 84.

When I administer Holy Baptism to the children of believers, then I do this as unto *heirs of the Kingdom of God and of His covenant, unto members of Christ's congregation*. And upon this ground I pray for the same blessings over them as over their parents, and declare unto them even as unto their parents *that God is their God*. I am completely one in this with the liturgical form of baptism, and I doubt seriously, whether those who have a broad administration of the seal of the covenant, are equally in agreement with that form.[15]

Scholte also disagreed with De Cock on the question of the nature of the covenant. De Cock maintained that those born within the church and baptized by the church were a part of the church visible and were only externally a part of the covenant community. They could be said to be outwardly in the covenant, but they were not actually in the covenant until they came to the assurance of faith. Scholte disagreed. At a Provincial Gathering of Lower Gelderland on March 8, 1837 (only three years after the Secession had begun), Scholte submitted the following:

Article 8. All those who according to God's promise belong to God's covenant, that is, *all believers* and their children may and must be baptized. The believers must be recognized by the marks of Christians, that is, by *confession and walk*, according to God's Word. Everyone who shows these marks should be recognized and dealt with as a member of the church, and thus should receive the signs of the covenant for himself and for his seed. However, those who do not show such marks may not be recognized as members and must together with their children, be denied the Sacraments until their conversion.[16]

I have quoted from Scholte at length because the issues brought up were so crucially important in subsequent history.

---

15. Quoted in Ibid., 104.
16. Ibid., 105.

The disagreements on other issues within the camp of the Secession are to be traced to the views of Helenius De Cock, a son of Hendrik De Cock, who took over the chair of theology in the seminary in Kampen in 1860.[17] While first Helenius agreed with his father, he gradually changed his position and adopted a radically different view of the covenant. While he did not abandon his views on election, he pushed election aside and said that the truth of predestination was irrelevant to the administration of the covenant in time.[18] And pushing election aside in the administration of the covenant, Helenius De Cock took the position that the promise of baptism was a promise to all the children baptized, so that all are in the covenant, though outwardly, and are participants of the covenant. Their unbelief cannot invalidate God's covenant, although it deprives them of the blessing of the covenant.[19] Thus, all the promises of the covenant (as outlined in the first part of the Baptism Form) are given to all the children, though only objectively. And the baptized children are "sanctified in Christ" only objectively, that is, they are only separated from other unbaptized children by the mark of baptism.[20]

Because Helenius De Cock took the position which he did on the question of baptism, it was not strange that he also adopted the view of the well-meant offer of the gospel, which

17. Ibid., 34.
18. Ibid., 55, 56.
19. Ibid., 56, 57.
20. Ibid., 59, 60. The "Baptism Form" referred to is the Form in use in Dutch Reformed churches from the time of the Synod of Dordt, although many have adopted new Forms in the last fifty years or so. The blessings spoken of in the Form include: (1) God's witness that He makes "an eternal covenant of grace with us, and adopts us for his children and heirs, and . . . [provides] us with every good thing . . . ;" (2) Christ's assurance that He washes us "in his blood from all our sins, incorporating us into the fellowship of his death and resurrection . . . ;" and (3) the Holy Spirit's promise "that he will dwell in us, and sanctify us to be members of Christ, applying unto us that which we have in Christ . . ."

teaches that the gospel is offered to all who hear it as an expression of God's intention or desire to save all.[21]

The very same issues which were to be so crucial in the history of the PRC were issues of long standing in the Reformed Churches in the Netherlands. But what is more important is the fact that, throughout the history of these Reformed churches, the most orthodox theologians took positions identical with the position for which the PRC have fought in the years of their existence.

The *Doleantie*[22]

Dr. Abraham Kuyper, one of the most influential men of the nineteenth century, and without doubt its greatest theologian, led an additional reformation movement out of the state church in 1886. He, too, was converted from modernism while in the ministry and saw the necessity of a thorough reformation of his church, which had become apostate in doctrine, liturgy, and church government.

In many respects Kuyper's movement was in agreement with the Secession of fifty-two years earlier. Both were a return to the confessions of the Reformed churches; both were a return to the old liturgy adopted by Dordt; and both were a return to the Church Order of Dordt and Reformed church polity.

But for all the similarities, there were also striking and important differences. We need not go into all these

21. Ibid., 56, 57. If the promise made in baptism is to all the children baptized, that promise, because it is of God, expresses God's desire to save all these children, even though many go lost. So also the gospel offer expresses to all who hear the preaching God's earnest desire to save them, even though many go lost.

22. I use the Dutch word here for the reformatory movement of Dr. Abraham Kuyper. It is difficult to find a suitable English word to take its place. *Doleantie* literally means "aggrieved," and the *dolerende kerken* were the aggrieved churches. Kuyper adopted this term because he wanted to emphasize that his movement was the true continuation of the Reformed Churches in the Netherlands, but that his followers were "aggrieved" by the apostasy found in the state church.

differences here.[23] It is sufficient for our purposes to concentrate on the two issues which were to be of great importance in the history of the PRC.

Kuyper was emphatically opposed to the well-meant offer of the gospel. He inveighed fiercely against it in his writings.[24] He had two objections. Because the well-meant offer taught that God desired the salvation of all men and made salvation available to all men, the offer implied a universal atonement. Kuyper insisted the atonement of Christ was for the elect only. The second objection of Kuyper involved another aspect of the offer. If God desires the salvation of all men, He is favorably inclined and gracious to all men. While Kuyper did hold to a certain "common" grace, he strongly repudiated the common grace of the offer.

Kuyper's Views on
Grace and Baptism

Nevertheless, Kuyper did hold to a common grace.[25] Kuyper taught a grace which was shown to the reprobate only, but had the effect on them of restraining their sin and enabling them to do a certain amount of good. This grace opened the door to cooperation between the people of

---

23. They involved differences over supralapsarian vs. infralapsarianism, immediate vs. mediate regeneration, and eternal vs. temporal justification—the Secession Churches holding to infralapsarianism, mediate regeneration, and temporal justification, and Kuyper holding to the other positions.

24. See his important work, *Dat De Genade Particulier Is* (That Grace Is Particular) in the book series *Uit Het Woord* (Out of the Word) (Amsterdam: J. H. Kruyt, 1884). For quotations from Kuyper to prove this point, see David Engelsma, *Hyper-Calvinism and the Call of the Gospel: An Examination of the "Well-Meant Offer"of the Gospel*, 2nd ed. (Grand Rapids: Reformed Free Publishing Association, 1994), 173–92.

25. The terms are different in the Dutch, and the difference cannot be adequately translated into English. The common grace associated with the well-meant offer was known as *algemeene genade,* or, general grace. Kuyper preferred to speak of *gemeene gratie,* or, common grace. His definitive work on the subject was, in fact, given the title *De Gemeene Gratie.*

God and the world, and made life possible in this present sin-cursed creation.[26]

On the question of the covenant, Kuyper held in general to the view that had prevailed among the best of the Dutch Reformed theologians. In fact, Kuyper, in his insistence that the covenant is only with the elect, reached back all the way to Olevianus, the co-author of the Heidelberg Catechism.[27]

Kuyper emphasized the sovereignty of God in the work of grace, and the immutability of God's covenant and promises. "With Kuyper's viewpoint one never risks making the covenant of grace a disguised covenant of works."[28] "The so-called conditions of the covenant are never, in Kuyper's view, conditions in the real sense."[29] And Kuyper's unconditional covenant promise stood in closest connection with his denial of the well-meant offer.[30]

Nevertheless, Kuyper threw confusion into the controversy when he taught that the basis for the baptism of all the children born to believing parents was presupposed regeneration. That is, Kuyper taught that the church must "presuppose" the regeneration of every child and must continue to presuppose this until the child himself showed emphatically that he was not a true member of the covenant.

This teaching of Kuyper was to hang like an albatross around the neck of the church for many years and is still a source of confusion today.

Dr. Klaas Schilder

The Secession of 1834 and the *Doleantie* of 1886 were almost inevitably destined for marriage. Both movements

---

26. See Herman Hoeksema and Herman Hanko, *Ready to Give an Answer* (Grandville, Mich.: Reformed Free Publishing Association, 1997), 55–62; See also Danhof and Hoeksema, *Van Zonde en Genade*, where Kuyper's views on common grace are described at length.

27. Smilde, *Een Eeuw van Strijd*, 82, 90, 92.

28. Ibid., 87.

29. Ibid., 88.

30. Ibid.

were, after all, reformatory movements, and they were, in spite of their differences, a return to the old paths of Dordt.

The marriage took place in 1892, and the new denomination became known as the Gereformeerde Kerk in Nederland (GKN) (The Reformed Church in the Netherlands).[31]

The marriage, however, was never really successful. The differences in doctrine were too many and too great. In 1905 the synod was almost entirely preoccupied with efforts to arbitrate and, if possible, resolve the differences. Out of these efforts came the Conclusions of Utrecht. This document played an important role in the subsequent history of the Reformed Churches in the Netherlands.[32]

Trouble broke out again in the 1930s over the views of Dr. Klaas Schilder.[33] Both sides blamed the other as the cause of the deepening rift, and both were partly right. Both charged the opposite side with wrong interpretations of the Conclusions of Utrecht. The disagreements, however, were chiefly over the doctrines of common grace, the place of children in the covenant, the nature of the covenant, and self-examination within the covenant.

Matters came to a head during World War II at the synod of Sneek-Utrecht (1943–1945). While adopting the

---

31. Not all the churches of the Secession went along with the merger; those that did not remained a separate denomination called *De Christelijke Gereformeerde Kerk* (The Christian Reformed Church). This denomination is a sister church of the Free Reformed Churches in America and Canada.

32. The copy of the Conclusions of Utrecht which I have before me is prepared by Henry Beets, Stated Clerk of the synod of the Christian Reformed Church in North America. It was an abstract of the CRC's Agenda for Synod 1942 (Part I, Reports), giving the Dutch and two English translations, 3–12. The English translation finally selected (see Appendix D) appears in the CRC's *Acts of Synod 1942* (Grand Rapids: Office of the Stated Clerk, Synod of the Christian Reformed Church), 352–54. The PRC never adopted these decisions as the CRC did. These "Conclusions" enter the discussion at a later date, and I will reserve treatment of them till then.

33. I shall give here only a brief statement of Schilder's position. Schilder played such a prominent role in the history of the PRC that it will be necessary to pay closer attention to his views in a subsequent chapter.

Kuyperian theory of common grace, the synod repudiated Schilder's position on the covenant. Schilder was deposed from office, along with the ministers who agreed with him, and the Liberated Churches (LC) began.

These Liberated Churches were the ones with which the PRC had contact in the years following World War II, and it was this contact which was the occasion for the trouble and schism in 1953 which reduced so greatly the already small Protestant Reformed (PR) denomination.

Summary

The history of the Reformed churches in the Netherlands and in this country shaped the life of the PRC. The Reformed faith which took root in the Netherlands shortly after the Reformation of the sixteenth century flourished in the first decades of its existence. It survived the Arminian crisis and successfully fought off that pernicious error. From that controversy emerged the Canons of Dordt. Although towards the end of the seventeenth century apostasy began to make inroads into the Dutch Reformed churches, and although for a time apostasy seemed to have gained the victory, God rescued His church through two church reformations. The church reformation at the time of the Secession in 1834 brought the church back to Reformed doctrine, liturgy and church government. The church reformation at the time of the *Doleantie* (1886) gave the church in the Netherlands an emphasis on sovereign and particular grace which was crucial for the defense and development of the faith.

Through it all, however, was woven the golden thread of the truth of God's covenant. This doctrine proved to be the most decisive in shaping the history of the PRC.

The reformation in Holland, Michigan, when the early settlers established the Christian Reformed Church because of their fears of the liberalizing tendencies in the

Reformed Church of America, was also important, for it was a reiteration in this country of what the Secession and the *Doleantie* had maintained.

It is not surprising, therefore, that doctrinal development in the PRC revolves around the truths of sovereign and particular grace, especially as they affect the truth of God's covenant.

CHAPTER 2

Roots in the Christian Reformed Church

Old Dutch Proverb

In 't verleden	In the past
ligt 't heden	lies the present
In 't nu	And today
wat worden zal.	holds the future.

Early History of the Christian Reformed Church

The immigrants from the Netherlands who formed the first Christian Reformed congregations were not the first Dutchmen to settle in the United States. Over 200 years prior to the beginning of the Christian Reformed Church (CRC) the Dutch had settled in the area of what is now Manhattan Island, New York City, eastern New York, and northeastern New Jersey. Because the settlements were established in the early part of the seventeenth century, these settlers were from the state church in the Netherlands.

As more and more people from Holland came to America and as the country became more settled, the Reformed Church grew rapidly and became known as the Reformed Church in America (RCA). This denomination had, from time to time, struggles which closely resembled those which were to give birth to the PRC. The doctrinal issues were often the same.[1]

When the immigrants from Holland who belonged to the Secession of 1834 sought refuge in America, the RCA, established strategically in the East, was in a position to help these immigrants and did so freely and generously. The RCA not only provided food, lodging, and money for the immigrants, but assisted them in getting established in a new world which was foreign to them in every respect.

One could list many reasons for the immigrations which led to the establishment of the CRC, but several were chief among them.

Generally speaking, the people who followed De Cock, Van Raalte, Scholte, and the others out of the state church were the lower classes of people, the poor and uneducated. For them life in the Netherlands had always been very difficult, and the future held little hope of improvement for their families. Conditions were ripe for many to venture across the seas in search of new lands that gave promise of enough to eat, especially in light of the general poverty that characterized so many of these people and the terrible potato famine which stalked Europe.

Further, the people of the Secession of 1834 were severely persecuted by the government of their homeland because of their departure from the government-approved church. De Cock himself had to endure imprisonment and large fines, and rough and sometimes cruel soldiers were quartered in his home. Thus, the sorry plight of the Secessionists was made worse by persecution, and many determined to escape by sailing across wide seas in search of a land where they could worship their God according to the Scriptures without fear

---

1. I will discuss the issues themselves in connection with the controversies of 1924.

of mobs or police to disturb them and drag them off to prison.

Two large migrations were led, respectively, by H. P. Scholte and A. Van Raalte. Scholte settled in what is now Pella, Iowa, on the vast western prairies along the shores of the Skunk River. There, because Scholte was himself strongly inclined to independentism, a congregation was established which never sought affiliation with any other denomination, but which ceased to exist shortly after the death of Scholte.

The other settlement was in Holland, Michigan, where Van Raalte led his brave band of settlers and where, through perseverance and courage, a flourishing community was carved out of forests and swampland in little more than one generation. Out of this small settlement came the CRC.

Van Raalte himself, for whatever reasons, favored membership in the RCA for his struggling followers. He soon persuaded his followers to join the RCA, although some did so reluctantly. Undoubtedly a sense of gratitude toward the RCA for the generous care the immigrants had received when they first arrived on American shores and settled in Holland had something to do with joining. But their reluctance was understandable nonetheless. The RCA was a daughter church of the denomination from which these very immigrants had departed just a few years earlier. Returning to the RCA was like returning to the state church, which had persecuted them and which they considered to be a false church.

The doubts of the settlers concerning the wisdom of their decision were not lessened by reports from the East that all was not well in the RCA. Some churches there did not administer the sacraments in the divine worship services. Lodge membership was not at all uncommon. Hymns were sung in place of the Psalms. A certain spirit of worldliness and willingness to conform to American ways was common. It all added up to the conclusion on the part of many that they had made a serious mistake in joining the RCA.

Although Van Raalte himself remained in the RCA until his death, a number of his followers, along with hundreds of new immigrants who had followed the early pioneers, decided they were compelled before God to separate from the RCA and to form a new denomination. The movement began in Graafschap, a small community near Holland, in 1857. It grew rapidly, fed by new waves of immigrants and by internal growth.

The CRC quickly became a large denomination.

It is the mother church of the Protestant Reformed Churches.

**The Doctrinal History
of the RCA**

It is necessary to take a brief look at some of the doctrinal issues which, even before the birth of the CRC, troubled the RCA. These issues will make clear that the doctrines of common grace and the well-meant offer, which gave rise to the PRC, are of long standing in the church.

The doctrine of the covenant never occupied the attention of the RCA as it did churches of the Netherlands and the CRC. The reason for this can probably be found in the fact that the RCA had its origins in the state church in the Netherlands at about the time of the synod of Dordt (1618–1619). Covenant theology had not yet become a part of the church's theological agenda. Nor, for that matter, has covenant theology ever been seriously discussed and developed, either within the state church in the Netherlands or in the RCA.

But the same cannot be said about the doctrines of common grace and the well-meant offer of the gospel. These were issues in the RCA which proved to be of critical importance and which influenced greatly the beginning of the CRC.

Although it may very well be that some form of common

grace had been taught in the RCA for years,[2] the matter itself
and the issues relating to it came to a head in the case of Rev.
Wm. Van Eyck.[3] Van Eyck was charged with teaching that the
atoning sacrifice of Christ had a certain universal character
about it, because only by being in some sense universal could
Christ's sacrifice serve as the necessary basis of an offer of the
gospel.[4]

The synod exonerated Van Eyck and approved of his
teachings. When various members of the RCA protested
this decision of synod, the protesters were disciplined and
eventually left the RCA and formed Classis Hackensack.[5]

A certain RCA minister, Rev. Fraeligh, clearly saw the
relation between common grace and the well-meant offer.
He denied both and taught that "temporal blessings were a
curse to the reprobate," because "strictly speaking, the offer
of salvation is not to be made to all who hear the gospel."[6]

The universalizing of salvation by the synod of the RCA

---

2. Wm. O. Van Eyck, *The Union of 1850: A collection of Papers by the Late Wm.
O. Van Eyck, Esq. on the Union of the Classis of Holland with the Reformed Church in
America, in June, 1850*, selected and ed. by Permanent Committee on History
and Research of the General Synod of the Reformed Church in America (Grand
Rapids: Wm. B. Eerdmans Publishing Co., 1950). Van Eyck is quoted in these
papers as saying that common grace was not only held by all the Reformed and
Presbyterian churches, but had been in the RCA for 100 years.

3. For information on this case, see: Wm. O. Van Eyck, *Landmarks of
the Reformed Fathers* (Grand Rapids: The Reformed Press, 1922). Van Eyck,
significantly, wrote this book to criticize the people in Holland, Michigan, for
leaving the RCA and establishing the Christian Reformed Church.

4. Van Eyck's own words were: "I believe . . . that not one of the non-elect
perish in consequence of any defect in the sacrifice of Christ upon the cross, or of
any want of sincerity of God in the offer, but wholly on account of their obstinate
rejection of the mercy offered. Hence I believe that the perfect sacrifice of Christ
is the grand foundation upon which the offer of salvation is indiscriminately made
to all . . ." (Ibid., 169).

5. Ibid., 172.

6. Ibid., 179. Common grace has always been a part of the well-meant offer
package, because if the well-meant offer declares that God's desire is to save all
men, then that desire on God's part is indicative of his favor to all men. In the
quotation given here, Fraeligh referred to the offer of the gospel in that sense, that
is, in the sense that God desires to save all men, or, at least, all who hear the gospel.

quickly opened the door to other errors. Many defenders of common grace now felt free to state openly their erroneous views. Van Eyck himself claimed that the doctrine of election and reprobation, which was taught by those who had left the RCA, was a "dangerous medicine against which the fathers of Dort had warned."[7] Many defended a universal atonement and used it as a ground for maintaining that it was possible for even heathen to be saved without faith in Christ.[8] In fact, the universality of the atonement became the judicial ground for favors and mercies, gifts and works of the Spirit, given to all men. The whole world benefited from Christ's work.[9]

Those who were critical of the RCA's official position on this question and who ultimately departed from the denomination held more firmly to a Reformed conception of salvation. If we may judge by the criticisms which were made of them by Van Eyck, they indeed stood in the line of Dordt and the great Reformed theologians in the Netherlands. They were criticized, for example, for "an inordinate emphasis on predestination, and an insistence that justification was eternal because it was rooted in election."[10] They were accused of holding to a strictly particular atonement, that is, a death of Christ for the elect only; of holding to the perfect righteousness of the justified sinner; of denying that man is a free agent; and of denying an offer to all and a grace common to all.[11] The condemnation by their accusers was the strongest proof of their orthodoxy.

In later years the greater part of Classis Hackensack joined the CRC.

---

7. Ibid., 196, 197.
8. Ibid., 179, 180.
9. Van Eyck, *The Union of 1850*, 116ff.
10. Ibid., 113, 115.
11. Van Eyck, *Landmarks*, 179. The seceders of Classis Hackensack were quoted as saying that temporal blessings were "in their nature and design curses to the non-elect" (p. 206).

The Beginning of the
Christian Reformed Church

The CRC had its origins in the wilderness of Holland, Michigan. Albertus Van Raalte had led his small band of Reformed believers out of the Netherlands and away from affiliation with the Secession churches in the Netherlands to a new land of promise. This scraggly but devout band had been met in the East by members of the RCA who had given them help and advice and lodged them until they could travel into the heartland of America.

After arduous journeys, the "Gideon's band" had settled in the forests of Western Michigan and, with unbelievable endurance in the face of great hardship, had carved out a home. Because church had been and continued to be at the very center of their lives, they faced the question of their church obligations as soon as they had erected some shack-like shelters.

On the very first Lord's day that the settlers were in their new place of residence, they came together to worship under the leadership of Rev. Van Raalte. But broader ecclesiastical fellowship was soon brought to their attention. It seems as if the initiative was taken by the RCA itself. The congregations in the East had befriended Van Raalte's band when it landed on the East Coast. But soon the RCA contacted the immigrants to offer them a broader denominational church home in their adopted country. Arguments could be made on both sides. Against joining the RCA was the very obvious objection that the RCA was a sister church to the state church in the Netherlands, which church in the Netherlands had expelled them and persecuted them. Further, not all that the immigrants had learned of the RCA was to their liking.

On the other hand, in favor of joining the RCA were these considerations. The RCA churches in the East had befriended them in a time of great need. The men from the RCA who visited them in their colony were very sincere in offering them a denominational church home. The settlers were in a strange country where the bitter antagonisms of the Secession were unknown. And their own leader, Rev. Van Raalte, was strongly in favor of joining the RCA.

Van Raalte's influence on the settlers was great. He was their leader and source of encouragement and hope in times of despair. He was their preacher and pastor, who ministered to them on the Lord's day, buried their dead, comforted them in sickness, and brought God's Word to them in season and out of season. He kept their courage from failing when the efforts to settle the forests of Western Michigan seemed more than they could endure.[12]

Although many had reservations and became a part of the RCA only with great reluctance, the union did take place.[13] But it was of short duration. Unsettling reports from the East continued to trouble the immigrants. Dissatisfaction with the union was never completely overcome. And so in 1857 some of the immigrants left the RCA to establish the CRC. The denomination grew rapidly, fed by new waves of immigrants from all parts of the Netherlands.

The question we face, although it may be impossible to give a definite answer, is: To what extent were the immigrants in Holland under the leadership of Van Raalte aware of the doctrinal position of the RCA? A related question is: How much did those who left the RCA to form a new

_____

12. The documents which have been preserved from this period are, without exception, evidence of the high esteem in which Van Raalte was held by the immigrants. Indeed, one cannot read these documents without being impressed with the remarkable leadership which Van Raalte gave the colony. See Henry S. Lucas, ed. and comp., *Dutch Immigrant Memoirs and Related Writings* (Grand Rapids: Wm. B. Eerdmans Publishing Co., 1997).

13. A question remains whether the immigrants in fact authorized the union with the RCA. Van Raalte was present at the synod where the immigrants were accepted into the fellowship of the RCA, and Van Raalte himself expressed the willingness of the settlers to enter this union. But whether he was given official sanction by the colonists to commit them to union with the RCA is not at all clear from the records. See D. H. Kromminga, *The Christian Reformed Tradition* (Grand Rapids: Wm. B. Eerdmans Publishing Co., 1943), 102–06.

denomination know about the disputes in the RCA over common grace and the well-meant offer?

Van Raalte himself was not strong theologically. He was of the weak wing of the Secession, and he not only led the settlers into the RCA without any qualms, but remained in the RCA when many of the settlers left that denomination to form the CRC. He apparently did not share the concern of his followers to remain doctrinally faithful to the Reformed faith. After a study of Van Raalte's sermons, one has said: "In his treatment of 'common grace' one detects an unresolved tension which forms part of the historical-theological controversies surrounding these doctrines in Reformed circles in the twentieth century."[14] But the very mention of common grace in Van Raalte's sermons indicates an awareness of the issues on the part of the settlers. It was undoubtedly because many among the immigrants did not consider common grace to be a significant error that they stayed with Van Raalte in the RCA.

But what about those who left to form the CRC? One difficulty in determining the doctrinal position of those who left the RCA to form the CRC is to be found in the reasons for their departure from the RCA. It was apparent when the split finally came that such issues as hymn singing in the worship services and lodge membership dominated.

It would seem that the fledgling denomination, at least in principle, rejected common grace and the well-meant offer. The split of Classis Hackensack from the RCA over the question of common grace and the well-meant offer certainly underscored the doctrinal orthodoxy of the members of Classis Hackensack. And the fact of contact between the Seceders and Classis Hackensack is verified by Van Eyck

---

14. Gordon J. Spykman, "The Van Raalte Sermons," *Reformed Review* 30, no. 2 (Winter 1997): 100. This entire issue was devoted to "Albertus Christiaan Van Raalte 1811–1886–1976."

himself who, in condemning the settlers in Holland for leaving the RCA, accuses them of having contact with the Seceders in the East.[15]

At the same time, however, various views on common grace and the offer of the gospel, which were very similar to those approved by the RCA, appeared relatively early in the CRC. By the end of the nineteenth century and the early part of the twentieth century an offer of the gospel, in the sense of a desire of God to save all, was commonly preached.[16]

It appears that, while indeed the CRC in its early years was sound and deeply committed to the doctrines of sovereign grace, nevertheless the weaknesses that were present in the Secession movement in the Netherlands soon appeared in the CRC as well.

A little thought will show that this was almost inevitable.

We have seen earlier that the Secession always had a weaker side, one that was represented especially by Brummelkamp and Helenius De Cock. Their influence among the Seceders in the Netherlands was strong and widespread. It is not surprising, therefore, that as immigration not only continued but increased in numbers, and as most of the immigrants from the Netherlands who belonged to the Secession churches joined the CRC, these influences of Brummelkamp and Helenius De Cock would also enter the thinking of many in the CRC.

Add to this the fact that the CRC, in its early years, called and obtained many ministers from the Netherlands who had been taught and trained in theology by Helenius

---

15. Van Eyck, *Landmarks*, 202, 203. Van Eyck claims this was true particularly of the Seceders in Graafschap, who were the first to leave the RCA and who constituted the first CRC congregation. Graafschap is a suburb of Holland, Mich.

16. See my syllabus, "The History of the Free Offer." On pp. 173 and 174 I have quotations taken from reading sermons prepared, published, and used in those days, which clearly teach an offer. See also Oostendorp, *H. P. Scholte: Leader of the Secession*, 123, 124, especially footnote 16.

De Cock,[17] and it is not difficult to see that many of these men became infected by the ideas of common grace.

It must be understood, however, that most of the time this drift towards common grace and an offer did not come as a conscious and deliberate adoption of a view which was knowingly quite at odds with historical Reformed thought. One could almost say that the issues were really lost in the shuffle brought about by events that were a crucial part of establishing a new denomination in a new land and in the midst of a strange culture. Even as late as the beginning of the PRC in 1924, many, if not most, people had no idea what common grace was all about, and, if they had been asked to define it, would have been at a total loss to do so. The issues simply were not on the agenda of the ecclesiastical assemblies of the church prior to the 1920s.[18]

How then could common grace have become the issue that led to the formation of the PRC?

The answer to that brings us to another chapter in the history of the CRC, a chapter dealing with the arrival on these shores of those who belonged to the *Doleantie* and were followers of Abraham Kuyper.

The Influence of Kuyperians

Abraham Kuyper, in his development of common grace, had differed markedly from those views which were taught among the members of Secession churches.[19] Kuyper's development of this doctrine was motivated by a desire to establish a doctrinal foundation for his involvement in

---

17. Helenius De Cock, son of Hendrik De Cock, was professor of theology in the seminary of the Secession churches in Kampen, Netherlands.

18. When Herman Hoeksema, as editor of a column in the *Banner*, wrote critically of common grace in the last part of the decade prior to the split of 1924, no one raised a whisper of opposition. It simply was not thought strange that common grace was attacked.

19. For Secessionist view, see pp. 8–9 of chapter 1.

politics, which led to a brief career as prime minister of the Netherlands; and by a need to establish a foundation for Kuyper's coalition with the Roman Catholics in the "Second Chamber" of the Dutch Parliament that made Kuyper's election as prime minister possible.[20]

The tradition of the Secession churches was markedly different from what became known as the "Neo-Calvinism" of Kuyper. The Secession churches had emphasized piety, godliness, and a life of the antithesis, which emphasized separation from the world. Kuyper and his followers were fearful of this position and thought it led to an unwillingness to influence for good the culture in which the church found itself. The Pietists, as they were sometimes called,[21] concentrated all their attention on the church and her calling to preach the gospel as the God-ordained way in which the elect would be gathered. They had little regard for the "world" about them and rightly considered the world with all its institutions to be not only antithetical to the kingdom of Christ, but also downright dangerous.

The obvious reason for this suspicion and righteous fear of the world was the Reformed doctrine of total depravity, in other words, that the unregenerated man was incapable of doing any good at all, so that no virtue, true knowledge, or wisdom could be found in the world. Cooperation with the world in any sense could lead only to approval of the ungodliness of the world, and thus it ran the grave threat of being contaminated with the world's wickedness.

---

20. ". . . to be active in modern culture and society . . . had . . . stimulated Kuyper's advocacy of the concept of common grace, as a means both of justifying the attitude and of directing it towards positive social and political ends." Peter S. Heslam, *Creating a Christian Worldview: Abraham Kuyper's Lectures on Calvinism* (Grand Rapids: Wm. B. Eerdmans Publishing Co., 1998), 122.

21. James D. Bratt, *Dutch Calvinism in Modern America: A History of a Conservative Subculture* (Grand Rapids: Wm. B. Eerdmans Publishing Co., 1984). Bratt's book discusses the conflicts and tensions between those whom he calls Pietists and the Neo-Calvinists.

The Neo-Calvinists, on the other hand, were concerned with making culture Christian and transforming it so that all of culture would be based upon and imbued with the principles of Reformed Christianity.[22] These followers of Kuyper considered the position of the "Pietists" to be seriously flawed. The flaws manifested themselves in especially two ways: (1) the Pietist position led to a spiritual arrogance on the part of the redeemed, which manifested itself in a "holier-than-thou" attitude towards all the non-saved; and (2) the Pietists emphasized beyond reason an approach to life rooted in principle, in other words, in principles found in Scripture.[23]

Out of these charges leveled against the Secessionists arose the broader charge of Anabaptism. Kuyperians were wont to speak of the "sickly Anabaptist plant" growing in the Reformed garden, which led the church to world-flight by teaching God's people to ignore science, art, and culture, and which could, if not stemmed, destroy the Reformed faith.[24]

But if the church was called to the work of transforming culture, such a call had to have a firm doctrinal basis before the attempt could be made. The doctrine that was invented

---

22. This position had, according to some, post-millennial overtones. That is, it had about it the idea that the kingdom of Christ could in some sense be realized in the history of this present world. Referring to Louis Berkhof, who for many years occupied the chair of theology at Calvin Theological Seminary, Grand Rapids, Zwaanstra writes that Berkhof pressed for a social gospel because "the church was God's chosen instrument to prepare [God's people] for eternal life, but also to implement as much as possible the kingdom of God on earth." Henry Zwaanstra, *Reformed Thought and Experience in a New World: A Study of the Christian Reformed Church and Its American Environment* (Kampen, Netherlands: J. H. Kok, 1973), 197.

23. Ibid., 19.

24. That charge of Anabaptism became a kind of battle cry with which all opponents of Kuyperian common grace were confronted. Hoeksema himself was repeatedly charged with Anabaptism when he raised his objections to common grace. Labeling is always an easy way to discredit the position of others without entering into the real issues involved. Anabaptism is always wrong. If one can make such a label stick, one has gone a long way towards discrediting the opposition, and the need for a biblical examination of the doctrines is made less necessary.

to accomplish this goal was the doctrine of common grace.[25]

The basic ingredients of the common grace which Kuyper taught were these: immediately after the fall God intervened with His common grace to mitigate and restrain the effects of sin so that the original creation mandate could still be carried out. Thus, common grace enabled the unregenerate wicked to subdue the earth, discover true wisdom, develop true knowledge, and perform many works of virtue. Not only was it possible for the church to benefit from these excellent accomplishments of the wicked, but the ability of the wicked to do such good created a large morally neutral zone in which elect and reprobate, regenerate and unregenerate, could work together for a common cause.[26]

---

25. Here we must think of *gemeene gratie*, the Kuyperian common grace, to be distinguished from the common grace of the general and well-meant offer of the gospel.

26. Common grace "restrains the power of sin" and enables "knowledge and virtue to flower in the absence of true religion" (Bratt, *Dutch Calvinism in Modern America*, 19). Common grace sanctions human endeavor, blesses heathen culture, makes societal institutions means of grace by restraining sin, and opens the doors for cooperation with unbelievers (Ibid., 20). "Common grace came to be the linchpin for the entire transformation of consciousness Kuyper was trying to effect" (Ibid., 20). Bratt points out that Johannes Groen, minister in Eastern Ave. CRC prior to Hoeksema's coming, and ardent Kuyperian, argued on the basis of common grace that the laws of social development were rooted in creation, not redemption. The antithesis was only in the sphere of redemption; hence the Christian might and ought to operate in the same social sphere as the wicked (Ibid., 76). Groen also argued that natural law was imbedded in the consciousness of every man and that, aided by common grace in the world and special revelation to the church, it was possible for the Christian to cooperate with the world (Zwaanstra, *Reformed Thought*, 268). Henry Stob, in his discussion of the antithesis, insists that common grace did not destroy the antithesis, but that the antithesis, modified by common grace, does not make neutrality impossible. Common grace is rooted in man's creation, preserves man's natural powers so that sin does not diminish man's physical, psychological, or mental powers in any significant way, and thus "the antithesis rests upon the basis of a nonantithetical, universally shared, increated, and common grace-supported rationality." "Observations on the Concept of the Antithesis" in *Perspectives on the Christian Reformed Church* (Festschrift for John Henry Kromminga), ed. Peter De Klerk and Richard R. De Redder (Grand Rapids: Baker Book House, 1983), 248–51. It is interesting that in this book Stob also points out that the great difference is that

Immigrants who were followers of Kuyper came into this country in increasingly large numbers until they constituted a sizable part of the CRC. But the differences between the immigrants who traced their roots back to the Secession of 1834 and the immigrants who were followers of Kuyper were great. The "Pietists" were content to live their lives in relative separation from the American culture around them, and many were satisfied with a transplantation of their homeland to America. The followers of Kuyper were aggressive, eager to adapt to the American way of life, and quick to get on with the task of using the tool of common grace to transform the new culture in which they now lived.

The latter began to publish their own paper, *Religion and Culture,* and even succeeded in getting some of their own men into teaching positions in Calvin College, Grand Rapids, Michigan, even though the college had been started and originally staffed with those who belonged to the tradition of the Secession.

The division led to disputes and controversies, sometimes so severe that some questioned whether the church could long survive in its present form. But at the heart of all the controversy was the important difference over the doctrine of common grace.

It is well to bear in mind that many could be found in the church who, if not specifically opposed to common grace in any form, were at least deeply committed to the truths of sovereign and particular grace. They came from both traditions: the Secession and the *Doleantie.* That there was no active opposition to common grace on their part was to be explained by the fact that they had never given the whole question any serious thought and had little idea of how threatening common grace could be—in whatever form it was propagated.

Hoeksema, beginning with election and reprobation, defines the antithesis as a spiritual gulf between believer and unbeliever (pp. 245–47).

But Herman Hoeksema, a minister in the CRC, along with others, saw that also Kuyperian common grace posed a threat to the church. They saw that Kuyper had, with his common grace, done nothing other than build a bridge across the chasm of the antithesis, which enabled the people of the church to run over and consort with the ungodly, and which enabled the wicked world to infiltrate the church.

The two streams of common grace, one of which could be traced back to the Secession churches, and one of which could be found in Kuyper's influence, were both in the CRC.

In summing up the general doctrinal condition of the CRC, Hoeksema later wrote:

> Even before this time [1918], it must be recorded, the Christian Reformed Churches had never been wholly purged from the leaven of Pelagianism and Arminianism. The churches were, indeed, officially Reformed, united on the basis of the Three Forms of Unity as their standards, but the actual condition was by no means in full accord with this official stand. The error of two irreconcilable wills of God, according to which, on the one hand, God willed that all men should be saved, while, on the other hand, He had predestinated His own from before the foundation of the world and reprobated the others, had found a ready acceptance in the churches. So deeply had the error, that the gospel of salvation is a well-meaning offer of grace on the part of God to all men, struck root, and so generally was it accepted as Reformed truth, that it had become the general tenor of preaching and instruction, that it was openly and officially taught in the Theological School of the Christian Reformed Churches, and that denial of this evident error was considered a dangerously extreme or one-sided view, if not a downright heresy . . .

But, while such ideas were to be traced to the tradition of the Secessionists, Kuyperian common grace had also worked its evil leaven. Hoeksema went on to say:

About the time of which we are writing other evils developed. There was a gradually growing spirit of confessional indifferentism, largely caused by ignorance of the Reformed truth and not infrequently manifesting itself in open disdain of and antagonism against the Reformed principles; and as might be expected, there developed a pronounced tendency toward a falsely conceived "broadmindedness" together with the manifestation of a spirit of worldly-mindedness, that would hide behind the name of "Calvinism" as a shield. Especially during the years of the World War, of which several of the leaders of the Christian Reformed Churches were enthusiastic supporters, with its spread of much false and pernicious propaganda, its confusion of the truth with purely humanistic philosophy, its hastening of the inevitable process of Americanization of the churches, long, perhaps, too long restrained, these evil tendencies received a new impetus and asserted themselves with a new confidence and emphasis. There began to appear what may be called a latitudinarian party in the churches, a group of men that assumed a certain leadership, who opposed the antithesis, stood for a "broader" view of the Christian's life and calling in the world, and strove to bridge the gap between the world and the Church. These men were wont to speak of the urgent need of a "restatement" of the truth; they lauded the movement of the *jongeren* in the Netherlands, who clamored for something new though they knew not what; and they frequently appealed to the alleged development of a "new mentality," that required new methods of approach, new forms and new truths. This "broadminded" party, it must be recorded, did not appear to have any sympathy with the views of Doctor Abraham Kuyper Sr., until they discovered that his theory of *Common Grace* offered them a philosophy that would support their latitudinarian views in the name of Calvinism. The antithetical conception of Kuyper they fairly disdained. Common grace became the warp and woof of their life-view. "Calvinism" and "Common Grace" became synonymous. Only they that believed and emphasized the theory of common grace were the true Calvinists. And all that opposed them and refused to believe and proclaim this theory of common grace, they proudly and disdainfully branded as

Anabaptists! By a dexterous hocus-pocus, Calvinism, always known the world over for its doctrine of predestination and particular grace, had been changed overnight into a philosophy of common grace!

Those who made the discovery and propagated this conception of Calvinism were, generally speaking, the men of *Religion and Culture*, which was the name of a magazine they published and in which propaganda was made for the "broader" views.[27]

The Janssen Controversy

The issue of common grace came to a head in the CRC through the Janssen controversy.[28] This assertion is not immediately evident because common grace is not even so much as mentioned in the official decisions of the synod of the CRC in 1922 which dealt with the teachings of Professor Janssen. It nevertheless remains a fact, not only that common grace lay at the heart of the issue, but also that there never would have been a common grace controversy in 1924 if the Janssen controversy had not first taken place.

Dr. Ralph Janssen, born and raised in the CRC, educated in some of the most prestigious universities of Europe, and an extraordinarily able scholar and teacher, was appointed to the chair of Old Testament at Calvin Theological Seminary in 1914.

It was not long after Janssen began his teaching duties that his fellow professors began to suspect him of higher critical views of Scripture.[29] These suspicions proved correct.

---

27. Herman Hoeksema, *The Protestant Reformed Churches in America: Their Origin, Early History And Doctrine* (Grand Rapids: First Protestant Reformed Church of Grand Rapids, [1936]), 14–16.

28. Issues relating to the doctrine of the covenant also were discussed and debated within the CRC, but I will wait with treatment of them until the time when they became real issues in the PRC.

29. For a detailed discussion of the entire Janssen controversy, see my thesis, "A Study of the Relation between the Views of Prof. R. Janssen and Common Grace" (Th.M. thesis, Calvin Theological Seminary, Grand Rapids, Mich., 1988). This is available in syllabus form from the bookstore of the Theological School of the Protestant Reformed Churches, Grandville, Mich.

Among Janssen's teachings, the following errors stood out and formed the basis for his condemnation by the synod of the CRC in 1922. Janssen taught that the inspiration of Scripture was "organic," by which he meant that it was not verbal, but that God gave the writers thoughts which they were able to express in their own words and within the context of their own cultural beliefs. This approach led Janssen to question the canonicity of such biblical books as Ecclesiastes and the Song of Solomon.

He also taught that the monotheistic religion, which was developed by Israel in the wilderness, and the laws which Israel used to govern the nation's national, political, and social life were in some measure adaptations of the religions and laws of surrounding heathen nations.

Such a view led to various other conclusions. Janssen did not believe that all the stories of the Old Testament heroes of faith (such as the exploits of Samson recorded in the book of Judges) were, in fact, historical. He considered them to be fables and myths developed by the nation of Israel so that Israel might have its own national heroes, as did the Greeks and other nations.

The issue which more than any other of Janssen's views brought about his condemnation in the church was his denial of the miracles. He did not believe that the water in the rock at Rephidim, for example, was especially created by God, but that the water was always present. It was released for Israel's use by the blow of Moses which broke the rock open. The manna in the wilderness with which God fed the nation and which was a type of Christ was not miraculously provided, but commonly grew in the desert through which Israel wandered. The walls of Jericho did not fall by God's direct hand, but by an earthquake, perhaps brought about by the rhythmic march of the Israelites around the city.

The so-called Janssen case would not be all that significant for us if it were not for the fact that Dr. Janssen based his entire defense on the doctrine of common grace. In various articles which appeared in the *Banner*[30] and in various pamphlets which he wrote it is clear that he was simply applying Kuyper's doctrine of common grace to biblical studies.[31] It is true that Janssen, being the able scholar that he was, did this in a novel and original way, and certainly in a way which would probably not have been approved by Kuyper. But the fact remains that the novelty and originality of Janssen's position was not a fundamental distortion of Kuyper's common grace, but an application of the doctrine to the sphere of biblical studies.[32]

It is worth our while to examine briefly how Janssen used common grace as the basis for his views of Scripture.[33]

According to Janssen, Israel, throughout all its history, was

30. The official paper of the CRC.

31. These pamphlets are: "De Crisis in de Christelijke Gereformeerde Kerk in Amerika" (The Crisis in the Christian Reformed Church in America) (Grand Rapids: n.p., 1922); "De Synodale Conclusies" (The Synodical Conclusions) (Grand Rapids: n.p., 1923); "Het Synodale Vonnis en Zijne Voorgeschiedenis Kerkrechtelijk Beoordeeld" (The Synodical Verdict and Its Previous History Church Politically Judged) (Grand Rapids: n.p., 1922); "Voortzetting van den Strijd" (Continuation of the Controversy) (Grand Rapids: n.p., 1922).

32. Although Janssen's views were condemned by the CRC, his approach gained wide acceptance, and today it is not at all uncommon in the CRC to make use of critical studies of Scripture.

33. While Janssen clearly, emphatically, and specifically based his defense on common grace, it is also true, as one learns from reading his pamphlets, that Janssen himself never actually made specific the connections. He described his view of common grace in a general way and was quick to accuse his accusers of denying common grace. My description of the specific connections is, therefore, my conclusion concerning Janssen's reasoning rather than Janssen's own carefully defined position. In such an enterprise there is, of course, always the possibility of misinterpretation. But a scrutiny of the writings of later Janssen supporters will bolster the legitimacy of my conclusions. I refer to three Harry R. Boer articles: "Ralph Janssen After Fifty Years," *Reformed Journal* 22 (December 1972): 17–22; "The Janssen Case: Aftermath," *Reformed Journal* 23 (November 1973): 21–4; and "Viewpoint In Religion," *Grand Rapids Press* (April 25, 1987): D4. I also refer to Quirinus Breen, "My Reflections on Prof. Ralph Janssen and on the Janssen Case of 1922" (several undated typewritten sheets in Quirinus Breen file, Archives, Hekman Library of Calvin College and Calvin Theological Seminary, Grand Rapids) and to George Stob, "The Christian Reformed Church and Her Schools" (Th.D dissertation, Princeton Theological Seminary, Princeton, N.J., 1955).

influenced by the nations surrounding it and by the culture in which it found itself. Such influence extended even to Israel's views of Jehovah. But when the religions of the surrounding nations were instrumental in shaping and molding Israel's own religion, such influence did not necessarily have a bad effect upon what the nation believed. While in many respects the religion of the heathen was wrong, nevertheless it contained a core of truth which was present in these heathen religions because of common grace. And, while the elements in heathen religions which Israel took over had to be baptized and purified within the sphere of special revelation, nevertheless, these elements were in themselves truth. These cultural influences and virtues of the heathen, having their origin in common grace, constituted that overlapping area of which Kuyper had made so much, and in which believers and unbelievers could meet on common ground.

When it came to Janssen's denial of miracles, he applied the doctrine of common grace in a slightly different way. Here the whole question of scientific endeavor was involved.[34] Janssen firmly believed that all miracles in Scripture had to be explained in such a way that they were in harmony with science, because science and its discoveries were the fruit of common grace. Thus, when the believer cooperated in his scientific endeavor with unbelieving science, he was doing nothing more than recognizing God's work of grace in the wicked which enabled them to discover truth.

Applied to a specific miracle, this principle makes clear why Janssen denied that God created water at Rephidim or manna in the wilderness. Science teaches that the amount of matter and energy in the universe is constant. To say that God

---

34. Although Janssen seemed not to have lectured much at all on the first chapters of Genesis and the doctrine of creation, a passing reference here and there to creation indicates that Janssen did not, for scientific reasons, believe in creation in six days of twenty-four hours.

created the manna or the water which gushed from the rock is to deny the scientific principle of the conservation of matter and energy. And so, because science is the product of common grace, the miracle itself had to be explained so as not to contradict science.

It was, all in all, an amazing performance on Janssen's part.

The synod of the CRC in 1922 condemned Janssen's higher critical views of Scripture. But the synod said nothing about Janssen's underlying argument, common grace.

Synod was guided in its decisions by the majority report of a committee which had been appointed by the Theological School Committee to study the Janssen issue. On that committee were men who held to common grace and men who repudiated common grace. In fact, two men who were deposed in 1924 for their denial of common grace and who were the spiritual fathers of the PRC were on that committee. They were Revs. Henry Danhof and Herman Hoeksema. And it is not an exaggeration to say that these two were chiefly responsible for preparing the majority report that recommended condemnation of Janssen's views.

These two men opposed common grace, and they had openly voiced their opposition prior to the resolution of the Janssen case. It was known throughout the churches that they disagreed fundamentally with Kuyper's and Janssen's position.

Yet the issue was not mentioned in the report of the committee, either in the Majority Report or the Minority Report. This is somewhat puzzling, but can, perhaps, be explained by the fact that the majority of the committee, while agreed in its condemnation of Janssen's errors, was divided on its views of common grace. And the committee almost certainly must have reasoned that to bring their disagreements over common grace to synod would distract the synod from the need to condemn sharply and unambiguously Janssen's heresies.

In any case, Herman Hoeksema himself later regretted that the CRC did not deal with the issue of common grace in connection with Janssen's views. Hoeksema wrote:

> In the light of subsequent history it was evidently a mistake on the part of the Reverends H. Danhof and H. Hoeksema, that they co-operated with the four professors (Janssen's colleagues in the Seminary who were the first to bring charges against Janssen) in the Janssen controversy, rather than oppose his views separately and from their own standpoint . . .[35]

Janssen was condemned by the synod of the CRC meeting in Orange City, Iowa, in June of 1922. He was by the same synod dismissed from his teaching post in the seminary. But nothing was said about common grace.

The stage was set for the next controversy.

Summary

Controversies over the doctrines of common grace were a part of the history of the Reformed churches on the North American continent long before the PRC came into existence. Questions concerning common grace were present in the RCA and in the CRC, although Kuyperian common grace was unique to the CRC because it had been imported to America through Kuyper's followers who had found a church home in the CRC.

The issues which brought about a separation between the RCA and the CRC in 1857 were not primarily doctrinal, but of a more practical sort: lodge membership, preaching the Heidelberg Catechism on the Lord's day, hymn singing, etc. Besides, those who left the RCA to form the CRC were in the Holland, Michigan, area and had been there only a few short

---

35. Hoeksema, *The Protestant Reformed Churches in America*, 24. By the expression "from their own standpoint" Hoeksema refers to their own standpoint on common grace.

years. They really knew very little about the doctrinal position of the RCA and had no way of finding out.

It is more likely that the issues of common grace and the well-meant offer arose in the CRC because new immigrants carried these doctrines as part of their ecclesiastical luggage when they set sail for the new world. Common grace and the well-meant offer had been a part of the teachings of some of the churches of the Secession almost from the beginning, but had become more pronounced under the influence of Brummelkamp and Helenius De Cock. These teachings were easily assimilated into CRC thought.

A new kind of common grace arose out of the teachings of the notable theologian Dr. Abraham Kuyper. It was a common grace that wanted nothing of the well-meant offer; but it was a common grace that broke down the walls of the antithesis between the church and the world and created an area of common endeavor between Zion and Athens, believers and unbelievers, in which both could labor for their mutual advantage. This doctrine of common grace also became a part of the thinking of the CRC through a new stream of immigrants who had come under the persuasive influence of Kuyper and who, with zeal and enthusiasm, were ready to put Kuyper's common grace into practice in America.

Kuyperian common grace was forced onto the church's agenda when Dr. Janssen began to apply Kuyper's common grace to higher critical studies of the Bible. His extremely important position in Calvin Seminary served as a central staging area for spreading the noxious doctrines of common grace through the churches. Especially because of the thorough study of the problem by Rev. Herman Hoeksema, and under his capable leadership, the church summoned up its courage and condemned Janssen's views. But the church did so without saying anything about common grace, the one doctrine on which Janssen had built his entire defense. The failure of the synod of 1922 to deal with common grace was a manifestation of the deep divisions which existed in the CRC over the old common grace of the Secession churches with their emphasis on the well-meant offer, and the new common grace of Abraham Kuyper which had only recently been introduced into the church.

The church was badly divided over these issues. They had to be resolved. The doctrines were too important. They had to do with the very heart of the Reformed faith. Is the grace of God particular—for the elect alone? Is it sovereign in its operations, so that God accomplishes His determined purpose? Or is grace very generally distributed to all men in the world, so that elect and reprobate alike share in such bounties? But then, too, is salvation, at a decisive point, dependent upon the will of man?

The issues had to be decided. The question whether the CRC was to be a Reformed church was at stake. Within two years after Janssen had been condemned, the CRC made up its mind. In doing so, it adopted the very common grace to which Janssen appealed in defense of his position, and merged that common grace with the common grace of the Secession churches. It put it all together into one doctrinal statement. And it made the statement binding on all its ministers. The CRC won the battle with Janssen, but it lost the war.

PART 2:
The Origin of the Churches

CHAPTER 3

The Beginning
of the Protestant
Reformed Churches

The friends of Doctor Janssen, realizing that their idol had been irrevocably cast down, and [Janssen's] foes, acting from the . . . motive of fundamental agreement [with common grace] . . . now combined their attacks upon [Revs. Danhof and Hoeksema].
—Herman Hoeksema, *The Protestant Reformed Churches in America*

Whereas the Synod of 1924, assembled in Kalamazoo, Mich., adopted three points of doctrine, which, according to our most sacred conviction, are in direct conflict with our Reformed Confessions and principles; Whereas, by the actions of Classis Grand Rapids East and Classis Grand Rapids West, we are denied the right to discuss and interpret said three points of doctrine of said Synod . . . be it resolved . . . that we adopt as our common basis the Three Forms of Unity and the Church Order of the Reformed Churches . . .

—Act of Agreement

The Shape of the Controversy

In the first section of their book *Van Zonde en Genade* (Concerning Sin and Grace), Revs. Herman Hoeksema and Henry Danhof give a brief historical survey of the history of the church of Christ from the time of Augustine in the fifth century to the time the book was written (1923). Their concern was to demonstrate that, from a doctrinal point of view, the history of the church is characterized by a prolonged struggle to maintain the doctrines of sovereign and particular grace. They point out that these issues concerning the character of God's grace were on the forefront in the Pelagian controversy of Augustine's time, were profound issues at the time of the Reformation, were the one great reason for the synod of Dordt, were the basic causes of the Secession of 1834, and were finally the issues in the controversy which vexed the Christian Reformed Church in the early 1920s.

Sovereign grace and particular grace are two sides to the same coin. One who believes that grace is sovereign must believe that God's grace is also particular, that is, only for the elect. The opposite is also true: particular grace means sovereign grace. But the negative is equally valid. It is impossible to hold to the idea that grace is common without also denying its sovereign character. A common grace is a grace that does not save and cannot save. A grace common to all men is an ineffectual grace, a resistible grace, a grace over which man has power. But the more fundamental and more important difference between a sovereign and an ineffectual grace involves a question concerning God's own being, for grace is the grace of God. Is God alone God, who does all His good pleasure? Is God everything and man nothing? Or, is man a smaller sovereign who can influence the Most High? Is man perched, be it precariously, on the edge of God's throne? Is man a contributor in God's work of salvation, and God dependent on him?

These issues, as Hoeksema defined them even before he was expelled from the CRC, were the basic issues in the controversy over common grace. These resulted in the formation of the Protestant Reformed Churches.

**Early Discussions of
Common Grace**

Although the Janssen controversy had brought the doctrines of common grace sharply into focus, the issues themselves had been discussed earlier. Not only did the differences over common grace between the immigrants of the Secession and the immigrants who were followers of Kuyper form a constant subject of discussion, but Rev. Herman Hoeksema had, even before the Janssen controversy, subjected the views of Kuyper to public scrutiny and criticism. He had, as editor of a department in the *Banner* called "Our Doctrine," discussed Kuyper's view of common grace over a period of more than two years, and he had sharply criticized it in the light of Scripture and the confessions.[1]

Because Dr. Janssen's critical views of Scripture had become known in the churches, and because Dr. Janssen had defended his views with an appeal to Kuyperian common grace, it was quite natural that Hoeksema's articles soon began to deal with specific criticisms of Janssen as well.[2] This was especially true after Hoeksema had obtained a fairly complete set of the students' notes taken in class during Janssen's lectures.

The church knew, therefore, what Hoeksema believed concerning the doctrine of common grace; they knew he denied the doctrine, and some determined to oppose him on this ground.

Hoeksema suggests strongly that the opposition to his teachings was rooted in the fact that, although Ralph Janssen had been dismissed from his post in Calvin Seminary, he had many supporters within the CRC who now came to his

---

1. The first article appeared in the *Banner* of October 31, 1918, and the last January 6, 1921 (spanning vols. 53–56). This was before the *Banner* was shut to Hoeksema's further discussion of the question.

2. These articles were written after the 1920 synod of the CRC. That synod had exonerated Janssen, not so much because it was persuaded that Janssen's views were biblical and confessional, but because no investigation of these views had ever been made, and no one was sure exactly what he had taught. Janssen had produced no public writings defending his views of higher criticism, and the only records which could be found containing these views were student notes. These student notes were finally, after careful study and comparison, used as the basis for Janssen's condemnation.

defense. Because the synod had spoken, these supporters could not very well defend Janssen's views without opposing the synodical decisions. But there was one thing they could do: they could take hold of Janssen's appeal to Kuyperian common grace and make that the issue. They could press hard to defend it, and in doing so, they could, at the same time, secure their condemnation of Hoeksema.[3]

The battle began with an exchange of pamphlets and books. Two characteristics of this early skirmishing stand out. The attacks against Hoeksema involved a charge that Hoeksema was Anabaptistic in his denial of common grace, and that Hoeksema's Anabaptism put him outside the line of the Reformed faith as it had developed over the centuries in the Netherlands.[4]

But the controversy could not remain on this level.

Hoeksema's views on sovereign and particular grace seemed to have been developed and sharpened in the years he served in Eastern Ave. CRC.[5]

---

3. "The friends of Doctor Janssen, realizing that their idol had been irrevocably cast down, and his foes, acting from the subconscious motive of fundamental agreement with the underlying principle of the instruction they had opposed [the reference here being to Janssen's four colleagues in the seminary who had brought the original charges against him], now combined their attacks upon the two ministers that had performed the lion's share of the work in the Janssen controversy and borne the brunt of the battle" (Hoeksema, *The Protestant Reformed Churches in America*, 25). Much of the historical material that follows is from this book.

4. Karel van Baalen, whose two books were most influential in the debate. They are: *De Loochening der Gemeene Gratie: Gereformeerd of Doopersch?* (The Denial of Common Grace: Reformed or Anabaptist?) (Grand Rapids: Eerdmans-Sevensma Co., 1922) and *Nieuwigheid en Dwaling* (Novelty and Error) (Grand Rapids: Eerdmans-Sevensma Co., 1923). Henry Danhof and Herman Hoeksema responded to the first book as co-authors of *Niet Doopersch maar Gereformeerd* (Not Anabaptist but Reformed) (n.p.: by the authors, n.d.) and *Langs Zuivere Banen* (Along Straight Paths) (n.p.: by the authors, n.d.). Danhof was involved in all these exchanges because he joined Hoeksema in opposing common grace.

5. Herman Hoeksema was ordained in 1915, served in Fourteenth St. CRC, Holland, Mich., until 1920, and served the Eastern Ave. CRC until his deposition, shortly after which time the group following Hoeksema from Eastern Ave. CRC became known as the First Protestant Reformed Church of Grand Rapids, Mich.

Hoeksema had been born and instructed in the tradition of the Secession churches in the Netherlands and had come to appreciate the deep piety which characterized these people. But in his teens he had found a friend who attended a church founded by the followers of Kuyper. With this friend he sometimes went to church and soon regularly accompanied him to its Young Men's Society. At one of the conventions of young men's societies, he heard Dr. Abraham Kuyper and was attracted to Kuyper's emphasis on sovereign and particular grace.[6]

From that time until his departure to America, Hoeksema became an admirer and student of Kuyper. He saw clearly that the Kuyper of particular grace stood in the line of the Reformation, Dordt, and Reformed Dutch theology. And he made particular grace the heart and soul of all his own work in developing the truth.

Already in his studies at Calvin Seminary Hoeksema was somewhat troubled by some of the instruction which he received. He had received extensive training in the doctrine of the covenant by Professor William Heyns,[7] and had concluded that Heyns' covenant conception was a distortion of Scripture's emphasis on sovereign grace and a concession to Arminian theology. But he was himself unsure what direction was the biblical one.

It was in Eastern Ave. CRC that all his thinking crystallized, prodded no doubt by the Janssen controversy, and sharpened by the exchange of pamphlets and books which followed. Especially his preaching took on a stronger emphasis of all the truths of sovereign grace.

It was not surprising, therefore, that protests against his teachings came first of all from his own congregation.

---

6. Gertrude Hoeksema, *Therefore Have I Spoken: A Biography of Herman Hoeksema* (Grand Rapids: Reformed Free Publishing Association, 1969), 32.

7. I will consider Heyns' views later.

Protests and Appeals

In the early part of 1924 various protests were filed against the teaching and preaching of Rev. Hoeksema. They came from three members of his congregation. They were later followed by three additional protests from ministers of the gospel, colleagues of Rev. Hoeksema, but men who were strong defenders of common grace. One of these colleagues was Rev. J. K. van Baalen, author of the book in which Hoeksema had been charged with Anabaptism, and Hoeksema's sharpest critic. He filed a protest against the teachings of Henry Danhof as well. This protest was filed with the consistory of First CRC of Kalamazoo, Michigan, of which Danhof was pastor.

The contents of the protests are of interest and concern to us.

If I can sum up the main objections against the position of Hoeksema that were found in the protests, especially five points emerge.[8]

First of all, objections were lodged directly against Hoeksema's view of particular grace. The emphasis in all Hoeksema's writings and preaching had been on the truth that God's grace is for the elect only. The protests objected to this and defended the position that God's grace was for all men. Because God's virtues are one in Him, God's grace includes His mercy, love, benevolence, etc. Hence, God's grace to all men means also that He is merciful towards all men, loves them, and blesses them.

The second element in the protests was an objection against the emphasis in the preaching and writing of Hoeksema and Danhof on eternal predestination. This was strange from one point of view, because an emphasis on

---

8. Hoeksema, *The Protestant Reformed Churches in America*, 34–41. What follows is a summation of the material with which the classis had to deal.

eternal predestination had always been characteristic of Calvinism: of Calvin and Dordt, and of Reformed theologians in the centuries following. But, from another point of view, such objections were not strange after all, because the doctrine that God loves all men cannot, in any possible way, be harmonized with the doctrine of election and reprobation. If one wanted a universal love of God, election and reprobation had to be pushed into the background, for reprobation teaches God's hatred of the wicked.

Thirdly, the protests, with Abraham Kuyper's common grace obviously in mind, objected to a strong affirmation of the doctrine of total depravity and a consequent denial of the good deeds of the ungodly. The objection was made, again following Kuyper, that such a view of total depravity made social reform impossible.

In the fourth place, the objections were concerned with the fact that Danhof and Hoeksema, in denying the gracious and well-meant offer of the gospel, denied also the invitation of the gospel extended to all men to come to Christ. Those who pressed the issue of a well-meant offer insisted that it was part of God's gracious love towards all men, inasmuch as the gospel offer revealed His desire to save all.[9]

And finally, the protestants were offended that Hoeksema should stress so strongly God's hatred of the reprobate and man's obligation to "hate them that hate" God (Ps. 139:21, 22). Hoeksema, so it was said, negated the basic command of the second table of the law: "Love thy neighbor as thyself."

It is clear that all the issues of common grace vs. particular grace were already defined in the protests lodged in the first five months of 1924.

---

9. While I will discuss the issues involved more specifically in a later chapter, the fact is that this question of the gracious offer of the gospel became the chief point of controversy. It was called *Het puntje van het eerste punt* ("The main point of the first point" of common grace). It is the issue around which, more than any other, controversy still swirls today.

Adjudication of the
Protests and Appeals

In the spring of 1924 the protests and appeals went to Classis Grand Rapids East, the classis in which Eastern Ave. CRC resided, and to Classis Grand Rapids West, the classis in which First CRC of Kalamazoo of the CRC resided. One can point out many church political irregularities in the classical treatment of the material, but the end result was the same: both classes sent most of the material to synod, which was scheduled to meet in June of that same year.

And so, two years after the Janssen controversy and synod's refusal to deal with common grace, the synod of the CRC was, after all, confronted directly with the issue.

The discussions on synod were long and sometimes rancorous. Synod had to recess at times to give advisory committees opportunity to work. The professors from the seminary who had supported Hoeksema during the Janssen controversy were now his opponents. The fact that many were unable to follow the debates and discussions made it fairly obvious that much uncertainty existed in the churches concerning the real nature of common grace—if, indeed, there was such a thing. Postponement of the issue would have been wise. But synod refused to be delayed.

Perhaps one of the greatest injustices perpetrated by synod was its consistent refusal to allow Rev. Hoeksema to speak in his own defense, even though the protests and appeals were directed against him.[10] Such treatment of a defendant

---

10. A protest, which was also before synod, had been lodged against Rev. Henry Danhof, but Danhof was a delegate and had, therefore, the opportunity to speak. Rev. Hoeksema was given one opportunity to speak, but then only because he promised that if synod would allow him to speak just once, he would not ask for the floor again. He spoke for two hours in an evening session in the packed auditorium of Oakdale Park CRC, Grand Rapids. A footnote to this is that when obvious injustices were being done to Hoeksema on the floor of the synod, and when he asked again for the floor to defend himself, he was reminded of his promise.

is worse than one receives in a worldly court of law and cannot help but reflect on the integrity of the synod. Nor can it do anything else but serve as a kind of barometer of the antagonism against Hoeksema.

The decisions of the synod, as they finally emerged, were rather lengthy. The first section of the decision was the doctrinal statement, with an appeal to Scripture, the confessions, and Reformed theologians,[11] and was intended to define the doctrine of common grace. This doctrinal statement was divided into three parts, so that the entire doctrinal decision would henceforth be known as the "Three Points." See Appendix B for text and proofs.

The first point of this first section was a statement of common grace held by those in the CRC who were from the tradition of the Secession of 1834. It spoke of God's attitude of favor (grace) towards all creatures, including all men; and the gracious offer of the gospel was referred to as an instance of this common favor of God towards all.[12]

The second and third points had to do with the common grace of Abraham Kuyper. Point two spoke of God's gracious

---

11. No actual examples of the Reformed theologians were mentioned.

12. The first point reads:"Regarding the first point, touching the favorable attitude of God toward mankind in general and not only toward the elect, synod declares that according to Scripture and the Confession it is established, that besides the saving grace of God shown only to the elect unto eternal life, there is also a certain favor or grace of God which He shows to His creatures in general. This is evident from the Scripture passages that were quoted and from the Canons of Dordt, II, 5 and III, IV, 8, 9, where the general offer of the gospel is set forth; while it also is evident from the citations made from Reformed writers belonging to the most flourishing period of Reformed theology that our fathers from of old maintained this view." Hoeksema, *The Protestant Reformed Churches in America*, 84. (For the primary source of the three points, see *Acta der Synode 1924*, Art. 132, pp. 145–46.) The references in this point to God's attitude of favor towards all men, and to the well-meant gospel offer are a summary of the form of common grace as taught among the Secessionists. The second and third points established Kuyperian common grace as official dogma. The three points of common grace taken together, therefore, had a twofold purpose: the condemnation of Hoeksema's denial of common grace, and the healing of the rift in the CRC between the Secessionists and the Kuyperians.

restraining power in the hearts of all men (except the elect) which prevented the full effects of man's fall from manifesting themselves in unregenerate man's life.[13]

Point three expressed synod's opinion that, because the Holy Spirit restrained sin in the hearts of all men, all men were capable of performing good deeds which met God's approval and were of use and benefit to the church.[14]

The second section of the decision was a rather peculiar one. It expressed essentially two opinions concerning the writings and teachings of Hoeksema and Danhof. On the one hand, their teachings were criticized as being too strong and as contradicting Scripture and the confessions in their denial of common grace; on the other hand, synod acknowledged that the motivation of the two ministers was defense of the Reformed faith, and that they were Reformed in their teachings, although they tended to be one-sided.

The third section was basically a series of admonitions: an admonition to Revs. Danhof and Hoeksema to be more moderate in their expressions and to submit to the decisions

---

13. The second point reads: "Regarding the second point touching the restraint of sin in the life of the individual man and of society in general, synod declares that according to Scripture and the Confession there is such a restraint of sin. This is evident from the Scripture passages that were quoted and from the Netherland Confession, Arts. 13 and 36, which teach that God by a general operation of His Spirit, without renewing the heart, restrains the unbridled manifestation of sin, so that life in human society remains possible; which the citations from Reformed authors of the most flourishing period of Reformed theology prove, moreover, that our fathers from of old maintained this view" Hoeksema, *The Protestant Reformed Churches in America*, 84–5.

14. The third point reads: "Regarding the third point, touching the performance of so-called civic righteousness by the unregenerate, synod declares that according to Scripture and the Confession, the unregenerate, though incapable of doing any spiritual good (Canons of Dordt, III, IV, 3) are able to perform such civic good. This is evident from the Scripture passages that were quoted and from the Canons of Dordt, III, IV, 4, and from the Netherland Confession, Art. 36, which teach that God without renewing the heart, exercises such an influence upon man that he is enabled to do civic good; while it is, moreover, evident from the citations made from Reformed writers of the most flourishing period of Reformed theology that our fathers from of old maintained this view" (Ibid., p. 85).

on common grace; to all the ministers of the denomination not to be one-sided in their preaching and teaching; and to the churches in general to take to heart the warnings against worldliness, which synod thought might be a danger to the church now that common grace had been established as dogma.

And finally, synod urged on the churches to make the subject of common grace a matter of study and development so that the church could come to a clear consensus on the doctrine.[15]

It was, in a way, a strange decision. On the one hand, synod emphatically insisted that common grace was the teaching of Scripture, the Reformed confessions, and the glorious heritage of the church of Christ. But on the other hand, synod said that those who opposed and denied such a crucial doctrine were nevertheless still Reformed, although they tended to be somewhat one-sided. And not only was such an important doctrine commended to the churches for purposes of additional study and development, but because common grace could easily encourage worldliness, the churches ought to be warned against this implication of the doctrine.

It is a strange truth of Scripture and the heritage of the Reformed faith indeed which one can deny without losing his Reformed character. And it is a yet stranger truth which has in it the potential for such deadly consequences as worldliness.

Decisions of Classis

The synod of 1924 had made its decisions on common grace, but it had failed to settle the matter from a church political viewpoint. While declaring common grace to be biblical, confessional, and the teaching of the best Reformed theologians from the time of the Reformation, synod failed to

15. Ibid., 84–94, where the entire decision is quoted.

deal with Revs. Hoeksema and Danhof, who had openly stated on the floor of the synod that they did not agree with the decisions on common grace, and, in fact, that they would never teach these views, but instead would openly oppose them.[16]

Strictly speaking, when these two ministers had so clearly expressed their opposition to synod's decision, synod was obligated, morally and ecclesiastically, to advise the consistories of Revs. Danhof and Hoeksema to discipline them. If the decisions were indeed biblical and confessional, as synod insisted, those who opposed the decisions were opposing Scripture and the Reformed creeds.

The issue is even somewhat more complicated by the fact that a motion was on the floor of the synod to discipline Hoeksema and Danhof, but it was rejected. By that rejection synod expressed its unwillingness to discipline those who militated against its decisions—at least its decision on common grace.[17]

This was very peculiar on the part of synod and is difficult to explain. Admittedly I speculate when I suggest that the reason for synod's refusal to discipline was rooted in some uncertainty on synod's part that common grace was indeed the teaching of Scripture. Perhaps a majority were sufficiently doubtful and so hesitated to do anything as serious as discipline.

While surely only a suggestion, the idea is supported by two considerations. In the first place, in its very lengthy decisions on common grace, the synod had also commended the whole doctrine to the churches for further study and reflection. Synod did so in the hope that such study would, in a few years, "lead to a consensus of opinion in this matter, and thus it will gradually prepare the way in our churches for a united confession concerning Common Grace."[18]

---

16. Ibid., 88, 89, 94–96.
17. Ibid., 78, 79.
18. Ibid., 92–94.

Secondly, a hesitation can be detected on the part of synod in its decision that the ministers who repudiated common grace were, after all, fundamentally Reformed, even if they had a certain tendency towards one-sidedness.[19] An ecclesiastical body does not quickly discipline one whom the body itself calls Reformed.

In the line of synod's hesitancy or equivocation, it is not surprising that the ministers involved interpreted synod's decisions to mean that, while the churches had officially expressed themselves on common grace, members of the church were still permitted to hold to their own views and express publicly their opposition to these doctrines.

But that interpretation soon brought trouble for Hoeksema and Danhof.

Within the Eastern Ave. congregation people were under discipline. The synod had also failed to resolve that problem.

It is all rather complicated, and I shall have to be brief in describing what happened.

The reader will recall that protestants from his own congregation had charged Rev. Hoeksema with public sin for denying common grace. As a result of this charge, the consistory of Eastern Ave. had placed these people under censure and had begun disciplinary proceedings.[20]

The synod had said nothing about the censure of these people, and the matter was still not settled within the Eastern Ave. Church. Nor did the protestants withdraw their protests. In a way it is understandable that they maintained their protests, because the synod itself had adopted their doctrinal views and had condemned the

---

19. Ibid., 86. It would have been far preferable that synod wait until a consensus and united confession had been reached on common grace before a decision was taken and made binding.

20. It is doubtful whether this discipline imposed on these protestants was, from a church political point of view, a correct procedure. I shall have opportunity to take a closer look at the matter in a later chapter.

views of their pastor. And so the charge of public sin stood, as far as the protestants were concerned.

But the consistory of Eastern Ave. also had a certain basis in synod's decision for maintaining that these people had to withdraw their charges of false doctrine against their pastor. The synod had very clearly refused to discipline Rev. Hoeksema for any sin; and the synod had, in fact, said of him that he was "Reformed."

So an impossible dilemma confronted the congregation of Eastern Ave.

That dilemma was resolved by classis. Where synod feared to walk, classis boldly rushed in.

The protestants from Eastern Ave. appealed their censure to a meeting of Classis Grand Rapids East in which the Eastern Ave. congregation resided and asked that their censure be lifted. The classis, meeting in August of 1924, after considering the matter, decided that the consistory indeed ought to lift the censure of those who were being disciplined.

But such a decision did not bring peace to the Eastern Ave. congregation any more than the synodical decisions, for the charges of false doctrine were not retracted. And so a special classis meeting was called in November to deal further with the matter.

In the meantime, Revs. Hoeksema and Danhof had become the editors of a new paper which they called the *Standard Bearer,* and in which they were free to publish their views and give their reasons for their doctrinal opposition to common grace.[21] The *Standard Bearer* contained attacks against the doctrine of common grace, yet the defenders of common grace took the opportunity to force, upon pain of discipline, the doctrine of common grace on those who opposed it. The classis decided, not only that the discipline

---

21. This magazine, still published today more than seventy-five years later, became an important instrument in the doctrinal development of the PRC.

of the protesting members had to be lifted, but that the officebearers (elders and minister) in Eastern Ave. had to express agreement with common grace.[22]

The classis adjourned till December to give the consistory and minister of Eastern Ave. opportunity to comply. When, at the December meeting, the elders and the minister informed classis that they could not in good conscience comply with the classical demands, classis made its final decisions.

The classis suspended and then deposed Rev. Herman Hoeksema from his office of minister of the gospel in the Christian Reformed denomination; and the classis declared the elders of the Eastern Ave. congregation outside of the denomination because of their sin of insubordination.[23]

The Beginning of the Protestant Reformed Churches

The Protestant Reformed Churches really had their beginning with these decisions of Classis Grand Rapids East.

The actions of this classis were followed very shortly by similar actions taken in Classis Grand Rapids West. In this classis Rev. Danhof resided. He was pastor of First CRC of Kalamazoo. He had, as a delegate to synod, expressed his disagreement with common grace, and he had joined Rev. Hoeksema on the editorial staff of the *Standard Bearer*. Also belonging to this classis was Rev. George M. Ophoff, recently installed pastor of the Hope Riverbend CRC in what is now called Walker, Michigan. He too had joined the editorial staff of the *Standard Bearer*, and had thus become a marked man.

Classis Grand Rapids West wasted little time. The sole question set before these men and the elders of their

---

22. For the full decision see Hoeksema, *The Protestant Reformed Churches in America,* 154–59.
23. For the full decision see Ibid., 206, 207, 225–29.

congregations by the classis was: Will you promise to adhere to the decisions of the synod of 1924 with respect to common grace? When they refused, they too were summarily deposed from office by the classis.[24]

In the beginning of the history of the PRC, matters were a bit more complicated than the above short narrative would seem to indicate. Several factors made matters somewhat cloudy and obscure.

Synod had made ambiguous decisions, as I have pointed out, and it was a very real question whether either of the two CR classes involved had the right to take it upon itself to interpret synod's decisions. It would have been far better if the classes had waited till the next synod so that synod could itself speak on issues which it had refused to address in June 1924.

The difficulty was, and everyone can sympathize with the problem, that synod met only once every two years. When people are under censure, they are deprived of the sacraments. They cannot wait for another two years to have their discipline cases resolved. Nor could the tensions that had built over common grace in the Eastern Ave. Church be so easily set on a back burner to await adjudication two years hence.

But these were not the only difficulties. It was a very real church political question (and remains such today) whether a classis in a Reformed church has the right to exercise discipline over officebearers. Classes had deposed ministers and elders. Was this right? Were these depositions right? Were these officebearers in fact deposed? Was this exercise of the keys of the kingdom of heaven, done on earth, actually sealed in heaven?[25]

Ordinarily, when officebearers, whether elders or ministers, are deposed from office, and these officebearers do

---

24. For the documents and decisions see Ibid., 230–47.
25. See Matthew 16:19. I will examine these questions more closely in chapter 5.

not agree with their deposition, they are required to submit nonetheless. This does not mean that their case is hopeless and that they have no recourse to justice, but it does mean that they must appeal their unjust deposition to a broader ecclesiastical body for further adjudication and submit while their case is being treated. The officebearers of Eastern Ave., who had been deposed by classis, under ordinary circumstances should have submitted and appealed their cases to synod. That is, they should temporarily have laid aside their duties, acquiesced in what classis did, and, appealing to synod, plead with synod for righteous judgment. But in this case that was not so easy to do; nor was it necessarily wise.

In the first place, the deposition was terribly unjust by all standards of Reformed church polity. The officebearers could confidently believe that classis had stepped outside its God-given jurisdiction and that heaven had not sealed the discipline done on earth.

Secondly, the pastors and elders who were deposed served in congregations, two of them very large, in which most of the members were as displeased with the decisions of the classes as the officebearers were. If the officebearers had ceased their work, all these hundreds of people would have been like sheep without a shepherd.

Undoubtedly, the classes would somehow have appointed others to take the places of the deposed ministers, but these others would have been men who themselves believed in common grace, and who themselves agreed with the unjust depositions which classes had perpetrated. The end would have been bitter indeed, for faithful shepherds would have been turning over their sheep to the care of men who had proved to be unscrupulous. While two years would go by, their congregations would be turned over to others while they sat passively waiting for a body who could adjudicate their claims.

There was one other alternative. And that was the one they took.

The officebearers repudiated the unjust and wrong decisions of the classes and continued to function in their offices in order to care for the needs of their congregations.

But such a course of action as Hoeksema, Ophoff, and Danhof chose to take had its own price to pay. By refusing to submit to the decisions of the classes and by continuing to function in their offices, the consistories and ministers involved were separating themselves from the denomination which they had previously served.[26]

It is true that when the three congregations banded together to form in effect what was a new denomination, they called themselves "Protesting Christian Reformed Churches." They did this as long as their protests were still pending with the synod.

It is also true that, strictly speaking, by leaving the CRC and forming a new denomination, they had lost their right of appeal to the synod of 1926. They were fully aware of this, because, before the synod of 1926 met, they had already signed an "Act of Agreement" on March 6, 1925, which made them a denomination with a separate identity (see Appendix C).

They maintained their appeals to give the CRC one more opportunity to repent of its terrible sins. The CRC did not listen. The appeals were rejected.

The "Act of Agreement" was an important document.[27] The document joined the three churches in a repudiation of the doctrinal errors of common grace and the church

---

26. This is a perfectly proper thing to do and in keeping with Reformed church polity. When one believes before God and the church that decisions have been made which are contrary to God's Word, he may, without ecclesiastical penalty, leave that church. The final adjudication will take place in the judgment day before the face of Christ.

27. For the full text see Hoeksema, *The Protestant Reformed Churches in America*, 256, 257.

political errors of classes' unrighteous depositions. It united the three churches on the common basis of the three confessions of the Reformed churches,[28] and it united them in the common task of deciding matters of mutual interest and getting on with the important work of church reformation.

Such was the humble beginning of the Protestant Reformed Churches.

Summary

God's providence works in mysterious ways, for, as the Lord Himself said through Isaiah His servant: "My thoughts are not your thoughts, neither are your ways my ways" (55:8). The formation of the PRC came about through these mysterious ways.

It was not surprising that those in the CRC who were in agreement with Dr. Janssen should turn their wrath upon Herman Hoeksema, for he was the leading figure in the forces which opposed Janssen and sought his condemnation. Nor is it surprising that these supporters of Dr. Janssen should use the issue of common grace to secure Rev. Hoeksema's condemnation. Everyone in the church knew that Hoeksema opposed common grace. He had expressed his dissatisfaction with the doctrine in the *Banner*.

It was something of a surprise that the four professors in the seminary who had brought the original complaint against Janssen[29] and who had sought Hoeksema's help should now turn against him. One may argue that, from the very beginning of the Janssen case, these four professors were,

---

28. The Confession of Faith, the Heidelberg Catechism, and the Canons of Dordt. Reproduced in "Three Forms of Unity" (n.p., Mission Committee of the Protestant Reformed Churches in America, 1991). These confessions had, of course, been the creedal basis of the CRC. But the three congregations were convinced that the decisions on common grace were contrary to all that was taught in the creeds.

29. Professors Louis Berkhof, William Heyns, Samuel Volbeda, and Foppe Ten Hoor.

on the whole, supporters of common grace, and that, now that the doctrine became an issue in the churches, they were conscience bound to defend it. But two considerations must be taken into account. The first is that Janssen himself was not sure whether all the four professors believed common grace and expressed doubts about their commitment to the doctrine which was the cornerstone of his defense. But in the second place, the four professors knew full well, as did the rest of the church, what Hoeksema's views on common grace were. Their knowledge that Hoeksema denied common grace did not prevent them from securing his help when they needed it in their opposition to Janssen. It is surprising, then, that they should now seek his condemnation.

It is also strange that the synod of the CRC should adopt a doctrinal statement about a doctrine over which there was so much disagreement and which had not really risen out of the life of the churches. It would have been better if synod had postponed decisions on the matter and given time for discussion and debate so as to arrive at a mature decision. But all the activities of synod, as well as Classes Grand Rapids East and West have the air about them of haste. On the classical level the need for haste seemed even more urgent than on the synodical. Even though synod had hesitated over discipline, the classis was not to be deterred in its determination to bring the issues to a head and rid the churches of those who opposed common grace.

From several points of view, it seems as if the establishment of the PRC was premature. But the issue was forced, and one can only say that behind it was the hand of God, who directs all things according to His eternal purpose, and for the good of the church which He loves.

This must be our conclusion as we consider the beginning of the PRC.

CHAPTER 4

Common Grace or Particular Grace

[Our calling is] to preserve the truth that the grace of God is always particular, to defend that truth with all our power, to develop it in all its riches, to impart it to the generation to come, and to give testimony outside of the pale of our churches of that very truth in word and in deed, in the midst of the church and in the midst of the world.
—Herman Hoeksema, *The Protestant Reformed Churches: 25th Anniversary 1925–1950*

Introduction

When Herman Hoeksema attempted to find one doctrine which, more than any other, defined the beginning of the PRC, he found it in the truth of the particular grace of God. That issue stood out clearly in 1925 when the PRC began. It remains a distinguishing mark of the churches today. Those who teach that grace is not particular, but common, believe that God's grace is shown to all men. The PRC believe that Scripture and the Reformed confessions teach that God's grace is for His people only and that the wicked never receive so much as an ounce of grace.

To many, the issue may not seem important. But the issue is a crucial one which ultimately involves the whole truth of God's Word. It involves directly such other doctrines as the sovereignty of God in the work of salvation, the extent of the atoning sacrifice of Jesus Christ, the free will of man, and even the truth of God Himself. This latter is demonstrated by an event which took place on the floor of the synod of 1924 which adopted the Three Points. In the course of the debate, the president of the synod, Rev. I. Van Dellen, made the following remarks: "I cannot refute all heretics, even my own brother who is a Baptist. But my Reformed antennae tell me that Danhof and Hoeksema proceed from a wrong idea of God, and that therefore their doctrine is dangerous for our churches to consider."[1]

Yes, even the nature and being of God are involved in this matter. The president of the synod was correct. The question was and is: Who is God and what kind of God is He?

Grace for All

The very name "common grace" indicates that those who hold to this view believe that the grace of God is "common" or general, that is, that grace is for all men. God shows His grace to all men without exception. This is what the CRC approved as official doctrine when it adopted the three points of common grace.

Because the grace of God is God's favor and blessing, God is favorably disposed to all men. He looks with kindness and good will upon all men without distinction. He is favorably disposed to every one. His face smiles with pleasure towards all. But, because God's attributes are all one, the attribute of grace includes many other attributes, which the defenders of common grace used at random and as being synonymous with grace. They spoke of God's benevolence and kindness, of God's love and mercy, of God's goodness and lovingkindness—all in the same breath, as it were. All these attributes of God are shown to all men without distinction.

It is true that those who taught these views did not believe that these attributes are saving, though they are called by the

---

1. Henry Danhof, "God Is God" *SB* 1, no. 1 (October 1924): 4.

same names as those attributes which God shows towards His people. They are temporal blessings which end when the wicked die and which become, after death, nothing but the horror of eternal punishment in hell. But they are blessings indeed.

The blessings of God upon all men are of various kinds, according to those who held these views. They include the good things of the creation: rain, sunshine, plentiful harvests, prosperity, health, a good family, and all such things as are pleasant and to be desired in this world.

Included also in the favor and love which God shows to all men is a certain postponement of judgment. God does not immediately send His curses upon the wicked, even though they deserve it. He gives them instead many years in which they are relatively free from these curses. He postpones until the day of their death the dark clouds of judgment in which the storms of His anger break upon them.

Various texts were appealed to in support of this view, chiefly texts which speak of God's good gifts to men.[2] By interpreting texts which speak of God's good gifts to men in such a way that they taught God's grace to all, the synod identified good gifts with grace, as if the two were identical.

The good gifts which God gives to men were clearly designated as non-saving gifts. But this did not mean that they are to be considered as unrelated to salvation. They are inseparably connected to the work of salvation and have as their goal the salvation of all those who receive such gifts. Herman Bavinck, for example, spoke of common grace preparing the heathen for the reception of the gospel.[3] And,

---

2. See Matthew 5:45; Acts 14:17; Psalm 145:9.

3. "It is common grace which makes special grace possible, prepares the way for it, and later supports it; and special grace, in its turn, leads common grace up to its own level and puts it into its service. Both revelations, finally, have as their purpose the preservation of the human race, the first by sustaining it, and the second by redeeming it, and both in this way serve the end of glorifying all of God's excellencies." Herman Bavinck, *Our Reasonable Faith*, tr. by Henry Zylstra from the

in fact, part of common grace, which is, according to CRC theologians, an aid to salvation, is the common grace of general revelation. God reveals Himself to all men in creation as a preparation for the preaching of the gospel.[4]

Grace in the Offer

More explicitly, common grace was connected with God's work of salvation in the well-meant offer of the gospel, of which the first point made mention. In fact, the first point appealed to the well-meant offer of the gospel as an evidence of God's favor and grace towards all men.

The point is important enough to take special note of it. The well-meant offer of the gospel means that God desires and intends to save all who hear the gospel. That desire of God is God's common grace, or general attitude of favor to all. But common grace itself cannot save. Nevertheless, though it cannot save, it is indicative of God's intent to save all who hear.

If one investigates the writings of the theologians of the CRC, he discovers that this grace which comes to all men through the preaching of the gospel means three things. It means, first of all, that God expresses His own personal desire and will to save all who hear the gospel. He wants every one to know that, for His part, He longs for their salvation.

This idea of a gracious offer of the gospel was reaffirmed by the CRC at its synod of 1926 when the protests of Revs. Danhof and Hoeksema were considered. The synod affirmed "a goodness or grace of God in causing to go forth a well-meaning offer of salvation to all to whom the preaching of the gospel comes," as well as of a "certain grace or goodness

---

Dutch book *Magnalia Dei* (Grand Rapids: Wm. B. Eerdmans Publishing Co., 1956), 38.

4. Ibid. See also William Masselink, *General Revelation and Common Grace* (Grand Rapids: Wm. B. Eerdmans Publishing Co., 1953). As the title indicates, the entire book deals with this question, but see, for example, 84.

or favorable inclination of God" which "is revealed toward a group of men broader than the group of the elect, and that is, among other things, also evident from the fact that God well-meaningly calls each one to whom the lovely invitation of the Gospel comes."[5]

Secondly, while God's desire to save every one who hears the gospel is really the main grace which God shows to all men, there is more. Many people, by the preaching, are brought up in the "sphere" of the gospel. In other words, they are brought up in a church and home and school where the gospel is preached and taught. These people, without exception, receive many tokens and gifts which indicate God's love, for they receive instruction in Scripture, the signs and seals of baptism and the Lord's Supper, education in Christian schools, training in catechism, the fellowship of church and home, and the shelter of a covenant community. These are, so it is said, good gifts of God, and, therefore, indications of God's love for them whether they be wicked or righteous.

Thirdly, in addition to all these things which the gospel offer brings to everyone who hears the gospel, one more grace must be added. That grace is the grace of God in the hearts of all who hear the gospel. It is a kind of subjective or preparatory grace which is worked by the Holy Spirit, and which really makes it possible for a man to accept or reject the Christ offered in the gospel.[6]

---

5. Christian Reformed Church, *Acts of Synod 1926*, quoted by Homer C. Hoeksema in "The Protestant Reformed Churches and What They Stand For Doctrinally" in *God's Covenant Faithfulness: The 50th Anniversary of the Protestant Reformed Churches in America*, ed. Gertrude Hoeksema (Grand Rapids: Reformed Free Publishing Association, 1975), 32 of Section II.

6. This was a view of long standing in the church, both in Reformed churches and Presbyterian churches. With respect to the latter, it could be found in the teachings of the Marrow Men, who were condemned by the Presbyterian Church of Scotland in the eighteenth century. See my syllabus, "The History of the Free Offer," 94–121. This same error was taught by the Arminians in the Reformed Churches in the Netherlands in the sixteenth and seventeenth centuries and was

When one takes all these things into account, it is not difficult to see that common grace has many implications of the most important kind. It affects the whole of life, the whole of one's conception of the truth of Scripture, the whole of one's idea of God Himself. The doctrine is not one to take lightly.

Grace Which Restrains Sin

A common grace which was defined in terms of God's attitude of favor towards all men was not, by any means, the whole teaching of those who supported common grace. Other influences were present in the CRC, and other ideas were incorporated into the final decisions.

Within the CRC many followed the teachings of Abraham Kuyper, who had developed a theory of common grace in the Netherlands quite different from the ideas I defined above. In fact, Kuyper himself did not accept the doctrine of God's general attitude of favor towards all men. Nor did Kuyper want anything to do with a gracious offer of the gospel. His common grace was for the reprobate only, never for the elect, and was only very indirectly connected to God's work of salvation.

In his earlier years, Kuyper emphatically repudiated common grace.[7] It was only later that he began to formulate a doctrine of common grace in connection with his desire to find for the Reformed people in the Netherlands a place

---

condemned by the synod of Dordt. See Canons of Dordt, III & IV, B, 5.

7. Henry Danhof and Herman Hoeksema, *Van Zonde en Genade*, 86–114. Hoeksema expresses agreement with Kuyper and even commends him for strict adherence to Reformed thought. *Van Zonde en Genade* is an extremely important book because it was written in 1923, before the PRC were established; and because in it one finds Hoeksema's basic position outlined, a position which he held all his life. I am going to be relying heavily on this book. A translation of it is being prepared for publication by the Reformed Free Publishing Association.

in politics and in the world.[8] To make advances in politics, to elect members to the Dutch Parliament, and to secure, if possible, the office of prime minister, it was necessary for the Reformed people, working through a Christian political party, to form a coalition in government with the Roman Catholics. But such a coalition had to be justified. Common grace became that justification.[9]

Kuyper himself said that no one, not even Calvin, had developed the doctrine of common grace; and he freely admitted that it was not taught in the Reformed confessions.[10] But, Kuyper claimed, it was essential for the correct development of the Reformed faith that the doctrine be developed and taught.

Basically, in Kuyper's thought, common grace was a reversal of the consequences of the fall of Adam.[11] The consequences of sin were severe. God pronounced death upon those who disobeyed Him. But, said Kuyper, it was worse than that. If common grace had not intervened, man would have become a beast and the creation a wilderness. The poison of sin was fearful.

But common grace is an antidote which God administers to man and through man to the creation. That antidote has some amazing results. It postpones the judgment of eternal

---

8. Herman Hoeksema, "Sketches on the History of Doctrine: Dr. Abraham Kuyper and Common Grace," *SB* 6 (April 1, 1930): 304, 305.

9. Heslam writes: "Kuyper and his followers had proved it was possible to be active in modern culture and society without compromise to their principles, and they had even enjoyed a certain measure of respect from the world outside their own circle. This encouraged a less hostile and defensive attitude towards the unbelieving world, and this in turn stimulated Kuyper's advocacy of the concept of common grace, as a means both of justifying the attitude and of directing it towards positive social and political ends." Heslam, *Creating a Christian Worldview: Abraham Kuyper's Lectures on Calvinism*, 122.

10. Danhof and Hoeksema, *Van Zonde en Genade*, 67.

11. For a full description of Kuyper's view, see, Ibid., 114ff. See also Henry R. Van Til, *The Calvinist Concept of Culture* (Grand Rapids: Baker Book House, 1959), 117–136.

death;[12] it preserves man as a man and prevents him from becoming a beast; it preserves sufficient spiritual strength in man to fulfill the original creation mandate to subdue the earth; it seeps from Adam to the whole of Adam's posterity and enables them to continue Adam's work of carrying out the so-called cultural mandate; it preserves the creation from becoming a wilderness and maintains the creation as a relatively beautiful place; and it enables sinful man to accomplish a great deal of good in the world.

This good which common grace enables the wicked to do is of great value in Kuyper's judgment. In an article in a Dutch paper called *De Heraut*, Kuyper maintained that common grace was more important than particular grace,[13] and that these fruits of common grace would last eternally.[14] No wonder the people of God could profit significantly from them!

The result of this massive dose of common grace was a threefold principle at work in the world. The principle of sin and its operations in man continued to operate in some measure; the principle of saving grace by which God gathered His church was also present; and the principle of common grace which made an earthly and worldly development of good possible in the life of the wicked was active. Sin still worked, but its effects were sharply mitigated. God still maintained His purpose in Christ in the salvation of the church, but this was a development in the world wholly apart from the original creation mandate and the development of culture in the world of sin. The crucial development in history took place because common grace operated in such a

---

12. Kuyper spoke of the fact that God's words, "The day that thou eatest thereof thou shalt surely die," were not a threat, but a prediction of what would happen if sin were not restrained by common grace. Danhof and Hoeksema, *Van Zonde en Genade*, 259–270.

13. Ibid., 146.

14. Ibid.

way that the whole of culture blossomed and flourished and produced fruits that would be preserved for heaven.[15]

A relation did, however, exist between the development of culture in the world and the development of the church in the sphere of God's special grace. That relation was pretty much a one-way street. The world benefited very little from the church, but the church benefited tremendously from the world. The culture developed by the world was of enormous benefit to the church. The church benefited not only from the world's discoveries and inventions, but also from its knowledge, philosophy, science, music, art, architecture, and sculpture. All was the fruit of grace. To turn one's back on it was to spurn God's own grace operative in a thousand places in the halls of wicked men.

Just as importantly, common grace created an area which was morally neutral and in which the world and the people of God could cooperate for mutually acceptable goals. Common grace, restraining sin and enabling the unregenerate to do good, made cooperation with the world a possibility and a calling for the people of God.[16]

And so the way was paved for the Christian to march eagerly into the world, cooperate with wicked men in all spheres of life, and make a social, economic, and political impact on this present creation and its development. Common grace formed the theoretical basis for a world and life view which turned the believer's attention to making this world a better place in which to live. And the believer could confidently expect that the fruits of common grace in a world made beautiful by common grace would be preserved in the age to come.

---

15. Ibid.

16. It is no wonder that Danhof and Hoeksema solemnly predicted that, should Kuyper's view of common grace ever become the accepted doctrine in the CRC, it would lead to every form of worldliness. They write: " ... this doctrine (Kuyperian common grace), if it is not opposed, will weaken practically all real Christian action and send a tidal wave of world-conformity throughout our churches." Ibid., 82.

This view was imported into the CRC by immigrants from the Netherlands who carried Kuyper's visions to a new land. These enthusiastic followers of Kuyper were eager to put Kuyper's views into effect in America, and, as I have mentioned before, they established a magazine, *Religion and Culture*, to accomplish their task.

Calvin College was to be the center of this endeavor. As one professor put it: ". . . Jerusalem and Athens . . . should dwell together in holy matrimony. These two shall dwell together in peace and harmony within the walls of Calvin College in order that the whole man may be equipped for the true service of God."[17]

One writer, in describing what Kuyperian common grace meant to the CRC, points out how Kuyperians saw common grace as both an antidote for Pietism, with its emphasis on the antithesis, and a powerful tool for cultural transformation.[18] Pietism, emphasizing heavily the antithesis, ignored science, art, and culture. Common grace, so he writes, was developed to counter the flaws in the doctrine of the antithesis, which flaws were: (1) spiritual arrogance; (2) abuse of principial analysis.[19] The power of common grace, according to this author, was to restrain "the power of sin" and enable "knowledge and virtue to flower in the absence of true religion."[20]

So common grace sanctioned human endeavor, blessed

---

17. Quotation from a speech delivered by Professor Ralph Stob, commented on by George M. Ophoff in "Calvin College, or Jerusalem and Athens," *SB* 10 (October 15, 1933): 43.

18. The reference is particularly to the Pietism of those who had their roots in the Secession of 1834, the people who founded the CRC and controlled its life for the first forty or so years of its existence.

19. Bratt, *Dutch Calvinism in Modern America*, 19. It is not completely clear what Bratt means by "principial analysis," but it is likely that he refers to the fact that many within the tradition he is describing wanted to live their entire life out of the principles laid down in God's Word. They "analyzed" everything in the world in terms of these principles.

20. Ibid., 19.

heathen culture, made societal institutions means of grace by restraining sin, and opened the doors for cooperation with unbelievers.[21] "Common grace became the linchpin for the entire transformation of consciousness Kuyper was trying to effect."[22]

Rev. Herman Hoeksema's predecessor in Eastern Ave. CRC, Rev. Johannes Groen, argued on the basis of common grace that the laws of social development were rooted in creation, not redemption. The antithesis was therefore only operative in the sphere of redemption. But because of common grace, the Christian ought to and could operate in the same social sphere as the wicked to accomplish mutually acceptable goals.[23]

Kuyper's view of common grace was officially adopted by the CRC in 1924 and is embodied in the second and third points which speak, respectively, of the restraint of sin by the Holy Spirit in the hearts of all men, and the good that unregenerated sinners are capable of doing.

Common grace was a grace given to all men which was surprisingly successful in making man a virtuous and capable person able to accomplish much of value not only for this life, but also for heaven—even though he himself would never get there.

Some General Considerations

The purpose of this chapter is not to engage in a debate over the question of particular vs. common grace by coming to the defense of the position of the PRC. The purpose is, rather, a summary of the arguments that were raised in the 1920s against common grace, along with additional arguments which have appeared in PR writings through

---

21. Ibid., 20.
22. Ibid.
23. Ibid., 76. Groen used this argument in support of membership in the neutral labor unions.

the seventy-five years of the church's history. The summary shall have to be brief. One interested in a detailed study can consult the many writings that the PRC have produced.

Such a summary of arguments against common grace is not enough, however, if the arguments are and remain only negative. The positive truth which the PRC holds is also important. What does the PRC stand for in contrast to common grace? To be against common grace is one thing; to stand for the truth of God over against common grace is quite another.

Fundamental to PR objections to common grace is the claim that the doctrines are denials of Scripture and the confessions of the Reformed churches. The CRC did appeal to both Scripture and the confessions to support its doctrines of common grace. But the PRC insist that this appeal was unjustified because the interpretation of both Scripture and the confessions, which was implied in an appeal to them, was incorrect. In every instance serious misinterpretations were involved.[24]

The PRC also objected to the fact that the CRC was setting forth as official dogma doctrines which had been refuted by the church throughout most of its new dispensational history. Although the decisions on common grace had appealed to the fact that the doctrines adopted by the CRC were those of theologians "in the most flourishing period of Reformed theology," an impartial reading of all theology in the tradition of the Reformation would reveal that such a claim was spurious, and that quite the contrary was true. Yet much of the debate centered on that very question.[25]

---

24. It is a significant aspect of the decisions on common grace that although appeal was made to various scriptural and confessional passages, no exegesis or explanation was ever offered by the synod. The interested reader can find concise and brief explanations of the debated texts and passages from the confessions in Hoeksema and Hanko, *Ready to Give an Answer*, 63–159.

25. See Herman Hoeksema, *Calvin, Berkhof, and H. J. Kuiper: A Comparison* (Grand Rapids: Reformed Free Publishing Association, 1930).

I shall not deal with these questions here, but shall concentrate on summaries of the PR position. I shall treat three aspects of the doctrine of common grace: the good gifts which God gives; the well-meant offer of the gospel; and the Kuyperian doctrine of the restraint of sin and the good which the unregenerate do.

Common Grace and God's Good Gifts

The position which the PRC took with respect to the gifts of God was sometimes misinterpreted by the defenders of common grace. No one among those who denied common grace ever so much as hinted that the gifts of God to men were bad gifts, as some defenders of common grace claimed. Everyone agreed that God gives men only good gifts. Not only does Scripture teach this,[26] but various passages even emphasize this. Psalm 73, it was pointed out, clearly states, in the complaint of Asaph, that the wicked have more of these earthly things, which common grace called blessings, than God's people. God never gives bad gifts. When God gives the wicked the things of His creation, He gives good gifts because He is the overflowing fountain of all good and because "every good gift and every perfect gift is from above, and cometh down from the Father of lights, with whom is no variableness, neither shadow of turning."[27]

But God is also good to His creation because it is His creation. Although the wicked abuse it, mutilate it, try to lay claim to it for their own benefit, and use it to sin, God still preserves His creation, takes care of it, and is, in fact, so good to his creation that He redeems it in Christ and makes it into the new heavens and the new earth.

---

26. It is clear that Psalm 145:9, a text quoted in support of common grace, teaches God's goodness over and to all His works.

27. James 1:17.

But these ideas were not what common grace was all about. Common grace held that these good gifts were demonstrations and evidences of God's favor and love to all men. This is quite a different matter. And this the PRC denied.

Common grace is exactly what it says it is, a grace of God given to all. But this position is not only contrary to Scripture; it inevitably leads to problems—problems which are serious because they involve the very experiences of life in the midst of the world. One problem is: If the good things in life, of which, generally speaking, the wicked have more than the righteous, are really indications of God's favor towards all men, what are God's judgments, which also come upon elect and reprobate alike? Are they expressions of God's wrath? wrath upon elect and reprobate?

The question never was answered; indeed, the proponents of common grace never attempted an answer.

The matter is put in its clearest terms by Hoeksema. "If gifts as such were grace, this grace would still not be very common. The wicked are fatter than the people of the Lord. But the whole idea is wrong. Grace is not in things, but purely in the good favor of God. Even as suffering and grief and adversity as such are not wrath and curse, so also gold and silver, rain and sunshine, gifts and talents are not as such, grace. Grace can very well work in all things, yet it always remains particular and is granted only to His people."[28]

God's attitude towards wicked man is one of unchanging hatred and wrath. Whether he receives many of God's good gifts or receives very few of them; whether he receives health or diseases which plague him all his life long, God remains a God of wrath towards the wicked. The curse of the Lord is always in the house of the wicked (Prov. 3:33), and though

---

28. Danhof and Hoeksema, *Van Zonde en Genade*, 244. Bratt maintains that Hoeksema's position—that it is inconceivable that God shows favor to the reprobate—was an idea "that came to haunt Hoeksema." Bratt, *Dutch Calvinism in Modern America*, 111. Bratt offers no proof for this, and it is manifestly false.

the wicked receive many good things in this life, they are added ice on the slippery slope of life down which the wicked speed into everlasting destruction (Ps. 73).

But God's love and favor remain on His people in all their life, and every experience of life is given sovereignly by God as an expression of His love. Not only are health and prosperity tokens of God's favor, but also cancer and poverty are sent in love. God's attitude cannot be determined by things.

Another aspect of this question must be considered. When God gives good gifts to the wicked, the result is that the wicked more and more show how wicked they really are. Every good gift becomes an additional occasion to sin. Every good gift underscores their hatred of God as they sneeringly claim to have acquired these gifts by their own power and refuse to acknowledge that it is a gift of God. But this is also God's purpose which He sovereignly executes. God puts the wicked on slippery places. God does this by giving them good gifts. He is executing His counsel.[29] God never shows favor to the reprobate, but His curse is always with them.[30]

It is different with God's attitude toward the elect. Indeed, God sends His judgments upon the earth in the form of tornados, floods, cancer, war, and drought. The righteous are not spared these calamities. But God loves His people. He sends them these afflictions, which He uses as chastisements that they may be taught the ways of the Lord.[31] He will not allow any evil to hurt them.[32] Though the wicked gain the world as their own, while God's people have nothing, God will guide His own by His counsel and afterward take them to glory.[33] Christ bore their judgment on the cross, and from

---

29. Psalm 73:18, 19.
30. Proverbs 3:33.
31. Hebrews 12:5–11.
32. Psalm 91:10.
33. Psalm 73:24.

the cross rivers of blessing stream to them, blessing which comes in everything they receive, for all things are for their good when they are called according to God's purpose.[34] The blessing of God is in the habitation of the just, even when this habitation is a hovel, there is little food on the table, and the mother is dying of cancer.[35] Judgment in the form of chastisement must come on God's people, for Zion is always redeemed through judgment, and her converts with righteousness.[36]

Grace is particular and sovereign, always saving, always for the good of those who are the objects of God's favor.

An additional question which was put to those who so vehemently defended common grace was: What is the judicial basis for common grace? This crucial question presupposes, of course, that God is just and righteous in all His ways. God must be and is just in all His dealings with men, even to the extent of giving His own Son to the death of Calvary to pay for sin. How, then, can a just God love, be kind, and give good gifts to reprobate wicked—unless somewhere and somehow these blessings are earned?[37] Where are they earned?

For a few decades this question proved to be extremely embarrassing. The legitimacy of the question could not be denied. But the answer was difficult. To claim, as was the reasonable conclusion, that Christ earned these benefits for

---

34. Romans 8:28.
35. Proverbs 3:33.
36. Isaiah 1:27.
37. Hoeksema apologized to a Dutch theologian, Valentine Hepp, for using the expression "overflow of grace" with reference to the reprobate in connection with the atonement of Christ. Even then he taught that God's good gifts were common, but grace was particular. Danhof and Hoeksema, *Van Zonde en Genade*, 251. It must be remembered that all this was written while Hoeksema was still in the CRC. Indeed, in his articles in the *Banner* he had proposed the idea that the good gifts which the reprobate receive are overflows from the work of Christ on the cross. See my work, "A Study of the Relation between the Views of Prof. R. Janssen and Common Grace," 92. The material referred to there can be found in Herman Hoeksema, "The Fallen King," *Banner* 53 (October 31, 1918): 789.

all men on the cross was to deny a point which Reformed people had maintained since the time of Calvin: that Christ's death on the cross was for His elect only and in no sense for all men. Common grace forced the church to deny limited atonement.[38]

Common Grace and the Well-meant Offer

The second part of the first point of common grace deals with the well-meant gospel offer. Also against this doctrine serious objections were raised.

One such objection was the same as that raised against the idea of a common goodness of God: What is the judicial basis for this gracious and well-meant offer? If God offers salvation in such a way that He expresses His desire for all to be saved, and He earnestly beseeches all to accept the salvation promised, that salvation must surely be available. The salvation offered must be earned.[39]

This question too was for a long time met with silence. But it would not go away. It was there demanding an answer. And finally it was answered by the very teaching that had formerly been condemned as heresy, namely that the atoning sacrifice of Christ was indeed for all men. The CRC was, by the force of its own decisions on the gracious offer of the gospel, driven to a universal atonement.[40]

---

38. John Murray had no hesitation in finding the judicial basis for common grace in Christ's cross. John Murray, *Redemption—Accomplished and Applied* (Grand Rapids: Wm. B. Eerdmans Publishing Co., 1955). He writes: "The unbelieving and reprobate in this world enjoy numerous benefits that flow from the fact that Christ died and rose again" (p. 71).

39. Herman Hoeksema, *Een Kracht Gods Tot Zaligheid, of Genade Geen Aanbod* (A Power of God unto Salvation, or Grace Not an Offer) (Grand Rapids: Reformed Free Publishing Association, 1932), 12. A translation of this important book has been prepared in syllabus form (Grandville, Mich.: Theological School of the Protestant Reformed Churches, 1996). Page 12 refers to this translation.

40. The decision was made in connection with the "Dekker Case." It came to synod in the form of protests against writings of Prof. Harold Dekker which had

The objection was also raised against the doctrine of the gospel offer that it implies that God has two wills, which are in conflict with each other. The reason for this objection is clear enough. Claiming to be Reformed, the CRC insisted that it believed in election and reprobation, according to which God wills to save only those whom He has chosen from all eternity to be His people, while damning others in the way of their sin. This is straight-forward Calvinism. But the gracious offer of the gospel teaches that God wills to save all men to whom the gospel comes. So God wills to save His people and damn others, and God wills to save all men. God has, in His own divine being, two wills.

An attempt was made to answer this objection, but the answer was very feeble. It consisted of appealing to "apparent contradiction," by which was meant that Scripture teaches truths which apparently contradict each other, but which we must accept anyway. If we refuse to accept them, we become rationalistic and refuse to bow before Scripture. God's mind sees no contradiction, and two seemingly opposite truths are harmonized in the mind of God.[41]

---

appeared in the *Reformed Journal*, and in which Dekker had defended a universal love of God rooted in a universal atonement. The matter was treated at many different synods, but finally Dekker was exonerated completely. I was present at the final debate and remember that more than one speaker appealed to the well-meant offer of the gospel in support of Dekker's universalism and argued that a well-meant offer could only be genuine if Christ died for all. The pertinent decisions are found in *Acts of Synod of the Christian Reformed Church, 1967*, Art. 177 (found in the minutes of a continued session of the synod), and in *Acts of Synod 1968*, Art. 98.

41. I shall investigate later the charge of rationalism which was leveled against Hoeksema. Not only were some prepared to say that there are indeed two wills in God, but they even openly spoke of theology as being a "two-track" theology. This was, for example, the claim of J. K. van Baalen, *De Loochening der Gemeene Gratie*, 35–38. W. Heyns put his solution in a slightly different form. He wrote, on facing the question of whether a well-meant offer implies a universal atonement: "[the question of the atonement] concerns the question for whom the satisfaction of Christ is intended in God's decree to bring deliverance. This is a question which concerns the secret things. The second, however, concerns the question: to whom is salvation in Christ offered? And this is a question which concerns the revealed

It was clear at the beginning of the history of the PRC, and it is clear today, that a gracious offer is nothing but Arminian free-willism. If God expresses His desire to save all men, does all He can in His grace towards all to save them, and many who hear the offer are, after all, not saved, then the gospel is reduced to an invitation, God is reduced to begging, and salvation turns on the choice of man's free will.

The truth, therefore, of both Scripture and the confessions was and is very simple. God chose His people from before the foundation of the world. He gave them to Christ and Christ died for them, and for them alone. Throughout all the history of the world, the gospel is preached as the power of God unto salvation.[42] God knows His elect, and God knows where they are. He causes the gospel to be sent to them, and He causes that gospel to be efficacious by the work of the Holy Spirit in the hearts of the elect, so that the elect, inwardly called, are brought through the gospel to faith and repentance. By that same gospel, they are preserved and kept in the world until they are finally brought into glory.[43]

The enemies of this truth concerning the gospel laid many and grievous accusations at the door of the PRC. Some were: (1) the PRC preaches only to the elect—which is the same as

---

things. In Arminianism is an effort to bring the secret and revealed things into agreement. This is done by distorting the secret things in such a manner as the revealed things seem to demand it. This may not be done. To do the same in the other direction by holding that only to the elect is well-meant grace offered, is no less a distortion of the gospel." By secret things Heyns refers to God's secret or hidden will, sometimes called the will of His decree, which includes election and reprobation. By God's revealed will, also called the will of His command, Heyns refers to that which we know concerning God's purpose, which includes the well-meant offer of the gospel. William Heyns, *Manual of Reformed Doctrine* (Grand Rapids: Wm. B. Eerdmans Publishing Co., 1926), 197.

42. Romans 1:16.

43. For most of the material here and in what follows, I have depended on Hoeksema, *Een Kracht Gods Tot Zaligheid*. But see also Hoeksema's *Het Evangelie: Of De Jongste Aanval op de Waarheid der Souvereine Genade* (The Gospel: or, The Latest Attack on the Truth of Sovereign Grace) (Grand Rapids: Mission Committee of the Protestant Reformed Churches, 1933).

Hyper-Calvinism;[44] (2) the PRC neglect the command of the gospel which comes to all men; (3) the PRC are unable to do mission work. These charges were not only brought against the PRC at the time of the controversy, but continue to be brought today. Hoeksema put these charges to rest, however. Charging those who made them with dishonesty, Hoeksema wrote: "The preaching is made into an offer of grace on the part of God to all mankind. When they [the defenders of that view] are attacked they answer that all that they are interested in is that the gospel be preached to all mankind without distinction along with the command to repent and believe . . . But in the meantime they still continue to speak of a general offer of grace on the part of God to all mankind. Under that slogan they still continue to pour into people the pernicious poison of the Pelagian error. Such juggling must stop. We must know where we stand."[45]

Hoeksema goes on to say,

> If I preach in my congregation: I promise ten dollars to all who have no work and are in need, if they come to me, then that is a general proclamation of a particular promise. The proclamation is general, the promise is particular. It is a particular offer. When God says: to all those who labor and are heavy laden, who come to Me, I will give rest, then that is indeed a general proclamation, but the promise is particular. When God calls: Ho, all ye that thirst, come to the waters, then this is proclaimed in general, but the promise concerns only the elect. When God says: Turn unto me all ye ends of the earth, then it may be remarked in the first place, that all the ends of the earth do not include every one head for head; but in the second place, that God promises salvation to those who turn to Him, who repent, so that also here you have a particular promise. And since it is God Himself who must work the true laboring and

---

44. See Engelsma, *Hyper-Calvinism and the Call of the Gospel,* for a refutation of this idea.
45. Hoeksema, *Een Kracht Gods Tot Zaligheid,* 75.

thirsting and repentance, it is as plain as day that all these passages basically concern only the elect.

However, with a well-meant offer on the part of God one means no less than that God's intent with the preaching of the gospel is to save all.

Otherwise why do they always speak of a mystery when they compare this offer to the doctrine of election and reprobation? Indeed there is no mystery whatever in the teaching that God causes His gospel to be preached to all without distinction in order to save the elect and harden the others. The calling through the gospel makes the reprobate wicked responsible, places the depravity of his sinful heart in the clearest light and increases his judgment. That is God's intent. *The result answers completely to God's intent.* And God carries out His counsel. He still maintains man's responsibility and the justice of God. What is so very incomprehensible here? This is the clear teaching of the Scriptures . . .[46]

No, the incomprehensibility, the nonsense of the presentation is created when you try to bind the Arminian teaching of a general offer to the Reformed teaching of particular grace. Then you say, God desires to save only the elect; Christ brought atonement only for them; God gives His grace and works conversion only in them; but yet God offers His grace well-meaningly, with the intent of saving them, to all mankind; and if this grace is not accepted the result does not answer to the intent!

This is not a mystery. It is nonsense. It is so nonsensical, because the latter is not true, while the former is true; the latter is not in harmony with Scripture, the former is; the latter is not Reformed, the former is thoroughly Reformed. You want to join the lie to the truth. Therefore you end with a so-called mystery.[47]

In answer to the charge that the PRC wanted to preach only to the elect, Hoeksema insisted that as often as men

---

46. Ibid., 76, 77.
47. Ibid., 77.

make this charge, they are shooting at a straw man.[48] The gospel must be preached to all men, that is, to those to whom God is pleased to send the gospel. The gospel is never in all history preached to all men head for head. Millions have lived and died without ever hearing the gospel. But it is certainly preached to far more than the elect. God wills this because Christ must be presented as God's way of salvation, and men must be confronted with the command to repent of their sin and believe in Christ. On the basis of their rejection of Christ, they are condemned and justly punished.

It is by means of this command of the gospel that sin is shown for the horrible power that it really is, for man will never of his own power repent and believe. He cannot, for he is totally depraved. And he will not, for his heart is at enmity against God. But behind the preaching is God's eternal decree of reprobation. Through the preaching God accomplishes His purpose, for through the gospel the reprobate are hardened in their sin.

When God confronts man with the command to repent and believe in Christ, God is very serious about it. He means exactly what He says.[49] It can, therefore, be said that it is the "will" of God that all who hear the gospel do indeed turn from their evil way and repent of their sin.

But this point created confusion in the entire controversy.[50] Many took Hoeksema's denial of the well-meant offer of grace to mean that he did not believe that the gospel, with a command to repent and believe, came to all men. But even when the distinction was made clear, they persisted in their

---

48. Ibid., 30.

49. Canons of Dordt, III & IV, 8.

50. See Hoeksema, *Een Kracht Gods Tot Zaligheid*. At various places in the book this confusion comes through. Not only was this confusion evident in the writings of Rev. Keegstra, against whose editorials in *De Wachter* the book was written; but this same confusion was evident in various criticisms of the book which were made in the Netherlands, one by the son of Dr. Abraham Kuyper.

criticism, obviously finding a certain delight in attempting to give some plausibility to the charge of Hyper-Calvinism.

But the problem went a bit deeper than that. If Hoeksema spoke of the fact, as he did, that the command to repent, with which all men are confronted, is serious on God's part, then it seems to follow that God not only wills to save the elect, but He also wills that all men repent. And, if He wills that all men repent, He wills, after all, the salvation of all men.

Or, if I may put the matter a bit differently, the question really is: Did not Hoeksema find himself in a dilemma by denying the well-meant offer? If Hoeksema agreed that the gospel commanded all to repent, then it is indeed God's will that all repent and be saved; and that is only what the CRC had insisted on. If, on the other hand, Hoeksema denied that God's will is that all be saved, then he also is forced to deny the command of the gospel (or, at least, the seriousness of that command); and that denial put him in the unenviable position of teaching that the gospel could only be preached to the elect. That is Hyper-Calvinism.

The question is an important one. And Hoeksema recognized it as such. But he did not see it as a dilemma at all. The differences were clear and striking between Hoeksema's position and that of his accusers.

The position which was staked out by the PRC and remains their position till the present is first of all an emphatic rejection of the preaching of the gospel as grace to all. It must be remembered that the well-meant offer is said to be grace to all who hear. This the PRC deny.

Secondly, the PRC insist that the command of the gospel must come to all who hear the gospel, not as an expression of God's grace, but as an expression of God's holiness and justice. God had originally created man holy and upright. Man had fallen into sin. He no longer is able to obey God; he no longer even wants to obey God. Man's will is depraved along with the whole of the nature, and he cannot will the good. Yet God maintains the just demands of His holy law, which were first revealed in Paradise. Man's inability to obey does not alter God's just demands. God must, in keeping with the integrity and righteousness of His own being, insist on obedience. If, for example, God should say to depraved man: "I am sorry that you fell. I had not intended it that way. I could justly destroy you. But, because I am kind and merciful, I will no longer require of you that which you cannot perform."—if God should say something like that to man, God's own righteousness would be denigrated. God cannot and will not change His holy demands because of man's sin.

Through the gospel, God comes to man with the command to repent of sin, obey God, believe in Christ. If the excuse is made that man can no longer do this, God's answer is: "I made you capable of obeying me. It is your own fault that you cannot. I still insist that you do."[51] God's command is not rooted in a universal love towards all men; it is rooted in His own justice and the original command of the creation ordinance.

In the third place, it is quite correct to make a distinction between the will of God's decree and the will of God's command. God decrees to save His elect and to damn the wicked. God also wills that all men obey Him and forsake their evil ways.[52] But between these two there is no conflict.

---

51. This is precisely the teaching of the Heidelberg Catechism in Lord's Day IV. It is striking that both Arminians and Antinomians teach that God requires from man only that which he is capable of doing.

52. It is, however, confusing to speak of God's hidden will as synonymous with the will of God's decree, and of God's revealed will as synonymous with the will of God's command. Many things about the will of God's decree are revealed as, for example, God's election and reprobation (even though we do not know who are elect and who are reprobate). Further, God makes known in the Holy Scriptures a multitude of details concerning what He has decreed to do throughout the course of history (even though many details of our own personal lives are not made known to us before God's counsel is executed). Many appeal to the fact that God's counsel is hidden, not only to affirm that those who are elect and those who are reprobate are not known to us, but to deny election and reprobation altogether. Or, if they do not deny it, they insist that since we know nothing about it, we do best to ignore it.

In fact, it is not even correct to speak of two wills of God. God has one will, in which the distinctions we make are combined into one great purpose of God.[53] God sovereignly determines to save His church and to damn the reprobate in the way of their sin. He accomplishes this purpose sovereignly through the preaching of the gospel. By that gospel God demonstrates His power to save His church and thus reveals the riches of His grace towards the elect. But He also hardens the reprobate as they manifest their hatred of God by their refusal to obey the commands of the gospel to abandon their sinful way and believe in God's Christ.

Thus the grace of God through the gospel is always particular and sovereign. It always accomplishes God's purpose. It saves His people and condemns the wicked.

Particular Grace and Providence in Human History

The very peculiar and philosophical views concerning common grace which Kuyper taught and which were adopted by the CRC in the second and third points of common grace were an open and frontal attack against the truth of God's particular and sovereign grace. Already as editor of the "Our Doctrine" column in the *Banner* and in a book published in 1923, Hoeksema attacked these novel views of Kuyper.[54]

Hoeksema was scathing in his denunciation of what Kuyper taught. He accused Kuyper of proposing a dualism in history composed of the development of mankind by

---

53. Calvin already insisted on that in his treatise on "The Eternal Predestination of God," sometimes called the *Consensus Genevensis*. It was written by Calvin at the time of the controversy with Bolsec, a heretic who made God's predestination conditional. Translated by Henry Cole, it has been republished by the Reformed Free Publishing Association, along with Calvin's treatise on "The Secret Providence of God," under the title *Calvin's Calvinism* (Grand Rapids, 1987).

54. The book was *Van Zonde en Genade*. Most of what I include in what follows is taken from this book. Although it was co-authored by Danhof and Hoeksema, the latter was undoubtedly its primary author.

common grace as men fulfilled the original cultural mandate, and the development of the church by special and saving grace. These two streams of development, both of which run independently, never meet. Even though the church benefits in many ways from what is happening in the history of the development of common grace, the two remain forever different streams. Kuyper claimed, therefore, that God has two purposes in history. This dualism Hoeksema called nonsense.

Worse, common grace is an effort to build a bridge over the spiritual chasm that exists between the church and the world.[55] Hoeksema warned against this bridge-building as the means whereby worldliness would be brought into the church.[56] He was quite frank in accusing many in the church of engaging in such bridge-building in order to establish a neutral area where church and world could cooperate.[57] But he assured the church that such cooperation would not lead, as many dreamed, to a purifying of the world and the establishment of Christ's rule over every institution of society, but would rather result in the destruction of the church under the onslaughts of worldliness.

The fall of man in Paradise, Hoeksema insisted, resulted in man's total depravity. From henceforth man was incapable of doing any good whatsoever and was inclined to all evil. No common grace came to mitigate that depravity. Man is as wicked as it is possible to be.

---

55. Quirinus Breen, a minister in the CRC and a follower of Ralph Janssen, used that very expression to describe the church's calling. In fact, he maintained that Herman Bavinck—Dutch theologian who moved from the seminary of the Secession, which was located in Kampen, to Kuyper's Free University in Amsterdam—died young in working at the enormous task of constructing that bridge (Danhof and Hoeksema, *Van Zonde en Genade*, 228, 229). There is truth to this. The Bavinck who taught in the Free University is quite different from the Bavinck who wrote *Gereformeerde Dogmatiek* (Reformed Dogmatics).

56. Danhof and Hoeksema, *Van Zonde en Genade*, 229.

57. Ibid., 60, 61.

Man continues to live in God's world, even subduing the creation. But he uses it in every instance to develop in sin, establish his own kingdom of wickedness, and become increasingly opposed to God until all his efforts culminate in the kingdom of Antichrist.[58] Never can any good proceed from the wicked. Wicked man may help his fellow man, may build hospitals, may perform many different deeds which seem to us to be good. But because that which is good in the sight of God is only that which proceeds from a true faith, is according to God's law, and is to God's glory,[59] these good deeds are only an outward conformity to God's law performed out of self-interest in society.[60]

God's purpose in this world is not to be explained in terms of a host of wicked who actually fulfill the original cultural mandate and accomplish much good in the world. God's purpose is always and only to save His church through Jesus Christ. The church is the important institution. The church is the number of God's elect on whom God pours His grace. The church is gathered throughout all time in Christ and brought finally into heaven.

The salvation of the church is not only God's real purpose in the creation; it is also God's only purpose. Creation, the fall, reprobation, the development of sin: all are subordinate to the one great purpose of God in Jesus Christ accomplished in the salvation of the elect.

---

58. Hoeksema spoke of this as the organic development of sin. The term "organic" is used so frequently by Hoeksema and in so many different relationships that I am devoting a special chapter to what he meant by that term.

59. Heidelberg Catechism, Q & A 91.

60. Danhof and Hoeksema, *Van Zonde en Genade*, 142, 150–54. See also Danhof and Hoeksema, *Langs Zuivere Banen*. All the truths which I am here discussing are treated in detail in Herman Hoeksema, *A Triple Breach in the Foundation of the Reformed Faith: A Critical Treatise on the "Three Points" Adopted by the Synod of the Christian Reformed Churches in 1924* (no publication data given). See especially pp. 75, 76 for a reference to the nature of the "good deeds" of the ungodly. In a 1992 reprint (made from an earlier 1942 reprint) by Grandville, Mich.: Evangelism Committee of Southwest Protestant Reformed Church, this material is found on pp. 64, 65.

It is true that throughout all history the whole creation is shared by wicked and righteous; nevertheless, between the two is the spiritual-ethical antithesis which sharply separates them from each other.[61] The wicked live out of the principle of sin; the elect live out of the principle of regeneration, which is God's gracious work in their hearts. Between the two is no area of cooperation, for Israel shall dwell in safety alone.[62]

Kuyper had maintained that common grace preserved the creation from becoming a wilderness and preserved man from becoming an animal. Hoeksema wanted nothing of that. Man sinned and man fell *as man*. He remained man, though sinful man. He retained his mind and will, even though these natural powers were diminished because of the curse. Man's problem was not that he was no longer man; it was that he was a wicked man.

These natural powers of mind and will are what the confessions call "natural light."[63] By such natural light man is still able to know the difference between good and evil, and thus he remains responsible before God. And it is by that natural light that man is able to subdue the creation and develop culture. But the culture he develops is used exclusively in the service of sin.

Thus, while the righteous and the wicked live side by side and share all the things of the creation, a spiritual, ethical chasm yawns between them which separates them spiritually for time and for eternity. No grace comes to the wicked; all things are grace for the elect.

Hoeksema did not deny a restraint of sin. But he found restraint of sin in God's providence, as God controlled and directed all the circumstances of the life of men. Restraint

---

61. This idea of the antithesis is another crucial idea in Hoeksema's thought. I shall return to it later.
62. Deuteronomy 33:28.
63. Canons of Dordt III & IV, 4; Confession of Faith, Art. 14.

of sin was not grace, for it was under God's providential rule that man developed in sin throughout the ages. Sin is restrained outwardly by all the circumstances of life which are determined and executed by the decree of God's providence.[64] The only gracious restraint of sin is in the hearts of the elect. And that grace is a sanctifying and saving power.

Summary

By its formulations of common grace the CRC seriously compromised the truth of Scripture and the Reformed confessions. The CRC committed itself to a doctrine which taught that God is gracious to all men. Because grace includes all God's ethical attributes, common grace taught that God loves all men, is merciful to all men, is longsuffering towards all men, and wants to save all men. While such general grace is not itself a saving grace, it nonetheless has as its goal the salvation of all. Such a presentation of the grace of God puts one in an impossible bind because, obviously, not all men are saved. Why not? The only answer can be that God, who longs to save them, is unable to do so. And, if one would again ask, Why cannot God save? the only answer can be that salvation, in a decisive way, is left to the will of man.

Hoeksema from the very beginning of the common grace controversy charged the proponents of common grace with Arminianism. The charge proved to be prophetic. Arminianism has run rampant through the CRC.

Kuyperian common grace was also officially adopted in the second and third points of the synod of 1924. Kuyperian common grace is a common grace which restrains the sins of the ungodly so that they are able to fulfill the original cultural

---

64. It has been correctly said that common grace confuses the work of the Holy Spirit with that of the policeman.

mandate given to Adam before the fall. This ability to fulfill the cultural mandate creates a large area of cooperation in which the wicked and the righteous can work together for common ends.

Kuyperian common grace was disastrous for the doctrine of the antithesis. It built a bridge over the chasm which spiritually separates God's people from the world, and because the bridge is two-way, the world rushed into the church, and the church dashed over the bridge to fling itself into the waiting arms of the world. Worldliness became a way of life in the church.

Kuyperian common grace destroyed the truth of total depravity because it was God's power in the reprobate which enabled them to do good. Total depravity is then an abstraction. No totally depraved man has ever existed in the world.

The Three Points form a unity. It has been said that the second point, which deals with the restraint of sin, can stand the test of orthodoxy if permitted to stand by itself. There is an element of truth in this. Surely the heresy of the second point is not nearly as evident and great if it is divorced from the first and third points.[65]

The Three Points are the three doctrines adopted by the CRC concerning common grace. The restraint of sin is also grace. Because the restraint of sin operates in the reprobate, the second point also teaches a grace to the reprobate which makes their depravity less than total and enables them to do good in the sight of God.

The heirs of common grace who stood in the tradition of the Secession of 1834 did not want Kuyperian common grace. Nor did the majority of the Kuyperians want a general

---

65. The second point of the Remonstrance of the Arminians, adopted by them in 1610 and to which the five canons of Dordt were the answer, can also stand by itself. It affirms total depravity. But in the context of the other four points, it could not possibly have a correct interpretation, as the synod of Dordt clearly saw.

attitude of God's favor towards all, shown especially in the well-meant offer of the gospel. These two factions in the church, prior to 1924, could not agree on fundamental points of doctrine and life. The decisions of 1924, in addition to condemning the views of Herman Hoeksema, brought unity and peace between these two warring factions. They united on the basis of an erroneous doctrine and agreed to bury their differences over this doctrine.

On the other hand, Hoeksema, in his denial of common grace, showed the faithful within the church that, whether they were of the tradition of the Secession in 1834 or of the tradition of the *Doleantie*, they could put aside the differences which had traditionally separated the two groups and unite on the basis of the one truth of sovereign and particular grace.

This happened in the formation of the PRC. Within that one denomination were those who were supralapsarian and those who were infralapsarian. Some believed in mediate regeneration and some held to immediate regeneration. Some firmly believed in eternal justification, and some held tenaciously to temporal justification. But all believed in the sovereign and particular character of the grace of God. That is, all believed that salvation is by grace alone, given to the elect.

Faithfulness to Scripture and the Reformed confessions requires unwavering commitment to the doctrine of particular grace. It is a battle in which the church must engage to preserve the truth of Scripture. The importance of this battle for the truth cannot be overstated. Hoeksema wrote: ". . . We bemoan the fact that separation and a split has come between us [the PRC and the CRC]. That there must always be split and separation between those who should unitedly confess the Reformed truth—who would not bemoan that? Nor did we seek it or desire it. Our opponents were out to destroy us. They could not condemn and cast us out with Scripture and the confessions. Therefore they formulated the 'Three Points' . . . Here . . . the Reformed truth must be sought with a candle. And it is rapidly growing worse. It remains to be seen whether our Protestant Reformed Churches will be privileged to maintain the Reformed truth for a long time to come. But God the Lord calls us to battle."[66]

66. Hoeksema, Een Kracht Gods Tot Zaligheid, 70.

CHAPTER 5

ℛeformed in Church Government

In [ecclesiastical] assemblies ecclesiastical matters only shall be transacted and that in an ecclesiastical manner. In major assemblies only such matters shall be dealt with as could not be finished in minor assemblies, or such as pertain to the Churches of the major assembly in common.
—Church Order of Dordrecht

If anyone complain that he has been wronged by the decision of a minor assembly, he shall have the right to appeal to a major ecclesiastical assembly, and whatever may be agreed upon by a majority vote shall be considered settled and binding, unless it be proved to conflict with the Word of God or with the Articles of the Church Order . . .
—Church Order of Dordrecht

The Classis has the same jurisdiction over the Consistory as the Particular Synod has over the Classis and the General Synod over the Particular.
—Church Order of Dordrecht

Introduction

When God brings reformation to His church, it is because the church in which His people find themselves has chosen to walk the way of apostasy. Denominational apostasy, always irreversible, affects the church in its entire life: doctrine, worship, church government, and the walk of the members.[1]

---

1. The walk of the members of the church is important, not only because one's

That all aspects of the church's life are affected is not surprising since they are inseparably related to each other.

Reformation, therefore, includes reformation in doctrine, worship, church government, and the life and calling of the members of the church. It is in all respects, as Jeremiah 6:16 expresses it, a return to the old paths.

At the beginning of the history of the PRC, doctrinal errors in the CRC were certainly the major cause of separation. But issues of church government also occupied an important place in the turmoil, confusion, and final separation of the PRC from the CRC.

The issues in church government were clearly defined. The CRC had violated some crucially important principles; the PRC had upheld them, though with some hesitation and difficulty. Only after wrestling with these problems in later years were correct principles firmly imbedded in the life of the church. Reformed church government has become, under God's blessing, a distinctive mark of the life of the denomination of which I write.

Three church political issues particularly stand out. Each of them deserves some discussion.

Censuring Protestants

In the history of the Eastern Ave. CRC, the controversy over common grace was precipitated by protests from various members of the congregation. These protests expressed objections to the doctrinal content of the preaching of Rev. Herman Hoeksema.[2]

The protestants, after they had been admonished by the consistory to retract their charges, and after they refused to

---

life of sanctification is determined by and has its source in sound doctrine, but also because this walk of the members of a church is the witness of that church to those around it. It is probably for this reason that Article 29 of the Confession of Faith includes in its discussion of the marks of the true and the false church, a discussion of the marks of a true Christian.

2. See chapter 3, pp. 52 and 53, for further details.

do so, were put under censure by the consistory for falsely accusing their pastor of the sin of preaching heresy in the pulpit.

This matter of the censure of the protestants continued to be a central church political issue in the whole controversy. The protestants were kept under censure during the adjudication of the entire case on the classical and synodical levels, and the censure was maintained by the consistory even though synod had made common grace official dogma in the churches.[3]

When the consistory refused to lift the censure, even after synod made its decisions, the protestants appealed to Classis Grand Rapids East, which finally suspended and deposed Hoeksema and the consistory.

The question arises whether discipline of the protestants was a proper course of action for the consistory to follow. We are not concerned now with the irregularities in the protests themselves or in the way they were handled, which in many respects was contrary to Reformed church government; nor are we interested in the fact that the protestants had, over the course of the case, made themselves guilty of other sins which were brought to their attention by the consistory. We are concerned about just one question: Was it church politically right for the consistory to put the protestants under censure for protesting the preaching of their pastor?

Rev. Hoeksema defended this action of the consistory in some detail.[4] Nevertheless, such action was surely not proper according to the government of the church of Christ. The Church Order of Dordrecht which was adopted by the synod

---

3. Undoubtedly the reasoning of the consistory was that, although the synod had supported the case of the protestants by establishing common grace as dogma, the synod had also expressed the fact that Rev. Hoeksema was Reformed in his teaching, even though he showed an inclination to one-sidedness. The protests, after all, accused Rev. Hoeksema of being un-Reformed.

4. Hoeksema, *The Protestant Reformed Churches in America*, 30, 32.

of Dordrecht in its great meeting of 1618–1619 had included in it Article 31[5] which guaranteed the right of the individual believer to appeal to a broader assembly of the churches if he was aggrieved by a decision of his consistory and was not satisfied with the consistory's defense of its position.

Article 31 is an important part of the Church Order, for it is the one article in the entire Church Order which guarantees the right of believers to live in obedience to their consciences. The right of the individual conscience is one for which the Reformation, beginning with Luther, had fought fiercely.[6] Every believer must give answer before God for his own conscience. And he must, to have peace, live so that he has a good conscience before God. If the decisions of the church are, in his judgment, contrary to the Word of God (and the Reformed confessions) and he cannot, in good conscience, live under those decisions, then it is his solemn responsibility to show the consistory that the decision which troubles him is contrary to the Word of God. And if he does not succeed, he retains the right to appeal the matter to a broader judicatory of the churches.

This is what the protestants were doing when they protested the preaching of their pastor.

The protestants were, of course, wrong in the contents of their protest. Rev. Hoeksema's preaching was soundly Reformed—as even the synod later testified. But the simple

---

5. Article 31 reads: "If anyone complain that he has been wronged by the decision of a minor assembly, he shall have the right to appeal to a major ecclesiastical assembly, and whatever may be agreed upon by a majority vote shall be considered settled and binding, unless it be proved to conflict with the Word of God or with the articles of the Church Order, as long as they are not changed by the general synod."

6. In Luther's dramatic and courageous stand at the Diet of Worms he had appealed to his conscience. It must be emphasized, however, that he insisted that the conscience had to be enlightened by the Word. The conviction of his conscience was that what he believed was taught in the Word of God. And he insisted that he had to be shown from that Word that his position was false before he would change his views.

fact of the matter is that Hoeksema's doctrine was the point the protestants were contesting. They should not have been put under censure for challenging the Reformed character of the preaching and finally appealing their case to a broader assembly.

If the broader assemblies had decided in favor of the consistory, then indeed the protestants would have been required to retract their accusations. And if they still refused, discipline would have been necessary. But the fact of the matter is that synod waffled, declaring their accusations to be essentially true, but also affirming the Reformed character of their pastor. The point is that the censure should not have been imposed prior to the adjudication of their protests. Eastern Ave.'s consistory was wrong in its censure of the protestants.

The Autonomy of a Congregation

The most important church political issue which emerged from the controversy was the issue of the right of a broader assembly to discipline officebearers.[7]

The issue was hotly debated at the time when Classis Grand Rapids East was faced with Rev. Hoeksema's refusal to sign the three points of common grace and the consistory's refusal to lift the censure of the protestants. It was also debated on Classis Grand Rapids West when Revs. Ophoff and Danhof refused to subscribe to common grace. In the discussions which followed the organization of the PRC much was written by both sides concerning the issue.[8]

---

7. While the immediate question was the discipline of office bearers by a broader assembly, the more basic question was: May a broader assembly (classis or synod) discipline at all?

8. For the criticism of classical action by the men of the PRC, see: George M. Ophoff, "May a Classis Depose a Consistory: or, The Plain Truth about the Institution of Christ's Church," SB 4 (January 15, 1928): 179–87; 4 (February 15, 1928): 225–32; 4 (March 1, 1928): 250, 251; 4 (March 15, 1928): 273–80; 4 (April

The problem had been a question in the Reformed Churches both in the Netherlands and in this country. Defenders of both positions could be found and were often quoted.[9] Nevertheless, the fact remains that the broader principles of Reformed church polity forbid such action on the part of broader assemblies.

The broader principles of Reformed church government include the principle of the autonomy of the local church. That principle of autonomy became the central question around which the entire controversy swirled. Although everyone involved was ready to grant that the local congregation is autonomous, no one could agree on what autonomy means. It was especially in this area that the PRC developed an important principle of church government.

The principles which are at stake are clear enough. Christ is the Head of the church. He is appointed as such from all eternity and rules the church from His exalted position at God's right hand. The church is His body. It is a church only because Christ lives in it. And it remains a church only when it is ruled in all its life by its King.

Christ is not only Head of the whole church, which is His body, but Christ has also manifested His body in the world as an ecclesiastical institution. This institution is an organization with a constitution, a membership roll, officers, and an assigned task. That institution which is organized by Christ is the local congregation.

Each local congregation is a complete manifestation of the body of Christ and possesses all the attributes which

---

1, 1928): 299–305; and 4 (April 15, 1928): 327–32. See also Herman Hoeksema, "A Catechism on the History of the Origin of the Protestant Reformed Churches," *SB* 6 (September 1, 1930): 536–38; 7 (December 1, 1930): 111–14; 8 (July 1, 1932): 450–53. Also see Hoeksema, *The Protestant Reformed Churches in America*, 214–21.

9. The synod of the CRC in 1918 had, in fact, deposed Rev. Bultema, who had denied the kingship of Christ over the church in support of his pre-millennialism. Ralph Janssen had been dismissed by the synod of 1922 for his higher critical views of Scripture; but he had not been deposed, because he never was an ordained minister.

belong to the whole body: her unity, catholicity, holiness, and apostolicity. Its officebearers are ministers, elders, and deacons, appointed and called by Christ, and qualified for their work by the Spirit of Christ. Its constitution is made up of the principles laid down in Scripture for the government of the church. Its membership consists of all who manifest themselves as true believers and their children. And the task assigned to it by Christ, the one purpose of its organization, is to preach the gospel, administer the sacraments, and exercise Christian discipline.

It is to this local congregation in Ephesus with its officebearers and Timothy as its minister that the apostle refers when he writes: "These things write I unto thee, hoping to come unto thee shortly: but if I tarry long, that thou mayest know how thou oughtest to behave thyself in the house of God, which is the church of the living God, the pillar and ground of the truth" (I Tim. 3:14, 15). It is also of this local congregation that Jesus speaks when He says that where two or three are gathered in His name, He is in the midst of them (Matt. 18:20).

The Lord Jesus Christ is present with His church through the work of the officebearers. He is present through His Word, and His Word is brought to the church through those who are called to their offices: the minister in the preaching of the gospel and the administration of the sacraments; the elders in the rule, government, and discipline of the church; and the deacons in administering Christ's mercy in the care of the poor.

Hence, the congregation is *autonomous*. That is, it is, under Christ, self-ruling. It is complete in itself, self-determining, committed to the task assigned it by Christ.

Many local congregations who agree in doctrine, government, and worship come together in church federations. They do this on the basis of the practices of the apostolic church which are the rule of church government for the entire new dispensation church. The apostolic church came together to decide matters of mutual concern (Acts 15:1–31). The impetus for such forming of federations is the solemn and urgent calling that comes to the church to seek the unity of the Spirit (Eph. 4:1–3).

A federation is a union of autonomous congregations. But, because a federation is an expression of the unity of the body of Christ, it has the authority to maintain that unity among the congregations. The assemblies of the federation (classes and synods) have, therefore, a certain amount of authority. They have the right and duty to exercise that authority.[10]

May a Classis Depose Officebearers?

All Reformed churches in the tradition of the Reformed faith as practiced in the Lowlands were agreed on these principles of autonomy and federative unity. The principles are, in fact, embodied in the Church Order of Dordrecht.[11]

The disagreement that emerged from the conflict of 1924 and became a bone of contention between the CRC and the PRC was over the question: What is the relation between the authority of the federation and the authority of a local and autonomous congregation? Does the authority of the former limit the authority of the latter? Or does the authority of the

---

10. In larger denominations there are three such bodies: classes (each representing a group of congregations in geographic proximity), particular synods (each representing a group of classes), and a general synod (representing the entire denomination). In Presbyterian church government, the equivalent of a classis is a presbytery, and the equivalent of a general synod is usually called a general assembly.

11. Although various articles can be quoted in this connection, perhaps the most pointed one is Article 36: "The classis has the same jurisdiction over the consistory as the particular synod has over the classis and the general synod over the particular." Note that the article establishes the principle of the authority of a broader assembly over a narrower assembly (classis over consistory, and synod over classis), but it does not give the broader assemblies *the same kind* of authority as the consistory has over the congregation, which authority is the decisive authority of discipline.

congregation in all respects supersede the authority of the federation?

When these rather abstract questions were being considered at the time of the controversies in 1924–1925, the real issue was much more concrete: Does a classis have the authority to depose officebearers? Classis Grand Rapids East and Classis Grand Rapids West both said yes. And in keeping with this answer, they deposed the officebearers of Eastern Ave. CRC, Hope CRC, and First CRC of Kalamazoo.[12]

It was the position of the men deposed, and later became the position of the Protestant Reformed Churches, that no broader assembly had this right.

The wrong which the classes of the CRC perpetrated was very great. Three considerations underscore the wrong. First of all, the classes which deposed Hoeksema, Ophoff, and Danhof did what synod had refused to do. The question of the discipline of Herman Hoeksema had come up at the synod, but had been rejected by synod. It could not be right that a classis did something contrary to the express wishes of synod.[13]

In the second place, the wrong was great because the synod had declared that Hoeksema was fundamentally Reformed. It is a great evil to strip a man of his office after the church's broadest assembly had said concerning him that he was Reformed in preaching and doctrine.[14]

---

12. These decisions of the two classes were later approved by the synod of the CRC in 1926, which approval made these erroneous decisions the official position of the CRC.

13. One may very well ask: Why, if the synod of 1924 refused to discipline, did it approve of the discipline of classis at its meeting in 1926? This is, of course, hard to answer. The synod of 1926 did not even consider its failure to discipline in 1924. Perhaps the synod of 1926 was only eager to be done with the matter once and for all. Besides, it had become something of a moot point because those who had been disciplined and deposed from office had already, in effect, started a new denomination.

14. A confession of the Reformed churches, the Confession of Faith (Art. 29), says that one of the marks of the false church is that it "persecutes those, who live

But, thirdly, and from a church political point of view, it was a travesty of Reformed church government that a classis took upon itself an authority which Christ had given only to the local congregation.

The charge made against these actions was the charge of hierarchy. Hierarchy in its extreme form is practiced by the Roman Catholic Church where the local congregation (parish) has no say at all in the doctrine, government and worship of the church, but where the pope and the clergy have sole and exclusive authority. From that hierarchy the Reformation had delivered the church. But in 1925 in the CRC, the authority of a local congregation was taken away from it and assumed by classis as its prerogative.

To depose from office is to exercise Christian discipline. It is to declare one a sinner, and, because of his sin, to judge him to be unworthy to hold office in the church of Christ. But Christ gave discipline to the local congregation, not to broader assemblies. The discipline exercised by the classis was a great wrong.

It may very well be asked: What is a classis or a synod to do if a local congregation refuses to do what a classis or synod decides it must do?[15] The concrete case which Classis Grand Rapids East had faced can serve as an illustration. The classis had told the consistory of Eastern Ave. CRC to lift the censure of the protestants. It had also told the consistory to require of its minister, Rev. Herman Hoeksema, that he express full agreement with the doctrines of common grace as decided by synod. But the consistory informed the classis that it refused to do what classis required. And Rev.

---

holily according to the Word of God, and rebuke her for her errors, covetousness, and idolatry."

15. The authority of a classis or synod over the congregations in certain matters is embodied in the rule of the Church Order: " . . . Whatever may be agreed upon by a majority vote shall be considered settled and binding" (Art. 31). The key words here are "settled and binding."

Hoeksema informed the classis that, whatever his consistory did, he would never subscribe to common grace. What was classis to do?

Before I answer that question, it is well to understand that the rules of Reformed church government specify what a consistory or congregation is responsible to do if it does not agree with a decision of classis. Such a consistory must make its objections known to the classis, and if the classis does not alter its decision, the consistory must appeal classis' decision to synod.[16] If the synod should uphold the classis, the consistory has two courses of action before it: (1) The consistory may submit to the decision, something the consistory ought to do if the consciences of the officebearers would not be violated by submitting. In that case the decision is settled and binding for the consistory and congregation. Or (2) The consistory, to preserve the right of conscience, may leave the denomination.

The classes and synods have the obligation to insist that their decisions are indeed considered settled and binding because they have a calling to preserve the unity of the federation; and that unity is in doctrine, worship, and government. The consistories, on the other hand, have the obligation to rule in their congregations. And they must do so according to the rule of Christ in the Scriptures as their own consciences determine that Word.

But when disagreement comes, orderly rules for settling the disputes are laid down by the Church Order of the denomination.

What is a classis (or synod) to do if officebearers refuse to consider its decisions settled and binding? When the consistory of Eastern Ave. appealed to synod, the entire

---

16. The rule quoted earlier also states: "If anyone complain that he has been wronged by the decision of a minor assembly, he shall have the right to appeal to a major ecclesiastical assembly" (Art. 31 of the Church Order).

matter should ordinarily have been held in abeyance until synod had spoken. This Classis Grand Rapids East refused to do. It took matters into its own hands and insisted on submission—or suffer the consequences of deposition.

If a consistory refuses to submit to decisions of a classis (or synod), what is a classis to do? Never, under any circumstances, may a classis take it upon itself to exercise discipline. This is a solemn task given to the consistory alone. Discipline is part of the God-given task assigned to the consistory by the Head of the church, the Lord Jesus Christ. For a broader or major assembly to take it upon itself to do this is to usurp prerogatives which Christ has never given it.

Has a classis, then, no recourse? What can it do to a stubborn and recalcitrant consistory? All that classis is able to do is set such a consistory outside the denomination. Such a consistory has broken the unity of the federation; such a consistory must suffer the penalty of being dismissed. But never may a classis discipline.

Another point is at issue here. If a consistory (or congregation, or even an individual) leaves a denomination, that consistory or congregation may very well be guilty of the sin of creating schism in the church of Christ. And if a classis unjustly dismisses a congregation, it becomes guilty of breaking the unity of the church and so on its part creates schism. Such sin is always serious and one ought seriously to ponder the consequences when one is faced with such a painful decision.

But all of this is not discipline. An individual, congregation, or consistory which withdraws from a denomination for conscience' sake will have to answer to Christ for such action. A classis or synod which, to preserve the unity of the denomination, has declared people outside the denomination will also have to answer to Christ. In either case, however, there is a certain agreement to part ways which does not involve any kind of ecclesiastical penalty or discipline by an exercise of the keys of the kingdom.

Discipline is quite different. Discipline is opening or closing the doors of the kingdom of heaven. When discipline is exercised, Christ Himself excludes from the kingdom, for whatsoever is done on earth is also done in heaven. Christ has given the keys of the kingdom to the local congregation (Matt. 16:19). Such discipline is the prerogative of those officebearers whom Christ has set in a local congregation.

The CRC had violated a fundamental principle of church government in deposing officebearers. The principle is crucial because it involves the headship of Christ over the church. Thus, the principle of the autonomy of the local congregation was restored in the reformation that took place when the PRC was formed.

Later History

Nevertheless, this principle was maintained in the PRC only with some difficulty. The balance between the autonomy of the local congregation and the authority of the federation is a precarious one. It needs constant attention and careful practice. The PRC was not always successful in maintaining the balance.

In the early years of its history, in reaction to the gross hierarchy of the CRC, the PRC emphasized the autonomy of the local congregation so strongly that it tended to lose sight of the importance and authority of the federation.

Some evidence of this may be found in an event which took place in the new denomination soon after it had been formed. It is an interesting story.

A congregation had been formed in Hull, Iowa, and a minister by the name of B. J. Danhof had been installed as the pastor of the congregation. Very early in his ministry he came into conflict with some decisions of the denomination and was not satisfied with what the denomination had done.[17] B. J. Danhof took it upon himself to put a notice in a local newspaper informing the community that the Hull, Iowa, Protestant Reformed Church had always been an independent congregation, and that the congregation was no longer a member of the Protestant Reformed Churches.[18] This notice was protested by various members in the Hull congregation, and the classis decided that B. J. Danhof had done wrong.[19] The result was that the pastor, with the majority of the members from Hull church, left the Protestant Reformed Churches.

This strange announcement which the pastor of Hull published was born out of a view of the autonomy of the local congregation which did violence to the federation and unity of the churches.

In subsequent history the emphasis on the autonomy of the local congregation at the expense of the authority of the federation manifested itself in especially two different ways.

First of all, the tendency was to deny the judiciary nature of the broader assemblies. That is, the tendency was to deny that they possessed any authority at all. In 1930, for example, Hoeksema wrote, "May a synod be called the highest judicatory of the church? By no means; the different churches thus voluntarily entering into a federative union acknowledge no other judiciary power than that which is lodged in their respective consistories. The power of a synod is always derivative and advisory."[20]

---

17. The churches in these early days were few in number, and the only broader assembly was "combined consistories," in which assembly delegates from all the consistories came together to make decisions. In a few years, this assembly became a single classis, and in 1940 the churches were divided into two classes, and a synod was organized.

18. Combined Consistories, Minutes of the meeting of November 3, 1926.

19. Combined Classis, Minutes of the meeting of February 2, 1927.

20. Herman Hoeksema, "A Catechism on the History of the PRC," *SB* 7 (December 1, 1930): 111.

Secondly, the autonomy of the local congregations was interpreted in the sense of a limited congregationalism or independentism.[21] This became manifest especially in an interpretation of Article 31 of the Church Order which was then generally held.

The Church Order, in Article 31, requires that decisions of ecclesiastical assemblies be considered "settled and binding" *unless* they are shown to conflict with the Word of God. The word "unless" in this article was interpreted to mean that if anyone had a disagreement with the decision of an assembly and exercised his right of appeal, he did not need to consider the decision which he appealed settled and binding. The appellant considered the decision wrong; he was in the process of appealing it; he maintained the right to agitate against the decision with which he disagreed, make propaganda against it, and attempt to gain as many to his view as he could. For him the decision was not settled and binding at all.

What was true for an individual was also true, it was argued, for a congregation. A congregation, if it considered the decision of a consistory or classis to be wrong and was appealing that decision, had a perfect right to ignore and even defy the decision with which it disagreed. It had no need to consider the decision "settled and binding." The autonomy of a local congregation, so it was said, required this interpretation.[22]

At the same time, there is also evidence of a certain hesitation in the churches for such an unrestricted interpretation. From time to time circumstances required a classis to exercise a certain amount of judicatory power.

---

21. This form of church government, practiced widely among Baptists as well as other congregations, really denies the legitimacy of church federations, at least insofar as broader assemblies have any kind of authority at all.

22. This position is argued in the series of articles by Ophoff: "May a Classis Depose a Consistory?"

In 1932, for example, the classis insisted on an explanation from the consistory of Hope PRC as to why the consistory did not comply with the previous advice of classis.[23] And when the Byron Center congregation had difficulties, and some members who were under discipline were received by the Hudsonville Church without confession of sin, synod not only upheld the decision of Classis East, which ruled that the consistory of Hudsonville was wrong, but insisted on compliance.[24]

In later years more emphasis began to be placed on the judicatory authority of the broader assemblies. This happened especially in connection with the trouble in the churches over conditional salvation and a conditional covenant. Those who eventually left the PRC appealed to the early history of our churches and the views on autonomy held then to support what amounted to a congregational form of church government. Many took the position that an individual or a congregation could accept or reject the decisions of a broader assembly and still remain in the PRC. This position was defended in court in Grand Rapids when the courts were asked to decide which group had legal claim to the property of First Protestant Reformed Church.[25] Over against such a perversion of the Church Order, the authority of the broader assemblies was emphasized.[26]

---

23. Classis East. Minutes of the meeting of June 1, 1932, Arts. 5–7.

24. *Acts of Synod of the Protestant Reformed Churches in America, 1944*, Arts. 70–72. The supplements contain the material of the case, pp. 54–64.

25. Confer the court records and especially the testimony of Rev. B. Kok, which testimony was refuted by Rev. Herman Hoeksema. The testimony of Rev. B. Kok can be found in State of Michigan Supreme Court, Appeal from Superior Court of Grand Rapids, Mich., in Chancery in the matter of First Protestant Reformed Church of Grand Rapids, Mich. (plaintiff) vs. Hubert De Wolf, et al. (defendants and appellants) and Herman Hoeksema, et al. (cross-defendants and appellees). Record on Appeal, 1953 (Grand Rapids: American Brief and Record Company, 1953), vol. 1: 117–54 and vol. 2: 461–682. Rev. Hoeksema's refutation is found in the vol. 2 pages.

26. Interestingly, the controversy centered in the question whether the word "unless," in the phrase "unless it be proved to conflict with the Word of God," also

To a certain extent, a brief and somewhat minor return to an overemphasis on autonomy at the expense of classical and synodical authority took place in the 1970s when overtures came to synod to change some of the constitutions of some of synod's standing committees. The constitutions of the mission committees had given to the synod the power to call a missionary. This, the overtures correctly pointed out, was contrary to the concept of autonomy, which implied that ministers and missionaries held their office from Christ only in a local congregation.

The constitutions, under the weight of the arguments, were duly changed, but the result was that some congregations which called a missionary took the position that the synod had nothing to say about the field of labor or work of the missionary. Synod was there only to pay the bills, even though the Church Order made missions the work of the churches in common.

These differences of opinion demonstrate that keeping a proper balance between the autonomy of the local congregation and the judicatory power of the broader assemblies is not such an easy matter. And the churches do well to keep this in mind as practical questions are settled in the churches.

Preaching after Deposition

One other incident in the early history of the PRC requires some attention. It is closely related to the question of the relation of an autonomous congregation to a denomination of churches.

After Rev. Herman Hoeksema was suspended and deposed along with his elders by Classis Grand Rapids East, he

---

implied "until." That is, is it proper to interpret Article 31 to mean that a decision is to be considered settled and binding "until it be proved to conflict with the Word of God . . . "? That is, the protestant is required, if this interpretation is correct, to submit to a decision during the time he is appealing it to a broader assembly even though he disagrees with it.

continued to preach in his congregation. This, it was claimed, was in violation of Reformed church polity.

Deposition from office means to be stripped of one's office and to be forbidden to exercise the duties of the office. That decision of Classis Grand Rapids East was, according to the Church Order, settled and binding. Rev. Hoeksema had the right to appeal the decision of classis to synod; but while the appeal was in process, submission was required. This Rev. Hoeksema did not do. He ignored the decision of classis and, though he appealed to synod, he continued to preach, and the elders, also deposed, continued to function in their offices.

Rev. Hoeksema explained his reasons for doing what he did.[27] He pointed out a number of circumstances that required that he continue to preach. For one thing, the decision of the synod on common grace had contained in it an ambiguity in that Rev. Hoeksema, who emphatically repudiated common grace, was declared officially to be Reformed, and a decision to discipline him was rejected. Classis had run roughshod over this, which made the decision of classis wrong.

In addition to that, the classis had acted illegally in taking upon itself the power to depose, an action which only a consistory has the Christ-given right to do. Thus the deposition, as the sentence of Christ who seals all the discipline of the church, was invalid. Christ Himself did not depose Rev. Hoeksema.

Thirdly, Hoeksema pointed out the fact that the synod did not meet for another two years, and the matter of his deposition could not be adjudicated until then. What was he to do? And what was his responsibility towards his congregation? The classis had made no provision for the care of the congregation. Most of the congregation supported their pastor. He could not, before God, leave them without a

---

27. See Hoeksema, *The Protestant Reformed Churches in America*, 219, 220.

shepherd, easy prey to the ravening wolves which would soon enter the flock and tear the sheep.

Nevertheless, the point was made that, as wrong as classis' decision was, Hoeksema was bound by the Church Order to submit until his appeal could be heard on synod.

Rev. Hoeksema knew and understood this. The consequences of his conduct were serious. But by continuing to preach and thus ignoring classis' decision, he was taking a course of action perfectly in keeping with Reformed church polity: in effect, leaving the Christian Reformed denomination. This was his right and prerogative. If one cannot, in good conscience, abide by a decision of a broader assembly, he always retains the right to leave that federation of churches. And he has the right to leave without ecclesiastical penalty. This is the right of the individual conscience before God.

That Hoeksema knew he was leaving the CRC and establishing a new denomination is evident from the fact that the congregation in which he was pastor, along with three other congregations, signed an "Act of Agreement," took a different name,[28] and proceeded to organize other congregations throughout the United States, mostly from people who had been members of the CRC.

When the synod of 1926 adjudicated the case, it basically refused to treat the appeal of Hoeksema on the grounds that Hoeksema was no longer a member of the CRC. This was technically correct, although it would have been morally upright to treat a case which arose out of the confusion which the synod itself created.

---

28. The name was "Protesting Christian Reformed Churches" to indicate that they had an appeal pending with the synod of the CRC. The claim that the CRC cast out the men who founded the PRC, a claim insisted upon by the PRC, rests upon the fact that all three ministers were deposed from office, which discipline would have had to be followed by further discipline should they not have submitted to the decision of classis.

Summary

The three aspects of the church's life—its doctrine, its government, its liturgy—always belong together. The three are closely united because all three really involve doctrine. The government of the church is an expression of the truth of Scripture concerning the way Christ rules in His church. Liturgy is an expression of how Scripture directs Christ's church to worship God. No wonder, then, that when a church departs in doctrine, it departs from God's Word in the government of the church and in its liturgy. It need not surprise us that, when the CRC departed from the truth of particular grace, it departed from Scripture's principles of church government as well. It gave to higher assemblies the power to exercise discipline over officebearers. It robbed the local church of authority which Christ had Himself given to the congregation. This was serious, so serious that reformation in this matter was required, for such error is ultimately destructive of the church. When the leaven of hierarchy is allowed to develop in the church, no longer do elders rule in the church of Christ, but broader assemblies take over the rule, and when broader assemblies do the work of elders, the rule of the church is put into the hands of committees and boards. Christ does not rule His church through committees and boards; He rules through elders.

It is Reformed to maintain firmly, as the PRC does, the autonomy of the local congregation, while at the same time giving the broader assemblies their right to exercise judicatory authority in the federation in order to preserve the unity of the denomination. But such exercise of authority must never usurp the right of the local church to preach God's Word, administer the sacraments, and exercise discipline.

Through the struggles to be faithful to Scripture in church government, the PRC once again gave to the important principle of the autonomy of the local church its proper meaning and emphasis, and have, on the whole, held it in its correct tension with the principle of the authority of the broader assemblies.

One more point ought to be made by way of summary. The PRC has contended over the years that the CRC cast out the leaders of the PRC and forced them to form a new and separate denomination. The PRC have contended that the CRC was guilty of casting out faithful men of God of whom the CRC itself witnessed that they were Reformed, left them without a church home, and forced them outside the instituted church of Christ. The horror of this may be seen in the fact that the church is the mother of the faithful. The people of God are brought forth by mother, nourished at mother's breasts, disciplined, comforted, instructed, and cared for throughout life under mother's gracious protection. But in the instance of the CRC's deposition of faithful officebearers, mother banished faithful children from her household and told them, in effect, to fend for themselves. Mother wanted no part of them any longer. And the only reason that can be deduced for such cruel treatment is that faithful men rebuked mother for her sins.

The CRC has argued that these men who were disciplined were not expelled from the denomination, but left by their own volition. These men left when they refused to submit to the decisions of the classes which deposed them, while appealing their case and unjust treatment to synod. This is technically correct. The option was there for Revs. Hoeksema, Ophoff, and Danhof to cease to preach in their congregations, appeal to synod, and allow other ministers to work in their churches during the long two years they would have to wait before their cases could be adjudicated.

These deposed ministers refused to do that. Their refusal was, in the final analysis, rooted in their deep conviction that they were responsible for their congregations and for the sheep which were entrusted to their care. It would have been negligence of the worst sort to abandon their sheep and turn them over to shepherds who had proved to be unfaithful by their willingness to subscribe to the error of common grace. They were true shepherds who were willing to pay any price for the safety and welfare of the flock.

And so the technical point fades into insignificance. They were truly cast out of mother's house. They were told in effect: We will not have you in our house unless you submit, contrary to Scripture and the confessions, to God-dishonoring decisions. We will prevent you from serving your sheep. We will put shepherds over your flocks who will deceive and lead astray. We require of you that, if you do not submit to mother's decisions, we will let you stand helplessly on the sidelines while others take care of your sheep.

Hence, Hoeksema, Ophoff, and Danhof were truly expelled, for they could not do what the CRC demanded. The welfare of Christ's sheep is always first. This decision will be honored by Christ who loves His sheep when all appear before His throne.

PART 3:
The Positive Development of the Truth

CHAPTER 6

Introduction

The history of dogma has its principium in Holy Writ, even as in the closed canon it has its starting point. That which develops in the history of dogma is not the truth of revelation, for it is complete and the canon is closed; to what is revealed no tittle or iota can be added. But the reflection of that truth in the believing mind of the church and its systematic expression and definition is characterized by progress and development . . . Dogmas are born as soon as the believing mind of the church concentrates and logically systematizes the truth of revelation.
—Herman Hoeksema, *"History of Dogma"*

The Protestant Reformed Churches have often been charged with making their objections to common grace the only point of concern in their writings and preaching. The charge is that the leaders of the PRC, stung by decisions of the CRC which threw them out for denying common grace, can talk of nothing else, as if common grace is the only point in all Reformed theology worth speaking about.

That allegation is untrue. It cannot be denied that in the early history of the PRC a great deal of attention was paid to the issues which brought about the beginnings of the denomination. This is understandable. The CRC, as if in justification of its conduct, devoted an extraordinary amount of time and energy to defending common grace and criticizing those who denied it. These attacks against sovereign and particular grace had to be answered.

Besides, the leaders of the PRC believed that it was their calling to bring to the attention of all whom they could reach that the issues were important and crucial in the life and calling of the people of God. They believed that the decisions taken by the synod of the CRC in June 1924 brought apostasy into that church, from which it was unlikely that the church would repent. Such apostasy could only lead to further apostasy and deterioration, and those who remained in such a denomination were imperiling their souls and the souls of their children.

Nevertheless, it was by no means true that the controversy which erupted over common grace in the CRC occupied all the attention of the PRC in the years following 1924. It is not even true that it occupied most of the attention of the leaders and the people. And it is certainly not true that the PRC took such a negative position that they were only "against" certain views, and that no one ever really knew what these churches were "for."

Such a thing never happens if the reformation of the church is true reformation.

It is true that a church which, though historically manifesting the church of Christ on earth, departs from the truth and chooses to go the abysmal way of apostasy, rarely, if ever, returns. One can search the pages of the history of the church in vain to find instances. It seems almost certain that the rule of God is that once a church departs, it sets itself on a path that leads steadily downhill into deeper and deeper heresy.

For this reason, the true church of Christ cannot long endure in such an apostatizing denomination; it has to come out of an unfaithful church to survive as the church of Christ. Thus Christ calls the faithful out, as He called the faithful from the lukewarm church of Laodicea before He spit it out of His mouth (Rev. 3:14–22). And thus the faithful must reestablish the church so that the truth of God may continue to have witnesses in the world. The church, according to Paul, is, after all, the pillar and ground of the truth (I Tim. 3:15).

Such coming out of an apostatizing denomination is church reformation. It was for Luther and Calvin. Such reformation took place in the British Isles when Presbyterianism was established over against Anglicanism, and when the faithful left apostate Presbyterian churches in the nineteenth century to reform confessional Presbyterianism. Faithfulness demanded departure from an apostatizing denomination in the Netherlands in the reformations under H. De Cock and A. Kuyper. The same was required in 1924 when the PRC began its separate existence.

Because an unfaithful church has departed from the faith once delivered unto the saints, a certain "going back" is always required in church reformation, a return to what Jeremiah calls the "old paths" (Jer. 6:16). The church must recover what has been lost, not only of the tried and true faith from earlier centuries, especially laid down in the confessions of the church, but also of true worship and government in the church. In other words, it is not only a return to true doctrine, but also to a biblical liturgy and church government.

But once the church returns to these old paths, it cannot live in the past. It must engage in that great task assigned to her of uncovering in greater measure the riches of Holy Scripture. A church which lives in the past becomes an anachronism. A church which does nothing else but rave against evils perpetrated by those who cast her out becomes as stagnant as a dead pond which is polluted and choked by algae. Only a church which, having gone back, once again moves forward is an institution worthy of the name "church."

One crucial aspect of the calling of the church to develop the truth must never be forgotten. The development of the truth in which the church of Christ must engage may never be a development of the truth which is cut off from the truth of the past. The false church denies the past, divorces itself from history, and in the name of relevancy repudiates its heritage. It consigns the confessions to museums and criticizes the formulations of these confessions as outdated expressions of ideas held many centuries earlier, but irrelevant to modern times. It begins anew in the work of theology and finds new ways to make itself capable of addressing the problems of a more modern day.

In making itself guilty of such foolishness the false church denies that the truth of the past is the fruit of the Spirit of Christ, mocks the studious labors of godly theologians who spent their lifetime wrestling with Scripture, condemns the work of the church of the past to the dust heaps of history, and in so doing, empties the churches of faithful members and commits ecclesiastical suicide.

The truth of God is one—confessed from the beginning to the end of time. It is that one grand truth which unites the church of all ages in a unity of the body of Christ. Of that development of the truth there is no end on this side of the grave. But that development, the ongoing work of the church, is like the gradual opening of a rose bud which slowly reveals all the aspects of its beauty. It takes all the centuries of the history of the world, and especially of the new dispensation, for the rose bud to unfold; but it is the same rosebud.

Almost always when a church which has engaged in genuine church reformation continues its important work of developing the truth, it does so prompted by the experiences which brought about the reformation in the first place. In 1924 the main doctrinal issue was particular vs. common grace. It is not strange that the doctrinal developments of various aspects of the truth should have their occasion in the defense of particular grace and a refutation of common grace.

Many of these developments were significant contributions to the whole body of Reformed truth. To understand that God used the PRC to develop them is not only to appreciate more fully our Reformed heritage, but it also enables us to see our God-given reason for existence as a separate denomination.

In the following chapters I shall pay attention to various areas in which the truth of God's Word was developed in the PRC.

CHAPTER 7

The Sovereign Grace of Miracles

A wonder belongs entirely as to its idea in the sphere of grace. In general we would circumscribe a wonder as that act of God whereby He raises the whole of His creation, fallen in sin and under the curse, into the glory of His eternal kingdom and everlasting covenant.

—Herman Hoeksema, *Reformed Dogmatics*

The Janssen Controversy Bears Fruit

In chapter 2, I described the major role which Rev. Herman Hoeksema played in the Janssen controversy. Although Janssen, by his higher criticism, denied the divine character and some of the factual data of Scripture, it was his denial of the miracles which especially secured his condemnation in the church. If the people could not always follow the intricate arguments of Janssen on various other higher critical issues, they certainly understood his denial of the miracles. Such denial was, in their minds, unforgivable.

To Hoeksema, however, the interesting point of the whole matter was that Janssen appealed to Kuyperian common grace in support of his denial of the miracles.[1] Many have

---

1. Janssen argued, our readers will recall, that since scientific discoveries were the fruit of common grace, when these discoveries conflicted with the testimony of Scripture, the church was required to reexamine its explanation of Scripture to make it harmonize with science. If this sounds far-fetched to some readers,

taken the position that Janssen, in appealing to this kind of common grace, was attempting merely to invoke the support of an outstanding theologian who had many followers in the CRC. He was attempting by this ploy to divert attention from his views and concentrate them on another subject. He was dragging a red herring across his trail.[2]

The synod of 1922, while condemning Janssen, did not deal with the question of common grace. But the irony of the whole matter was that the synod of 1924 adopted the very basis of Janssen's heresy as biblical and confessional dogma and threw out of its fellowship those who denied it. The defeat of Janssen's pernicious errors was a Pyrrhic victory: the battle was won, but the war was lost.

The close connection between Janssen's denial of the miracles and common grace led Hoeksema to examine the whole question of miracles, especially as they had been defined and developed in past Reformed thought. And the consideration he gave to the question of miracles was from the perspective of the doctrines of sovereign and particular grace.[3]

Miracles and Providence

Hoeksema treated the doctrine of miracles under the general heading of providence. This in itself is not so

---

the CRC very recently approved of an evolutionistic interpretation of the origin of all things with an appeal to common grace. See *Acts of the Synod of the Christian Reformed Church, 1991*, Arts. 83, 86, pp. 762–65.

2. See my thesis, "A Study of the Relation between the Views of Prof. R. Janssen and Common Grace." When the time came to defend my thesis before the faculty of Calvin Seminary I was quizzed rather closely on this point. Those of the faculty engaged in the questioning insisted that Janssen's appeal to common grace was totally without warrant, in other words, that there was no intrinsic connection between Kuyperian common grace and a denial of the miracles. The history of the CRC has proved otherwise.

3. For the material which follows, I rely on the rather lengthy discussion of miracles found in Herman Hoeksema, *Reformed Dogmatics* (Grand Rapids: Reformed Free Publishing Association, 1966), 227–44. I consider Hoeksema's treatment of miracles to be one of the most significant and beautiful treatments of the subject to be found anywhere.

strange, for that was the place in Reformed dogmatics where miracles had usually been discussed. But, while treating miracles and providence together, many theologians set both doctrines outside of the doctrine of salvation in Christ. These Reformed theologians did not see the connection between providence and salvation and, as a result, made providence a work quite independent of God's work of saving grace. Providence and the salvation of the church ran in two different riverbeds, or along two different tracks. And the relation between the two was tenuous, intermittent, and incidental.

All this led to a kind of dualism in the works of God. It was taught that God, in His providence, upheld and ruled the world. But God had also an additional work which He performed when He saved His people in Jesus Christ.[4]

It is not difficult to go from such a dualism to a position which ascribes providence to the area of common grace, and the salvation of the church to the area of special grace. Providence was considered a general and non-saving work of God which embraced all creation. Providence brought rain and sunshine, health and prosperity. So also common grace, which included rain and sunshine, belonged to providence and not to the work of salvation.[5]

According to dualism, history runs in two channels: the channel of providence and common grace, and the channel of salvation and special grace. Only occasionally and somewhat incidentally do the two meet, and only arbitrarily does God's

---

4. Providence and salvation were not, of course, completely separated in Reformed theology. Scripture is too clear on the fact that all things work together for good to those who love God and are called according to His purpose (Rom. 8:28) to deny that providence must ultimately serve the salvation of the church. But no intrinsic connection was found.

5. See the first point of common grace, quoted in footnote 12 of chapter 3, which referred to Matthew 5:45 as proof of God's favor towards the wicked in rain and sunshine. The same decision also referred to Psalm 145:9 and Acts 14:17 as proof of the same favor.

providence specifically serve the salvation of the church and common grace serve special grace.[6]

This whole conception was abandoned by Hoeksema. He insisted that Scripture taught only one purpose of God in all that God did; and that purpose was being realized from the very beginning of time. The original Paradise, the creation of man and his subsequent fall were all subservient to God's purpose in the salvation of the church.

And included in the salvation of the church was also the salvation of the entire creation, fallen under the curse, but also redeemed in Christ and brought to the greater glory of the new heavens and the new earth.[7]

Providence, in all aspects, is God's work which He performs in order that His church might be saved in Christ. That is, providence itself is part of the revelation of God in Jesus Christ because all things are under the rule of Christ, and Christ rules over all for the one purpose of saving His church and bringing the whole of God's creation to its final perfection. These considerations were fundamental in Hoeksema's thought.

---

6. It can be argued that the basic divorce of providence from salvation was something of a conclusion derived from infralapsarianism. Infralapsarianism defined the order of God's decrees as being the same as the order of history. That is, God first determined to glorify Himself through Paradise the first; but the temptation and fall of man effectively prevented the realization of that purpose. So God determined to glorify Himself through Jesus Christ and the salvation of the church.

The usual interpretation of providence, especially as it was defined in later years by Abraham Kuyper in his views of common grace, was one which made providence a kind of preservation of God's original purpose through common grace. God does not abandon His original purpose but preserves it through common grace, while He works out an additional purpose in the salvation of the church.

Kuyper's view seemed strangely inconsistent, for Kuyper was strongly supralapsarian in his early ministry when he was a powerful defender of particular grace.

7. I shall have more to say about this in a later chapter, for these ideas form, in a certain sense, the heart of PR theology.

Miracles and Particular Grace

In his treatment of miracles, Hoeksema discusses, first of all, various interpretations of miracles which have been offered in the past and which are in harmony with the generally accepted ideas of providence. They can be summed up as follows.[8]

Miracles were explained in terms of violations of, or interferences with, natural law. The creation operates according to fixed laws imbedded in the creation at the time when God formed it. These laws have been discovered by man and are known to him. The entire operation of the universe can be explained in terms of them.

But on occasion God intervenes in such a way that natural laws are suspended and God works in ways other than these laws. While usually the earth takes twenty-four hours to rotate on its axis, in the days of Joshua and in answer to his prayer the day was much longer, so that Israel might defeat its enemies. Usually when a man dies, that is the end of his earthly existence, but God suspended this law at certain times and brought men who had died back into this life.

Hoeksema pointed out two serious objections to this view of miracles, though both are related.

In the first place, such a view tends to deny that all that happens in the creation is by the direct hand of God operating in His own world, and not the result of natural law. While Hoeksema did not deny that God usually worked in a regular and predictable way in His creation, he insisted that the concept of natural law as usually described was basically a deistic idea that pushed God out of His own world and explained the world in terms of forces operating independently of God.[9]

---

8. Hoeksema cites the views of C. Hodge, J. J. Van Oosterzee, L. Berkhof, and G. Vos as examples of the views he criticizes. He speaks favorably of the views of H. Bavinck. Hoeksema, *Reformed Dogmatics*, 237, 238.

9. Deism is that heresy which views the world much like a clock. The clockmaker fashions the clock, winds it up, and lets it run on its own, which it

In the second place, Hoeksema insisted that all things which take place, whether the "normal" events of the creation or the miracles, were equally and in the same way God's work. God made the walls of Jericho fall, but that work was no more a work of God than the course of a planet in the solar system, the trail of a snowflake falling from leaden skies, or the path of an ant across the sidewalk in front of one's feet. God's providence not only means that God continues to give life and existence to every creature, but it also means that God so rules that His counsel is carried out in the minutest detail. Nothing is left to chance or natural law; God's hand moves every creature so that it serves His purpose.[10]

Closely connected with the view that defined miracles as being violations or suspensions of natural law, miracles were often viewed as works of God which we are unable to understand—apparently in distinction from works of God which we can understand. The idea was that, while most of the time we are able to explain what happens in terms of the natural laws discovered by science, some works of God, defying science, are beyond explanation. While we can explain how an apple tree grows from an apple seed, we cannot explain how the gourd which shaded Jonah outside Nineveh grew in a few hours and perished in a few hours. That is, we cannot explain it in any scientific terms.

Once again, the idea here is that of natural law, with which science has to do and which forms the explanation of

---

is perfectly capable of doing. So God creates the world with its natural laws, withdraws from His creation, and permits the creation to operate on its own. He may intervene occasionally to "set the clock more accurately," but His intervention is on rare occasions and only when absolutely necessary. Such a deism in the eighteenth century led to a complete denial of all miracles, of angels and demons, and of the miraculous work of Christ.

10. I well remember how this was often demonstrated to us in class by Hoeksema's animated reading of Psalm 29: "The voice of the Lord is upon the waters: the God of glory thundereth: the Lord is upon many waters . . . The voice of the Lord breaketh the cedars . . . The voice of the Lord shaketh the wilderness."

all things which take place. Those events are called miracles which are a suspension of natural law and are, for this reason, beyond explanation. To find the explanation of miracles along these lines is to fail to recognize the true nature of all the works of God.

Hoeksema reminds us that in very fact there is not one work of God in all His creation which can be understood by us. Science may offer some limited explanation, but science, with all its boasting, cannot explain the mysteries of the universe. Science cannot explain in terms of natural law how a blade of grass grows, how an oak tree comes from an acorn, how a human eye operates, how a baby is formed in the womb of its mother. All these works of God defy explanation because they deal with the deepest mysteries of life itself. We cannot understand how 5,000 people could be fed with five loaves and two fishes; but we cannot understand either how a seed of corn dies when it is put in the earth, and that it must die to bring forth a new corn stalk. This is because everything is God's work directly and immediately, and everything which God does lies beyond human understanding.

Miracles indeed belong to providence, but only because providence is to be understood as God's sovereign guidance over all His creatures so that all His creatures, including wicked men and devils, serve the salvation of His church.

All that God does in His providence is for the purpose of the revelation of His sovereign and particular grace in the salvation of the church. The ship of the creation, a figure Hoeksema often used, is guided through history by God so that it arrives at the shore of eternity. All things serve the salvation of the elect in Christ, even reprobate men and angels. They are the chaff necessary for the growth of the wheat, but burned with fire when the wheat is gathered into the granary.

Miracles belong to this work of grace.

Miracles took place in the creation because God was saving

His people and the creation in Christ. By Adam's sin the creation itself fell under the curse and all men became totally depraved. Gloom, despair, hopelessness, and dark judgment hung over all. But God's purpose is not realized in the first Adam; it is realized in the second Adam, our Lord Jesus Christ. And so, from the beginning of time God announced His purpose to send Christ and through Christ to save the elect and the creation which man had ruined.

Miracles are the signs of that work of God.

A sign is something that happens in this earth but which points to something heavenly. Miracles are such signs. Signs attract people's attention because they are different from the ordinary. God usually makes the sun come up and go down again at predictable times. But God, without any additional effort on His part or without laboring, can suspend the sun and moon and make the day twice as long as it normally is. That attracts people's attention because it is not God's usual way of working. And so it becomes a sign.

Men born blind usually remain such all their lives. But once in a while these blind were made to see by the mere command of the Lord. Usually the water of the Nile was fit for drinking, washing, and irrigation. But once it was made blood. That captured people's attention.

All men, of course, see the miracles. But the wicked do not like miracles. Miracles make them uncomfortable because their cozy universe is suddenly invaded by alien and inexplicable forces. And indeed miracles remind the wicked of what they really know all along to be true—that God rules sovereignly and demands to be worshiped. So they deny the miracles.

But God's people are able to see and understand the miracles. They are signs of God's great work in Christ. God reaches down into this sin-cursed creation and with a mighty arm rescues it and His elect by a powerful work of grace in Christ. Every miracle is a ray of heavenly light in the gloom, a word of salvation in the curse, a glimpse of God's great power to save.

Every miracle points to Christ, the Light of the world, the Power of God unto salvation to all who believe, the Daystar that arises in our hearts, the Sun of Righteousness with healing in His wings. Every miracle points to Christ's work. Christ makes the spiritually blind to see, the spiritually deaf to hear, the spiritually dead to come forth from their graves. Christ makes the stars in their courses fight against Sisera, and the sun and moon fight against Joshua's enemies, so that the church may be saved. Christ raises up kings and princes, even mighty Cyrus, so that the church might be brought back from captivity.

Miracles are, therefore, signs which are given by God to point us to the great miracle of all time, the miracle of salvation in Christ. God comes in Christ into this sin-ravaged world to bring all His elect and all the creation into the glory and blessedness of the everlasting kingdom of Christ in the new heaven and the new earth.

Such salvation of the elect and of the creation was God's eternal purpose, which He had determined before the foundation of the world. To that purpose all that God does must be subservient. This includes the original creation, the fall, and all the history of this present creation.

As the history of this world unfolds, it appears to be the history of a fallen world in which sin reigns and in which all the consequences of sin must be endured by the human race. Disease, death, war, suffering, pain—all speak eloquently of the wrath of God against sinful man and of the sure execution of God's sentence: "The day that thou eatest thereof thou shalt surely die." Hospitals, rest homes, nursing institutions for the aged, mental institutions, prisons, cemeteries, and blood-soaked battlefields all testify to God's burning wrath against the sinner.

But immediately after the fall, God preached the gospel of salvation to our first parents (directing, strangely enough,

His words to Satan): "I will put enmity between thee and the woman, and between thy seed and her seed" (Gen. 3:15). That Word of promise spoke of the coming of Christ and the great things God would do through Christ. But God always accommodates Himself to the weakness of the faith of His people and the doubts and fears that plague their souls. He condescends to cater to their stupidity and inability to understand spiritual things. This was true especially in those days when the completed Scriptures were not in the possession of the church and the church had no objective and infallibly inspired record of the gospel in Scripture.

God gave the church signs of what He was doing and would do so that the church could have some tangible evidence of God's mighty works.[11] They would have something which their eyes could see and which would help them understand God's great works. In the old dispensation God gave them help in understanding things by the signs of miracles. Israel was surrounded by miracles.

Of course, only the people of God in whom the work of God's grace had been performed could see and understand these miracles. The wicked never wanted them nor would believe them. The Jews of Jesus' day were abundant proof of the inability of the wicked to see and understand the miracles. They saw all Jesus' works, which testified of Him, and they were witnesses of the mighty miracles which He performed. And yet, with the crassest arrogance, they asked for a sign to prove Jesus' claims. When the Lord cast out devils, they said He did it in the name of Beelzebub the prince of the devils, and they came perilously close to committing the unpardonable sin. When a voice from heaven

---

11. God gives His church such signs also in the new dispensation in the sacraments. These sacraments are added to the Word so that we, of weak and wavering faith, and of spiritual inability to understand, may have tangible and visible testimonies of what God does for us in Christ.

testified that Christ was God's beloved Son in whom God was well-pleased, they muttered that it had thundered.[12]

But God's people saw in these miracles God's testimony of His mighty works. They saw pictures of God's purpose to save His creation and His elect in Christ. And they looked in hope beyond the miracles, which were only signs of the reality which they could expect when Christ would come.

God performed miracles to provide for the needs of His people. The manna in the wilderness during Israel's wandering and the water from the rock in Rephidim pointed to Christ the Bread of Life and to the Spirit of Christ who comes to the church to save them. The miracle of the destruction of Sennacherib's hosts by the angel of Jehovah pointed believing Israel to the preservation of the church by Christ Himself so that no enemy could overcome them.

Cyrus' decree that Judah could return to its own land demonstrated to the people of God how God makes the wicked serve the salvation of His church—even though they storm and rage against God's people.

The miracles of the sun standing still and the hail that killed Israel's enemies—as well as the star in the East that summoned the Magi—were eloquent testimonies that the creation itself was at the service of the church saved in Christ. The toppling of Jericho's walls and the complete rout of David's enemies showed the saints that their victory over all the forces of sin and evil was guaranteed by the victory of Christ on the cross, for faith is the victory that overcomes the world.

Miracles of healing recorded in both the Old and New Testament Scriptures spoke directly of salvation worked by the Holy Spirit. The lame walk as a sign that God gives

---

12. Things have not substantially changed in recent centuries. Dedicated attempts have been made by those who despise miracles to give natural explanations to them. Janssen did this in the early 1900s. It is common today.

grace to His people to walk the way of faithfulness to Him, which leads to heaven. The blind see, for, as Jesus told His disciples: Blessed are your eyes for they see the mysteries of the kingdom of heaven spoken of in parables. The dead were raised because Christ raises His people from the spiritual death of the curse and hell that they may live with Him forever.

After the Scriptures were completed, the church no longer needs the signs of miracles because the Scriptures, infallibly inspired, are the unfailing testimony of God's work of grace. We have something solid, something objective, a work of God profound and wonderful to which we can cling. Alleged miracles will not and cannot add to those Scriptures. Indeed, such miracles, as is evident from the entire charismatic movement, detract from Scripture and lead God's people away from the sure rock of Scripture's testimony.

But what need has the church of miracles any longer when the one great miracle of the ages has been performed by God? Christ has come and now sits on the throne of the universe to accomplish all that God has determined to do. That miracle is the possession of the people of God, for the Spirit of Christ is within them to give them all the riches of salvation as Christ earned it on His blessed cross. We only wait for the final chapter of that miracle to be written when Christ comes again upon the clouds to destroy the wicked, take His church to glory, make all the creation new, and dwell with His people in the blessed marriage relation of God's covenant, world without end.

Summary

One will never understand the miracles of Scripture unless one understands in each miracle a sign of the work of God in Christ to save His church. They are signs which God gave to point to the great work of God which He performed. Imbedded in history and a part of history, they defy history's gloomy and downward course to destruction. They come as the voice of God from another world, from heaven itself, to tell of grace in a sin-cursed world, of hope and light where all is hopeless and dark. That light shines from heaven itself, and will engulf all the elect and all the creation when God makes all things new in the day of Christ. But miracles must be a part of history because Christ—in His birth, His cross, His resurrection from the dead, and His ascension—is in history as a part of history, in order to redeem history and bring it to its grand finale at the end of time.

Such a conception of miracles requires that they be considered in the light of sovereign and particular grace. One can never deny them, as Janssen did and as so many do today, without denying ultimately the one great miracle of Christ and salvation in Him. Understanding miracles, therefore, in their true biblical significance, one cannot imagine how anyone can possibly speak of a grace common to all. They all testify of what God does graciously in the work of salvation, and that for His elect people in Christ.

CHAPTER 8

Sovereign Grace and Revelation

We know [God] by two means: first, by the creation, preservation and government of the universe; which is before our eyes as a most elegant book, wherein all creatures, great and small, are as so many characters leading us to contemplate the invisible things of God, namely, his power and divinity . . .

—Confession of Faith

The relation between [general and special revelation] is such that the handwriting in nature declares in earthly symbols what the revelation of God in Scripture expresses in plain human language.

—Herman Hoeksema, *Standard Bearer*

Background

The idea of "general revelation" had long occupied an accepted and honored place in Reformed theology. The term was used to define God's speech concerning Himself in the creation. It was one of the two speeches of God present in this world and available to men, the other being God's speech in Scripture. It was said to have confessional sanction in Article 2 of the Confession of Faith.[1] In the early years of

---

1. Article 2 reads: "We know [God] by two means: first, by the creation, preservation and government of the universe; which is before our eyes as a most elegant book, wherein all creatures, great and small, are as so many characters leading us to contemplate the invisible things of God, namely, his power and divinity, as the apostle Paul saith, Rom. 1:20. All which things are sufficient to

the PRC, the idea of general revelation was taught as a part of the doctrine of the church. It was included in a lesson in a catechism book in Reformed doctrine prepared by Rev. Hoeksema and used for the instruction of the young people of the covenant in their advanced doctrine class.[2]

But in spite of the fact that he included the doctrine in his catechism book, Hoeksema had some reservations concerning it. While still in the CRC, Hoeksema had expressed concern that "the life of the Reformed people has simply been steeped with the spirit" of the principle of common grace. One of the results of this influence of common grace was, Hoeksema observed, that "general revelation" was given a significance far beyond its divine intention. Proponents of common grace claimed that general revelation contained in it valuable elements for the faith of the people of God, so that in the New Testament church reconciliation had taken place between "the science of revelation" (special revelation in Scripture) and the "science of nature" (general revelation in creation). Christianity, as a result, was considered to be the fulfillment of heathendom.[3] A wrong view of general revelation, Hoeksema insisted, was inseparably connected to common grace.

General revelation was commonly accepted and found in works of many different writers.[4] And, indeed, it was not

---

convince men, and leave them without excuse. Secondly, he makes himself more clearly and fully known to us by his holy and divine Word, that is to say, as far as is necessary for us to know in this life, to his glory and our salvation."

2. Herman Hoeksema, *Essentials of Reformed Doctrine: A Guide in Catechetical Instruction* (Grand Rapids: n.p., 1927), a book of questions and answers for memorization along with questions which required some thought and research to answer. The book was written in its original form by Herman Hoeksema. It underwent some revision, although no significant change. The latest printing was in 1982.

3. Danhof and Hoeksema, *Van Zonde en Genade*, 81.

4. Schaff, for example, speaks of the *logos* present in creation, which was clear enough to enable the heathen to come to a sufficient knowledge of God to look forward with some measure of eagerness for the coming of Christ. Philip Schaff, *History of the Christian Church*, vol. 1 (Grand Rapids: Wm. B. Eerdmans Publishing Co., 1956), 74–6.

infrequently connected to common grace. Herman Bavinck, for example, devoted a fairly lengthy section to a discussion of the relation between general revelation and common grace in his book *Our Reasonable Faith*.[5] It is possible that even Albertus Van Raalte adopted a similar position.[6] But it had become explicit in W. Masselink's book *General Revelation and Common Grace*.[7]

It is not surprising, therefore, that as Hoeksema pondered the close connection between common grace and the generally accepted view of general revelation, he also saw that to abandon common grace was to face the need to modify his doctrine of revelation.

How Common Grace and General Revelation Were Connected

The idea of general revelation is based primarily on Romans 1:19, 20: "Because that which may be known of God is manifest in them [the context here makes clear that the reference is to the heathen who have not the gospel]; for God hath shewed it unto them. For the invisible things of him from the creation of the world are clearly seen, being understood by the things that are made, even his eternal power and Godhead; so that they are without excuse." Clearly the text points out that God makes Himself known even to the heathen who live and die without ever hearing the gospel. They know who God is, and they know that He must be served as the only true God. "God hath shewed it

---

5. Bavinck, *Our Reasonable Faith*, 37, 38. Herman Bavinck was a late nineteenth and early twentieth century theologian, a contemporary of Abraham Kuyper.

6. Spykman, "The Van Raalte Sermons," 100. Spykman claims that Van Raalte's sermons show evidence of a "two-level, nature / grace framework" in which Van Raalte defended a kind of dualism between "worldly knowledge" and "true wisdom." This, according to Spykman, resulted in an "unresolved tension" in Van Raalte's thought between common grace (which must be connected to worldly knowledge) and special grace (which must be connected to true wisdom).

7. Masselink, *General Revelation and Common Grace*.

unto them," and God showed these things to them "by the things that are made," that is, by the creation itself. Hence, in addition to the revelation of God in Scripture, God also speaks concerning Himself in creation.

No one had any objection to this view as such, and it was the view incorporated in the catechism book which Rev. Hoeksema prepared. The trouble came when this idea of God's speech in creation to all men was connected to common grace.

The connection was made in many ways. In the first place, the most basic point was that this speech of God in creation which all men could and did hear was common grace because revelation in creation was evidence of God's favor towards the heathen, who were, because of their sin, to be considered under God's wrath. God's wrath was softened by an attitude of favor, and God's attitude of favor was evident in God's willingness to show Himself to the wicked.

In the second place, this grace was not only objectively present in God's speech in the creation, but, through that speech in the creation, grace was also subjectively bestowed upon the wicked, so that they received this grace in their hearts. Kuyper especially had developed this idea in his *Gemeene Gratie*,[8] and it had been at least implied in the three points of common grace adopted by the synod of the CRC in 1924. This latter was evident from the fact that the synod, in an effort to find confessional support for Kuyper's common grace, had referred to and quoted Canons III & IV, 4 and the Confession of Faith, Article 14.[9] The Canons speak of

---

8. Abraham Kuyper, *De Gemeene Gratie,* 3 vols. (Amsterdam: Höveker and Wormser, 1902). See also Hoeksema, *Van Zonde en Genade,* where Kuyper's views are described in detail.

9. Canons of Dordt, III & IV, 4 speaks of "glimmerings of natural light, whereby [man] retains some knowledge of God, of natural things, and of the differences between good and evil," and the Confession of Faith, Art. 14, speaks of man's retention, even after the fall, of a few remains of the excellent gifts with which he had been endowed when he was created.

a knowledge of God which the heathen possess. And the Confession of Faith mentions gifts which it calls "excellent."

In the third place, God's grace given to the heathen outside the gospel was such a powerful grace that it enabled fallen and totally depraved man to do a great deal of good. Ralph Janssen, for example, had used this idea of grace to the heathen through "general revelation" as the explanation for his view that the Israelites, in the development of their religion, adopted many ideas from the heathen which surrounded them. Bavinck spoke of a common grace, shown through God's speech in creation, which gave such a significant knowledge of God to the heathen that these heathen became dissatisfied with their own idol worship, began to thirst for the true God, and thus were prepared spiritually for the advent of the gospel which was brought to the nations after Pentecost.[10]

This close relationship between "general revelation" and common grace has continued over the years among those who hold to the concepts. A striking example of this is to be found in a decision of the CRC justifying theistic evolution. When theistic evolution was being taught in Calvin College, and when protests were lodged on the synod against this teaching, synod said that, because of common grace, the speech of God in creation had to be received as valid. And the speech of God in the creation spoke of a very old earth, which had developed over innumerable millennia by the processes of evolution.[11] The argument was that we have two speeches of God, one in creation and one in Scripture. These two must agree because they are both speeches of

---

10. Bavinck, *Our Reasonable Faith*, 37, 38.

11. See David J. Engelsma, "Creation and Science . . . and Common Grace," *SB* 67 (February 15, 1991 and March 1, 1991): 221–223 and 245–247 for an analysis of the report submitted to synod. For the report itself and the decisions of the CRC, see *Acts of Synod of the Christian Reformed Church, 1991*, Arts. 83, 86, pp. 762–765.

God. And so when the speech of God in creation tells us that the earth is very old and that it developed through various evolutionary processes, then we must accept that as God's own Word.[12]

The moral law of God is also a part of God's speech in creation. This is taught in Romans 2:14, 15 in the same general context as Paul's words in Romans 1. This passage reads: "For when the Gentiles, which have not the law, do by nature the things contained in the law, these, having not the law, are a law unto themselves: which shew the work of the law written in their hearts, their conscience also bearing witness, and their thoughts the mean while accusing or else excusing one another."

The proponents of common grace, however, claimed that this moral law, embodied in creation, is also evidence of common grace. Again, Canons III & IV, Article 4 was appealed to in support of this position, especially the words: "There remain . . . in man since the fall, the glimmerings of natural light, whereby he . . . discovers some regard for virtue, good order in society, and for maintaining an orderly external deportment."[13]

---

12. The irony comes in when the two speeches of God appear not to agree. The speech of God in Holy Scripture tells us that the earth is very young, only about 6000 years of age. The proponents of evolution apparently consider the speech of God in creation (even though it is fallible and heard by sinful men), to be more trustworthy than the speech of God in Scripture, which is God-inspired. And so, the interpretation of Scripture is altered in fundamental ways to make Scripture agree with science. One would think that it is apparent that science should be made to agree with Scripture since science is man's word and subject to repeated alteration, modification, and amendment. But the opposite is done, and Scripture is made to agree with science.

13. When the synod of 1924 quoted this article in support of common grace, it quoted only the first part and omitted the second, a part which would, if quoted, have disproved their interpretation of the article. The first part was quoted as proof that the depraved sinner can do civil good. The omitted part reads: "But so far is this light of nature from being sufficient to bring him to a saving knowledge of God, and to true conversion, that he is incapable of using it aright even in things natural and civil. Nay further, this light, such as it is, man in various ways renders wholly polluted, and holds it in unrighteousness, by doing which he becomes inexcusable before God."

Moral law was said to be rooted in and a part of general revelation. In relating it to common grace, it was argued that this moral law was revealed in creation and imbedded in the consciousness of every man. In fact, it was argued that, because this revelation of God's moral law was grace, the natural man was capable of doing the "works of the law." This ability to do the works of the law, in turn, made it possible for the Christian to cooperate with the world in certain areas of life. Johannes Groen, Herman Hoeksema's predecessor in Eastern Ave. CRC, even argued that the Christian could legitimately join "neutral" labor unions because they were governed by "precepts and regulations derived from general revelation."[14]

It is not surprising, therefore, that the whole concept of general revelation was subjected by Hoeksema and the PRC to renewed study in the light of Scripture and the confessions in order to free it from the shackles of common grace.

The Positive Development

Hoeksema's lack of enthusiasm for general revelation showed itself even before the establishment of the PRC. When he took issue with Kuyper's common grace in 1923, Hoeksema dealt also with Canons III & IV, 4 and the concept of glimmerings of natural light which fallen man retains. He insisted that this natural light could not possibly be identified with any natural goodness in fallen man, as Kuyper claimed, but rather that it refers to a certain ability to know, which man retains simply because he remains man, even though he is fallen man. It also refers to the knowledge of God which the natural man actually does possess through creation, namely, God's eternal power and Godhead, but which man holds down in unrighteousness.[15]

From time to time one can find references in Hoeksema's

14. Henry Zwaanstra, *Reformed Thought*, 268, 271.
15. Danhof and Hoeksema, *Van Zonde en Genade*, 161–68.

writings to some aspect of this question as, for example, in an article entitled "The Wrath Revealed from Heaven: Romans 1:18ff." Here Hoeksema pointed out that one could hardly call God's general revelation "grace" when the text itself is discussing "the wrath of God revealed from heaven."[16] But what is striking is the fact that Hoeksema's mature view of so-called general revelation came out when he was compelled by developments in the Reformed churches to write against various forms of theistic evolution raising their ugly heads in the Christian colleges and schools. In an important article, written already in 1928, Hoeksema explained and sharply repudiated evolution: "It makes no difference what form of the evolution theory you accept, on its basis you have no revelation of God in the universe."[17]

The main point of Hoeksema's criticism, however, is his objection to the idea of two kinds of revelation: general and special. He calls this idea "dualism" because it does not reckon with sin as determined by God's immutable counsel. Such a view of general revelation presupposes that if sin had not entered the world, revelation in nature would have been enough for man's ultimate entry into heaven.[18]

Hoeksema insisted that the two speeches of God in creation and in Scripture are basically one. God never intended to reveal Himself fully in creation. As Hoeksema pointed out, already before the fall of Adam and Eve, God used special revelation to speak directly to Adam.[19] God eternally determined that sin should enter the world in order

---

16. *SB* 2 (September 1, 1926): 412–15.

17. Herman Hoeksema, "God's Handwriting In Nature," *SB* 5 (September 15, 1929): 572.

18. Ibid., 573. The dualism with which Hoeksema charged the defenders of evolution became abundantly evident when it was admitted that the "speech of God in creation" sharply contradicted the "speech of God in Scripture" on the question of the age of the earth and the way in which God formed all things.

19. Ibid., 573, 574.

for a fuller and more perfect revelation of Himself through Jesus Christ to be given and recorded infallibly on the pages of Holy Scripture.

This revelation of God through Jesus Christ is the full revelation of God. It is the revelation of God's eternal purpose to redeem His church as well as the entire creation in Christ in the new heavens and the new earth. Hence the earthly is created after the pattern of the heavenly in order to point us to that heavenly creation which is the ultimate purpose of all God's works. The result is that the speech of God in creation is directly related to and serves the greater purpose of God's revelation in Scripture.

Scripture points out this close relation between the earthly and the heavenly in different ways. Jesus could compare the kingdom of heaven with a sower who went out to sow, a fishnet dragged through the sea, a pearl of great price, and a wedding feast to which many guests were called. A Roman infantry soldier with armor and weapons can give us some idea of Christian warfare and of a Christian's defense while under the attack of Satan and his hosts (Eph. 6:11–17); a dove can be a symbol of the Holy Spirit who descended upon our Lord (Matt. 3:16); an earthquake can point to the final destruction of this earthly creation to make way for the new (Hag. 2:6, 7); and God Himself can be seen in the immovable rock which resists the pounding of the seas and in which people can find a refuge in time of storm (Ps. 61:2).

But, because of the spiritual blindness of fallen man, we must, as Calvin reminded us, put on the eyeglasses of Scripture to see these things. Those eyeglasses are made usable by the enlightening power of the Spirit who gives us eyes to see. Thus Jesus says of us: "Blessed are your eyes, for they see" . . . the mysteries of the kingdom of heaven locked up in these parables of the earthly creation.[20]

---

20. For an eloquent statement of the relation between the earthly and the

To demonstrate that the speech of God in creation is the same as the speech of God in Scripture, Hoeksema appealed to both Scripture and the testimony of creation itself. Expressing his dissatisfaction with the entire concept "general revelation," and referring to it as a "*so-called* general revelation,"[21] he insisted that the two were related: ". . . the relation between the two is such that the handwriting in nature declares in earthly symbols what the revelation of God in Scripture expresses in plain human language."[22]

The creation is, after all, adapted to the work of salvation. The Psalms repeatedly speak of this truth when they tell us of the mercy of God and the wonders of salvation made known in creation. A striking example which Hoeksema chose in order to demonstrate this point was the antithesis. The spiritual separation between the wicked and God's people of which the Psalms speak so eloquently is found over and over again in the creation itself.[23]

A natural religion is, therefore, forever impossible, for, although the wicked can see God's power and Godhead in creation, they are unable to see things heavenly and spiritual, for these are foolishness to them.[24] The conclusion is that

---

heavenly, see Milton S. Terry, *Biblical Hermeneutics* (Grand Rapids: Zondervan Publishing House, 1976), 244ff.: "May we not safely affirm that the analogies traceable between the natural and spiritual worlds are parts of a divine harmony which it is the noblest mental exercise to discover and unfold? . . . Trench has the following profound observations: 'It is not merely that these analogies assist to make the truth intelligible, or, if intelligible before, present it more vividly to the mind . . . Their power lies deeper . . . They are arguments, and may be alleged as witnesses; the world of nature being throughout a witness for the world of spirit, proceeding from the same hand . . . All lovers of truth . . . know that the earthly tabernacle is made after the pattern of things seen in the mount; and the question suggested by the angel in Milton is often forced upon their meditations—"What if earth / Be but the shadow of heaven and things therein / Each to other like, more than on earth is thought?"'"

21. Hoeksema, "God's Handwriting in Nature," 573.
22. Ibid.
23. Ibid., 574. One can find such a striking example in Psalm 1, which Psalm is the major theme of the entire Psalter.
24. Hoeksema, "God's Handwriting in Nature," 575.

"even in this respect there is no general or common grace. The heathen have the revelation of God in nature without the light of Scripture. And they also lack the spiritual light of the grace of God in their hearts. They are without excuse for they know God, all things revealing Him in His eternal power and Godhead and proclaiming that He must be feared and glorified."[25]

These important ideas are also discussed in Hoeksema's Introduction to *Reformed Dogmatics*. He comes very close in this Introduction to denying that God's speech in creation can even be called "revelation" in any sense when the wicked are involved, because revelation implies someone "who can receive and understand God's speech."[26]

Although surely, before the fall, Adam and Eve were able to hear and see the speech of God in creation, the fall had serious consequences for such revelation. On the one hand, the speech of God in creation is drowned now by another word of God, the word of the curse. God's speech continues, but it is the speech of wrath. "God is the terror of the creature that hears His speech."[27]

On the other hand, sin so affected man himself that he is no longer capable of hearing that speech. This is not due to a loss of man's natural faculties, but is due to the awfulness of sin. Sin makes man spiritually blind to God's revelation because man's hatred of God makes the confession of God's power and Godhead impossible. Wicked men hold the truth in unrighteousness, according to Paul in Romans 1:18.[28]

Hence two things are required for revelation to take place. One is God's gift of the Holy Scriptures, which reveal God in Jesus Christ and which are the key to unlock the knowledge of God in creation. The other is the enlightening power

---

25. Ibid.
26. Hoeksema, *Reformed Dogmatics*, 17.
27. Ibid., 18, 19.
28. Ibid.

of the Holy Spirit in the hearts of God's people, by which power the darkness of sin is destroyed and God's people are enabled to know spiritual things. Appealing to I Corinthians 2, Hoeksema insists that the natural man can never know God, while the spiritual man who possesses the Spirit is able to appropriate revelation.[29] There is no revelation in the true sense of the word where those who are in the presence of it are blind. One may "reveal" a beautiful painting to an audience, but if everyone in the audience is blind, there is no revelation at all.

The wicked surely do possess glimmerings of natural light and some remnants of the excellent gifts with which they were originally endowed when created in Adam. But this only means, according to Hoeksema, that they were men before they fell, that they remained men though they fell, and that, therefore, they continue as rational and moral creatures, though totally depraved. The glimmerings and remnants are the powers of mind and will which enable them to know that God is God and that He must be served, leaving them without excuse when they suppress the truth in unrighteousness.

But even this natural light and these excellent powers are only glimmerings and remnants of what Adam possessed before he fell. They are like the tattered remains of a fur coat badly eaten by moths in the course of a summer. Even these remains are used by man to sin, and they make him all the more guilty before God. They are not a common grace from God to man, as the Arminians said,[30] and as the CRC maintains.

Thus the truth that God's grace is both sovereign and particular became crucially important for the doctrine of revelation. The fact that the force of the argument

---

29. Ibid., 20, 21.
30. Canons of Dordt, III & IV, B, 5.

demolished all theories of evolution was almost incidental.[31] God does not show grace to the ungodly, but wrath, in His speech in creation (Rom. 1:18). The speech which the ungodly are able to hear concerning God's eternal power and Godhead is sufficient to leave them without excuse (1:20). But even that speech the wicked hold under in unrighteousness and change the glory of the incorruptible God into an image like unto corruptible creatures (1:23, 25). Before these they bow in worship. And God, just and righteous in His wrath against sin, gives men over to every unspeakable lust, especially the horrible sin of homosexuality (1:26, 27).

God does give grace. But He gives grace to His elect people, sovereignly and efficaciously. He gives that grace to His people objectively in giving them the Holy Scriptures, in which are revealed all the riches of God's truth and love in Christ Jesus as the God of salvation. And in these same Scriptures He gives the key which unlocks the speech of God in creation so that God's people are able to see that, even in creation, Christ is revealed in all His work. The heavens declare the glory of God and the firmament showeth His handiwork, for the stars point us to Christ, the Bright and Morning Star, and the sun going forth from its chambers speaks eloquently of the Sun of Righteousness who arises with healing in His wings. With eyes to see, God's people are always pointed to Christ. They see Christ in the Lion of Judah's tribe, the Rose of Sharon, and the Lily of the Valley. They see in the rainbow God's covenant with creation. In the seed that dies in the ground before it can produce a stalk

---

31. I do not mean "incidental" in the sense that the heresy of evolution is not important. It is a crucially important heresy which ultimately destroys the whole of Scripture, because it will not take literally God's own narrative of creation. But it is "incidental" because it was not the main point of the argument in Hoeksema's discussion of revelation. Yet it is true that if one understands correctly the nature of God's speech in creation, evolution becomes nonsense, and Scripture's description of the creation of all things becomes that which we accept by faith in the Word of God.

of corn, they see a witness to the resurrection of the body. And in the change of a caterpillar in a chrysalis to a beautiful butterfly, they hear the eloquent speech of God concerning the change in their bodies from earthly to heavenly, conformed to Christ's glorious body. All created things sing a joyful doxology of praise to Him who has promised to save the creation—and us.

Thus, the speech of God comes in all its beauty and majesty to sinners saved by grace. They hear the powerful voice of God coming to them in Scripture; but, putting on the eyeglasses of Scripture, they are able to see the salvation of God even in all the things that are made.

Summary

Perhaps no single concept is more basic to PR theology than the concept of revelation. Even God's eternal covenant of grace rests solidly on the truth that God reveals Himself. He is in His own triune life a covenant God, who has perfect fellowship in Himself and enjoys the blessedness of His own fellowship. The covenant of grace which He establishes with His people in Christ is but the *revelation* of His own infinitely blessed life. He reveals the riches of His own covenant life by taking His elect people into that covenant life through Jesus Christ.

God does not reveal Himself by two different and unrelated speeches: one in creation and one in Scripture. Nor does God adapt His speech in creation to the unbelieving, while giving the Scriptures to the church, so that each possesses his own book. Nor is the speech of God in creation "common" grace, while Scripture conveys "special" grace.[32]

---

32. It is doubtful whether even the proponents of common grace would consistently maintain such a distinction. While Dr. Abraham Kuyper spoke of common grace as belonging only to the reprobate, the Secessionists held to a common grace which was shared by elect and reprobate alike. This view of the Secessionists is proved by the fact that the well-meant offer of the gospel was a

God has one purpose in His eternal counsel. That purpose is to glorify Himself and His own great name. God determines, freely and sovereignly, to glorify Himself through the revelation of His infinite perfections and His eternal blessedness. All that revelation of His greatness and glory is through Jesus Christ and only through Him. Because God's purpose is one, God did not first decide to reveal Himself through the first Paradise and make salvation possible through that original work of creation.[33] God was not frustrated by Adam's unwillingness to cooperate or by his blatant disobedience in forming an alliance with Satan. Adam did not force God into a serious alteration in His plans in order to attempt to make something from the mess Adam brought into the world. Christ and God's revelation in Christ is not another speech intended to undo the failed attempts of God in the original creation.

God's purpose is one great and glorious purpose: to reveal the riches of His own being through Jesus Christ. For Christ is the highest and best, the most wise and most perfect revelation of God. All things are subordinate to that purpose of God: creation, Paradise, Adam, the fall, the history of the world, the organic development of sin, and the salvation of the church.

Creation still reveals God, but only to the elect. This is the real point of Article 2 of the Confession of Faith, which has often been wrongly quoted as proof of two revelations. It must be remembered that this article is part of the confession of the faith of God's people. Hence, Article 2 begins with the words: "*We* know [God] by two means . . ." Not all men know God by two means, but we—in other words, God's people who confess their faith in the world—know Him by two means.

---

particular manifestation of common grace to all men, elect and reprobate alike.

33. This original salvation would then be accomplished by a kind of covenant of works.

It is true that the article speaks of this book of creation leaving all men without excuse. This is the very clear statement of Paul in Romans 1:18ff. But this speech of God in creation is not grace to the wicked, but wrath. It is part of the wrath of God revealed from heaven. God sovereignly accomplishes His eternal purpose in reprobation and the revelation of His wrath from heaven by seeing to it that the wicked are without excuse.

The wicked never come to any true spiritual knowledge of God by means of creation, for they are spiritually blind. They are spiritually incapable of knowing and perceiving spiritual things—as Paul makes clear in I Corinthians 2.

God formed with great care the original creation, so that all that He had made was very good, perfectly adapted to serve His purpose in Christ. He erected the stage on which would be enacted the great drama of sin and grace. He built it with care and precision so that it might serve to be the backdrop of all history. Into that history Christ entered to save the cursed creation and the elect. In Christ and all that He redeems, therefore, God reveals all His infinite perfections so that He may be praised and glorified forever.

Creation was such a perfect stage for this divine drama that the stage itself was a harmonious and grand symbolic display of the heavenly. The earthly was formed and fashioned after the pattern of the heavenly. The earthly speaks of heavenly things and helps us in our earthiness to understand what God's purpose is all about. Everything is rich with this heavenly beauty. Everything reveals heaven's streaming light. Jesus, aware of this, spoke in parables. Scripture, taking up this glorious song, always leads us to contemplate the heavenly by means of the earthly. Creation is a symphony of heavenly themes.

But the music can be heard and the instruments in the orchestra can be seen only by the people of God who have been given eyes to see and ears to hear. This is a work of sovereign and particular grace wrought as a part of salvation. Because of this great grace, the choir of the redeemed lift their voices, accompanied by the symphony of God's glorious world, to sing the song of Moses and the Lamb. Then God is glorified, for He has sovereignly revealed, through the Lamb slain from the foundations of the world, the riches of His grace and mercy and love and greatness.

CHAPTER 9

The Doctrine of Scripture

Verbal inspiration therefore must be understood in connection with the complete system of Christian doctrine. It may not be detached therefore, and a fortiori it may not be framed in an alien view of God. Verbal inspiration is integral with the doctrines of providence and predestination.
—Gordon Clark, *God's Hammer*

Through the Scriptures, the Holy Spirit works in the hearts of the people of God. The preaching of the gospel, setting forth the content of the Scriptures, is the power of God unto salvation to all who believe. By the Scriptures faith is worked. Through the on-going power of the Scriptures, God's people receive grace for every sorrow, every trial, every need. Always those Scriptures are, to use some of Scripture's own metaphors: bread for the hungry soul; cool and refreshing water to him that thirsts; a shield to protect one from the fiery darts of the devil; milk to enable the babe in Christ to grow; a surgeon's scalpel which cuts away the sin and corruption that would destroy us; indeed, a lamp unto our feet and a light upon our pathway.
—Homer Hoeksema, *The Doctrine of Scripture*

The History of the Doctrine

In the writings of the founders of the PRC on a large variety of subjects, less attention is paid to the doctrine of Holy Scripture than most other subjects. Until the 1980s no books were written on the subject; few sermons were printed dealing with it; almost no articles in the *Standard Bearer* were devoted to it.[1] Even in his magisterial work *Reformed Dogmatics* Herman Hoeksema does not discuss the doctrine at length, but only mentions it in his Introduction.

It is certainly possible to deduce reasons for this somewhat strange silence. The chief reason was, no doubt, that, even though the truth of the infallible inspiration of Scripture had been under fierce and relentless attack for over a century in many liberal and evangelical churches, it had not been a serious issue in Reformed churches until near the middle of the twentieth century. Generally speaking, all agreed on the question of the infallible nature of the inspiration of God's Word. Ralph Janssen had questioned it in his higher critical attacks on Scripture. He had spoken of an "organic inspiration" of Scripture, by which he meant that God had given to Scripture's authors, in a somewhat general way, the ideas He wanted incorporated in His Word, but had left the formulation of these ideas to the secondary authors themselves.[2] But these views had been condemned by the CRC, and the issue did not come up again for many years.

This silence on the doctrine must, however, not be interpreted as meaning that no doctrine was maintained and taught among the ministers and leaders of the PR churches. The traditional doctrine of Holy Scripture, commonly taught in conservative Reformed and Presbyterian churches, was maintained. It was believed that Scripture came to us through divine inspiration, but in such a way that men were employed in its writings. Thus one could speak of a divine and a human factor in inspiration, and a divine and a human element in Scripture itself. The divine element guaranteed Scripture's

---

1. Herman Hoeksema wrote a series of articles in vol. 8 of the *Standard Bearer* in which he discussed a controversy in the Netherlands concerning Scripture. In this series he developed some ideas of his own. See footnote 4 in this chapter for the references.

2. Hanko, "A Study of the Relation between the Views of Prof. R. Janssen and Common Grace," 57–64, especially 62, 63.

infallibility, but the human element explained how each author wrote in his own style, using his own unique gifts, and expressing himself in a way compatible with the cultural circumstances of the time and place in which he lived. Moses reflected in his writings his education in the courts of Pharaoh. David knew sheep and could write Psalm 23. Amos left the indelible mark of a herder of cattle on his prophecy. Paul wrote as one trained under Gamaliel, but converted by his vision of Christ on the road to Damascus. Asaph wrote as an Old Testament Psalmist preparing music for the temple service. John wrote as a profoundly intuitive student of the unique ministry of the Lord Jesus in the dispensation when all was fulfilled.

B. B. Warfield suggested a certain analogy between the incarnation of Christ Jesus and the inspiration of Scripture.[3] That is, Warfield had supported the idea of a certain analogy between the divine and human natures of Christ on the one hand, and the divine and human elements in Scripture on the other hand. But this analogy did not really take hold in the thinking of Reformed apologists, although it seemed, on the surface, to explain forcibly the fact of a human and a divine part in Holy Writ.

I am guessing, therefore, when I suggest the possibility that Ralph Janssen's appeal to common grace in defense of his critical approach to Scripture was a spark which led Herman Hoeksema to give some thought, from time to time, to the doctrine of inspiration and infallibility. While his thinking in this area was never systematically published, he did lay the groundwork for a Reformed view in a lengthy series of articles in the *Standard Bearer* as early as 1931 and 1932. These articles were an analysis of the views on

---

3. Homer C. Hoeksema, *The Doctrine of Scripture* (Grand Rapids: Reformed Free Publishing Association, 1990), 58, 59. The quotation is from Benjamin B. Warfield, *The Inspiration and Authority of the Bible* (Philadelphia: The Presbyterian and Reformed Publishing Co., 1948), 162, 163.

Scripture and the Reformed confessions by a Dr. Ubbink in the Netherlands.[4] And, addressing the very practical need for more Bible reading and study in the home, Hoeksema wrote a series of editorials on the subject in which he dealt with some of the questions involved in the doctrine of inspiration and infallibility.[5] But both series were for different purposes than a development of the Reformed doctrine of Scripture.

A View Inherent in Preaching and Teaching

Nevertheless, various practices in the churches and various truths taught in the catechism classes indicated very clearly that without exception all the ministers and teachers in the PRC held to an infallible Bible.

The preaching from the very beginning of the PRC was characterized by very careful and painstaking exegesis of the original Hebrew and Greek texts, which took into account the significance of every word. This was done in the firm conviction that the inspiration of Scripture was verbal inspiration, in other words, that God the Holy Spirit, the Author of Scripture, never chose one word over another arbitrarily. In every word, He had His purpose. A deep reverence for the sacred Scriptures characterized all the teaching in the church, the Christian schools, and the home. The Scriptures were accepted as the only rule of faith and life, and the people of God were taught to bow before the authority of Scripture because it was of divine origin. Even if no detailed view of Scripture had been developed in the

---

4. Herman Hoeksema, "De Nieuwe Belijdenis Aangaande Schrift en Kerk" (The New Confession Concerning Scripture and the Church), also titled, in some issues, "Dr. Ubbink's Proeve Eener Nieuwe Belijdenis" (Dr. Ubbink's Example of a New Confession). A series of thirteen editorials from *SB* 8 (February 1, 1932) through 8 (September 15, 1932), skipping issues 17, 22, and 23. Articles start p. 4 of each issue.

5. Herman Hoeksema, "Bibles and Bible Reading," *SB* 11 (October 15, 1934): 28; 11 (November 1, 1934): 52–3.

churches, an attitude of awe and reverence before the sacred volume was common and gave evidence of a strong faith in the infallibility of Scripture.

All the ministers whose preaching was so carefully expository had been taught in the Theological School of the PRC and thus reflected the views of Scripture held by their professors. Not only were they taught a hermeneutics which maintained the unique character of Scripture as God's infallible Word, but they were taught to put this truth into practice in exegesis and homiletics.[6] And a great deal of exegesis of Scripture was given to the students in chapel talks and lectures,[7] all of which could not help but give to the students practical instruction in the truth of infallible inspiration.

An interesting event took place in the mid-1950s which demonstrates the commitment to the doctrine of Holy Writ on the part of the leaders in the PRC.

When the committee for the translation of what was later to become the New International Version (NIV) of the Bible was being formed, the PRC was invited to participate. Synod approved of this and appointed a committee to do the work. An executive committee for this work sent to the committee of the PRC a questionnaire, the purpose of which was to ascertain the views of the participating churches on how the work of Bible translation was to be done. From the questionnaire it was soon apparent that the executive committee favored a theory of translation which was known as "dynamic equivalence." That is, the executive committee

---

6. "Hermeneutics" is the study of the rules of biblical interpretation; "exegesis" is the actual work of interpretation; "homiletics" is the science of sermon-making.

7. Many of these chapel talks are available in syllabus form from the bookstore of the Theological School of the Protestant Reformed Churches in Grandville, Mich. They show very careful and thorough exegesis of Scripture which breathes a spirit of reverence for the sacred text.

favored, not a literal translation, but a translation which took the general thought of the original and put it into an equivalent English thought. The committee of the PRC, disagreeing with that theory, answered the questionnaire in such a way that they brought strong objections against the theory of dynamic equivalence and made their case for a more literal translation.

In 1961 and 1962 the committee of the PRC reported to synod that it had not heard further from the translating committee; and in 1964 synod decided to discontinue its committee.[8]

The Development of the Doctrine

Through the labors of subsequent professors in the seminary, particularly the work of Rev. Homer Hoeksema, the actual development of the doctrine of Scripture continued.[9] Two forces gave impetus to the work. One was the increasingly influential works of higher critics in formerly conservative churches, who adopted some forms of literary and historical criticism and taught them openly in the seminaries of Reformed and Presbyterian churches. The other goad to the development of the doctrine was the departure from the doctrine of infallibility in these churches and the adoption of unbiblical views on certain matters, which required that the truth of infallibility be modified. Such modification was, for example, the case in the CRC when, because Scripture's infallibility was no longer maintained, evolutionistic views of Genesis 1–11 were approved, and women were given the right to hold ecclesiastical office in the church.

---

8. *Acts of Synod of the Protestant Reformed Churches in America*: 1958, Art. 134; 1959, Art. 138; 1960, Art. 79; 1961, Art. 40; 1962, Art. 192; 1964, Arts. 63, 64.
9. Homer Hoeksema, *The Doctrine of Scripture*.

The Central Issue

Scripture is closely related to the doctrine of revelation, because Scripture is the infallibly inspired record of the revelation of God in Jesus Christ as the God who saves His elect church. If revelation itself is God's speech concerning Himself and His works in Christ, it would seem to follow that the record of that revelation would also be God's work.

Because of this connection between revelation and Scripture, the question arose in the development of this doctrine: Is there really an element in Scripture that can be called "human"? No one in the history of the church had ever taught that the Bible had miraculously fallen from heaven, or that men whom God used to write the Bible were nothing but stenographers. This was so obviously out of keeping with the nature of Scripture itself that to hold to this kind of a "dictation theory" of inspiration would have been crass foolishness.

Nor did anyone deny that the old Reformed doctrine of inspiration as maintained in both the Westminster Confession and the Confession of Faith was right in its definition of inspiration. In fact, the creeds were important in this ongoing development of the doctrine of Scripture because they never so much as mention a human element in inspiration, although the Confession of Faith speaks of human instruments of divine inspiration.[10] In this, they reflect the Scriptures

---

10. The Westminster Confession of Faith speaks of inspiration thus: "It pleased the Lord . . . to commit the same wholly unto writing" (I, 1); "The authority of the Holy Scripture . . . dependeth . . . wholly upon God . . . : and therefore it is to be received, because it is the Word of God" (I, 4); "The Old Testament . . . and the New Testament . . . , being immediately inspired by God . . ." (I, 8). The (Belgic) Confession of Faith speaks of our need to receive the Scriptures "because the Holy Ghost witnesseth in our hearts, that they are from God" (Art. 5); it puts in the mouth of believers the confession that the Word of God comes to us because "holy men of God spake as they were moved by the Holy Ghost," and that "God commanded his servants . . . to commit his revealed word to writing" (Art. 3); it warns against considering "of equal value any writing of men . . . with those divine Scriptures" (Art. 7).

themselves, which, in the two classic passages on inspiration, describe Scripture in every part as "God-breathed,"[11] and as not of any private interpretation,[12] because the will of man was not involved in the work of inspiration, but men sanctified by God spoke as they were carried along by the Spirit.[13]

As I mentioned earlier in the chapter, an analogy between the incarnation of Christ and the inspiration of Scripture did not really take hold. But Hoeksema did find an analogy between the work of salvation in the hearts of the elect and the inspiration of Scripture.[14]

The analogy suggests itself because Scripture is an integral and essential part of God's salvation of His church in Christ. God's revelation, infallibly recorded in Scripture, was God's speech concerning His eternal purpose to save a church in His own Son through the work of the cross, the resurrection, and the ascension of Christ. And Scripture, in infallibly recording that revelation, is the authoritative Word of God which, when preached, is God's means to gather, defend, and preserve His elect church.[15]

---

11. II Timothy 3:16. The Greek "God-breathed" was rendered "given by inspiration of God" in the KJV.

12. II Peter 1:20. That is, not expressing any human opinion about anything.

13. II Peter 1:20, 21: ". . . prophecy came not in old time by the will of man . . ."

14. Homer Hoeksema, *The Doctrine Of Scripture*, 80, 81. The analogy, which was rejected, between the incarnation and Scripture, that is, between the union of the divine and human natures of Christ on the one hand, and the union of a divine and a human element in Scripture on the other hand, was used to charge those who denied a human element in Scripture with Docetism. The name seemed to fit because Docetism is an ancient heresy, found especially among the Gnostics, which denied the reality of Christ's human nature. Docetists claimed Christ's human nature was only an appearance.

15. In other words, a distinction must be made between revelation and inspiration of Scripture. Revelation took place throughout the entire period of sacred history. The Heidelberg Catechism speaks of our knowledge of our Mediator, Jesus Christ, as given to us through "the holy gospel, which God himself first revealed in Paradise; and afterwards published by the patriarchs and prophets, and represented by the sacrifices and other ceremonies of the law; and lastly, has fulfilled it by his only begotten Son" (Answer 19). God caused a record of that revelation to be recorded in Scripture by means of inspiration.

Another interesting aspect of the development of the doctrine was the joining of the inspiration of Scripture to the idea of the miracle.[16] The relationship was this. The central miracle which God performs is God's wonder of grace in Christ by which He sovereignly reaches down into this sin-cursed creation to save, through Christ's perfect work, His elect church and the entire creation and make it glorious as He is. The Scriptures, inspired by God as the authoritative book to be preached for the purpose of the gathering of the church, belong to that miracle.[17] The Scriptures themselves are miraculous in their origin and formation. They are miraculous, not simply because their inspiration cannot be explained in earthly terms, but because they are part of the miracle of salvation in Jesus Christ.

The analogy, therefore, if there is to be one at all, is between God's work of salvation and inspiration.

God's work of salvation in the hearts of God's people is of such a kind that it is wholly and completely of grace without the works of men. We are saved by grace, through faith. That salvation is not of us, but is the gift of God (Eph. 2:8, 9). This does not mean that we do not do good works as a result of our salvation, but our good works are God's work in and through us. For we are God's workmanship. We are created in Christ Jesus with a view to good works. God has foreordained those good works from all eternity, and has foreordained that we should walk in them (Eph. 2:10). We are to work out our salvation with fear and trembling. And we are able to do this because God works in us not only the will to do it, but the actual doing as well (Phil 2:12, 13). God is the Author of faith which is worked within us by the Holy Spirit, but He is also the Author of our very act of believing (Canons III & IV, 14).

---

16. See chapter 7 of this book.
17. Homer Hoeksema, *The Doctrine of Scripture*, 11–14, 83–86.

It is, therefore, impossible to speak of a human element in salvation. All is of God. And all remains *of* God, even though the works of the believer are His own works. That is the miracle of salvation, that which the Canons call a "supernatural work, most powerful, and at the same time most delightful, astonishing, mysterious, and ineffable; not inferior in efficacy to creation, or the resurrection from the dead" (Canons, III & IV, 12). Indeed, the will of fallen and sinful man, "being evil, disobedient, and refractory," God makes "good, obedient, and pliable," so that, "like a good tree, it may bring forth the fruits of good actions" (Canons, III & IV, 11). And the will, "thus renewed . . . becomes itself active," so that "man is himself rightly said to believe and repent, by virtue of that grace received" (Canons, III & IV, 12). So all the works of man remain his works, though worked by God.

So it is with Scripture. Paul's writings bear the unmistakable imprint of Paul's gifts, personality, work, and cultural milieu. And David's Psalms are the fruit of his own poetic soul and his high position as king of Israel and type of Christ. Psalm 84 is unmistakably different from Romans 5. But the Holy Spirit wrote them all and used men in such a way that the product was His work, not man's, though He used man in a way wonderful, mysterious, delightful, and perfectly suited to the salvation of the elect church of Christ.

This very doctrine of inspiration became a basis for a warning against Arminianism. Just as Arminianism is the introduction of a "human element" into the work of salvation, so to introduce into the inspiration of Scripture a human element is to do injustice to the work of God the Spirit in Scripture's inspiration. The opposite is also true: the only way to preserve consistently the truth of infallible inspiration is to do so on the basis of the sovereignty and particularity of grace in the work of salvation. If one becomes Arminian in his soteriology, he will soon lose the infallibility of Scripture as well. Countless churches, ravaged by higher criticism, will have to trace their spiritual demise to an introduction of the corroding influences of Arminian thought into their theology.

Inspiration and Common Grace

Common grace "commonized" the Bible. It opened the door to higher critical attacks on it.

Ralph Janssen had begun this already. Educated in universities in Europe where higher critical studies were common, he had drunk deeply at these wells and had carried over to Calvin Seminary the fruits of his studies. He insisted that common grace made his kind of critical work a necessity. God had, in grace, revealed His truth to the heathen as well as to Israel. Israel, in the formulation of its own monotheism, doctrines, and laws, borrowed from the heathen, because Israel was compelled to make use of the fruit of God's common grace among the heathen. Thus Scripture was the product of general revelation given in God's common grace to the heathen, and of special revelation given in saving grace to Israel. Israel's religion was a synthesis of Babylon and Jerusalem, of Egypt and Canaan. And critical studies were essential to find those "human" elements in Scripture and to discover the origin of these human elements in the nations who lived in the lands around the people of God.[18]

Janssen's position pushed open the door to all the critical studies which have destroyed the truth of infallible inspiration in so many Reformed and Presbyterian churches. What seminaries still repudiate literary and historical criticism consistently? All have gone after the siren call as foolish sailors lust after Lorelei's beautiful and seductive songs, only to be shipwrecked on the rocks of a Scripture with a "human element."[19]

---

18. Hanko, "A Study of the Relation between the Views of Prof. R. Janssen and Common Grace," 52.
19. Ibid.

Proof of Infallibility

Some important truths concerning Scripture's inspiration and content emerge from the doctrines of Scripture which are a part of the PR heritage.

Perhaps one of the most important is the truth that the proof for Scripture's inspiration and infallibility must come from Scripture's testimony of itself and not from empirical proof.[20] It is argued that Scripture's self-testimony as to its divine authorship and infallible contents is an inadequate argument because it is "arguing in a circle." A short imaginative discussion with an unbeliever will demonstrate what is meant by this.

Is Scripture the Word of God?
Yes!
How do you know?
Scripture says so.
How do you know that what Scripture says is trustworthy?
Scripture says so.

Yet, while this may sound like an argument in a circle, in fact it is not. A human book such as the *Institutes of the Christian Religion* claims for itself to have been written by John Calvin. No one in his right mind ever challenges that. The testimony of the book itself is sufficient. And the evidence of such self-testimony is acceptable in any court of law and cannot be overthrown. How much more is this not true of Scripture? Every page testifies that it is written

---

20. Homer Hoeksema, *The Doctrine of Scripture*, 11. It is a fact that most Bible scholars, even of a conservative bent, seem enamored with the idea of "proving" Scripture's inspiration by other means than by the testimony of Scripture itself. What these scholars do in relation to the inspiration of the whole, they do also in connection with questions concerning individual books, such as date, authorship, canonicity, etc. A clear example of this is the "proof" that is adduced to establish the fact that the apostle Paul wrote the epistle to the Galatians. Scripture's own self-testimony is that Paul wrote the book (Gal. 1:1). That makes all other arguments superfluous. Indeed, to rely on other arguments opens the door to the attacks of higher critics, who also have abundant "proof" that Paul did not write the book.

by God Himself through the Holy Spirit. Such testimony is overwhelmingly certain and cannot be gainsaid.

The difficulty lies not in the "proof"; the difficulty lies in the fact that wicked man rejects every claim of God in Scripture and in creation. If the angel Gabriel would testify publicly that the Scriptures are God's infallible Word, men would reject that "proof" as well. Men have Moses and the prophets; that is, Scripture itself testifies of Scripture's divine origin. If they will not hear Moses and the prophets, they will not be persuaded though one rise from the dead (Luke 16:31). God's people, in whom is faith, do not need proof; the wicked will not accept proof.

The Miracle of Inspiration

The second great truth implied in the doctrine of Scripture as held in the PRC is that Scripture is itself a miracle. There is the closest possible connection between the miracle of inspiration and the miracles recorded in Scripture. Because of the close relation between the miracle of inspiration and the miracles of Scripture, a denial of one leads to a denial of the other. Hence, if one does not hold to the truth of infallible inspiration, the denial of other miracles follows. So, when the miracle of creation is denied by all forms of evolution, including the theistic variety, then the miracles of deliverance and healing are denied; and then the great miracles of Christ's own work through His virgin birth, His atoning sacrifice, His bodily resurrection, ascension, and exaltation are also soon denied.[21]

Notice that even the doctrine of creation is included as a miracle. This is an important point in the doctrine of Scripture. It is often argued that it makes no essential difference whether one believes in a creation in six literal days of twenty-four hours, or whether one believes in an old

---

21. Ibid., 11.

earth in which creation took place by evolutionary processes. One's interpretation of Genesis 1–3 has nothing to do with the gospel and faith in Jesus Christ.

But such an argument is deceptive. Hoeksema makes the point that creation itself also belongs to the miraculous, to the wonder of grace in Jesus Christ.[22] While Hoeksema does not argue the point here, the truth implied is that the creation has no significance by itself. The creation narrative in Scripture is not an isolated bit of information divorced from the revelation of God in Christ. Rather, the doctrine of creation belongs to the whole of the wonder of salvation in Christ. God created heaven and earth and all that they contain because it was to be the setting in which would be shown the work of salvation; the background of a marvelous portrait of Christ; the stage on which would be enacted the entire drama of sin and salvation by grace. Even that creation, now under the curse because of man's sin, shall be delivered from the bondage of corruption into the glorious liberty of the sons of God (Rom. 8:19–22).

Scripture As an Organism

The third truth we must notice is that, because all Scripture reveals God in Christ, it is an organic unity.[23] By using the term "organic" in connection with Scripture, Hoeksema meant to say that the Scriptures, composed as they are of many different parts, nevertheless are bound together in one unifying theme: the revelation of Jehovah God in Jesus Christ as the God of the salvation of the elect.[24]

But more is meant even than that. So much is Scripture an organism that, even as an entire oak tree of full size is completely to be found in an acorn, so is the whole of the

---

22. Ibid., 12.

23. I shall deal with the truth that Scripture is an organism in a later chapter.

24. A Bible teacher I had in high school would often remind us that "wherever the artery of Scripture is cut, it flows with the blood of the Lamb."

truth of Scripture found in every part of it. From the time God spoke His promise of salvation to His people (Gen. 3:15), these people had in their possession the whole Word of God in principle—even before the entire Scriptures were prepared.[25] They had that Word of God in Christ just as surely as the entire oak tree is included in an acorn.

Further, predestination and providence must be taken into account in the origin and writing of Scripture. God chose His people in Christ from eternity. He determined to save them through Christ by the knowledge of Himself revealed in Christ.[26] The Scriptures were conceived in the mind of God eternally as the record of that revelation of God in Christ. They were conceived as a whole, a unity, a complete record of all revelation so that they might serve God's purpose in saving His people.

Predestination, therefore, included all the way of salvation,[27] and the Scriptures as a part of that way. Included, therefore, in God's decreeing purpose are all the means by which the Scriptures would be written. God determined the men whom He would use, the time of their birth, the circumstances of their birth, home, upbringing, education, etc. He determined the time they would live, the work they would do in His church, the circumstances in the church to which they would address their writings. All was determined, but in such a way that when the Scriptures would be completed, they would be perfect, complete, the whole record of God's revelation.

Providence also must play a key role because providence is God's sovereign work by which He carries out His counsel and brings to pass in history all that He has determined to do. The decree concerning the Scriptures is infallibly carried

---

25. Homer Hoeksema, *The Doctrine of Scripture*, 78–90. This last idea is on page 80.
26. John 17:3.
27. Canons of Dordt, I, 8: ". . . the Scripture declares the good pleasure, purpose and counsel of the divine will to be one, according to which he hath chosen us from eternity . . . to salvation and the *way* of salvation . . ."

out in time, and the result is that priceless gift of the Word of God which is the very life of the church.

One final matter should be mentioned. As I stated in an earlier chapter, God's revelation in Jesus Christ is always particular. Because Scripture is the inspired record of that revelation, Scripture is also written with the church in view. It has been called, and properly so, Christ's love letter to His elect bride. Its theme is "Comfort ye, comfort ye my people, saith your God" (Isa. 40:1). Its purpose is to give to God's people the knowledge of God Himself through Jesus Christ, whom to know is life eternal. Its goal is to provide the spiritual food which God's people need in all their earthly pilgrimage. More than that, Scripture itself makes use of many different metaphors in order to tell God's people of the marvelous gift which the church possesses in Scripture. It is as perfect a food as a mother's milk (I Pet. 2:1, 2; Isa. 55:1, 2). Yet, it is also meat for the adult Christian (I Cor. 3:2). It is a surgeon's scalpel, which performs spiritual operations to cut away the cancerous growths of sin (Heb. 4:12). It is a powerful sword by which we can gain the victory in our spiritual warfare (Eph. 6:17). And so I could go on. That Word of the Scriptures is all the believer needs to attain the great salvation God has prepared for him in Christ. And its end is attained when these people are brought safely to glory, where they shall need the Scriptures no longer, for they shall see the Christ of the Scriptures face-to-face.

Conclusion

Anyone who goes to Scripture must go with humble faith in the Word of God. If he thinks he knows better than Scripture, or if he comes in order to make Scripture teach what he wants to find, the Scriptures are a closed book to him. But he who comes in the childlike faith that Scripture is God's Word, and who prays as he enters the chambers of God's own revelation, "Speak, Lord, for thy servant heareth"

(I Sam. 3:9)—he will find in that Scripture Jesus Christ Himself. The believing child of God goes to Scripture with a willingness to hear God. He goes to learn from Scripture the teachings of the Holy Spirit.

Higher criticism comes to Scripture in quite a different way. With its emphasis on a human element, it wishes to explain Scripture from a human point of view. It wishes to learn from Scripture what Paul had to say on a given subject; what "Johannine Eschatology" is; what Peter believed concerning the coming of Christ at the end of time. And so books can be and are written on "The Theology of Paul."[28] It may even be that Johannine Eschatology contradicts Pauline views of the end, and such contradictions must be examined for clues as to the state of eschatological thinking in the post-resurrection church.

The believer is fundamentally not interested in what Paul, or Peter, or Isaiah believed, and Scripture will not help him in that regard, for Scripture is not of any private interpretation (II Pet. 1:20). The believer is interested in what "the Spirit saith to the churches" (Rev. 3:22).

The Scripture, Paul tells us, is like a mirror in which is reflected the One whom we shall see face-to-face in glory (I Cor. 13:12). Because Scripture is God's book, it is not just a biography of someone whom we have never met; it is the living Word of God and brings us, in the reading of it, face-to-face with Christ Himself. After all, because Scripture is God-breathed, it is, therefore, profitable for doctrine, for reproof, for correction in righteousness. It has the power to make the man of God wise, thoroughly furnished unto all good works (II Tim. 3:16, 17).

It has the power to do this to "the man of God." In a way,

---

28. Herman Ridderbos, *Paul: An Outline of His Theology*, tr. by John Richard De Witt (Grand Rapids: Wm. B. Eerdmans Publishing Co., 1975). The Dutch original was titled *Paulus*.

every man who opens the Scriptures comes face-to-face with Christ—even the ungodly. But it is for them a terrible thing. For they are confronted with One who puts to them the inescapable question: What will you do with Christ? Their answer is: We will crucify Him again—even on the cross of our own higher criticism. But also in that unbelief God accomplishes His purpose to harden the reprobate.

But to those who put their trust in Him, the Scriptures are a never-failing source of all blessings. These blessings are theirs through the all-sufficient Savior revealed on its precious pages.

CHAPTER 10

𝕋he Doctrine of the Antithesis

Thus our calling is . . . as the body of Christ and of believers individually to realize [our] part of the covenant of God, to live antithetically in the midst of and over against an ungodly world from the principle of regeneration.
—Herman Hoeksema, *The Protestant Reformed Churches: 25th Anniversary 1925–1950*

The Importance of the Doctrine

The problem of the antithesis plagued Reformed and Presbyterian churches already in the nineteenth century, as well as throughout the twentieth. In almost every case, the most important question was whether or not an area of neutrality existed in this world in which the believer and the unbeliever could meet on common ground and join in various common endeavors.

The great Presbyterian theologian B. B. Warfield took issue with Abraham Kuyper on the question of the antithesis in science, and maintained not only that Christianity is subject to scientific proof, but that the regenerate and the unregenerate are able to work together in finding absolute truth in creation and in building a science.[1] Kuyper insisted

---

1. George M. Marsden, *Understanding Fundamentalism and Evangelicalism* (Grand Rapids: Wm. B. Eerdmans Publishing Co., 1991), 124. Marsden refers to *Selected Writings of Benjamin B. Warfield*, ed. John E. Meeter, vol. 2 (Nutley, N.J.:

that the regenerate and unregenerate do science from fundamentally different viewpoints and within basically different frameworks.[2] Kuyper's antithesis was between a Christian world view and the humanism of the Enlightenment.[3]

But Kuyper's view of the antithesis also left much to be desired. Driven by dreams of a return to those glorious days when Calvinism held sway in every area of the Dutch republic, Kuyper wanted to claim the whole of modern culture and every institution of society for Christ so that all could be brought again under the banner of the Reformed faith. He considered the possibility to be very real that a Reformed man could be active in modern culture and society without compromise of principle. He wanted the respect of the world outside his own circle, and he persuaded his followers to be less hostile and defensive towards unbelievers. But this attitude had to be justified, and Kuyper found his justification in his theory of common grace.[4] In other words, common grace was used to modify sharply the idea of the antithesis.

Such a modification of the antithesis by common grace is also the view of others. James D. Bratt points out that Kuyper was fearful of the incipient Anabaptism in the Pietism of the people of the *Afscheiding* (Secession of 1834), which ignored science, art, and culture.[5] As we noticed earlier, Kuyper, according to Bratt, with the Anabaptistic tendencies of Pietism in mind, developed his common grace to open the way for cooperation with the unbelieving world. The

---

Presbyterian & Reformed Publishing Co., 1973), 101, 102, 106–23.

2. Marsden, Ibid.

3. The Enlightenment was a powerful movement in Europe which arose in the latter part of the seventeenth century and first part of the eighteenth, which really carried the humanistic principles of the Renaissance to their ultimate conclusions. It spawned rationalism, the French Revolution, deism, and higher critical studies of Scripture.

4. Heslam, *Creating a Christian Worldview*, 122.

5. Bratt, *Dutch Calvinism in Modern America*, 31.

ground was that the world's endeavors, through the power of common grace, were similar in fundamental respects to the efforts of the church.[6]

But, says Bratt, Kuyper created a "fundamental ambiguity between common grace and the antithesis."[7] This ambiguity was taken over by Kuyper's followers in America. These followers despised Hoeksema's views and condemned him as being Anabaptistic.[8]

The charge of Anabaptism was repeatedly made in the controversy over common grace in 1924. Especially Jan Karel van Baalen made use of this charge and wrote a book in which he attempted to prove his point.[9] Viewing world-flight as one of the fundamental principles of the Anabaptists, van Baalen accused Hoeksema of such a view when Hoeksema denied common grace and insisted that the antithesis was sharp and unbridgeable. According to van Baalen, to deny the operations of God's grace in the unregenerate was to flee from them into isolation.

In an important essay, written many years after the common grace controversy, Henry Stob described with his usual precision what the differences were between Hoeksema and the CRC.[10] After pointing out that the term "antithesis" was first used by Kant and Hegel,[11] and made

---

6. Ibid., 20.

7. Ibid., 30.

8. Ibid., 110. Bratt does not hesitate to say that the charge of Anabaptism was used to get at Hoeksema and his views, and that, finally, Hoeksema was abandoned by the Pietists as well as the Kuyperians.

9. The title of the book was *De Loochening der Gemeene Gratie: Gereformeerd of Doopersch?* (The Denial of Common Grace: Reformed or Anabaptist?). Hoeksema and Danhof responded with a book entitled, *Niet Doopersch maar Gereformeerd* (Not Anabaptist but Reformed). The controversy continued in van Baalen's book, *Nieuwigheid en Dwaling* (Novelty and Error). This was answered by Danhof and Hoeksema in two books: *Langs Zuivere Banen* (Along Straight Paths) and *Om Recht en Waarheid* (Concerning Right and Truth). *Om Recht en Waarheid* was published just prior to the CRC Synod of 1924.

10. Henry Stob, "Observations on the Concept of the Antithesis," 248–51.

11. Two eighteenth century philosophers who cast a long shadow over subsequent thought.

popular, though in a different sense, by Abraham Kuyper and Groen Van Prinsterer,[12] he proceeds to distinguish the view of the CRC from that of Hoeksema.

Stob points out, correctly, that Hoeksema began his construction of the antithesis with the decree of election and reprobation. But, Stob insists, this is incorrect, for God's universal love and well-meant offer of the gospel make reprobation only punitive, in other words, only just punishment for rejecting the gospel. In any case, predestination is abstract because it has no definite denotation; in other words, no one can possibly know who are elect and who are reprobate.[13]

The antithesis, says Stob, does not make neutrality impossible, because common grace preserves man's natural powers so that sin does not diminish man's physical, psychological, or mental powers in any significant way.[14] Hence, "the antithesis rests upon the basis of a non-antithetical, universally shared, increated, and common grace supported rationality."[15] Thus common grace, in creating this arena of neutrality, makes cooperation between the church and the world possible and desirable.

The Role of the Antithesis in 1924

Before the suspension and deposition of Rev. Herman Hoeksema by Classis Grand Rapids East of the CRC, Hoeksema already seriously warned the churches in his public writings of the danger of common grace destroying the antithesis. He spoke of the fact that not only he, but others in the church as well, were alarmed at the increase in

---

12. A contemporary of Abraham Kuyper who was the head of the Anti-revolutonary Party, which later voted Kuyper into the legislative assembly in the Netherlands. Van Prinsterer exercised great influence on Kuyper's political thinking.

13. Henry Stob, "Observations on the Concept of the Antithesis," 246.

14. Note that the Canons of Dordt, III & IV, 4 and the Confession of Faith, Art. 14, speak of these powers as "remnants" and "glimmerings" only.

15. Henry Stob, "Observations on the Concept of the Antithesis," 251.

a spirit of broad-mindedness and worldly-mindedness, which spirit openly defended the need for the Dutch churches to become more American by adapting themselves to and becoming involved in American culture. This could be done only by mixing religious and humanistic principles. A number of concerned men and ministers even met monthly for a time to discuss what could be done about the matter.[16]

The broad-mindedness which concerned Hoeksema and others was justified by appeals to Kuyperian common grace, and all who disagreed or dared to raise a voice of protest were branded Anabaptist.[17]

Already in 1923 Hoeksema publicly warned the churches once again, with all the seriousness he could muster, of this tendency to erase the spiritual separation between the church and the world.[18] He characterized common grace as that which bridged the gap between the church and the world, an expression which is literally found in the writings of one of the Janssen supporters.[19]

Janssen was himself an example of how the antithesis was broken down by the theory of common grace. And, although the Janssen party had been defeated in 1922, his defenders rose again to attack Hoeksema because of his outspoken insistence that common grace lay at the root of Janssen's errors. Opposition to Hoeksema was, at least in part, personal hostility,[20] but common grace was the issue, and Hoeksema's alleged Anabaptism was the charge.

Repeatedly, after 1924, Hoeksema predicted that, if

---

16. Hoeksema, "A Catechism on the History of the Origin of the PRC," *SB* 6 (September 1, 1930): 537, 538.

17. Ibid., 537.

18. Danhof and Hoeksema, *Van Zonde en Genade*, 228, 229.

19. Ibid. The Janssen supporter was Rev. Quirinus Breen, who resigned from the ministry in the CRC after Janssen's condemnation by the synod of 1922. He is quoted at some length.

20. Hoeksema, "A Catechism on the History of the Origin of the PRC," *SB* 6 (September 1, 1930): 539.

the CRC did not abandon its views on common grace, worldliness in every form would engulf the church. And in these prophecies he proved only too accurate.[21]

Common grace broke down the antithesis in two areas. First, it was maintained that, as a fruit of common grace, a great deal of truth was present in the world of the reprobate, which truth could be appropriated by the church and incorporated into her own body of belief. Thus the truth as it ultimately emerged was a combination of what the wicked had discovered by common grace and what the righteous had uncovered in Scripture by means of special grace.

The second area was the area of Christian living. There is something of a contradiction here. On the one hand, common grace enabled the reprobate to do much good from which the elect could profit. This was true especially in the field of culture: science, the arts, technology, etc. Worldly culture could be of benefit to and for the enjoyment of the church, as, for example, in the film arts.

But in something of a different sense, common grace created a grey area of moral neutrality, in which area the people of God and the children of Satan could work together in common causes, for common goals and purposes. This area of neutrality included, for example, "neutral" labor unions, as they were called. Christians could belong to them along with the wicked, for these unions were morally neutral. Christians

---

21. Apparently the prophecy stung, for a reference of the synod of the CRC to this prophecy of Hoeksema can be found in his *The Protestant Reformed Churches in America*, 88. The synod said in its official decisions: "In as far as the pastors H. Danhof and H. Hoeksema in their writings warn against worldlimindedness, synod judges that there is, indeed, reason for such warning with a view to a possible misuse of the doctrine of common grace . . ." (*Acta der Synode van de Christelijke Gereformeerde Kerk, 1924*, Art. 132, p. 148). An instance of such a prophecy of Hoeksema subsequent to 1924 can be found in Hoeksema, *The Protestant Reformed Churches in America*, 93. That worldliness of which Hoeksema warned has been officially approved by decisions of later synods of the CRC which favored dancing and the film arts. Strikingly, common grace was used as the doctrinal support of these decisions.

could cooperate with ungodly men in the pursuit of better working conditions in the shop.

But, Hoeksema warned, the result of such cooperation would not be that the church would make the world more Christian, but that the world would all but destroy the church in making the church like itself.

The doctrine of the antithesis has become an integral part of the thinking, the theology, and the life of the PRC. Students in the seminary are taught to preach antithetically, in other words, in such a way that the truth of Scripture is set over against the lie.[22] God's people are admonished to think antithetically, so that they are conscious of the many attempts to destroy the truth with the lie, and so that they learn to defend the truth over against the lie.

They are also called to live antithetically in the world, for preaching in the PRC is not only doctrinal preaching, but it is emphatically a practical bringing of God's Word to bear on every aspect of life. As the practical implications of God's Word are brought before God's people, it is the antithesis which is constantly called to their attention. One great theme of the practical calling of God's people is found in Moses' words to Israel: "The eternal God is thy refuge, and underneath are the everlasting arms . . . Israel then shall dwell in safety alone" (Deut. 33:27, 28).

---

22. So important is this that the Church Order of the Protestant Reformed Churches refers to this calling of ministers in a very sharp and pointed way. Art. 55 reads: "To ward off false doctrines and errors that multiply exceedingly through heretical writings, the ministers and elders shall use the means of teaching, of refutation or warning, and of admonition." In the Formula of Subscription, which all officebearers are required to sign, a minister solemnly before God swears an oath "diligently to teach and faithfully to defend" the doctrines in the creeds "without either directly or indirectly contradicting" them. He also promises to "reject all errors that militate against this doctrine," to be "disposed to refute and contradict these, and to exert" himself "in keeping the church free from such errors."

The Nature of the Antithesis

One who goes through the writings of the PRC in the *Standard Bearer*, in other brochures and pamphlets, and in books and articles for other magazines will find repeated references to the antithesis. It would be impossible to count the references made to this important doctrine. It has dominated the thinking of the PRC from the very beginning. And this doctrine of the antithesis as it is taught in the PRC is interwoven with the truth of sovereign grace.

In an early article on the subject,[23] Herman Hoeksema developed the idea of the antithesis and its doctrinal character. It is an important article which lays down fundamental truths from which Hoeksema, in the course of his life, never wavered.

The destruction of the antithesis by means of common grace was his starting point. At one time, he maintained, it was characteristic of Reformed people to hold to an absolute antithesis. Later, this absolute antithesis was modified so that "it was absolute in spiritual principle, but by virtue of the operation of a common grace there is also a certain practical synthesis in this world . . ."[24] Later, even that disappeared, and the "antithesis is forgotten in theory and in practice."[25]

In explaining precisely what the antithesis is, Hoeksema spoke of it as a term which signifies contrast or opposition, and described the contrast or opposition as being that "between light and darkness, between good and evil, between God and the devil, between the Church and the world."[26]

The antithesis is not dualism, Hoeksema went on to say. Dualism, throughout the history of philosophy, pagan

---

23. Herman Hoeksema, "Antithesis, Synthesis and Dualism," *SB* 4 (May 1, 1928): 353–57.

24. Ibid., 353.

25. Ibid.

26. Ibid.

religions, and even sometimes Christianity, has set good and evil, matter and spirit, and God and sin over against each other in such a way that they are two independent powers, both struggling for mastery, and both engaged in such vicious warfare that the outcome is uncertain—although, generally, "good" succeeds in defeating evil.

Dualism is present in much of the thinking in the church, such as when men "speak of God and Satan, as if the two were eternal and were two independent sources, the one of good, the other of evil."[27] This is a perversion and corruption of the antithesis which denies the sovereignty of God.

But a Reformed man starts with God.[28] To begin with God means to insist that in God is only light, which light is His infinite holiness. This light of God's infinite perfection God chose to reveal to the glory of His own name. But this glory must be revealed antithetically. God's purity shines in greater glory when it is revealed against the background of evil. And so God "determines from everlasting not only to reveal that He is Truth, but to do this in opposition to the lie; not only to manifest that He is Righteousness, but to accomplish this in opposition to Unrighteousness; to reveal that he is Holiness, but in contrast with corruption."[29]

Thus God is sovereign over good and evil. He reveals "that He loves the truth and hates the lie, that He loves righteousness and holiness and hates unrighteousness and corruption." Because the "Most High determines in His everlasting counsel to make [this] manifest," we must "certainly maintain that in His eternal counsel God has willed the darkness and all that is connected therewith, but always in such a way that He conceives of it as an object

---

27. Ibid., 354.

28. This is an important point, not only in Hoeksema's discussion of the antithesis, but in all Hoeksema's writings. He was, above all, theocentric, in other words, God-centered in his theology. I shall pay a bit closer attention to this in the next chapter.

29. Hoeksema, "Antithesis, Synthesis, and Dualism," 354.

of His hatred and displeasure, that the glory of His Name may be extolled. Never does darkness appear in God's counsel as the object of His love and pleasure. He has no pleasure in sin and corruption. But neither may we explain the existence of evil as independent of God's eternal will and decree."[30]

Revealed in Election and Reprobation

That the decree of election and reprobation is Hoeksema's starting point in his definition of the antithesis was noticed by everyone who took the time to read him. Bratt describes Hoeksema's view as proceeding from election and reprobation, so that history must be explained as the development of the two, which have nothing in common but the creation.[31] Although inexplicably lumping Cornelius Van Til and Hoeksema together on this point, Stob too says that Hoeksema constructed his view of the antithesis in terms of election and reprobation.[32]

This analysis is certainly correct. God wills, Hoeksema maintained, to form for Himself a covenant people to manifest His glorious virtues, and, because it is God's purpose to reveal His glory antithetically over against the darkness of the lie and corruption, God also wills that "this power of darkness must be there in the vessels of wrath and the children of light must be brought into closest connection with them."[33] God is the potter and man is the clay. From this clay God makes vessels of honor and dishonor. Pharaoh is raised up for the purpose of revealing God's glory. This is election and reprobation.

Yet these two are not "coordinate parts of God's counsel,

---

30. Ibid.
31. Bratt, *Dutch Calvinism in Modern America,* 103. This position, Bratt goes on to say, led him to attack common grace.
32. Henry Stob, "Observations on the Concept of the Antithesis," 245.
33. Hoeksema, "Antithesis, Synthesis and Dualism," 354, 355.

but the latter serves the former. Reprobation serves both to bring out the glory of election and to lead in a way of opposition and sin God's covenant to highest conceivable glory."[34]

The Execution of the Antithesis in Time

This antithesis is executed in time. It is first of all executed in time in the creation of Adam, who, as God's friend-servant, and of God's party, must serve God in saying "yes" to God's commands and "no" to that which God prohibits. Thus the antithesis for Adam was to say "yes" to God's command to subdue the earth, but to say "no" to eating the fruit of the tree of the knowledge of good and evil. God decreed the tree of the knowledge of good and evil in order for the antithesis to be expressed in Adam's life; but God decreed as well the fall of Satan and his appearance in the garden to tempt Adam and Eve. And God determined that Adam and Eve should fall.[35]

Thus God's purpose never was intended to be attained in the first Paradise. God had chosen a people in Christ, the second Adam, of whom the first Adam was but the type. The fall took place under the control of God, and henceforth the antithesis is revealed in two seeds: the seed of the woman and the seed of the serpent. The one is constituted of the elect, the other of the reprobate. The one are the objects of grace, the other of wrath.[36] The purpose of God in this is the realization of the antithesis in history, so that the virtues of God's great goodness are revealed the more perfectly against the background of His hatred of the sinner.

These two seeds have all things in common from a natural

---

34. Ibid., 355.
35. Ibid. See also Herman Hoeksema, "The Antithesis in Paradise," *SB* 1, no. 1 (October 1924): 7–9.
36. Hoeksema, "Antithesis, Synthesis, and Dualism," 355.

point of view. "They are both part of the natural organism in Adam, of the same flesh and blood. They have the same natural life, the same body and the same soul, the same mind and will, the same talents and powers. And they live in the same world. They till the same soil and receive the same rain and the same sunshine; they work in the same factory and often at the same bench. Not infrequently they live in the same home and are most closely related from a natural point of view. They develop the same institutions, are subjects of the same state, members of the same society, speak the same language as members of the same nation, and even are not so infrequently members of the same Church."[37]

But (and here is the great "but"): "All this is nothing more than the battleground upon which light and darkness clash, upon which the powers of sin and grace develop and come to manifestation."[38] And this is true because in the one, the elect in Christ, is "the new life, the life of regeneration, the life of the risen Christ,"[39] while in the other is "the principle of enmity against God."[40]

These two principles dominate their lives so completely that, from a spiritual point of view, the two seeds have nothing in common. And so the elect are called, not to leave the world, but to be in the world, in all the world, in every sphere of the life of this world, on the whole of its battleground, but living from the principle of grace and the life of regeneration.

"Living as children of light the darkness will hate them and will employ the powers and means of darkness to overcome them. Outwardly they may also seem to be submerged in the battle and to be defeated by the powers of darkness, even as Christ on Golgotha. But spiritually they have the victory.

37. Ibid.
38. Ibid.
39. Ibid., 355, 356.
40. Ibid.

They are of God's party. God fights His battle through them. And God through Christ will give them the ultimate victory, in the day when all the powers of darkness shall only prove to have worked together for the most glorious revelation of the Name of the Most High!"[41]

This is the antithesis as taught in the PRC.

The Practical Application
of the Antithesis
to Union Membership

The development of the doctrine of the antithesis is not abstract in the PRC. It is preached from the pulpits, it is on the agenda of ecclesiastical assemblies, and it is put into practice in the lives of the people of God.

One of the earliest evidences of the practical implications of the antithesis was the question of membership in so-called neutral labor unions. Already in 1927 the consistory of the PRC in Munster, Indiana,[42] asked the combined classis at its June meeting to take a stand on the question of membership in labor unions. There seemed to have been no hesitation on the part of the classis at all. It decided that "a member of the Protestant Reformed Churches cannot be a member of a labor union."[43]

This position has remained the position of the PRC throughout their history. That does not mean that the decision was not the subject of a great deal of debate at later classical meetings and in various articles in the *Standard Bearer*.[44] But the debate did not have to do with the substance of the decision; the debate concerned various church political aspects of the decision.

41. Ibid., 356.
42. Later to become the Protestant Reformed Church of South Holland, Illinois.
43. Minutes of the Classis of June 1927, Art. 31.
44. Herman Hoeksema, "De Union-Kwestie onder Ons" (The Union Question among Us) *SB* 6 (May 1, 1930): 349–51; 6 (May 15, 1930): 371–74; 6 (June 1, 1930): 399–402; 6 (July 1, 1930): 455; and 6 (August 15, 1930): 515–17.

One problem was that the decision had not been made in connection with a definite and specific case that had come up in connection with the discipline of a member who belonged to a union.[45] Although such objections were made against the decision of 1927, and, although it is not clear from the records what classis finally did, the decision itself was never rescinded.

Another objection that was raised against the decision of 1927 was the fact that the original decision had been made without grounds. Although a committee was appointed to draw up grounds, the work was repeatedly returned to the committee for additional study. Again, it is not clear from the record what happened in the interim, but the classis of June 4, 1930,[46] decided that no decision be taken on the entire matter until Rev. Hoeksema, the editor of the *Standard Bearer*, had had opportunity to discuss the matter thoroughly in that periodical.

What is important is the fact that the truth of the antithesis was repeatedly appealed to in support of the original decision of 1927. Although the reports of the committee which appeared periodically on classis were never, for one reason or another, officially adopted, the decision itself was never revoked.[47]

One report of an appointed committee declared that any "union, gathering or association . . . whose position is spiritually and ethically in conflict with our principles must

45. This is an interesting objection. It was argued that Art. 30 of the Church Order (which requires ecclesiastical assemblies to treat only such matters as are of an ecclesiastical nature, or such as concern the churches in common) restricted ecclesiastical assemblies to taking decisions only on specific "cases," in other words, only on matters which arose in connection with the work of the church (or churches). This is why no consistory, classis, or synod may simply, willy-nilly, make decisions on anything about which it chooses to speak out about. It must have some ecclesiastical reason for making a decision on a given matter.

46. See especially Supplement 5.

47. See, for example, Minutes of February 1, 1928; June 5, 1929, Art. 24; February 5, 1930, Arts. 18, 19, and 22; and June 4, 1930, Art. 15.

be regarded as standing in the line of the development of the antichrist." Appealing to the principle of corporate responsibility, this same committee report stated that anyone who becomes a member of such an organization is responsible for all the decisions and actions of the organization, and holds to the notion that a solution to the problems of sin can be found elsewhere than in the cross of Jesus Christ.[48]

Direct mention is made of the antithesis in the articles which appeared on the question in the *Standard Bearer*. This was especially true of an article appearing in the June 15, 1930, issue, where the implications of union membership for the antithesis were fully discussed. Finally, although the original decision of classis was criticized for church political or procedural mistakes, the principle of that decision and the grounds that had been suggested in 1930 were officially approved.[49]

Specific practices and principles of labor unions were shown to be in opposition to the biblical principles governing a believer's walk in the world. Mention was made of the fact that the basic reasons for organizing unions are contrary to Scripture. Unions are formed to give power to the laboring man so that, in his efforts to resist the authority of the employer, he might have influence on the employer. This, it was argued, is contrary to the Scripture's solemn admonition that servants must obey their masters.

It was also pointed out that, because the unions were engaging in class struggle, their deepest motivations were the same as those of socialism, and thus contrary to God's Word. The church does not and may not involve itself in class struggle, but must seek the spiritual welfare of the people of God. Nor is the church in the world to solve the social

---

48. Minutes of meeting of classis, February 5, 1930, Supplement 5.
49. Minutes of meeting of classis, June 4, 1930, Art. 15, Supplement 5.

problems of the world, but it is here to preach the gospel, through which the church of Christ is gathered and prepared for glory.

No effort was made in these discussions to justify employers in their ill treatment of employees. It was specifically argued that greed, from a spiritual and ethical point of view, motivates employer and employee alike, and that Scripture solemnly warns against the great evil of covetousness.

Also the practices of the unions came under attack. The unions advocated boycott, strikes, closed shops, and threats to coerce employers to do their will. All such uses of force are condemned by God, who calls His people to submit to their employers even when they suffer injustices. God Himself, in His time, makes all things right.[50]

And the final advice was that classis ought to declare that, although it had erred church politically, the decision should stand that a member of the union could not be a member of the PRC; that, as a matter of fact, for classis to rescind the decision would leave the impression with the churches that classis had changed its mind on the matter.[51]

It was in connection with the whole discussion of union membership that other questions arose concerning membership in other organizations. Documents were brought to classis and questions were sent to the *Standard Bearer* asking about membership in such organizations as "co-ops" of dairy farmers, grain farmers, and cattle farmers. Again it was the antithesis which was appealed to in support of various answers which were given. As long as the organizations did not adopt principles and practices contrary to the Word of God, and as long as their purpose

---

50. This material can be found in various issues of the *Standard Bearer*; but see especially Hoeksema, "De Union-Kwestie onder Ons," *SB* 6 (May 1, 1930): 349–51.

51. Ibid. 6 (August 15, 1930): 515–17.

was to facilitate the work in which farmers were engaged, no objection could be raised against membership in them or the use of them. The antithesis was a spiritual division and separation which is expressed in spiritual and ethical principles of conduct.[52]

Discussions on various aspects of union membership appeared with remarkable regularity in subsequent issues of the *Standard Bearer*, and from time to time it occupied the attention of ecclesiastical assemblies. But the churches never wavered on the original decision of 1927. For the most part the questions dealt with such subjects as membership in the Christian Labor Association (CLA), which was a union of Christian employees, but which also, in its constitution, approved of the strike;[53] of the wrongs of the closed shop, that is, of places of employment in which the employer had been coerced into refusing to hire anyone but those who were or agreed to become members of the union;[54] and of the question of conscientious objectors.[55] On at least one occasion synod even addressed letters to members of the government in the executive, legislative, and judiciary branches, protesting against the closed shop.[56]

These discussions and decisions of the churches were an application of the antithesis which by no means took place

---

52. See, for example, Ibid. 6 (July 1, 1930): 455.

53. The discussion began in the *SB* 7 (July 15, 1931): 470–74 with the views of Albert Piersma and a reply by Gerrit Vos. The discussion continued off and on for many years. The *Indexes* to vols. 1–73 of the *Standard Bearer* will lead the interested reader to further articles.

54. See *Acts of the Synod of the Protestant Reformed Churches in America, 1941*, Arts. 84, 85, p. 28.

55. This latter question arose in 1956 in connection with the Taft-Hartley law, which forbade the closed shop, but required of those who were conscientiously opposed to union membership to pay an amount equal to union dues to some charity, which charity would be determined either by the employer, the union, or the employee, depending on the rules adopted. Confer *Acts of Synod of the Protestant Reformed Churches, 1957*, Arts. 139, 167, pp. 44, 47, 169–75.

56. See *Acts of Synod of the Protestant Reformed Churches, 1946*, Arts. 20, 21, pp. 29–31.

in a vacuum, so to speak. Oftentimes members of the church lost their jobs and means of livelihood for the sake of these principles. On occasion they endured mockery and scorn at the hands of fellow Christians from other denominations for their opposition to the union. And the churches suffered losses in membership because some would not give up their union membership when admonished to do so by their elders. Faithfulness to God required for some a great price.

The Antithesis and Worldly Amusements

The principle of the antithesis was early in the history of the PRC applied to worldliness and worldly amusements. Herman Hoeksema had prophesied that the adoption of common grace would result in bringing worldly entertainment into the church, and this prediction apparently affected the CRC sufficiently that the synod of 1924, along with its statement on common grace, warned the churches of the dangers of worldly-mindedness.[57]

The church is always threatened by world-conformity, and the battle against sin includes a constant battle against the manner of life found in the world. God's people are fully aware of the deceitful efforts of Satan to destroy them by persuading them to conform to the wicked about them. But common grace became, in the CRC, the basis for official decisions approving various forms of worldly conduct which, prior to 1924, had been condemned by the church.

In the PRC things were different. Already on the combined classis meeting of February 2, 1927, a request appeared for guidelines on worldliness. Although the minutes do not reveal what the decision of classis was, the subject was much discussed in the churches. One of the occasions for

---

57. See footnote 21 in this chapter for the part of the decision dealing with this warning.

such a discussion was a decision of the CRC on movies. While in 1928 the CRC condemned attendance at worldly movies, in 1966 this position of the CRC changed. This decision not only refused to condemn movies as being per se wrong, but also encouraged believers to be busy in subjecting the film arts to the dominion and rule of Jesus Christ.[58]

In an article entitled "A Compromise on Movies," Hoeksema made clear that the doctrine of the antithesis clearly implied that movie attendance was contrary to Scripture.[59]

In an article written and published in 1934, Hoeksema commented on a play on the life of Martin Luther performed publicly. He used the occasion to demonstrate that common grace was the real reason why such worldliness had entered the mother church. The play had been performed under the auspices of the Christian Reformed Young Men's Society and apparently had had the approval of the churches.[60]

The relation between movie attendance and common grace was clear when, in the CRC, a medical missionary from Rehoboth, New Mexico, appealed to common grace as justification for movie attendance. It is not surprising that this should once again elicit some comment from the editor of the *Standard Bearer*.[61]

58. See *Acts of the Synod of the Christian Reformed Church 1966*, Art. 61, pp. 32–6. See also my pamphlet, "The Christian and the Film Arts" (Grand Rapids: Sunday School of the First Protestant Reformed Church, Grand Rapids, n.d.), especially pp. 3–5. The grounds which the CRC used to support their decision of 1966 were: (1) Entertainment is a permissible activity in the life of a Christian; (2) The unregenerate world is capable of producing morally good movies because of common grace, particularly the moral restraint of the Holy Spirit in the hearts of all men, and the resulting ability to do good; (3) The movie is a legitimate cultural medium. That decision opened the door to unregulated and promiscuous movie attendance among the CRC constituency.
59. Herman Hoeksema, "A Compromise on Movies," *SB* 3 (April 15, 1927): 318–21.
60. Herman Hoeksema, "Dr. Martin Luther on the Stage," *SB* 4 (February 1, 1928): 197–99.
61. Herman Hoeksema, "Appeals to Common Grace," *SB* 18 (October 1, 1941): 4–6.

Articles continued to appear from time to time concerning the question of drama.[62] It is not strange that this should be so, for the doctrine of the antithesis implies that practical questions of the Christian life have to be decided on the basis of principle rather than on the basis of expediency or other practical considerations. Many who were opposed to worldly movies considered them wrong because so many were filled with adultery, murder, covetousness, and other moral sins. But such a condemnation is of *some* movies and on practical grounds rather than principle, and the believer is left to decide for himself which movies are good and which are bad. The antithesis requires a more fundamental approach to the question. That question involves the rightness and wrongness of drama itself. Is drama a legitimate activity for the Christian? Is drama to be considered one of the "arts" which is pleasing to God? Or is drama itself wrong? To put it simply, the question often discussed was this: Is it wrong for a Christian to act out the role of another, whether the other be ficititious or real? And, if it is wrong to engage in acting, does it not then follow that watching dramatic productions is also wrong?

This position that drama itself is wrong was vigorously defended. It was defended not only on the grounds that drama, historically, belongs to the world of sin, but also on the grounds that drama is wrong because it is an attempt to submerge one's own God-given personality in order to take on the personality of another. Further, drama is wrong because it is impossible to take on another's personality without also taking on the sins of that person.[63]

---

62. See, for example, Andrew Petter, "Is Christian Drama Possible?" *SB* 18 (October 1, 1941): 19–22.

63. Other arguments were also mustered to prove the point, such as the argument that an acting out of another's life was a sacrilegious act if it involved holy activities, for it was acting out such holy activities as prayer for the sake of entertainment. Various objections to a flat-out condemnation of drama were also discussed. It was argued, for example, that a position condemning drama would

The position that dramatic productions are wrong was held throughout the history of the PRC and remains so today, although no official decisions have had to be made on the question. The consensus was sufficiently strong that the position was never challenged in the church courts.[64]

Because card playing and other games of chance had also been one of the three cardinal sins listed by the CRC as those worldly forms of entertainment to be avoided by the Christian, it too came under discussion. In a couple of articles Herman Hoeksema faced the question of the right or wrong of games of chance, and finally found them wanting on the grounds that they are a use of God's special providence for trivial reasons.[65]

Conclusions

Although the PRC dealt with some of the practical implications of the antithesis in connection with worldly amusements, it is beyond doubt that the truth of the antithesis came to prominence especially in the area of doctrine. The antithesis sets the truth over against the lie. To maintain an antithetical walk requires faithfulness to the doctrine of Scripture.

This commitment to doctrine is not simply another aspect of the antithesis; it is the fundamental point. A godly walk

necessarily condemn writing plays, reading plays, writing and reading novels, etc. See the next footnote for interesting and helpful discussions of these and other points.

64. See such pamphlets as: Richard Veldman, "The Movie" (Grand Rapids: Sunday School of the First Protestant Reformed Church, Grand Rapids, 1956) and my pamphlet, "The Christian and the Film Arts." A series of articles appearing in the *Standard Bearer* by Barry Gritters, "Renewing The Battle," are to be found in *SB* 69 (April 1, 1993): 308–10; 69 (May 1, 1993): 351- 53; 69 (May 15, 1993): 379–81; 69 (August 1993): 446–48; 69 (September 1, 1993): 465–68; and 70 (December 15, 1993): 139–41. The *Indexes* to vols. 1–73 of the *Standard Bearer* may suggest other articles on the subject.

65. Herman Hoeksema, "On Card Playing" *SB* 10 (May 1, 1934): 342, 343; 10 (June 1, 1934): 388, 389; 10 (June 15, 1934): 412, 413.

in separation from the world is impossible without sound doctrine. Christian conduct flows from commitment to the truth. Faithfulness in life is an expression of faithfulness in confession.

And so the primary consideration of the PRC has always been an emphasis upon and commitment to the historic Christian faith. This antithetical doctrinal emphasis has not only been evident in the sharp rebuke of error whenever it threatened the churches, but has, from a positive aspect, been evident in the emphasis on doctrine in preaching and teaching, and in the development of the heritage of the Reformed faith. PR preaching is doctrinally oriented. It must remain that way. The antithesis will remain only when doctrine is proclaimed from the pulpits and taught in the catechism classes.

Out of deep commitment to the historic Christian faith has come a strong emphasis on living antithetically in all areas of life. The believer is not to be in this world to live as the world. He is, in his place of work, his home, his entertainment, his contact with his neighbor and his church, to live out of the principle of regeneration by grace. Living in this way, he condemns the world of sin, confesses the name of Christ, and reveals in all his life his citizenship in the heavenly kingdom of Christ. He is a pilgrim and a stranger in this world—as Peter reminds him in his first epistle. God's law is his song in the tent of his pilgrimage (Ps. 119:54).

This separation is spiritual. The believer does not crawl into the dank cell of a monastery. Nor does he mock God's gifts by refusing to use them. He marries and brings forth children. He goes to work at 7:00 A.M. and labors diligently. He takes his vacation in the summertime. He builds a house and buys a car. He enjoys his food and drink and gives thanks for them as good gifts of God sanctified by God's Word and prayer. He revels in the beauties and mysteries of God's creation. He appreciates the arts, painting and architecture, music and singing. But in all his life he serves the Lord Christ and seeks the things above where Christ is seated at the right hand of God. Above the doorway of his house you might find a sign which reads: "In this house, Christ is King." And even if the sign is not there, you need not have any doubt that Christ is served in that home, for ten minutes within its walls will convince you that parents and children alike bow before King Jesus. The conversation of parents and children, the books they read, the music they listen to on the radio, the programs they watch on television, if indeed they have one, the devotions at mealtimes—in short, the happiness and love, the perpetual mention of the name of God and His Christ—all these will show that indeed in this house Christ is King.

The things of this creation, while important for a time during the years of our earthly sojourn, are passing. The things of heaven endure forever. Those eternal treasures have captured the hearts and minds of those who live antithetically. And those treasures are their delight as they pursue their pilgrim's way to the Celestial City.

Illustrations

(covering the roots in the Netherlands
through the schism of 1953)

1

2

3

4

5

6

7

Hendrik DeCock (1), a leading figure in the *Afscheiding* of 1834 and minister of the Reformed Church at Ulrum, the Netherlands (2), drew people from far and near to hear his sermons. Simon VanVelzen (3), the theologian of the *Afscheiding*, lived to see the reunion of Secession and *Doleantie* churches in 1892. Albertus VanRaalte (4) led a small band of Reformed believers to a new land of promise in Holland, Michigan, the first congregation being organized in Graafschap (5) in 1849. Hendrik Scholte (6), leader of the Dutch settlement in Pella, Iowa, and Anthony Brummelkamp (7) represented a weaker side of the Secession movement.

9

8

10

11

Dr. Abraham Kuyper (8) led a
reformation movement out of the
Reformed Church in the
Netherlands in the 1880s. He was
undoubtedly the most influential
theologian of the nineteenth century. He founded the Free
University and was prime minister of the Netherlands from 1900-
1905. In theology he was a supralapsarian, who emphasized
especially the truth of sovereign particular grace. *DeHeraut* (9) was
the religious weekly through which Dr. Kuyper led the *kleine luyden*
(little folk) to return to the confession of their fathers as set forth in
the Three Forms of Unity. Herman Bavinck (10), contemporary of
Kuyper and son of the *Afscheiding*, was a professor at Kampen.
Helenius DeCock (11), son of Hendrik DeCock, was a preacher
and professor in the *Afscheiding* churches. Helenius adopted a
conditional view of the covenant of grace and promoted this in
the churches.

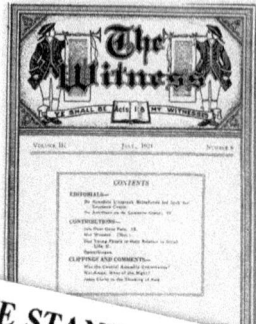

13

12

14

15

Religion and Culture (12) was a monthly
published by the proponents of Abraham
Kuyper's common grace views as these applied
to society in general. *The Witness* (13)—a monthly
with H.J. Kuiper, D. Swier, Y.P. DeJong, H. Hoeksema, H. Danhof,
and Profs. L. Berkhof and S. Volbeda on its staff—aimed at being
Reformed. *The Banner* (14), still published today, is the official
paper of the CRC. *The Banner* was closed to Revs. Hoeksema and
H. Danhof, as their views did not have the approval of, and were not
tolerated by, the leaders of the day in the CRC. *The Standard Bearer*
(15) was established as a free witness to the truth of God's Word.
In it Rev. Herman Hoeksema, Rev. Henry Danhof, Rev. George
Ophoff, and others engaged their opponents in a free exchange of
views. *The Standard Bearer* served then, as it does still today, as a
means of solid instruction in Reformed truth.

16

Henry Danhof (16)
Calvin Seminary, class of 1910,
and Herman Hoeksema (17)
Calvin Seminary, class of 1915.

17

SYNOD CONFRONTS VEXING PROBLEMS

Janssen Case and Question of Iowa Support of Calvin
Among Issues

SYNOD STILL BUSY ON JANSSEN CASE

Has Heated Debate on Doctrine in Church Periodicals.

JANSSEN OUT OF CASE, HE WRITES

Fair Trial Impossible, Declares Calvin College Professor Under Fire.

SYNOD SELECTS JANSSEN BOARD

(By Staff Correspondent)
Orange City, Ia., June 22.—
Christian Reformed synod Wednesday elected for the advisory committee in the first Janssen case

JANSSEN AGAIN REFUSES TO APPEAR.

Orange City, Ia., June 28.— Prof. Ralph Janssen of Calvin college refused Tuesday for the second time to defend himself against the charge of "heresy" made by some members of the Christian Reformed denomination. Rev. D. Kromminga, Janssen's defender, refused to act as advisor in the case unless given a declaration by synod in regard to the professor's request

JANSSEN CASE NOT ENDED BY SYNOD'S DECISION, IS BELIEF

Action Brings Widespread Comment Following Adjournment.

PROFESSOR IN PROTEST

Student Notes Unfair Basis for Condemnation, He Charges.

18   20

Ralph Janssen (18), appointed professor of Old Testament at Calvin Seminary in 1914, was deposed in 1922 by the CRC synod of Orange City, Iowa (19) for the naturalistic and modernistic views which characterized his interpretation of the Old Testament. Headlines (20) of *Grand Rapids Press* articles June-July 1922, highlighting the controversy.

19

23

21

22

24

In the Janssen controversy, these leaders, Louis Berkhof (21),
Foppe TenHoor (22), Samuel Volbeda (23), and William Heyns (24),
supported and were advocates of Hoeksema's opposition to
Professor Ralph Janssen. However, their convictions regarding the
antithesis became apparent soon after, when they supported the
three points and the deposition of Revs. Herman Hoeksema,
Henry Danhof, and George M. Ophoff.

25

26

Fourteenth St. CRC in
Holland, Michigan (25)
where Rev. H. Hoeksema was ordained minister in 1915 and where
he served until 1920. The Hoeksema family (26) at Fourteenth St.

Eastern Ave. CRC (27), where the common grace controversy
erupted. Welcoming program for their new pastor (28), and Rev.
Hoeksema in his study at Eastern Ave. (29).

27

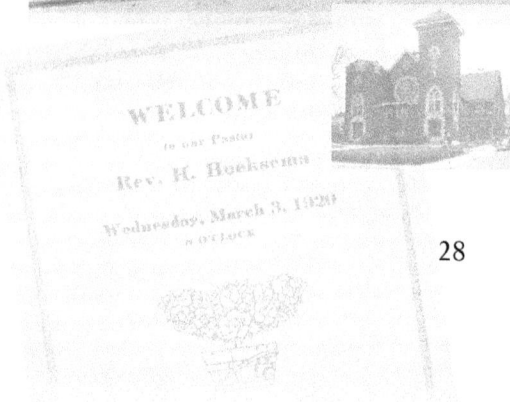

WELCOME
to our Pastor
Rev. H. Hoeksema
Wednesday, March 3, 1920
8 O'CLOCK

28

29

30

33

Hope CRC was organized in 1916 but existed without a pastor until Candidate George M. Ophoff (30) accepted their call in 1922. The original church building (31), built in 1917, architecturally symbolized the simplicity and humble beginnings of this rural congregation. A parsonage (32) was built in 1922 to house the newly-elected pastor and his family (33).

31

32

The CRC synod of 1924 (34), with Rev. Henry Danhof as delegate, was held in Kalamazoo, Michigan at First CRC of Kalamazoo (35). The synod was faced with protests against the Revs. Herman Hoeksema (36) and Henry Danhof (37) and their consistories over the issue of God's grace—particular or common.

The headlines (38) in the *Kalamazoo Gazette and Grand Rapids Press* kept the g eneral public informed of the controversial nature of the case. After three weeks of discussions in which much discord among the delegates manifested itself, the synod adopted the three points of common grace at a time when it was clearly evident that it was not at all prepared for such action.

34

35

36

37

PRICE THR

SYNOD NAMES BODY TO QUIZ REV. DANHOF

Doctrinal Teachings of Local Man and Grand Rapids Pastor Stir Row.

MAY MEAN HERESY TRIAL

Christian Reformed Church of America Committees Named; General Sessions Open Friday.

DOCTRINE DISPUTE AGITATES SYNOD

Controversy Over Common Grace in Hands of Committee at Kalamazoo.

WILL ATTRACT CROWDS

Kalamazoo. June 20.—The doctrinal controversy concerning common grace now raging in Christian Reformed church placed Wednesday in the hands of the synodical advisory committee and it is thought will be one of the questions to be discussed by the

SYNOD QUITS; SESSIONS LAST THREE WEEKS

Adjournment Taken at 1:00 Wednesday Morning; Rev. Danhof Protests.

(Continued From Page One)

The Rev. Danhof also declared in his protest that in two of its conclusions the synod did not at all clash with his views as expressed in his writings. He stated that the synod and the two pastors have not understood each other.

The protestant admitted that some

DISCUSSION OF H. DANHOF CASE TO BE LENGTHY

nal Teachings of Kalzoo and Kent Pastors under Fire.

mmittee of the Christian, Resynod has not as yet completed report for the consideration nied teaching on the doctrinal of the Rev. Henry Danhof and the Rev. Herbert

SYNOD LAYS LAWS DOWN FOR PASTORS

Christian Reformed Body Finds Hoeksema Not in Accord.

INTERPRETATIONS GIVEN

Kalamazoo. July 8—The Christian Reformed synod Monday took a definite

SYNOD MAY NOT STAGE HERESY TRIAL

Committee Advises Delay in Hoeksema-Danhof Common Grace Case.

38

The synod of 1924 had rejected its committee's advice to discipline those who rejected the teachings of common grace. But the classis of 1925 ordered consistories to query their ministers as to their full agreement with the three points of common grace. Revs. Danhof, Hoeksema, and Ophoff, all with firm resolve, expressed their rejection of this false doctrine.

CLASSIS DEPOSES REV. G. M. OPHOFF OF HOPE CHURCH

Christian Reformed Pastor Let Out of Meeting on Thursday.

HOEKSEMA DEPOSED, WHEN HE REFUSES TO MAKE DEFENSE

Eastern-av. Pastor Formally Barred from Christian Reformed Pulpit.

DECLINES TO APPEAR

CLASSIS HOLDS OFF DECISION IN CASES OF TWO MINISTERS

Men Who Disagree with Common Grace Tenet Still Wait Action.

OPHOFF PREFERS DEATH

Local Pastor Tells Christian Reformed Body He Will Not Subscribe.

Rev. G. Ophoff's reply to the question whether he would adhere to the three points summarizes the convictions and spiritual courage of the protesting pastors.

"Mr. President, if you were to place me before a gun to be shot or before me the three points to adhere to I would choose the former. I can't sign the three points. If I did I would be tearing the Bible into shreds. I would be stamping the Word under foot. I would be slapping God in the face."

39

40

41

The deposed pastors and consistories of Hope (39), Eastern
Avenue, and Kalamazoo, along with the larger portions of the
congregations who stayed with their pastors and consistories, were
outside the fellowship of the Christian Reformed Church.
Hope held worship services at the Blair (Riverbend) schoolhouse
(40) until June 1930. Kalamazoo used the facilities of the local
Congregational Church (41).

Eastern Avenue (Protesting)
Christian Reformed Church

Rev. H. Hoeksema, Pastor

42

43

The Eastern Ave. group first met in the Franklin Community House in Franklin Park. On January 29, 1925, the deposed consistories of Eastern Ave. (42), Hope, and Kalamazoo met to discuss unity and on March 6, 1925, they formed a temporary organization on the basis of an *Act of Agreement* (43) and adopted the name Protesting Christian Reformed Churches.

WEEKLY BULLETIN
Prot. First Christian Ref. Church

NEW HOME FOR THE PROTESTING CHRISTIAN REFORMED CHURCH SOCIETY.

Kal. Gazette 8-8-1925

44

In November 1926 the combined consistories met to organize a classis and adopted the name Protestant Reformed Churches. Rev. Danhof (44) withdrew from the new denomination, and he and the church of Kalamazoo continued independently as the Protesting First Christian Reformed Church of Kalamazoo (45).

45

46

NEW PROTESTANT REFORMED GROUP GROWING RAPIDLY

Three Churches in G. R. Form Nucleus for Young Denomination

The Protestant Reformed church, which may be called the youngest denomination among the churches of Reformed persuasion, has experienced a marvelous growth. Its origin is of recent date, 1924-25, when three ministers of the Christian Reformed church were deposed with their consistories, because of existing doctrinal differences. Since that time, the Protestant Reformed church was organized and now numbers 60 congregations, with 10 ministers of the gospel.

Three of these congregations are located in Grand Rapids. By far

REV. H. HOEKSEMA

the largest of these is the First Protestant Reformed church at the corner of Franklin st. and Fuller ave. This large congregation of 175 families is being served by Rev. Herman Hoeksema, the spiritual and inspirational leader of this young though promising denomination. Besides attending to his manifold duties as pastor of this large flock, he teaches at the Protestant Reformed seminary

Work Begins on New Church

The new Protesting Christian Reformed church to be located at the northwest corner of Franklin-st. and Fuller-av. Work started Tuesday of last week. Harvey H. Weemhoff is the architect. The basement will be completed in about five weeks and services will be held there until the church is completed. The church will cost $100,000.

47

In January 1925 the Eastern Ave. group began work (46) on a new church building and parsonage (47) on the northwest corner of Franklin and Fuller.

48

49

On December 22, 1926,
one year after the
congregation, pastored by
Rev. Herman Hoeksema
(48), had been forced from
their church building on
Eastern Avenue, they
dedicated the building of
the First Protestant
Reformed Church (49).

Dr. Klaas Schilder (50), brilliant theologian in the GKN (Netherlands), was deposed from his office as professor in the Kampen Theological School and as emeritus minister of the congregation in Delftshaven by the Synod of Sneek-Utrecht 1942-1944. His deposition in 1944 for his conditional views in regard to the covenant and the sacrament of baptism resulted in the founding of a new denomination commonly known as the Liberated Churches.

50

ED THEOLOGICAL CONFERENCE
AN — NOVEMBER 6-1947

PHOTO BY
CARL HARSHBERGER

51

Through his visits to America in 1939 and 1947, Schilder influenced many ministers and elders of the PRC to adopt his conditional covenant views. Given a voice within the churches, he became the occasion for schism in the PRC in the 1950s.

Dr. Schilder at the PRC theological conference in 1947 (51) and on the US capitol steps with Rev. and Mrs. Hoeksema after a conference with the Orthodox Presbyterians (52).

52

53 54 55

In the summer of 1949 Rev. John DeJong (53) and Rev. Bernard Kok (54) made an unofficial visit to the Netherlands (55) and represented the covenant views of Revs. Hoeksema and Ophoff as nothing more than their private opinions, not the official position of the PRC.

58

57

59

56

Rev. Andrew Cammenga (56) and Rev. Andrew Petter (57), contributors to the *Concordia* (58) and *Reformed Guardian* (59), led the western PR churches as a whole to reject the unconditional covenant of grace as defended by Revs. Hoeksema (60) and Ophoff (61).

61   63   60

Rev. Hubert DeWolf
(62), co-pastor in First
PR Church with Revs.
Herman Hoeksema
and Cornelius Hanko
(63), used the pulpit to
disseminate his
heretical views of
salvation by man's own
efforts. He became the
leader of the schismatic
movement in the East.

62

SUMMARY OF STATISTICS
of the
PROTESTANT REFORMED CHURCHES

CLASSIS EAST:

Churches	12
Michigan	9
Illinois	2
Wisconsin	1
Vacant	1
Ministers	17
Families	1014
Total Souls	4135

CLASSIS WEST

Churches	12
California	2
Washington	1
Iowa	7
Minnesota	1
Montana	1
Vacant	1
Ministers	11
Families	378
Total Souls	1928

— : — : — : —

DENOMINATION:

Churches	24
Vacant	2
Ministers	28
Home Missionary (Rev. Cammenga)	1
Families	1392
Total Souls	6063

64

Statistics show that numerically, the schism of 1953 decimated the PRC. The 1953 *Yearbook* (64) and 1954 *Yearbook* (65) from the PRC's *Acts of Synod* reveal that 33 percent of the churches, 50 percent of the ministers, and 61 percent of the total souls left the denomination.

SUMMARY OF STATISTICS OF THE
PROTESTANT REFORMED CHURCHES

CLASSIS EAST:

Churches 11
        (Michigan 8, Illinois 2, Wisconsin 1)
Vacant Churches 2
Ministers 11
Families 464
Individuals 10
Total Souls 1899
Catechism Enrollment 455
Communicant Members 1052

CLASSIS WEST:

Churches 5
        (Iowa 2, Minnesota 1, Washington 1, California 1)
Vacant Churches 2
Ministers 3
Families 99
Individuals
Total Souls 454
Catechism Enrollment 141
Communicant Members 209

DENOMINATIONAL TOTALS:

Churches 16
Vacant Churches 4
Ministers 14
Families 563
Total Souls 2353
Catechism Enrollment 626
Communicant Members 1261

65

Ministers in the PRC at the time of the schism of 1953 who remained faithful to the denomination.

1. John A. Heys
2. Marinus Schipper
3. Herman Veldman
4. Herman Hoeksema
5. Cornelius Hanko
6. George M. Ophoff
7. Homer C. Hoeksema
8. George C. Lubbers
9. Henry H. Kuiper
10. Gerrit Vos

$\mathcal{B}$iblical and Confessional, or Rationalistic?

The origin of our churches is to be explained in terms of our determination to remain faithful to the creeds; and we still want to be known as a creedally Reformed Church.
—Homer Hoeksema, *God's Covenant Faithfulness*

Introduction

One of the charges which the Protestant Reformed Churches have had to face over the years is the charge of rationalism. It has been made over and over again, and has come from different sources. The charge is a serious one, partly because rationalism is an exaltation of man's sinful reason to a position where it becomes the sole criterion of truth, and partly because it is, by its very nature, anti-biblical. A man cannot be faithful to the Scriptures and be a rationalist at the same time. He is one or the other. In fact, rationalism is unbelief; faithfulness to the Scriptures is saving faith.

The charge involves the method of theology which is used in the PRC. Are the PR theologians rationalistic or biblical in their theological work? What precisely is the theological method used in the PRC and how is theology developed? What role does Scripture assume? And, almost as important, what role do the confessions play in the work of theology which has been done and is still being done within the PRC?

These questions demand answers. It is our purpose to look into these matters in this chapter.

The Charge of Rationalism

The charge of rationalism against Herman Hoeksema's theology seems to have been made for the first time by a Christian Reformed minister prior to the split in 1924. The minister's name was J. K. van Baalen; the book he wrote was entitled *De Loochening der Gemeene Gratie* (The Denial of Common Grace).[1] His book was written during the common grace controversy and contained the charge that those who denied common grace were guilty of Anabaptism.[2] We are not particularly interested in the question of Anabaptism and its relation to common grace; but we are interested in another charge which van Baalen made, namely, that those who denied common grace were guilty of rationalism. Interestingly, van Baalen did this in connection with his own defense of a "two-track" theology.[3]

By a "two-track" theology van Baalen meant that theology runs on two parallel tracks which never meet. Or, to abandon the metaphor: theology consists of two lines of truth which cannot be harmonized. Common grace is one of these lines; other doctrines in the Reformed faith which seem to contradict common grace are the other line. To deny common grace was to deny the existence of two tracks by attempting to bring all the doctrines of faith into a consistent and harmonious unity. That effort was "rationalism" in van Baalen's opinion.[4]

---

1. The book was published in 1922.
2. The force of this charge was in van Baalen's insistence that a denial of common grace necessarily led to world-flight. It never was demonstrated in what sense Anabaptism taught world-flight, nor was it ever shown precisely how a denial of common grace necessarily resulted in world-flight. But the charge has stuck to the present.
3. van Baalen, *De Loochening der Gemeene Gratie*, 35–38. James Bratt refers to this charge of van Baalen in *Dutch Calvinism in Modern America*, 112. Bratt says that van Baalen not only accused Hoeksema of a single-track theology and of rationalism, but also of being guilty of the very same thing he condemned in Ralph Janssen—setting his own mind above Scripture.
4. Rev. R. B. Kuiper, professor in Westminster Theological Seminary and

The charge stuck. It was increasingly made, however, not so much with regard to a denial of common grace in general, but more specifically in connection with that one aspect of common grace called the well-meant offer of the gospel.[5] The trouble was that the doctrine of the well-meant offer seemed so totally at variance with traditional Reformed orthodoxy. We noticed earlier that those who defended the well-meant offer believed in the Reformed and Calvinistic doctrine of predestination, including both election and reprobation. But the well-meant offer teaches that God desires to save every one who hears the gospel. This is an intolerable contradiction. On the one hand, God determines to save only some, namely, those who are elect; and on the other hand, God desires to save every one who hears the gospel. So, with respect to given individuals, God both wants to save them and does not want to save them.

This contradiction is inherent in the well-meant offer. In his condemnation of the well-meant offer, Hoeksema pointed out that such contradictory ideas are nonsense. God cannot both will and not will the salvation of an individual. Or, to put it differently, God cannot both will to save a man and, at the same time, will to damn him. The contradiction is obvious and beyond solution. But his accusers, rather than abandoning the doctrine of the well-meant offer, charged him with rationalism, that is, with the sin of setting his own mind above the Scriptures. They considered this charge justified by the fact that he refused to accept contradictions in Scripture.

guest speaker at my college graduation in May 1952, demonstrated such two-track theology in his speech. The title of his address was "The Balance That Is Calvinism." He was at great pains to demonstrate that the genius of true Calvinism was its ability to hold in proper balance doctrines that were, as far as we could tell, mutually contradictory and, therefore, mutually exclusive of each other. Such doctrines were man's responsibility and God's sovereignty, and the well-meaning offer of the gospel and God's decree of election and reprobation, etc.

5. In fact, the charge of rationalism has so frequently been brought against those who deny the well-meant offer of the gospel that I shall use this doctrine as my chief example in discussing this question.

To fail to accept contradictions is to take a rationalistic approach to God's Word.

In defense of the position that contradictory views are taught in Scripture, appeal was made to what was called "paradox," or "apparent contradiction," or "mystery." All three terms were intended to mean the same thing, and all three were used to justify contradictions in theology. According to those who employed these terms, the point was this: The "contradictions" in Scripture are only apparent contradictions. They are paradoxes which we cannot solve, but which do have a solution. They seem to us to contradict each other, but on a higher plane they are in perfect harmony with each other. They are, therefore, "mysteries," which we cannot unravel.

But the defenders of such thinking went a bit further. They maintained that the reason why these doctrines seem to us to contradict each other is that our understanding is so limited that we cannot see the harmony. We must believe, as an act of faith, that in God's mind these two are perfectly harmonious and that no contradiction exists between them.

This appeal to the limited character of our knowledge in relation to God's omniscience sounds very pious and undoubtedly helped make the charge of rationalism plausible.

In the third place, another element was introduced into the discussion which resulted in further confusion, but which is crucial for an understanding of the whole problem. This element was the making of a distinction between God's "revealed will" and His "hidden" or "secret will."

This distinction went by different names. God's secret will was sometimes called God's "decretive will," or "the will of God's decree," while God's revealed will was called his "preceptive will, "or "the will of God's command."

But the terminology means the same thing. God had decreed that He would save only those whom He had chosen in Christ according to His sovereign decree of election. But

in His revealed will God makes known that it is His earnest
and serious desire that all men should be saved, and that this
desire manifests God's love for all men.

This was the distinction used by Professor W. Heyns,
which view the CRC followed. He writes:

> To whom is salvation in Christ offered? And this is a question
> which concerns the revealed things. In Arminianism we have an
> effort to bring the secret and the revealed things into agreement.
> This is done by distorting the secret things in such a manner as the
> revealed things seem to demand it. This may not be done. To do
> the same in the other direction by holding that only to the elect
> well meant grace is offered, is no less a distortion of the truth.[6]

The Position of
Cornelius Van Til

It is necessary at this point to introduce into the discussion
the view of Cornelius Van Til, late minister in the CRC
and professor of apologetics at Westminster Theological
Seminary in Philadelphia. Although Van Til did most of
his work during his years in Westminster, his position is
important for our discussion because, though Westminster
is a Presbyterian seminary, the Orthodox Presbyterian
Church was, in the late 1940s, locked in a controversy over
this very question. Because Herman Hoeksema himself had
been charged with rationalism, this controversy caught his
attention and he commented at length in the *Standard Bearer*
on it. In connection with these comments, he set forth some
of his own ideas on the issues involved.

The controversy swirled around the views of Gordon H.
Clark. Clark was charged with denying the incomprehensibility of God, with rationalism, and with a denial of the
well-meant offer of the gospel. His chief opponent in the
controversy was Cornelius Van Til.

---

6. Heyns, *Manual of Reformed Doctrine*, 197.

While Hoeksema thought the issue of the incomprehensibility of God to be rather abstract and more fitted for a theological discussion at a conference than for a controversy in church courts, he discussed at length the question of the well-meant offer, along with the whole question of apparent contradiction.[7]

It is not so easy to tell which of the issues that were discussed in the debate was the most important. Sometimes it seems as if the question of incomprehensibility was the chief one. But after reading the material, one is driven to the conclusion that especially Van Til, under the influence of his CR background, was interested in pressing the question of the well-meant offer, both in Westminster Theological Seminary and in the Orthodox Presbyterian Church.[8]

Gordon Clark denied the idea of the well-meant offer, and did so, in part, because it created contradiction in God. Clark's opponents insisted that, while the well-meant offer did indeed seem to create contradiction in God, this seeming contradiction was a paradox, a mystery, an apparent contradiction only. To deny that God expressed in the gospel His desire to save all men because it contradicted God's determination to save only the elect was to say that God is able to be fully comprehended. In other words, Van Til and those who agreed with him insisted that, because the chasm

---

7. Hoeksema's articles, published in the *Standard Bearer*, were later prepared in syllabus form by the Theological School of the Protestant Reformed Churches under the title "The Text of a Complaint: A Critique about the 'Clark Case'" (Grand Rapids: n.d.). The Trinity Foundation later published this syllabus as a book entitled *The Clark-Van Til Controversy* (Hobbs, N.M., 1995). The discussion and the issues involved are also referred to in John M. Frame, *Cornelius Van Til: An Analysis of His Thought* (Phillipsburg, N.J.: P & R Publishing Co., 1995), especially 220–23. On the broader issues of God's incomprehensibility, see Fred H. Klooster, *The Incomprehensibility of God in the Orthodox Presbyterian Conflict* (thesis, University of Amsterdam, published by Franeker, Netherlands: T. Wever, 1951).

8. Hoeksema himself suggests this in more than one place in The Trinity Foundation's book on the controversy: (Hoeksema, *The Clark-Van Til Controversy,* 33, 53) as well as elsewhere in the book.

between man and God is infinitely great, all that man can ever know about God is contrary premises. Man's limitations necessitate that his knowledge of God is essentially limited to seemingly contradictory propositions.[9]

When John M. Frame discusses the question of the well-meant offer in his book on Van Til, he himself makes a serious mistake in logical argumentation which is worthwhile to point out, since it is a mistake often made by those who criticize the position of the PRC for their rejection of the well-meant offer. In fact, it is precisely this mistake which gives a certain plausibility to the charge of Hyper-Calvinism.[10]

As I said, the defense of the well-meant offer involves an incorrect interpretation of the distinction between God's decretive will and His preceptive will. According to God's decretive will, God determines to save only His elect. According to His preceptive will, God desires to save all men. That there is contradiction between the two is justified on the grounds of the doctrine of paradox or apparent contradiction.

But there is a fatal flaw in the argument here, a flaw which is inexcusable in a man of Frame's ability. He argues that God often expresses a desire for something which He has not commanded. As an illustration of this, Frame points to the fact that although God determined that Cain kill Abel, nevertheless, the murder of Abel was against God's command.

No one committed to the truth of God's sovereignty would debate the proposition that, though God determined that Cain kill Abel, this deed was a terrible violation of God's command.

---

9. In his book *Cornelius Van Til*, Frame points out that the whole doctrine of paradox or apparent contradiction was a controlling principle in Van Til's theology; and, as a result, Van Til claimed that all truth was paradoxical. See pp. 63–95.

10. Ibid., 223.

Nor has the PRC ever denied that God commands all men everywhere to keep His law. Because all men have broken His law, God commands all men to repent of their sin and believe in the Lord Jesus Christ. This command, according to Canons II, 5, is set before men in the proclamation of the gospel: "This promise, together with the command to repent and believe, ought to be declared and published to all nations . . ." It is a point emphasized by the PRC as strongly as any proponent of the well-meant offer could wish.

But this matter of the command of the gospel is wholly beside the point. Precisely here Frame makes a subtle and, I hope, an unconscious shift in the language which is totally unwarranted. He identifies the *command* to repent and believe in Christ with God's *desire* to save all men. The argument seems to be: If God seriously commands all men to repent, God desires all men to repent. If God desires all men to repent, God desires (or wills) that all men be saved. If He wills that all men be saved, He loves all men and is gracious to all men. Neither Van Til, who made the same distinction, nor Frame, nor any other defender of the well-meant offer has any right to do this. Frame is speaking of the command of the gospel. That is fine. He is speaking of God's preceptive will as being the command of the gospel. We all agree. But then he must not include in that *preceptive* will, God's desire to save all men. God's desire is not His command. God's desire is that which He wills to do, that which He has eternally purposed in His counsel. God's desire is His decretive will. Just as soon as one speaks of a "desire" of God, one speaks of God's will, in other words, His decretive will.

Such lack of distinction as found in Frame is confusing and intolerable.[11]

---

11. This does not mean that God is not serious about the command to repent of sin and believe in Christ, which comes to all. God is totally earnest in this, so much so that He eternally punishes in hell those who refuse to repent. This is His preceptive will that He maintains. The Heidelberg Catechism, in Lord's Day

Nevertheless, this is not the chief issue which is my concern at the moment. The chief concern is that the whole doctrine of paradox or apparent contradiction was used to defend the well-meant offer of the gospel in Presbyterian circles as well as in Reformed churches.

Thus it happened that anyone who opposed the well-meant offer and who happened to mention that such a view as the well-meant offer created a contradiction in God was accused of rationalism, in other words, setting his own mind above Scripture.

It is this charge which needs to be examined in connection with what I may perhaps call the theological methodology of the PRC.

A Defense against Rationalism

It is ironic that the one theologian of the twentieth century who was, perhaps more than any other of the same century, a biblical theologian should be condemned for rationalism. And it is yet more ironic that the charge of rationalism should be laid at the feet of Hoeksema because of his denial of the well-meant offer of the gospel. This is especially true when we consider the fact that the Reformed tradition from the time of the Reformation repudiated the idea of a well-meant offer of the gospel, and that, insofar as it was taught, it was taught by those who had adopted the Arminian error.[12]

IV, points out that God must maintain the just demands of His law because His own righteousness demands it. He cannot tell the sinner: "I really no longer care whether you keep my law or whether you break it. Since you are totally depraved, I excuse you from obeying my righteous law." That would be out of keeping with God's divine majesty and righteousness. But we must not interpret this command that comes to all as a "desire" on God's part to save all. That moves the command from the preceptive will of God to His decretive will.

There is no conflict between a command that all must repent and a decree to save only the elect. This is exactly what Calvin is at great pains to demonstrate in his treatise "The Eternal Predestination of God" in *Calvin's Calvinism*.

12. See David J. Engelsma, *Hyper-Calvinism and the Call of the Gospel*, 127–92. See also my "The History of the Free Offer."

Hoeksema makes a point of showing that appeal is made to paradox, apparent contradiction or, as he calls it, "mystery," only because that is the only way to defend something as Reformed which is clearly Arminian.

> ... Why do they always speak of a mystery when they compare this offer [the well-meant offer] to the doctrine of election and reprobation? Indeed there is no mystery whatever in the teaching that God causes His gospel to be preached to all without distinction in order to save the elect and harden the others. The calling through the gospel makes the reprobate wicked responsible, places the depravity of his sinful heart in the clearest light and increases his judgment. That is God's intent. *The result answers completely to God's intent.* And God carries out His counsel. He still maintains man's responsibility and the justice of God. What is so very incomprehensible here? This is the clear teaching of the Scriptures ...
>
> No, the incomprehensible, the nonsense of the presentation is created when you try to bind the Arminian teaching of a general offer to the Reformed teaching of particular grace. Then you say: God desires to save only the elect; Christ brought atonement only for them; God gives His grace and works conversion only in them; but yet God offers His grace well-meaningly, with the intent of saving them, to all mankind; and if this grace is not accepted the result does not answer to the intent!
>
> This is not a mystery. It is nonsense ... You want to join the lie to the truth. Therefore you end up with a so-called mystery.[13]

What precisely is the position of the PRC on this whole matter? Are they rationalistic?

Let us start with the question of incomprehensibility. Is God incomprehensible?

In answer to this question, Hoeksema makes an important distinction between the incomprehensibility of God and the knowability of God.[14] He maintains that God is indeed

---

13. Translation of Hoeksema's *Een Kracht Gods Tot Zaligheid*, 76, 77.
14. Hoeksema, *Reformed Dogmatics*, 25–43.

incomprehensible because He is the infinite One, and we are but mere creatures. In this case, "incomprehensible" means "incapable of knowing completely or exhaustively." Even into all eternity, though God shall be the object of our everlasting contemplation, we shall never fully know Him, never even come close to knowing Him fully, never understand completely His works or His being. We shall never comprehend Him who is the infinite One.

But such incomprehensibility must not be confused with unknowability. It is true that we cannot know God at all of ourselves. We cannot climb the ladder of knowledge and make God the object of our investigation. God must reveal Himself. That is, God must speak of Himself to us in a way which we can understand.[15]

Revelation is centrally Christ Himself, who is the Word of God, the Word which God speaks (John 1:1–3). God makes Himself known in all His perfections in Jesus Christ, the Word become flesh. This revelation in Christ is infallibly recorded in sacred Scripture. It is not exhaustive of the truth as it is in God, for God remains the infinite One, while His revelation, adapted to us who are always finite creatures, is itself finite. But it is sufficient for our salvation; that is, we have from it sufficient knowledge of God in Jesus Christ that we may be saved.[16]

Because of revelation, God can be known, but only because His revelation is His speech to us in a way adapted to our

---

15. Hoeksema pointed out in his analysis of the Van Til-Clark controversy that the question was not really whether God is in Himself incomprehensible, but rather whether God's revelation is incomprehensible. In this respect the controversy never succeeded in clarifying the difference; and that failure to clarify the distinction between God as He is in Himself and God's revelation was a large part of the inability of the two protagonists to agree.

16. The Confession of Faith, Art. 7: "We believe that those Holy Scriptures fully contain the will of God, and that whatsoever man ought to believe, unto salvation, is sufficiently taught therein . . ."

creaturely understanding.[17] But our ability to know this revelation does not imply our ability to comprehend Him.

There is in this an important principle of all knowledge. Knowledge is not dependent on comprehension, if by comprehension one means total and exhaustive knowledge. Although I (and most other people) have not the knowledge of a rose which a biologist has, I do know a rose. I know it so that I am able to recognize one whenever I see one, and I know it sufficiently that I am able to enjoy it for its fragrance, beauty, and color. In fact, from a certain point of view, it is impossible for a man to comprehend any single creature in God's creation. Full knowledge, full understanding, exhaustive comprehension of even a leaf on a tree is beyond us. So much more is this true of Holy Scripture. Though it is finite, its depths are unfathomable, and though we study it all our lives, we know only a small part of it. Yet, beyond and behind Scripture stands the infinite God who has made Scripture, as well as the solar systems of the galaxies and the DNA molecule of a cell.

Rationalism is something quite different. It is the very opposite of the faith with which the believer comes to Scripture. The believer in the Word of God submits all his thinking to sacred Scripture. The rationalist claims to be able to discover truth apart from Scripture and with his own intellect. He gives powers to his intellect which it does not have and enthrones it so that it becomes the sole arbiter of truth. Rationalism exalts man. Rationalism abandons Scripture. Rationalism has no need of faith. To the rationalist, man's mind is sufficient.

Was Hoeksema ever a rationalist? If he were, one ought to be able to show that. One ought to be able to point out one passage in all his writings where Hoeksema sets the human mind above Scripture. Are the PRC rationalistic?

---

17. Calvin describes God's speech to us as "baby-talk."

It is not enough to show that the PRC are opposed to the idea that there is contradiction in Scripture. That is not rationalism. Rather than merely hurl the charge, one ought to demonstrate it from writings that have come from PR pens. Few writings in the last 100 years are as carefully based on Scripture as the writings from the PRC. And anyone who has visited PR churches in their worship on the Lord's day would have to admit that every sermon is a careful exposition of sacred Scripture and an earnest attempt to bring the congregation into submission to the Word of God.

Rationalism and Paradox

Nevertheless, in connection with the dispute over the well-meant offer, it has been repeatedly said that if one does not believe in paradox or in apparent contradiction, one is a rationalist. The reason behind this, so it is said, is that Scripture itself is full of apparent contradictions or paradoxes, and that faithful submission to Scripture involves, necessarily, a willingness to accept paradox.

The whole question of paradox or contradiction involves the question of logic. So to that we must pay a moment's attention.

This aspect of the question was extensively treated by Hoeksema in a lengthy analysis of Cornelius Van Til's book, *Common Grace*.[18] In a series of articles in the *Standard Bearer* Hoeksema analyzed Van Til's thought.[19] Some interesting points were made which indicate what the PRC consider to be a proper theological method, especially over against those who advocate paradox as being necessary.

---

18. Cornelius Van Til, *Common Grace* (Philadelphia: The Presbyterian and Reformed Publishing Company, 1947).

19. The series of editorials on "Common Grace" begins in vol. 19 (December 1, 1942) and continues through vol. 20 (October 15, 1943). Issues containing the editorials are 5–10, 12, 13, 15, 17 and 19 in vol. 19; and issues 1 and 2 in vol. 20.

Van Til had made a strange point about logic in the course of his writings. He had taken the position that the logic of unbelievers is different from the logic of believers.[20] Apparently, the reason why Van Til wanted to distinguish between a believing logic and an unbelieving logic was to make room within the believer's logic for contradictions, which, as everyone knows, do not exist in unbelieving logic.

Hoeksema repudiates that notion, although he admits that he is not sure exactly what Van Til means by the distinction.[21] He claims that the rules of logic are the same for a believer and an unbeliever, just as the theorems of geometry or the equations of algebra are the same for both.

This does not mean that the premises which believers use in their logical reasoning are not fundamentally different from those of unbelievers, for the latter begin with a denial of God as their most fundamental premise, while the believer begins with God. Thus the conclusions which a believer comes to are different from the conclusions to which an unbeliever comes. But the difference does not lie in the logic used. That is the same.

Secondly, Hoeksema also maintains that, because logic is logic, whether a believer or an unbeliever is using it, the law of contradiction holds for the believer as well as the unbeliever. Van Til maintains that in his thinking he can hold together both sides of a contradiction. Hoeksema said that that itself is a contradiction.[22] One cannot say that an apple is both an apple and an alligator at the same time and in the same sense. Nor can one say that an apple *is* an apple and is *not* an apple at the same moment in time and in the same sense of the word. That makes no sense and is, in fact, nonsense.

Yet such an illogical position is necessary if one is to say

---

20. Herman Hoeksema, "Common Grace" *SB* 19 (February 15, 1943): 221. See also Frame, *Cornelius Van Til*, 155.
21. Hoeksema, "Common Grace," Ibid.
22. Ibid.

that God does not love all men and that He does love all men in the same sense and at the same time, precisely the view of those who hold to the well-meant offer.

In the third place, Hoeksema does not deny "mystery." Scripture speaks often of mystery. But, according to Scripture, mystery is not a contradiction; it is something which cannot be known by man apart from revelation. And, in the nature of the case—for all the works of God are beyond our comprehension—a mystery is unfathomable.[23] But this does not mean that the mystery is unknowable. We know the great mystery of God become flesh. Can we fathom the greatness of it? No. Is it contradictory? By no means. Does it violate any laws of logic? Of course not. But it is the wisdom of God which is foolishness with men because men are unbelievers.

This point is carried out a bit further in Hoeksema's analysis of the Van Til-Clark controversy. In connection with the struggle that went on in the Orthodox Presbyterian Church over the incomprehensibility of God, Hoeksema makes the point that "either the logic of revelation is *our* logic, or there is no revelation."[24] He means by that statement that if revelation as it is contained in Scripture does not follow the laws of logic, then it is impossible for us to have any knowledge of it, for we cannot acquire knowledge of anything which defies the laws of logic.

Van Til had bolstered his point that God is incomprehensible by claiming that any proposition about anything at all has a different meaning for God than it has for man.[25] When God says something, He means by it something entirely different from what man means when he says the same thing. This follows from the fact that God's logic is

---

23. Ibid., 222.
24. Hoeksema, *The Clark-Van Til Controversy*, 8.
25. An example would be: "Two times two is four."

different from man's logic. Against this position Hoeksema said: "To say that any proposition does not have the same meaning for God as it has for man, is, it appears to me, a rationalistic contention. The complainants [against Gordon Clark] do not derive this from Scripture."[26]

If, therefore, Van Til's position is correct, God is not only incomprehensible, but also unknowable. That which is illogical is nonsense. That which is nonsense cannot be known. If all truth is illogical and nonsense, it cannot be known, and God, who is the truth, remains forever beyond our knowledge.

Rationalism and Scripture

When Hoeksema insisted that the main issues in the Van Til–Clark controversy (the incomprehensibility and unknowability of God) were nice subjects to discuss at theological conferences, but that the important issues (the well-meant offer of the gospel) were questions of Scripture and the interpretation of Scripture, he followed his own advice and proceeded to discuss the issues raised by the controversy as they touched on the Word of God.

The men who charged Clark with error, chief among whom was Cornelius Van Til himself, took the position that any attempt to harmonize Scripture with itself is per se rationalism. This position was, of course, in perfect harmony with their notion that the logic of faith is different from the logic of unbelief. They insisted that the logic of faith allows for contradictions; the logic of unbelief, which attempts to harmonize all truths into one consistent whole, is rationalism.

Over against this notion Hoeksema insisted that the idea of apparent contradiction is contrary to the nature of Scripture itself. If we are to know what Scripture teaches

---

26. Hoeksema, *The Clark-Van Til Controversy*, 12.

and are to understand God's revelation, Scripture can
have no contradictions in it. "Dogmatics proceeds from
the assumption that the truth revealed in the Bible can be
formulated into a logical system," wrote Hoeksema.[27]

This assertion that Scripture can be formulated into a
logical system means, according to Hoeksema, two things.
Scripture is one because God is one. Because God is one,
His revelation is one. And because His revelation is one, the
infallible record of that revelation is also one.[28] The second
implication is that Scripture must be understood according
to the *regula Scripturae*, the rule of Scripture, or, as it is
sometimes called, the analogy of faith.

Both of these ideas need a bit of explanation.

That God is one means not only that there is only one
God, but also that all God's works are one in Him, all His
attributes are essentially one, all His thoughts and the
purposes of His will are one. There can be no conflict, no
contradiction, no disharmony in Him who is alone God.

God's revelation is also one because God has determined
to reveal Himself through Jesus Christ, His only begotten
Son, our Lord. All of God's being, all of His works, and all
of His perfections are revealed through Christ, who is the
second person of the Trinity in our flesh. Just as God is one,
He who reveals God to us in His own person, natures, and
works is also one.

Thus, the record of that revelation in sacred Scripture
is also one. It is a perfect unity and harmony. It sings one
doxology of praise in which is no discordant note. This
assertion of oneness does not deny that Scripture contains
a great and glorious diversity. It has diversity of testaments,
diversity of languages, diversity of authorship, diversity of
literary genre, diversity of style, diversity of cultural milieus

---

27. Ibid., 26.
28. Ibid.

to which it is addressed. But its principle of unity is that the Scripture in all its parts is the record of the revelation of God in Christ. Scripture's diversity is that of a portrait. A portrait has a diversity of parts of the face, a diversity of personal traits, variety in the background, and diversity of color. But the diversity is united in the one principle that it is one perfect portrait of one person. So Scripture is one portrait of our Lord Jesus Christ.

If that portrait contains self-contradictory elements in it, it becomes unintelligible. If a portrait of an influential statesman contains the horn of a unicorn as well as a human nose, the barren wasteland of a lunar plateau as well as hair, the eyes of a fox along with human ears, the branches of a tree growing out of an ear, then one who looks at it says: "This makes no sense. I can know nothing about the statesman from this portrait."

Logic is nothing else but a description of the relationships in which things stand to each other. In the one unity of the creation every creature stands in a relationship to every other creature. Logic defines that relationship. Nothing more. When Scripture records the one truth of God in Jesus Christ, theology describes what each truth is and in what relationship each truth stands to every other truth.

And because the most fundamental, the most basic relationship in which all things in creation exist is their relation to God as Creator, that relationship in which creation stands to God becomes the one by which all things are truly knowable. So, because Scripture is the one record of the one revelation of God in Christ, so all the truths of Scripture are so related to each other that all point to the one God whom to know is life eternal.

To deny that characteristic of Scripture is to deny the possibility of any knowledge of God at all. To say that Scripture contains contradictions is to deny revelation.

The Analogy of Faith

That the truth revealed in the Bible can be formulated
into a logical system means, in the second place, that one
may speak of a "rule of Scripture," or an "analogy of faith."
Hoeksema writes: "The *regula Scripturae* means that throughout the Bible there runs a consistent line of thought . . ."[29]

The expression "analogy of faith" was used as early as the
Reformation of the sixteenth century, and the Reformed
churches have insisted on the principle until the present.[30]

The idea is certainly very much to the point. Scripture is
not a textbook on theology, but is the infallibly inspired and
written record of the revelation of God through Jesus Christ.
That revelation began in Paradise and was fulfilled in Christ.
That revelation begins, therefore, with the dawn of history
and continues till about A.D. 100. It is a revelation imbedded
in and a part of history. So Scripture records for us the
"history" of revelation.

Nevertheless, it is one portrait of the Lord Jesus Christ.
That one portrait contains many truths concerning Christ
as the revelation of God. These truths were revealed
immediately after the fall of our first parents, although
not fully. They were gradually made more fully known
throughout history.[31]

---

29. Ibid.
30. Thomas Miersma, "Scripture Interprets Scripture: Spiritually" *SB* 63
(November 1, 1986): 60–2. See also A. Skevington Wood, *Captive to the Word*
(Grand Rapids: Wm. B. Eerdmans Publishing Co., 1969). In this excellent book,
Wood has a chapter entitled "Luther and the Interpretation of Scripture." In it he
refers to Luther's doctrine of the "rule of Scripture," or the "rule of faith," or, as
Luther called it, "the analogy of faith," which Luther stated as follows: "Everything
must be weighed according to the analogy of faith." Luther also said, "The *analogia
fidei* is Scripture itself." What Luther means by *analogia fidei* is neatly expressed in
these words of his: "The interpretation has to be congruent with the general norm
of the Word of God" (p. 163).
31. My Old Testament history professor, Rev. George M. Ophoff, used to speak
of that revelation as a rose, which, when first begun in Paradise, was like a small
bud, but which grew and unfolded until the full flower of Christ Jesus in all His
glory was fully revealed.

The result is that every single truth, and all other truths, form the one great truth of Christ. These truths are found from the beginning of the Bible to the end. It is the task of the theologian to search the whole of Scripture, discover what any part of Scripture may say concerning a given truth, and bring all the truths together into one system of truth. To formulate such a system, the dogmatician must show the relationship between a single truth and all the other truths, in other words, the unique place which any given truth occupies in the portrait of the Lord Jesus Christ. This is the "rule of faith."

Directly from the rule of faith the most fundamental principle of biblical interpretation follows: Scripture interprets Scripture. Wood writes: "The formula of Scripture as its own interpreter was closely linked by Luther with another: that all exposition should be in agreement with the analogy of faith. Everything must be 'weighed according to the analogy of faith and the rule of Scripture.'"[32]

In the final analysis, this rule of faith is found in the confessions of the church. Luther already recognized that. According to Wood, "Creeds and confessions were of value only in so far as they embodied the rule of Scripture—as Luther believed the great historical affirmations to do. He demanded, however, that reference should be made to the Scripture as a whole and not merely to selected parts of it."[33]

---

32. Wood, *Captive to the Word*, 163. Wood, in explaining Luther here, gives the lie to Van Til's assertion about contradictions when he says: "All exposition should be in agreement with the analogy of faith."

33. Ibid. Wood makes use of a incisive quote from Luther: "The abominable sophists . . . support themselves with Scripture, because they would look laughable if they tried to force only their own dreams on men; but they do not quote Scripture in its entirety. They always snatch up what appears to favor them; but what is against them they either cleverly conceal or corrupt with their cunning glosses." How true today as well. In fact, the support for the well-meant offer is such a "snatching up of what appears to favor them"; and texts which teach the opposite of their interpretation of selected passages are pushed aside by an appeal to apparent contradiction.

Hoeksema concludes his discussion with some much needed reminders: "All sound, Reformed theologians and exegetes have always insisted that Scripture must be explained in its own light and that difficult passages must be explained in harmony with the current teaching of the Bible."[34]

The Confessions and the Theological Method of the PRC

Luther's reference to the confessions as an expression of the "rule of Scripture" necessarily brings up the question of the role of the confessions in the theological work of the church.[35]

It has been the position of the PRC since their inception that the proper way for a believer to go to Scripture is via the confessions of the church. That seemingly bold assertion has been challenged as giving to the confessions an authority which is greater than that of Scripture.

Nevertheless, this is not true, and one will see that it is not true if one will understand the importance of the confessions in all the work of theology.

The confessions are written and officially adopted by the church as statements of what the church believes to be the truth of Scripture. Sometimes those confessions deal only with one point of doctrine (as the Nicene Creed); sometimes with several points of doctrine directly related to each other (as the Canons of Dordt); and sometimes with most or all the truths of Scripture (as the Heidelberg Catechism or the Westminster Confession of Faith). But whether their contents are limited or include all the truth of Scripture, they are written according to the "rule of Scripture," or

34. Hoeksema, *The Clark-Van Til Controversy*, 53.
35. For a discussion of this point, see my article, "The Confessions in the Life of the Church" *SB* 58 (July 1, 1982): 416–19.

"the analogy of faith." They contain all that the Scriptures teach with respect to a given point of doctrine—insofar as the church understood it at the time the confession was written.[36]

If the truth of Scripture is to be understood in all its fullness, then it must be understood according to this "rule of Scripture." Because the confessions contain this "analogy of faith," the way to go to Scripture is by way of the confessions. That is, the proper way of studying Scripture in any given passage is with a thorough knowledge of and commitment to the confessions.

The alternative to this method is that every time one wants to learn the truth of Scripture, he must "start from scratch," begin all over, come to Scripture without any idea of the truth. But no one ever gets anywhere by that method, for he must in every text go to the whole of Scripture to learn what Scripture teaches. It took the church 2,000 years to get where it is now. A man who thinks he will accomplish in his own lifetime what the church worked at for 2,000 years is, to say the least, proud.

Besides, that truth which the church in the past has confessed is the direct fruit of the Spirit of Truth whom Christ promised to the church (John 14, 15, 16) and who has led the church into the truth. To ignore all the work of the church in the past is to ignore the work of the Holy Spirit as the Spirit of our Lord Jesus Christ.

The church of today builds on the church of the past. The

---

36. No confession and no theology will exhaust the knowledge of God as it is contained in sacred Scripture. But we must not conclude that the confessions of the church contain bits and pieces of the truth. The development of the truth through the ages is not like the collecting of bits and pieces from Scripture, pasted or welded together in an arbitrary way; the development of the truth is like the growth of a tree from the small sapling (contained in the Nicene Creed) to the great confessions of the sixteenth and seventeenth centuries. But whether that body of truth consists of a small sapling or a mighty oak, all the truth is in both the sapling and the mature tree.

theologians today stand on the shoulders of the theologians of bygone centuries—as they in turn stood on the shoulders of their forerunners. Kuyper stood on the shoulders of Calvin, and Calvin on the shoulders of Augustine, and Augustine on the shoulders of Athanasius.

The confession of the church grows into a mighty oak because the theologians of one generation take the confessions of a past generation, absorb them into their thinking, and then study Scripture anew in its profound depths to bring that truth of former times to yet greater clarity.

But does not this give the confessions an authority at least equal to, if not greater than, the Scriptures?

It does not.

The confessions are always to be compared to and measured against the Scriptures. The confessions only express what the church, through the work of the Spirit of Truth, has declared to be the teaching of the Word of God. These confessions do not teach what the Word of God says in one isolated passage; rather, they express what is the rule of faith—that which the whole of Scripture teaches concerning a given point of doctrine. But these same confessions, even though they have stood the test of time, must be continually subjected to the scrutiny of God's Word, for the Scriptures are written by God; the confessions are the product of the church, the work of fallible men.

The truth that the confessions are the fruit of the Spirit of Truth in the church does not change the fact that the confessions can be wrong. Just as the life of regeneration is wrought by the Spirit of Christ in a sinful person to whom much sin still clings, so the confessions are the work of the Spirit in the church to which much imperfection still clings. In full awareness of the imperfect understanding of God's people, the church has always provided ways in which the confessions can be brought more in harmony with the Word of God, should it be found that they are in error.

But to ignore and despise the confessions is to turn one's back on the Spirit of Christ and the superb work of the church in the past as led by the Spirit and to impoverish one's own understanding of the Word of God.

Faith and Theological Method

An important aspect of the theological work which has been done in the PRC is the doctrine of the role that faith plays in the true knowledge of God as it comes to us in Scripture.

Herman Hoeksema laid down the crucial importance of faith in true knowing, but the implications of this have been developed further. I include here some aspects of that development.

Although sin, when it entered the world through our first parents, had profound effects on the natural light with which men had been endowed by their Creator, sin did not rob men of their rationality. They remain rational and moral creatures. The problem of sin lies elsewhere.

Sin is a spiritual and moral depravity which gained control over the whole man. The result is that sinful man's heart is filled with hatred and enmity against God. In alliance with Satan, who seeks God's overthrow, man cooperates with Satan to work towards the realization of Satan's purposes, a kingdom of darkness in God's creation.

The problem with sinful man is not inability to know (rationality); it is a spiritual refusal to believe anything of God. Apart from grace, man is incapable of arriving at the truth, for the "light, such as it is, man in various ways renders wholly polluted, and holds it in unrighteousness" (Canons III & IV, 4); and "all the light that is in us is changed into darkness" (Confession of Faith, Art. 14). Paul speaks of "natural" men, and says of them: "But the natural man receiveth not the things of the Spirit of God: for they are foolishness unto him: neither can he know them, because they are spiritually discerned" (I Cor. 2:14).

Man's mind is, therefore, incapable of appropriating the truth. He may very well learn many things about the creation and the relationships in which various creatures stand to each other; but he denies the relationship in which all things stand to God. And so he has no true knowledge of anything at all.

We are delivered from such profound spiritual ignorance by the work of regeneration and conversion through the enlightening power of the Holy Spirit. In principle this involves that enlightening influence of the Holy Spirit which gives to the regenerated child of God the love of God in his heart, the desire to know God, and to walk in obedience to Him. Faith is a powerful and, ultimately, correct way of knowing. Faith is the one instrument whereby a person can acquire true understanding. Faith gives to those who possess it a knowledge which totally outdistances the knowledge of the most learned of unbelievers. This is the reason why the Psalmist can say: "I have more understanding than all my teachers: for thy testimonies are my meditation. I understand more than the ancients, because I keep thy precepts" (Ps. 119:99, 100).[37]

Faith is, first of all, the spiritual bond that unites the believer to Christ, and to God through Christ. As a bond, faith is also knowledge, the knowledge of Christ to whom the believer is united. Faith is knowledge because its object is the sacred Scriptures, in which Christ is revealed. Faith receives those Scriptures as God's very Word concerning all His works.

---

37. The Psalmist does not claim superior intellect, a higher IQ, so to speak. He claims "understanding." In other words, he understands even earthly things better than the most learned among the wicked. He, though relatively uneducated, understands, for example, how this creation came into existence through divine command in six days of twenty-four hours, and he understands God's purpose in all this creation to glorify Himself in the new heavens and new earth through Christ. Thus he understands things far better than the learned scientist with a Ph.D in physics who teaches that all things came into existence by virtue of a "big bang" some ten to fifteen billion years ago. The latter is a fool. He has no understanding.

When faith has as its object the Scriptures, faith believes what the Scriptures say. And, believing what the Scriptures say, faith leads to the One who is made known in Scripture, the Lord Jesus Christ. Faith always brings the student of Scripture to Christ Himself—by the Spirit of Christ in his heart. With this knowledge of Scripture, the believer has a true understanding of all things.

Thus faith is the personal, intimate, experiential knowledge of Christ, and of God through Christ. It is that kind of knowledge which a man has of his wife whom he dearly loves. It is reasonable knowledge, rational knowledge, intelligible knowledge—of course. But faith is a knowledge which transcends the knowledge of mere reason. Reason can help one who is regenerated[38] understand the truth, for reason can help him understand, for example, how Christ's atoning sacrifice is related to justification by faith and the final renewal of all things. But faith is first, and reason helps faith as a servant helps his master. The knowledge a believer has of Christ and of God is a transcendent knowledge of personal acquaintance. If a man would ask me to prove reasonably the existence of my wife at the moment I am sitting with my arm around her on the sofa, I would pity the poor man and tell him: "What kind of proof will you believe if you do not believe her existence when you see us sitting here together?" So the believer looks in pity on the unbeliever who asks for proof of God's existence. "What kind of proof shall I give you that will convince you, when trees and birds, flowers and the starry heavens speak of Him? And above all, the Scriptures speak of Him, and the Scriptures are themselves the Word of Him in whom we believe. If you will not believe that testimony, then there is no proof which will convince you.

---

38. While Luther could call reason "the devil's whore" when he referred to reason in its own strength, he could also refer to reason as "the handmaiden of faith."

The trouble with you is not that the proof is inadequate; the trouble with you is, as the proverb puts it: 'No one is so blind as he who *will* not see.'" Men have Moses and the prophets. Let them hear them. And if they will not hear Moses and the prophets, they will not be persuaded even if one should rise from the dead (Luke 16:29–31). That is, there is no proof to convince the unbeliever. Nor will he be convinced by proof. He needs grace!

Scripture is also received as God's by faith. One may very well ask: "You point us to Scripture, but how do we know that Scripture is reliable? How do we know that Scripture is the infallible Word of God?" The answer to that question is not to spend two years writing fifteen books to support with rational arguments that Scripture is reliable.[39] All the proof under the heavens may very well be mustered in an imposing manner so that no bit of evidence is left unreported. But who will be persuaded? The unbeliever? He cannot even see the kingdom of heaven apart from regeneration (John 3:3). His problem is not lack of proof. His problem is sin. Only when sin is removed will it be possible to "believe" the truth.

So, in a sense, the believer needs no proof. I need proof that Scripture is the Word of God no more than I need proof that a given letter I received today is from my wife. I *know* it is from her. It is her handwriting. It is the way she talks. She knows things that only she and I know. There is no amount of "proof" in God's world that can persuade me that this letter is not from her. I know her.

So the believer stakes out his claim for Scripture. How do I know that Scripture is the Word of God? Well, the Bible itself

---

39. I am not denying that the church ought to refute the contentions of higher critics. The church may surely do this on the ground of the foolishness of their contentions. But the Bible stands as the Word of God without the kind of proof which we call empirical. Empirical proof, in the nature of the case, is not needed by the believer and will never persuade the unbeliever. To attempt to do so is rationalism.

says so. The Author wrote His name on every page. This is the way He would write. This book contains things that only He would know. I know Him, and this is what He would say. There is no amount of proof which anyone can muster which would disprove what is obvious to faith.

The proof for the flood does not lie in the remains of a boat in some frozen lake on Ararat. It is in Genesis 6–9. If one will not believe that, a discovery of the old ark will not help. The proof for creationism does not lie in the fossils, or in the geological column, or in the atom—any more than the proof for evolution lies in these things. The proof for creation is in Genesis 1 and 2. "They have Moses and the prophets; let them hear them . . ." The believer knows because he is a believer. And that faith gives him more understanding than all his (unbelieving) teachers, or than all the (unbelieving) ancients. By faith we not only know, but also understand that the worlds were framed by the Word of God . . . (Heb. 11:3).

The PRC develop theology not in rationalistic ways, but by faith in the Holy Scriptures.

Theologically-centered Method

The theology of the PRC has been consistently God-centered. Such God-centered emphasis has resulted in God-centered preaching, God-centered catechetical instruction, and God-centered education in the seminary.

This emphasis on God and on His glory is the reason why the doctrine of the absolute sovereignty of God is so strongly emphasized in PR churches. God's sovereignty, which He exercises through His exalted Son, our Lord Jesus Christ, is a sovereignty that extends to all His works—in heaven, in this vast universe, and in hell. The decree of providence, which includes all that transpires, is sovereignly executed. Angels and devils are subject to His control. Nothing happens in all the creation which is outside of God's own work.

That sovereignty must be maintained in the work of

salvation as well. God's absolute sovereignty in salvation means that the whole work of salvation, from beginning to end, is so completely God's work that no room at all is left for man's work. Sovereignty excludes the freedom of man's will to choose for God. Sovereignty includes all the good works of God's people which are eternally prepared that the elect should perform them (Eph. 2:10). Sovereignty means that even the willing and the doing of good works is God's work, done according to His good pleasure (Phil. 2:12, 13). God's glory in the salvation of the church means absolute sovereignty in the work of salvation.

This truth, when preached from PR pulpits, in no way denies or even abridges man's responsibility. PR preaching is insistent on man's obligations to keep the precepts of God. But, holding to the truth of God's sovereignty requires that preaching always emphasize two truths. The one is that God holds all men accountable for their sin; and He brings this accountability to their consciousness by confronting them with the demands of the gospel to repent of sin and believe in Christ. The other truth is that the gospel is directed to the elect as the glad tidings of salvation. The precepts of the gospel, urged upon God's people, tell them that God has saved them by His power, that they are to walk in gratitude for such a salvation, and that they are to become more and more what grace has made them. The words of Augustine are the key to their walk in holiness: "Give what Thou dost ask, and ask what Thou wilt." This joyful obedience required of God's people is not something that is left to them to perform; they are taught in gracious and loving words to flee to the cross of Christ. In the cross they will find forgiveness for their many sins, and in that cross they will find the strength and grace merited for them and worked by the Spirit to enable them to do what God wills.

And, if one should say, "Yes, but their going to the cross is still their work," the answer is that God does not save His people as stocks and blocks[40] but as people who consciously and willingly glorify the God of their salvation. God brings them to the cross, yet in such a wonderful way that they themselves flee for refuge to their Savior.

This God-centeredness was the controlling principle in the theology of Herman Hoeksema. One cannot read in his *Reformed Dogmatics* without becoming aware of how the entire development of theology centers in God's work for His own glory. The emphasis on God's counsel and the supralapsarian viewpoint Hoeksema takes bring this truth home.[41] His doctrine of providence, which emphasizes that all things which take place are for the glory of God's name in Christ, strikes an identical note. In treating of the doctrine of God's everlasting covenant of grace, one is not surprised to find that Hoeksema begins the doctrinal development of that concept by an appeal to the fact that God lives a covenant life within His own triune being, and that the covenant of grace is but the revelation of that perfect life of blessedness which God lives in Himself.[42]

But perhaps nowhere is the truth of Hoeksema's God-centered theology more prominent than in his treatment of God's attributes.[43] After suggesting another distinction between God's attributes than the traditional one between incommunicable and communicable attributes, Hoeksema goes on very carefully to define each perfection of God. But in every case he is at pains to define these attributes as indeed attributes *of God*. God's grace, for example, receives full treatment as an attribute of God.[44] Hoeksema's primary

---

40. Herman Hoeksema was wont to say from the pulpit: God does not take us to heaven in the upper berth of a Pullman sleeper. He saves us as rational, moral creatures. He saves in this way in order that His people may glorify Him as they consciously come to know their salvation.
41. Hoeksema, *Reformed Dogmatics*, 153–65.
42. Ibid., 152.
43. Ibid., 61–130.
44. Ibid., 107–12.

interest is not in the question of the meaning of God's grace towards His people in Christ. Hoeksema's primary concern is to define grace, first of all, as an attribute of God which characterizes God in His own self-sufficient and eternally glorious being. God is, if we may put it that way, gracious to Himself. He is, within His own life, a God of grace. The grace which He shows to others is only a revelation through Christ of that attribute which belongs to God's own divine being.[45] In fact, we are unable to understand grace in its true significance, as the elect are the sole objects of it, unless we understand first of all that grace characterizes God's own being.

And so this emphasis on God and His glory becomes the starting point of all PR doctrine and life. It has its practical significance too. God's people are taught to pray, "Hallowed be Thy name"; that is, the hallowing and glory of God's name is more important than anything else. It does not matter, in the final analysis, what happens to us personally, so long as God's great name is glorified. So we must pray; so we must live; so we must be in submission to the sovereign will of God.

And, above all, in the glorious work of salvation man has nothing about which to boast. He has done absolutely nothing to gain or secure his salvation. He sings from the heart: "All that I am I owe to Thee . . ." (versification of Ps. 139). He always puts all boasting aside, for there is nothing of him in which to boast. He stands in constant awe and amazement at the wonder of grace which has saved him, a poor sinner. He considers all his life, with all its duties, responsibilities, work, obligations, sufferings and sorrows, as a part of salvation, to be a great privilege given by a loving God to prepare him for glory and the eternity that awaits him when God's glory shall fill all things and engulf him in its brightness and blessedness.

---

45. Ibid.

CHAPTER 12

The Meaning of the Concept "Organic"

This emphasis on the "organic" so exasperated their antagonist, Jan Karel van Baalen, that he angrily charged that all that Danhof and Hoeksema did was chant, "organic, ORGANIC, *ORGANIC": Yes indeed. But calling out, "organic,* ORGANIC, *ORGANIC" is not the same as an explanation of how we must conceive [of the term] . . . organic.*
—David Engelsma, *Protestant Reformed Theological Journal*

Introduction

One would be hard pressed to find in all the writings of the ministers in the Protestant Reformed Churches a word used more commonly and in a more widely-diversified way than the word "organic."

The term is used to describe the basic character of the original creation which was an "organic" whole. It is used repeatedly to define the relationship in which man stood to that creation, as an "organic" part of it. The word also appears in connection with Adam's relationship to the human race, for he was its "organic" head. But as the "organic" head of the human race, Adam was but the figure of Christ, who is the "organic" Head of the elect.

In a different way, the term is used to describe the development of sin from Adam's first transgression to the reign of Antichrist at the end of the ages. That development of sin is described as "organic." But the covenant of grace, which God establishes with His elect in Christ, also has an "organic" development due to the fact that God saves His people in the line of generations. And, in fact, this "organic" development of the covenant in the line of generations is the basis for the baptism of all the children of believers, even though not all are elect and true members of the covenant.

The term is also applied to Scripture. It is said that the proper interpretation of Scripture is possible only when one considers that the Scriptures are an "organic" whole.

The rather striking fact is, however, that one can search in vain for a definition of this word. Passages can be found in which some things are said about the term, and in which the writer made clear why the term could be applied to a given doctrine; but a definition cannot be found.[1] Yet because the term was used so often and because so much was said about it, it is possible to gain a clear idea of its meaning and importance in PR theology.

The History of the Term

None of the fathers of the PRC ever claimed that his use of the term "organic" was original with him. It was freely admitted that the term had a long history in Reformed theology. In fact, Hoeksema claims that the idea was already found in Augustine, though Augustine did not use the term itself.[2]

Although the whole idea of an organism was not used in the Middle Ages,[3] it reappeared at the time of the

---

1. Rev. Hoeksema often developed the term in his preaching on the pulpit of First Church, and in the sermons in which the term was important, he gave a definition in the context in which he was using it.

2. Danhof and Hoeksema, *Van Zonde en Genade*, 25–27. Augustine was one of the greatest of the early church fathers. He lived A.D. 354–430.

3. It becomes clear in subsequent discussions in *Van Zonde en Genade* that Hoeksema considered that the failure of the medieval church to deal with the concept was due to the Pelagianism to which the Roman Catholic Church had committed itself.

Reformation, and again, most clearly, in the synod of Dordt's affirmation of the great truth of sovereign predestination. As Hoeksema said, the choice which the church always has to make is the choice between predestination and the free will of man. Dordt chose the first, and in its powerful affirmation of predestination, Dordt suggested the organic view of the church as the number of the predestined. This was clearly in opposition to Arminianism.[4]

But, so Hoeksema claimed, Dordt's statement was only a suggestion, and the synod was weak on one aspect of the doctrine of organic unity: the organic relation of the elect to the creation.[5] Such "weakness" can, however, easily be explained: Dordt was dealing with Arminianism and its individualistic emphasis, and the synod had not time to develop carefully the positive aspects of the truth.

Hoeksema claims that even Kuyper was critical of Dordt in its failure to develop more fully the organic idea. But all are agreed that this weakness in Dordt, such as it is, is compensated for by our other confessions which are much more emphatic on the subject. The Canons, therefore, can be supplemented by the other confessions without doing injustice to the thought of the Canons.[6]

Hoeksema points out that Kuyper, especially in his earlier days, was deeply committed to the principle of organic unity and developed it in a beautiful and important way.[7] Kuyper, according to Hoeksema, even went so far as to develop this idea of an organic unity of the elect in his defense of the

---

4. Danhof and Hoeksema, *Van Zonde en Genade*, 31–39. Hoeksema means to stress here the extremely important point that Arminianism and Pelagianism are always individualistic, and thus opposed to an organic conception of things. I shall have more to say about this a bit later and shall have opportunity to explain these ideas more fully.

5. Ibid., 41, 42.

6. Ibid.

7. Ibid., 86–91. A lengthy quotation from Kuyper is included to prove the point.

antithetical life which the elect are called to live in relation to the unbelieving world.[8]

However, says Hoeksema, Kuyper took quite a different stand when he began to develop his common grace, for common grace was directly opposed to the biblical idea of the organic unity of the people of God and their antithetical life in the world.

According to Hoeksema, the same is true of Herman Bavinck, who adopted a common grace which excluded any development of the organic unity of God's people over against the world. Bavinck spoke of a goodness and mercy of God which operates even in hell. He insisted that both the fall of Adam and the coming of Christ, both good and evil, both elect and reprobate, cooperate for a common purpose.[9]

Leaning heavily, therefore, on past Reformed thought, Danhof and Hoeksema spent a great deal of time, even in their early years in the ministry, explaining this crucial organic idea. And so it came about that the term and the idea associated with it entered into the warp and woof of PR thought.

The Idea of an Organism

The importance of the term "organic" in PR theology cannot be denied. Nevertheless, the difficulty of describing precisely what PR theologians meant by this term is great. The reasons are two. In the first place, one looks in vain for a definition of the term. Its frequent use without careful definition seems to indicate that the authors of PR literature assumed a knowledge and understanding of the term on the part of the readers. Although the assumption may have been correct in earlier years, it is certainly not true

8. Ibid., 91–4.
9. Ibid., 176–86.

now.[10] Secondly, as I indicated above, the term has been used in different connections and even, perhaps, in different ways. These two facts make definition difficult.

Nevertheless, certain ideas concerning the term emerge.[11]

One crucial characteristic of an organism is that it is a collection of diverse parts united into one whole. A tree is an organism because it is composed of leaves, branches, trunk, and roots, which function as parts of the one tree and are united in it. A leaf of a tree has some of the characteristics of an organism in that, while it is dependent for its life on the tree as a whole, it too is composed of different cells, each of which has a function within the unity of the leaf. And each cell of the leaf is a complex structure of many parts working in harmony with each other. But together all the parts make up the one organism of the tree.

The various parts which make up an organism are related to each other. They are related in such a way that each single part of the organism is dependent upon every other part for its existence and for the accomplishment of its own unique purpose. A human eye in a human body is related to and dependent upon every other part of the body for its life and its work. A human eye, lying by itself on a table, has no meaning, does no good, has no purpose, and can accomplish nothing.

In an organism, there is a kind of perfection. This is not a moral and spiritual perfection, but a perfection of creation. To add something foreign to the organism as God created it is to destroy it. If one would add a branch of a tree to a

---

10. I have learned, sometimes to my dismay, that if I use the term "organic" in theological discussion, I am met with blank stares and puzzled looks. In fact, it is difficult to explain to others, unfamiliar with the term, what it really means.

11. In the material that follows, the attempt to give an explanation to the term "organic" is emphatically *my* attempt. The language and illustrations are mine. I believe that what I say correctly reflects the thinking of those whose views I am describing, but the description is my attempt to sum up the thinking of PR theologians.

human body, one would destroy the body. If one would add a human eye to a tree, one would destroy the tree—and the eye. In each case, one would not have an organism, but a monstrosity. Nor can anything be taken away from such an organism without, at the very least, making it less than it was intended to be. Take the roots from a tree and one destroys the tree. Amputate a leg, and, while the man can continue to live, his activities are curtailed.

The wide diversity of parts which make up an organism are united by one principle, which binds all the parts into a whole. Usually this principle of unity is some principle of life. This is important, for an automobile is also a unity of parts for one purpose—to carry one or more people from one place to another without too much effort on the part of the people being transported. But an automobile is not an organism; it is a mechanical device which has no principle of life. An organism has a principle of life. This life defines its unity and its purpose.[12] It pervades all the parts, binds all the parts together, makes every part dependent upon and related to every other part, and gives to the organism as a whole its identity and purpose.

God created living organisms with different principles of life, or, perhaps better, different manifestations of life. The life of a fish is different from that of a bird. The life of a tree is different from that of a man. But one principle of life defines the unity and purpose of each organism.

The Scriptures point us to the organisms in the creation as being pictures and earthly illustrations of heavenly and spiritual realities. We shall take a closer look at this later, but

---

12. In speaking of a principle of life as being characteristic of an organism, we must bear in mind that the term "organic" was used in a broader sense also. The Bible is said to be an organic whole, although it can be said to be "living" only in quite a different way than a tree or a person is living. The "organic" development of sin is an expression commonly used, but here too "organic" is used in a different way than, for example, when it is used to describe the church in I Corinthians 12.

here the principle of Scripture is followed that the earthly is created after the pattern of the heavenly.

The organism of a grapevine, for example, is used to picture the nation of Israel in Psalm 80 and John 15:1–3. The organism of the human body is a figure of the church in I Corinthians 12. The organism of a wheat plant with the kernel and the chaff is used repeatedly in Scripture as a picture of the church in its historical manifestation with both elect and reprobate in it.[13]

The organic idea is clearly a common idea in Scripture. It is not surprising, therefore, that it should find its way into Reformed theology.

The Creation As an Organism

When God formed this earthly creation, He formed it in such a way that it constituted an organism. Within that creation are an uncountable number of individual creatures, of seemingly infinite diversity, which God formed during the six days of the creation week. Yet the creation, especially in its original form, as it came from the hand of the Creator, was a unity.[14]

Within the unity of the creation, each individual creature is dependent upon and related to every other creature. Even if we can only dimly see this grand unity, this music of the spheres, we nevertheless are able to hear as from a distance the glorious symphony of the song of the creation.

The idea that the creation is an organism is already implied in the Greek word used in Scripture. The word is *cosmos*, and its most basic meaning is "a harmonious arrangement." The earthly creation is such a harmonious arrangement. In it the grand tune played by each part of

---

13. Hoeksema, *Reformed Dogmatics*, 574–75.
14. Sin and the curse have altered the creation in significant ways and destroyed some of its organic unity, but it remains basically a unity even under the curse. Ecologists are only just learning this. To disrupt one part of the creation is to affect every other part in surprising and often destructive ways.

the symphony is a doxology of praise and glory to God, the Creator.

The individual place which each creature occupies in the organism of the creation is defined by the Word of God by which it was created. That Word of God is, according to Psalms 19 and 119, to be identified with the law of God. Concerning that law of God for the creation, Hoeksema writes: "The law of God is not a mere code; it is the living will of God for the creature."[15] It defines the precise place in the whole organism of the creation which that creature occupies. It gives expression to that place which each creature occupies as it defines the relationships in which each creature lives to every other creature—how each creature is dependent upon the creation as a whole, and how it contributes to the creation as a whole. As such, that Word or law of God defines the precise way in which each creature, in relation to the cosmos, glorifies God and serves God's purpose. God saw all that He had made, and behold, it was very good; in other words, it was perfectly suited to accomplish the purpose for which God had created it.

The law of God for each creature is perfectly adapted to its nature; or, perhaps better, the nature of the creature is perfectly formed by God to fit in its own place in the unity of the whole. When the creature keeps that law, it lives and flourishes. When it breaks that law, whether it be tree, fish, bird, or man, it dies. It fails to serve God's purpose in its own unique place, and so cannot rightfully have a place in God's world any more. Take a fish out of the water, an environment to which its nature is adapted, and it dies. Pull a tree from the soil, and it dies. Lure man away from loving God, and he dies. He cannot fulfill his created purpose.[16]

Adam, as becomes especially evident in his naming of the

---

15. Hoeksema, *Reformed Dogmatics*, 212.
16. Ibid.

animals, was able to see the unique place in the creation which each creature occupied in relation to the whole. Adam could see that which we can no longer see: how each creature occupied its own place in the organism of the cosmos, and how that creature, in its very nature, served God's purpose of the glory of His name. In other words, Adam could see the Word of God in that creature and could give that creature a name which was an echo of God's speech. It was a name which fit because it was a name expressive of God's powerful and creative Word.[17]

Such is the organism of the creation.

Man As Organism

Man is, of course, a part of that organism of the creation. He was created of the earth earthy and is one creature among the great variety of creatures which God formed.

He is, however, also an individual organism within the creation.

He was a part of the organism of the creation itself. He was created by the Word of God which formed him from the dust of the earth and breathed into his nostrils the breath of life. He was created as a part of the organism of this earthly world so that he was related to all the creatures, dependent upon the creation for his existence, and capable of serving his purpose in the creation only as a part of the whole.

Yet he was created also as the highest of all creatures, for he was created in the image of God, in true knowledge, righteousness, and holiness. And, as image-bearer, he was also created as God's representative in the world to demonstrate in his life that this creation belonged to God, was created for God's glory, and had to be used in God's service. And so he was God's prophet, God's priest, and God's king.

---

17. Ibid., 63.

Thus, for him the law of God which defined his own place and purpose was to love the Lord his God with all his heart, mind, soul, and strength. When he loved God he fulfilled his purpose. When he failed to love God he was sentenced to death, for he had no rightful place in the creation any longer and had to be removed from it.

Thus man stood as an earthly creature in a relation to the whole creation; but he, as the highest of all God's creatures, also stood in a unique relation to God. As Hoeksema was wont to put it, the lines of the whole creation were united in the heart of Adam so that, through Adam, the whole creation could be a manifestation of and could be used for God's own glory. "In the heart of man lies the central point of the life of the creation . . . In man creation is centralized and finds its capstone. Man is not merely a microcosm, a miniature world, but he is prophet, priest and king. He makes God's will known to the creature, he devotes the creation to the Creator, he allows God's authority to be carried out in regard to the creature. And he carries out God's purpose and will concerning himself according to the free choice of his own will. In other words, man is friend and bond-servant of God."[18] "All creation serves man that man may serve God."[19]

Man, as he came from his Creator, was a part of the organism of the creation and was its head. As we shall presently see, man also remains organically a part of the creation and still retains his headship over the creation, but sin made many changes.

In the second place, within the organism of the creation was also to be found the organism of the human race. Adam was not only organic head of the creation which was put under his rule in God's name, but he was also organic head of the whole human race which came forth from him.

---

18. Danhof and Hoeksema, *Van Zonde en Genade*, 169.
19. Ibid., 170.

Hoeksema defines this relation of Adam to the whole human race as organic when he says, "[Adam] was the first father, the bearer of the entire human nature, so that organically the entire human race was in him." And again, "[Adam] is the father of us all. God created the whole human nature in him. In this sense Augustine was right when he taught that all men were in Adam: to be sure, there was in him not a multitude of individual persons, nor were there in him millions of individualizations of the human nature; but the truth is, nevertheless, that all human natures that ever would exist were organically in Adam, and they all developed out of him. God 'hath made of one blood all nations of men for to dwell on all the face of the earth' (Acts 17:26)."[20]

On the doctrine of Adam's organic relation to the whole human race rests the doctrine of Adam's legal relation to all his posterity.

The doctrine of Adam's legal relation to his posterity has been maintained in Presbyterian and Reformed circles since the seventeenth century and the development in that century of federal covenant theology. It is sad, to say the least, that this doctrine is so little known in our day. It is, in fact, often denied outright.[21] It is seldom preached from the pulpit, even in the churches which officially hold it. Yet, its importance is crucial. It is a mighty bulwark against all forms of Arminianism and Pelagianism, which are so emphatically individualistic in their theology. It is almost impossible to maintain a Reformed emphasis on sovereign grace without also holding firmly to the legal relationship in which Adam stood to all mankind.[22]

---

20. Hoeksema, *Reformed Dogmatics*, 223, 224.

21. See G. C. Berkouwer, *Sin* (Grand Rapids: Wm. B. Eerdmans Publishing Co., 1971). The Dutch book, *De Zonde*, was translated by Philip Holtrop. In this volume Berkouwer deals at length with the classical prooftext for original guilt, Romans 5:12–14 (pp. 453–465, 480–518) and attempts to disprove the doctrine by trying to show that this passage in Romans does not teach it.

22. As Romans 5:12–14 points out, Adam was the figure, in this respect, of

The doctrine is briefly this. Adam stood as legal representative of the entire human race which was to be born from
him. "[Adam] was not only the father of us all, so that the
whole human nature was created in him; but he stood also in
the unique position of being the legal head of the race in the
representative sense of the word."[23] What Adam did in his
calling with regard to the tree of the knowledge of good and
evil, he did as representing all men. Thus, when Adam ate of
the forbidden tree, he ate as the representative of the entire
human race.

Adam became guilty before God for the disobedience of
which he was the perpetrator. Guilt was legally imputed to
him. And the punishment for his guilt was death, a death
which included the spiritual death of total depravity.

Because the entire human race is legally represented in
Adam, the whole human race is guilty for the sin which Adam
committed. Every man born of Adam is guilty of disobedience to God for eating of the forbidden tree. Hence, the
punishment which was inflicted on Adam is inflicted upon
every man. Every man dies—spiritually as well as physically.
Total depravity is the just punishment of a righteous God
upon every man from the moment of conception, that is,
even before man himself performs one solitary act.[24] Thus the
organic relation of Adam to the entire human race is closely
connected to the legal and federal union between Adam and
all mankind.

The organism of the human race is itself composed of
smaller organisms within it. Just as the organism of a tree is
composed of the sub-organisms of a leaf, a root, a branch,

Christ. Adam was the legal head of the human race as a figure of Christ who is the
legal Head of the elect. "For as in Adam all die, even so in Christ shall all be made
alive" (I Cor. 15:22).

23. Hoeksema, *Reformed Dogmatics*, 224.

24. Ibid., 225. See also vol. 1 of Hoeksema, *The Triple Knowledge: An Exposition
of the Heidelberg Catechism* (Grand Rapids: Reformed Free Publishing Association,
1972), 147–50, 209, 210.

and a trunk, so is the organism of the human race composed of the sub-organisms of races, nations, clans, and families. And just as the organism of the human race is the basis for a federal relationship that exists between Adam and all men, so this same federal relationship exists within the sub-organisms.

Israel as a nation was guilty before God and responsible for the sin of Achan, even though most of the people in the nation knew nothing of what he had done. When Achan stole forbidden wealth from Jericho, Israel sinned (Josh. 7). Israel departed from God in serving the idols of the heathen, but Ezra and Daniel confess personal responsibility and guilt for the sin of the nation (Ezra 9; 10:1; Dan. 9). God visits the iniquity of the fathers upon the children unto the third and fourth generation of them that hate Him (Exod. 20:5).

So it is always. A government declares war, and whether or not a citizen agrees with his government, he suffers the consequences of that war. A drunken and fornicating father leaves the desolation of the consequences of his sin upon his wife and children.[25] Life is more than individual guilt; there is also corporate or federal responsibility. God deals with men, not only as individuals, but also as corporations, that is, as organisms within the organism of the human race with mutual responsibility.[26]

The way to escape the responsibility of the sin of others within the organism and corporate unity to which we belong is, as with all sin, the way of confession and repentance. We

---

25. Hoeksema, *Reformed Dogmatics*, 276–80. Hoeksema, in this section of his *Dogmatics*, develops this doctrine from Scripture and answers the many objections which have been brought against it.

26. The figure of a body is apt here. One may have cancer in the stomach, while the rest of the body is healthy. If the cancer is not removed, however, the entire body will soon be filled with the cancer and the whole man will be destroyed. So it is in the organisms within the organism of the human race. One man may preach heresy within a denomination. And, if that cancer of heresy is not removed but is allowed to remain in the body, the whole church will presently be affected to the extent that, in time, the whole church becomes apostate. The whole church is punished because all are corporately responsible for the heresy of one man.

are absolved from the sins of the nation when we condemn them and repudiate them, confessing them before God. We are absolved from responsibility for the sins of our fathers when we forsake those sins and turn to God in repentance and sorrow of heart. So true is this way of escape from corporate sin that the Heidelberg Catechism even says that we are to confess before God and express sorrow for our sinful natures against which we must struggle all our life long.[27] We are responsible for our sinful natures with which we are born because they are punishment for our guilt in Adam.

Our escape from such corporate guilt is possible only in Christ, of whom Adam was a figure. Christ is both the organic and federal Head of the elect. He so represents His people in His mighty work of suffering and dying on the cross that it is as if we ourselves are crucified, suffered the agony of hell, rose from the dead, and are now completely absolved from all the guilt of our sins.

If one denies the federal headship of Adam to the human race, one is compelled to deny the federal headship of Christ to His elect. This denial opens the door to Arminianism. If Christ did not die in the place of His people as their federal Head, He did not die in their place at all. If Christ did not die in the place of the elect, He did not obtain for them forgiveness of sins and life eternal. But if Christ did not acquire salvation for His people, then He died only so that God could make salvation available for all men; and thus salvation can be given only to those who through their own free will choose to believe in Christ.

Arminianism is an individualistic religion which has no sense of organic unity or corporate responsibility. In the work of salvation, because each man is a major contributor to his own salvation, the old adage holds: "Every man for himself, and the devil take the hindmost." God makes salvation possible to individuals who exercise their own free will. The

---

27. Q & A 56.

result is that a crowd, a conglomerate, a mass of individuals who accept Christ is saved, but not an organism, the organism of the body of Christ. This is a fatal flaw in Arminian and Pelagian thinking, as fatal as the error of free will.

The organic unity of Adam and the human race is a crucial biblical doctrine.

The Organism of Christ and His Church

Perhaps the closest definition of the term organic is found in Hoeksema's description of the organism of Christ and His elect church.

After pointing out that the church is not a crowd of people to which additions and subtractions can be made without spoiling the whole, nor a mere pile of stone and brick, but a harmonious and beautiful temple in which God dwells in Christ, he goes on to say,

> The church . . . is a living spiritual organism, of which Christ is the head, and all His people are members. This is expressed by the figures of the body, the vine and its branches, and the olive tree. The watch you carry in your pocket or on your wrist is also one whole. But it is a mechanism. It did not grow organically from a common principle. On the contrary, its parts were manufactured separately and afterwards assembled to constitute the watch. But an oak is an organism. The roots and trunk and branches and leaves were not mechanically put together, but developed from a common principle and grew from within. Thus also the church: it is a living organism, the body of Christ. Christ is first, and He is the head. In Him is all the life of the members of the whole body. From Him, through His Spirit, all the members receive their life and energy. He lives in them, and they live out of Him. His mind is their mind; His will is their will; His blessings are their blessings. His resurrection-life is their life. Apart from Him they are nothing and can do nothing. The church is that beautiful, harmonious, spiritual body of which Christ is the head and all the elect are members, that must serve

the purpose of revealing the glory of the life of the Triune God through Jesus Christ our Lord.[28]

That church in its entirety is an organism which was chosen in Christ from eternity. It is composed of the elect only. It is redeemed through the work of Christ, the Head of the church, who died for the sins of the elect and who earned everlasting blessedness for the saints. That organism is destined to live with God in covenant fellowship in glory for ever and ever.[29] The principle of the life of the organism of the church is the resurrection-life of Jesus Christ, which is His through His death and resurrection from the grave in Joseph's garden. That life is imparted to the elect through the work of the Holy Spirit, who dwells in the exalted and glorified Christ as the Head, and in all the elect as members of Christ.

The organic union is effected especially through faith. Faith is a bond that unites the elect to Christ, a kind of graft which puts dead branches into the living vine which is Christ, so that they live out of Him.[30]

Yet there are important additional truths to which we must give our attention.

The organism of the elect is a part of the organism of the human race. In order for it to become, in fact, the organism of the body of Christ, it must be extracted from the human race. That is, the elect must be delivered from the sin, guilt, and death which are their rightful due as a part of the generations of Adam, and be made members of the body of Christ. This is the work of salvation which God performs throughout history as He gathers His church from the human race.

---

28. Hoeksema, *Reformed Dogmatics*, 573, 574.

29. These ideas are so often emphasized in PR writings that one can almost turn to them at random and find this truth expressed in one form or another.

30. Hoeksema, *Reformed Dogmatics*, 479, 480. See also Hoeksema, *The Triple Knowledge*, vol. 1, 306–08.

But having said all this, I have not yet said enough. While God's people are in this present life, they are a part both of the organism of the human race and of the organism of the body of Christ. This is as God wills it. Hoeksema writes:

> [God] created that church from the beginning of the world organically, that is, within the organism of the human race, which, of course, included the reprobate element of humanity ... This reprobate shell in time lives under God's providence in natural organic relationship, as chaff with the grain, with the elect organism. Elect and reprobate are in a natural, organic sense of the word temporarily one. The reprobate shell serves the organism of the elect, of the church. The two are separated along the line of election and reprobation by an ever-continuing process, and in the end of the world the organism of the elect church will be finally and completely separated from the reprobate shell.[31]

The extraction or separation of the elect church from the reprobate world is an important part of the whole concept of organism. It is with good reason that the Scriptures use the figure of wheat and chaff to describe the organism of the human race divided by election and reprobation. For the wheat can be separated from the chaff only through threshing. While in Bible times that threshing took place either by oxen treading out the grain or by flailing the cut sheaves by hand, today the same process is carried out through threshing machines or combines. But however the work is done, the plant which is cut in the field has to be subjected to brutal treatment by the oxen, or the flailing, or the harvesters that are used today. The wheat kernel is so tightly bound up in the wheat plant that extraordinary means must be used to separate the two.

Scripture speaks repeatedly of the fact that the elect kernel can be separated from the reprobate chaff only by means of judgment. In predicting the captivity of Judah, Isaiah the

---

31. Hoeksema, *Reformed Dogmatics*, 574, 575.

prophet reminds Judah that captivity is necessary because "Zion shall be redeemed with judgment, and her converts with righteousness" (Isa. 1:27). Undoubtedly Peter has this same truth in mind when he says, "For the time is come that judgment must begin at the house of God: and if it first begin at us, what shall the end be of them that obey not the gospel of God? And if the righteous scarcely [that is, with great difficulty] be saved, where shall the ungodly and the sinner appear?" (I Pet. 4:17, 18)

Such judgments as God sent upon the nation of Israel and Judah were designed to separate the elect from the reprobate within the organism. Such is always the case in the history of the church. The Lord sends judgments upon the world because through these judgments the reprobate are destroyed and the people of God are saved. The reprobate shell perishes, but the organism of the human race is brought to glory.

Because an individual elect is an organism within the organism of the church, and because he himself is a sinner, though saved by grace, he too is delivered from the sin within him by judgment. Scripture sometimes calls these judgments "chastisements" (Heb. 12:5–13). They are manifestations of God's love and have as their purpose, correction. At other times Scripture calls these judgments trials, because the elect child of God is purified through them as gold is purified by fire (I Pet. 1:7). The organism of the elect must be saved through judgment.

Throughout his writings Hoeksema was careful to maintain a position which absolutely ruled out the notion that the salvation of the elect was an afterthought on God's part. The salvation of the elect was not a falling back on an alternate plan because God's original plan was spoiled by Adam's sin, an effort to rescue something worthwhile from the mess which Adam created by his disobedience. Hoeksema deals with this subject over and over again.[32] The gist of what he taught is found in this quotation:

> According to the infralapsarian presentation, God created a perfect and original organism in Adam. This original organism is marred and spoiled and corrupted by sin. And God restores this original organism in the church by recreation. Our chief objection against this mild Reformed conception is that according to it after all something falls really in the hands of Satan, and is lost. The devil after all gains a victory although God restores His marred creation and has the final victory. According to our conception [supralapsarian],[33] God from eternity purposed to create a church in Christ. That church was created in the loins of Adam organically, together with the reprobate shell of the human race. And in the line of election and reprobation God separates the pith from the shell and brings His elect church to glory. Nothing is lost. Sin and Satan must simply serve the purpose of realizing the church of Christ. And God maintains His counsel.[34]

The Organism of Christ and the Creation

I have not yet said all that PR writings contain on this important subject. Especially Hoeksema, as he developed these ideas, saw that they included much more than the salvation of the elect.

---

32. See, for example, Herman Hoeksema's syllabus, "Exegesis of Colossians," rev. ed. (Grandville, Mich.: Theological School of the Protestant Reformed Churches, 1997). See especially the first section, 1–9.

33. The question of supralapsarianism vs. infralapsarianism has to do with the order of the decrees of God's counsel. Generally speaking, while infras and supras alike agree that God's glory is the purpose and end of all God determines to do, infras believe that the decree of election and reprobation, and the salvation of the elect in Christ, follow the decree concerning the original creation and the fall. Supras believe that God determined before the creation and fall to glorify Himself through Christ and the salvation of the elect in Christ. Supras say the decrees of reprobation, creation, and the fall of man serve the purpose of the decree of salvation of the elect in Christ. The Reformed confessions are infralapsarian.

34. Hoeksema, *Reformed Dogmatics*, 575.

Adam was created in the beginning of time to serve as the prophet, priest, and king of God in this earthly creation. But God had also created a heavenly world over which Adam could not possibly serve as God's officebearer. That heavenly world was inhabited by angels, also rational, moral creatures among whom God also worked His eternal purpose of election and reprobation.

God's purpose in Christ is, indeed, to save His church which He has elected in Christ from before the foundation of the world. But it is far broader than that. The purpose of God is on a far grander scale.[35]

It was God's purpose from the very beginning that Christ should be the true Prophet of God, the true Priest in God's house, and the true King over all the creation. Thus Adam was only a figure of Christ who was to come, and could only dimly reflect the work of Christ as God's representative in creation.

To accomplish this purpose of God, Christ died for the whole creation which, because of Adam's sin, had come under the curse. God so loved the world that He gave His only begotten Son. That world is the entire cosmos which He formed in the beginning. That world is God's world. Satan makes his desperate attempt to wrest the creation from God, to usurp the throne of the universe and put himself upon it, and to drive God from His own creation. In this endeavor he enlists man. He does this because man is God's representative, apart from whom the devil can have no access to this creation. But God maintains His claims on His creation, and realizes His own purpose in redeeming it. This redemption, however, is accomplished through Christ, the One destined to be the glorious Head over all.

God established His covenant with the whole creation

---

35. For all that follows, see especially Hoeksema's "Exegesis of Colossians" (Col. 1:13–20), which contains a detailed description of these ideas.

through Noah at the time of the flood. The promise of salvation extends to all that God made (Gen. 9:10–19). The whole creation lives in expectation of the glory of the new heavens and the new earth (Rom. 8:19–22). And God's eternal Son, the Lord Jesus Christ, is He in whom all God's purpose is realized. For He is exalted as head over all for the sake of the church (Eph. 1:20–23; Col. 1:15–17).

But such exaltation of Christ is not only that Christ may be the second Adam, God's Prophet, Priest and King in this earthly creation. God's eternal purpose extends also to the heavenly creation, so that Christ is exalted above heaven and earth and all in them. Heaven and earth are made one. Elect angels and elect men are brought together in their proper relationships, where the angels serve the elect (Heb. 1:14). All is united in Christ as the exalted and glorified Lord.[36]

The organism of the creation is saved through Christ. The human race of God's election is saved through the power of Christ's mighty sacrifice. The elect angels are also reconciled to God through the cross. Heaven and earth now become one creation of God in which righteousness dwells and the everlasting kingdom of heaven is fully realized. All is by Christ and for Christ. And He, in all the blessedness of His glory, reveals God, so that God may be praised forever and ever, world without end.

This realization of God's glory through Christ was God's purpose from the beginning. Serving this purpose is creation, Adam as earthly head, the fall of Satan and his demons, the fall of our first parents, and all the history of the world. Everything serves that one great and glorious purpose of God. All is for God's glory.

---

36. Ibid., exegesis of Colossians 1:20, pp. 5–9, 19.

CHAPTER 13

The Organic Development of Sin

But parallel to [the positive line of election] runs the negative line. At the
same time and in the same manner as the work of God's elective love that
delivers, saves, and exalts to a fellowship of friendship, there is a separating,
banishing, rejecting, humiliating action of God's aversion, hate, wrath,
anger, and great displeasure in regard to the non-elect, along the line of
reprobation. This also takes place according to the immutability of God's
will . . . Emphasis must be laid upon the twofold operation of God's will:
from the will of God's eternal good pleasure proceeds the operation of
love, election, saving grace; but also the operation of hate, rejection,
wretchedness, banishment. Scripture speaks of life and death, of blessing
and curse, of light and darkness, struggle, victory, rest, salvation, and
the joy of the Lord, but also of increase in unrighteousness, hardening in
that which is evil, perishing, condemnation, suffering, punishment, and
everlasting fire. Living out of the principles of sin and grace, humanity is
divided into friendship and enmity toward God and toward one another.
The development of all things takes place along antithetical lines.
                    —Danhof and Hoeksema, *Van Zonde en Genade*

Introduction

In a rather surprising way the term "organic" was also applied
in PR literature and thought to the development of sin
throughout the history of the human race. This idea, as well
as that of the organic development of the covenant, appeared
early in the writings of PR men. Henry Danhof alluded to it

in 1919[1], but Danhof and Hoeksema dealt with this concept in detail in their book, *Van Zonde en Genade*.

As background to our discussion of the organic development of sin, we must remind ourselves of two things which were mentioned in the previous chapter: one is the organic unity of the human race; the second is the cleavage or division which God cut in the human race by the execution of His sovereign decree of predestination, including both election and reprobation.[2] God's covenant, which He establishes with His elect, develops organically therefore. But as God accomplishes His eternal purpose in reprobation, sin also develops until the cup of iniquity is filled and the world becomes ripe for judgment.[3] Hoeksema and Danhof write:

> But parallel to [the line of God's grace] runs the negative line. At the same time and in the same manner as the work of God's elective love that delivers, saves, and exalts to a fellowship of friendship, there is a separating, banishing, rejecting, humiliating action of God's aversion, hate, wrath, anger, and great displeasure in regard to the non-elect, along the line of reprobation.[4]

The line of reprobation is the line of the organic development of sin.

---

1. Danhof gave an address June 4, 1919, at a general ministers' conference in Grand Rapids. The text of it was published in a 42-page booklet, "De Idee van het Gendadeverbond" (The Idea of the Covenant of Grace) (Grand Rapids: Van Noord Publishing Company, 1920).

2. These ideas are expressly stated in Danof and Hoeksema, *Van Zonde en Genade*: "All the individual creatures collectively form one organic whole" (p. 169). The creation and the human race which is made out of one blood are also an organism because "in the heart of man lies the central point of the life of the creation" (p. 169). The spiritual separation between elect and reprobate takes place while mankind maintains its "natural relationship and organic fellowship" (pp. 195, 196).

3. Much of the following material may be found in *Van Zonde en Genade*. A section of this book pertinent to our discussion was translated by Cornelius Hanko and appears in the article "Concerning Sin and Grace" in the *Protestant Reformed Theological Journal* 31, no. 2 (April 1998): 27–42.

4. Ibid., 31.

The Idea of Organic Development of Sin

The application of the term "organic" to the development of sin may seem somewhat strange. Indeed, it is a somewhat different application of the term than one would expect.[5] Surely in the development of sin in the line of totally depraved sinners one can hardly speak of a unifying principle of "life." But in applying the term "organic" to sin's development, both Danhof and Hoeksema meant to demonstrate that the development of sin was a part of the development of the human race; and the human race, being itself an organism as it develops throughout history, develops sin in mutual cooperation, organic and federal unity, and even in the unity of their one purpose, namely to oppose God.

The following elements are a part of this development of sin.

Adam's sin is a root sin.[6] This means that Adam's sin was essentially disobedience, refusal to obey God, and direct and willful disobedience of God's command. Every sin which has ever been committed by man, which is now being committed, and which will be committed in the future is a sin which is also essentially disobedience and which grows out of Adam's one sin.

Nevertheless, Adam could not commit every single manifestation of the one sin of disobedience which Adam's children commit. He did not have the time for that, even though he lived 930 years, nor did he have the means to commit every possible sin. That one sin of disobedience could

---

5. David Engelsma calls attention to the fact that others have observed how the term "organic" is put to different uses. See Engelsma's "An Introduction to Henry Danhof's 'The Idea of the Covenant of Grace,'" *Protestant Reformed Theological Journal* 29, no. 2 (April 1996): 57, footnote 9.

6. Danhof and Hoeksema, *Van Zonde en Genade*, 112.

be and ultimately would be expressed in millions of ways in millions of different kinds of sin.

The human race itself develops. It develops socially, economically, politically, culturally. All this development is, however, in connection with the carrying out of the cultural mandate. God gave His command to Adam as king to subdue the earth. After the fall, man continued to perform that original cultural mandate. But he did so totally in the service of sin rather than in the service of God. The result is that sin develops as the cultural mandate is carried out and man subdues the earth. He invents many wonderful inventions and puts more and more of the marvelous powers of the creation to use so that they can be subordinate to his purposes and serve his goals. And so sin manifests itself in more and more ways. All is used to demonstrate fully and completely man's disobedience of God's commands.[7] Adam could not sin with television; modern twenty-first century man can and does. Cain could not sin with an automobile; today's generation can. Nimrod could not sin with an atom bomb; America does.

God wills that throughout history all the powers which He has put within the creation are uncovered by man and subjected to man's nefarious and God-dishonoring purpose. When the creation is completely subdued, then man will have sinned as much as it is possible to sin and will have expressed the root sin of disobedience in every possible way. Such a complete manifestation of sin takes place when the "man of sin" sets himself in the temple of God to oppose all that is called God and to make himself God (II Thess. 2).

This one root sin develops in such a way, therefore, that each generation builds upon the generation that precedes it, both by making use of past inventions and perfecting them, but also by finding different ways in which to use them to

---

7. A lengthy discussion of the development of sin as defined in Romans 1:18ff. is found in Ibid., 281ff.

sin. And as new inventions are added to the list, they are incorporated into the life of the human race and become part and parcel of the cultural life of mankind.

Through it all, God's purpose is accomplished. It is in the way of this organic development of sin, although under the sovereign control and direction of God's providence, that man becomes ripe for judgment. He shows in all his life that he will do nothing but sin—even when God gives him such great gifts as are to be found in the creation. The greater the gifts, the more man sins and the more terrible do his sins become. And thus man becomes worthy of his final punishment in hell.

Hence, in this sense, there is "organic" development of sin because it takes place along with and is inseparable from the organic development of the world of reprobate men.

The Organic Development of the Human Race and the Antithesis

Because within the one organism of the human race is the elect church (a new organism in Christ) and the world of reprobation, antithesis is created between the two kinds of people in the world and between the things they do.

I have discussed the antithesis earlier in this book, but I must return to the idea here. It forms an integral part of the doctrines developed in *Van Zonde en Genade* and influenced further thinking on the antithesis in subsequent PR writings.

I think it best to let the book *Van Zonde en Genade* speak for itself on this matter before us, and so I quote at length.

Danhof and Hoeksema speak of an antithetical organic development of sin, which means that:

Also here we should by all means follow the organic line, according to which the sinner develops in the wrong direction, while the regenerated child of God, through grace in Christ Jesus, walks in principle in the right direction. Possibly the two are not too far apart as far as their mere outward manifestation of life is concerned. But in the principle of the internal light of the heart they form a contrast, the contrast of light and darkness, of heaven and hell. And in the measure that you study more deeply and learn to know them, you will find that the world disappoints and the believing church surprises.[8]

The charge of Anabaptism, or world-flight, was laid at the feet of those who denied common grace. But Danhof and Hoeksema argued that the charge was nonsense simply because of the organic unity of the human race. The elect cannot flee the world even if they want to, for they are a part of it, organically bound to it, and required to live their life in it. But antithesis is something else. And that antithesis is possible because of this basic natural organic unity of all men.[9] The spiritual separation [of the antithesis] between elect and reprobate takes place while mankind maintains its "natural relationship and organic fellowship."[10] From a natural point of view they belong to one organism, that of the human race. As long as the church is on earth, that one organism of the human race continues. But from a spiritual point of view, the elect belong to a new organism, the organism of the body of Christ. Hence there is antithesis.

> But since all creatures in their organic fellowship, according to the counsel of God's providence, can experience from moment to moment God's sustaining and cooperating and governing power, whereby they can develop according to the idea, measure and place in the entirety of the organism and the eternal destination of each creature, a conflict is carried on in the very bosom of the creation, because of life out of two mutually exclusive principles. But these principles are of a spiritual, ethical nature, so that natural fellowship as such is not disrupted, but each party makes use of all that belongs to life in this present

8. Ibid., 163, 164.
9. For reference, see footnote 5 in this chapter.
10. Danhof and Hoeksema, *Van Zonde en Genade*, 195.

dispensation, in order to crowd out the life that proceeds from the opposite principle, and to cause its own principle to triumph. Therefore, although the regenerate and the unregenerate experience the same influence of divine powers in mutual, natural organic fellowship, and that according to each one's inclination and need, according to the demand of their natural and original destiny; and although their life here on earth is amazingly interwoven in all sorts of ways, Adam's children still, because of their different spiritual relationship to God, separate in principle always and everywhere, and form a contrast along the entire line of human activity, which keeps pace with the natural, organic development of the race and cosmic life, according to the nature of each dispensation and in harmony with the various circumstances of time and place, of life-sphere and relationship. The wedge of God's grace separates them.[11]

The antithesis between the people of God and the wicked is an antithesis which comes to expression in all of life. Both elect and reprobate live in this world and receive through providence the very same things. All these things which they receive under the providence of God are good gifts, for every good and perfect gift comes from God, who is the Father of lights, and in whom is no variableness or shadow of turning (James 1:17).

Because of the natural relationships in which all live, the wicked and the righteous have everything in common— except grace. The reprobate belong to the old organism of the fallen human race; the elect belong to the new organism of Christ's body. The old organism develops in sin; the new organism develops in righteousness and truth. The old human race fills the cup of iniquity; the new (and real) human race becomes the complete elect church. The old organism becomes ripe for judgment, the judgment of hell; the new organism, when complete, is taken to heaven.

---

11. Ibid., 195, 196.

While they are together in this world, the new organism of the church must be forcibly torn out of the organism of mankind of which it is, according to birth, a part. As that process takes place by the sovereign power of God, both live out of their own spiritual-ethical principle: the reprobate live out of the one principle of the root sin of disobedience; the elect live out of the new principle of the life of Christ, and they manifest themselves in God's world as those who live, in relation to all things, out of regeneration by grace.

Two things must yet be mentioned. One is that the reprobate organism always, even in history, serves the elect organism—as I already pointed out. The second is that Christ is not only the Head of the church, but of all things in heaven and on earth which are redeemed in Him. And that new organism of the elect and redeemed creation of heaven and earth (along with the elect angels) is brought into the tabernacle of God's everlasting covenant of grace in the new heavens and the new earth.[12]

12. Although somewhat incidental to our purposes, it is not superfluous to mention that this organic conception of all things is an absolute and decisive refutation of all forms of post-millennialism. According to this view, the history of this world gradually develops towards a glorious future in which the kingdom of Christ is realized in this present creation and, in some form or another, embraces the entire human race.

PART 4:
The Doctrine of the Covenant

CHAPTER 14

$\mathcal{T}$he Schism of 1953: Background in the Netherlands

It is our specific calling to preserve and to develop the truth that the God of the covenant establishes His covenant along the line of particular grace.
This we must emphasize.

We must not expect to become great in number. For therein does not lie our strength. But rather must we insist on the maintenance of the truth which God has entrusted to our care.

— Herman Hoeksema, *The Protestant Reformed Churches: 25th Anniversary 1925–1950*

Introduction

The controversy over conditional salvation was, without doubt, the most difficult and traumatic event in the seventy-five-year history of the Protestant Reformed Churches. The controversy itself created unrest, turmoil, and confusion in the churches. It made enemies of former friends. It divided families. It tore apart congregations. It resulted in a split in which over half of the total membership departed from the denomination. It left wounds from which the churches have, now some forty-seven years later, only just recovered.

When the toll is reckoned according to human reckoning, one can only conclude that the whole sad history was simply not worth the price that had to be paid. And many, especially those who did not live through it, will wonder whether blame should fall to human personalities, petty jealousies, and wicked bickerings more than the defense of principles and doctrines. Or, if principles and doctrines were involved, whether these are worth the great cost that had to be paid.

But these evaluations are made from a very human perspective, and one which ought not to be used in judging the history of the church of Christ. When weighed in the light of the church's calling and task, assigned to her from God, only one answer can be given: it was a battle that had to be fought. No price was too high to pay, no suffering too great to endure, no pain too severe to be borne. The alternative was unthinkable.

The doctrinal issues which were debated in homes and churches involved the most basic reasons for the existence of the Protestant Reformed Churches as a separate denomination. If the churches had refused to condemn the errors that were being publicly circulated, and if these errors had eventually received the official sanction of the ecclesiastical assemblies, the result would have been a complete repudiation of the origin of the churches in the controversies over common grace in the years preceding and including 1924. That is, if the churches had approved of the conditional theology which was being defended by various ministers within the PR denomination, honesty would have required that the denomination officially apologize to the Christian Reformed Church for establishing a separate denomination, and consistency would have demanded that all the people return to the mother church from which they had come out.

Although the issues took a slightly different form, they were basically the same as in 1924. The issues in the common grace controversy included a general desire on the part of God to save all men, and a general grace of God which enabled men to make their own choice with respect to the overtures of the gospel. The question in the controversy in 1953 over conditions in the covenant was the question of a general and conditional promise of God to all who are baptized, which condition had to be fulfilled by man before he could claim the promises for his own.

Both of these disputes included fundamental questions of the sovereignty of God in the work of salvation. In a general way, the truth of God's own glory through salvation by grace alone had to be defended against heresies which hand over the responsibility of salvation to man, even if it be in part only. Paul writes to the Ephesians that the reason why salvation is by grace through faith is that if it were of works, man would have reason to boast (2:8, 9). And such boasting must never be. God must have all the glory. The battle was for the glory of God. Any battle which is in defense of that truth is worth it—no matter what the price. But, in distinction from 1924, the controversy in 1953 involved a doctrine that had been especially a part of the heritage of the Reformed faith as developed in the PRC. This was the doctrine of the covenant.

The controversy in 1953 was unique. That is, it was uniquely PR and could not possibly have been fought anywhere else but in the PRC. It had a distinct PR flavor; it was an "in-house" matter; it dealt with the question of what it means to be Protestant Reformed. That made it the important debate that it was. And that fact brought up the one great question: Do the PRC have, before God and men, the right of a separate existence?

The story, the issues involved, the intricacies of the controversy, make the history a long one. I shall divide it into various chapters, this one dealing with the background in the Netherlands. The problem did not appear suddenly, as a thunderclap from a cloudless sky. It did not take everyone by surprise by coming without warning. It was the climax of a history that began in the Netherlands and was brought to this country by Dutch theologians, particularly the eminent Dutch theologian Klaas Schilder.

To the Netherlands we turn to begin the story.

In chapter 1 of the first section of this book I pointed out the deep differences in doctrine between the people of the Separation of 1834 and the people of the *Doleantie* of 1886. When these two reformatory movements came together in 1892 the differences did not disappear. They were, in fact, so severe that a special synod was called in 1905 to deal with them. This was the synod of Utrecht, which adopted the *Conclusies van Utrecht* (The Conclusions of Utrecht), which proved to be an unsuccessful effort to resolve the differences.

Although these differences were over various points of doctrine, the ones which concern us here are the differences over common grace and the covenant.[1] Generally speaking, the differences over common grace were the differences between *algemeene genade* (general grace, taught by many of the Separation of 1834) and *gemeene gratie* (common grace, taught by the followers of Dr. A. Kuyper).

The differences concerning the covenant were basic. The Kuyperians taught the following concerning the covenant: (1) it is unilateral, that is, one-sided in its establishment and in its maintenance; (2) it is unconditional; (3) only the elect are

---

1. For much of the following material I am dependent on Herman Hoeksema's unpublished notes on the church controversy in the Netherlands. See also the following articles by Hoeksema: "Loochening der Gemeene Gratie in Nederland" (Denial of Common Grace in the Netherlands) *SB* 12 (June 1, 1936): 391–95; "Bespreking der 'Algemeene Genade' in Nederland" (Decisions on 'Common Grace' in the Netherlands) *SB* 12 (September 1, 1936): 484–87 and 12 (September 15, 1936): 508–11; "De Kwestie 'Leergeschillen' op de Synode der Gereformeerde Kerken in de Nederland" (The Question of Differences in Doctrine in the Reformed Churches in the Netherlands) *SB* 13 (October 15, 1936): 35–9 and (November 1, 1936): 52–6; "Een Nuchtere Blik" (A Sober Glance), *SB* 13 (December 1, 1936): 100, 101; "Stemmen over de Synode in Nederland" (Opinions about the Synod in the Netherlands), *SB* 13 (December 15, 1936): 128, 129; "Professoren op de Synode" (Professors at Synod), *SB* 13 (January 15, 1937): 173, 174; and "Kastanjes Uit 't Vuur Gehaald?" (Chestnuts Pulled from the Fire?) *SB* 13 (March 15, 1937): 268, 269. Further articles included a discussion of a problem involving Dr. Valentine Hepp and what was thought to be an incorrect view of the relation between the divine and human natures in our Lord Jesus Christ. In all these articles Hoeksema comments at length on the problems in the Netherlands.

in the covenant; (4) baptism signifies that the elect children of the covenant are incorporated into it from infancy, as a general rule.

The people who traced their ecclesiastical origins to the Separation of 1834 taught: (1) a bilateral covenant, that is, one which took on the form of an agreement between two parties; (2) a conditional covenant in which man had to fulfill conditions in order to enter the covenant; (3) all who are baptized are included in the covenant in an objective sense; (4) baptism signifies that the promise of God is signified and sealed objectively to every baptized child.

Dr. Klaas Schilder took up his work in this unsettled situation.

The Teachings of
Dr. Klaas Schilder

Dr. Klaas Schilder was ordained a minister in the GKN and, after earning a doctorate, was installed as professor of theology in the seminary in Kampen, the Netherlands.[2] Although, generally speaking, Schilder followed the line of the people of the Separation of 1834 in his thinking, he was original in some respects and made contributions to the controversy which stamped the covenant views of the churches he founded with a "Schilderian" imprint.

For one thing, Schilder expressed a deep misgiving concerning any form of subjectivism, especially in regards to the question of assurance. While he considered the question of assurance an important one, he also thought the doctrine of assurance as promoted by the Kuyperians highly suspect. It was suspect because it was based on a vague and uncertain subjective testimony of the Holy Spirit. It could, in connection with Kuyper's other doctrines, lead to an assurance

---

2. For details of Schilder's life, see J. Faber, "Klaas Schilder's Life and Work" in *Always Obedient: Essays on the Teachings of Dr. Klaas Schilder*, ed. J. Geertsema (Phillipsburg, N.J.: P & R Publishing, 1995), 1–17.

based on a false subjective testimony which, in fact, was no voice of the Spirit at all. Schilder wanted something definite and specific, something objective—an objective Word of God to which one could cling.[3] He found an objective basis for assurance in the promise of God made, signified, and sealed at the time of baptism.

This promise of God is, therefore, for every child baptized. The child has that promise as an objective Word of God to which he can cling. Every baptized child possesses that promise as the ground of his assurance, so basing assurance on an objective Word of God.[4]

If, however, the promise of God comes to every child who is baptized, the question quite naturally arises how the promise of God can in fact come to all when not all are saved. Schilder found the answer to that question in his bilateral and conditional covenant. Although all the children of believers do indeed have the promise objectively, they do not receive the promise subjectively until they have fulfilled the condition of faith, which makes them heirs of the covenant and promise fully and completely.

Schilder insisted that only by stressing both the promise

---

3. Strauss writes, "How the two parts of the covenant function in the lives of the people of the covenant can be explained by what Schilder wrote about baptism. For baptism seals, in a sacramental way, the *promise* of the gospel." This promise is said to be given to every child baptized. S. A. Strauss, "Schilder on the Covenant" in *Always Obedient* (Ibid.), p. 28 of essay pp. 19–33. See also Andrew Petter, "The Covenant (Part IV)—Wrong Approaches," *Concordia* 4, no. 21 (December 25, 1947): 3. Petter argues, in describing Schilder's position (a position which Petter himself adopted) that if the covenant is for the elect alone, one must know he is elect before he can have assurance. But now the promise is for everyone baptized, so that everyone may know that it is for *him*, and thus have personal assurance. See also Leonard Verduin, *Honor Your Mother: Christian Reformed Roots in the 1834 Separation* (Grand Rapids: CRC Publications, 1988). Schilder, Verduin says, wanted no subjectivism, but an objective promise to all (p. 32).

4. Herman Hoeksema, "The Liberated Churches in the Netherlands," *SB* 22 (December 1, 1945): 100–02. In a lengthy series of articles, Hoeksema discussed the events in the Netherlands which resulted in the Liberated Churches. He criticized the views of Dr. Schilder and his followers and offered his own conception of the covenant of grace.

of God and the demand of faith was it possible to maintain man's responsibility.[5] Because the realization of the covenant subjectively is dependent upon the fulfillment of certain conditions, the warnings and threats of the covenant, as well as the promises, are real, and man's responsibility is adequately maintained.[6]

Schilder was also concerned to emphasize the importance of history over against the counsel of God.[7] For this reason he rejected the eternal decrees of God as a dogmatician's starting point. In effect this means that the eternal decree of election has nothing to do with the establishment and realization of the covenant of grace. It was wrong to say, as followers of Kuyper did, that the elect of God are the same as those included in the covenant.[8] Election belongs to the hidden things, and in the sphere of the covenant election plays no role.[9]

Schilder, according to Strauss, insisted that the covenant of grace is very much like the covenant of works in that both are an agreement between God and man, both are bilateral, and both are conditioned on faith. Strauss writes:

---

5. Strauss, "Schilder on the Covenant," 21.

6. Ibid.

7. Ibid.

8. See also Jelle Faber, "American Secession Theologians on Covenant and Baptism," essay in *American Secession Theologians on Covenant and Baptism & Extra-Scriptural Binding—A New Danger* (Neerlandia, Alberta, Canada: Inheritance Publications, 1996), p. 29 of essay pp. 15–54.

9. It is interesting that in connection with the relation of election to the covenant, Schilder repudiated the idea of Christ as the Head of the covenant. He was prepared to admit that Christ was Mediator *in* the covenant, but to hold to the teaching that Christ was the Head *of* the covenant was to bring election into the covenant after all, for the people of God are elect in Christ their Head. Jelle Faber, in his essay on seven theologians who came out of the Secession tradition and immigrated to North America (Ibid.), agrees with six of them who taught that the covenant of grace has no representative Covenant-head: "It is certainly good to abandon the concept of Christ as Head of the covenant of grace . . . It excludes any identification of covenant and eternal election or any confusion of God's covenant and His eternal counsel of peace," 37. See also Andrew Petter, "The Covenant (XV)—Solving the Problem," *Concordia* 5, no. 12 (August 19, 1948): 1, 3.

How the two parts of the covenant function in the lives of the people of the covenant can be explained with what Schilder wrote about baptism. For baptism seals, in a sacramental way, the *promise* of the gospel. But this promise, in fact, *demands* from us that we, in faith, appropriate for ourselves what is promised, and so make it our own. Due to this state of affairs, Schilder did not hesitate to speak about faith as a condition in the covenant ... What Schilder had in mind with his "Reformed doctrine of conditions" is that God has decreed that salvation can never be realized without faith. One's baptism, therefore, does not imply a dogmatic proclamation, for instance, that God confers salvation on the elect. But in my baptism I receive a concrete address from God, a message that God proclaims to everyone who is baptized personally: "if you believe, you will be saved."[10]

Schilder attempted to avoid the charge of Arminianism in his view of conditions. Strauss writes: "Of course, this does not mean *condition* in the Arminian sense of the word, as if man could earn something through his obedience, but *condition* in the Reformed sense. Faith, he writes, is indeed a gift of the God of the covenant, but it is, at the same time, also a condition set by Him."[11]

One more aspect of Schilder's doctrine of the covenant requires our attention. In many ways it is a crucial aspect, for it, perhaps as much as the whole concept of conditions, opened the way for the charge of Arminianism. This is the doctrine of a general covenantal grace.

William Heyns, professor at Calvin Seminary in the days when Herman Hoeksema was studying there, had adopted a view of the covenant which can be considered in some respects to be the mother of the Liberated view. Heyns found great importance in the promise, because the promise of God is really what the covenant is all about. And, proceeding from

---

10. Strauss, "Schilder on the Covenant," 28, 29.
11. Ibid.

that premise, he made the covenant all but identical with the promise.[12]

Heyns attempted to be Reformed. He spoke of the covenant as being one-sided, but explained this as meaning that God establishes His covenant with every baptized child so that each child is in the covenant and can become a covenant-breaker.[13] He spoke of the covenant as unbreakable, but only in the sense that it *may* not be broken; not in the sense that it *can* not be broken. He spoke of the covenant as unconditional, but meant by this that every child of believers is unconditionally in the covenant.[14]

But, on the other hand, the covenant is two-sided because its full blessedness depends on our accepting God's promise.[15] It is breakable because God's covenant is established with every child, so that there can be covenant breakers who reject the promise of God.[16] And so the covenant is conditional because keeping the covenant is essential for gaining its reward.[17] "Whether therefore that which is given to us will or will not really become ours depends upon our accepting or not accepting it."[18]

In keeping with his general approach to the doctrine of the covenant and his strong tendency to bring Arminianism

---

12. This idea whether the covenant of grace could be defined in terms of the promise became a crucial point in the debate in the PRC over conditions in the late 1940s and early 1950s.

13. Heyns, *Manual Of Reformed Doctrine*, 128.

14. Ibid., 131.

15. Ibid., 134.

16. Ibid., 128.

17. Ibid., 131.

18. Ibid., 134. It is significant that Heyns defended this position in connection with his vigorous and unwavering defense of the well-meant offer of the gospel. He specifically connects the two in his *Manual of Reformed Doctrine*, and indeed they are really the same. In the offer God expresses His desire to save all who hear the gospel. In baptism, a sign and seal added to the gospel, God expresses His desire and promise to save every child baptized. The general promise given in baptism is only the offer applied to the covenant.

into it, Heyns also refused to connect the covenant with eternal justification, for, Heyns claimed, to connect the covenant with eternal justification is to bring in the doctrine of election as the controlling principle.[19]

The result of all this is that, according to Heyns, there is an objective and a subjective covenant; the former, God gives to all baptized children in the same sense as the offer of the gospel; the second is realized only when the condition of faith is fulfilled. If one refuses and rejects the covenant given him in baptism, he becomes a covenant breaker.

But to all this Heyns added his doctrine of general covenantal grace. This grace was given to all the children baptized and was a prevenient grace which changed "the subjective spiritual condition of covenant children."[20] It was common grace applied to the covenant, and it was a grace which enabled each child to accept or reject the promise that was his through baptism. Faber also alludes to this view of Heyns and speaks of it as "a grace which does not insure salvation and yet takes from the covenant members all excuse." It is a "measure of life" to be found in all baptized children, whether elect or reprobate.[21] It is a grace which results in a modification of man's depravity so that "man's total incapacity by nature for the things that are of the Spirit of God is taken away," and so that "there is in the covenant child an initial or incipient capacity of covenantal nurture."[22]

I pointed out earlier that the starting point for the Schilderian view of the covenant was the question of the ground of assurance. Heyns also addressed himself to the question of assurance. We have, said Heyns, an objective assurance of being in the covenant by virtue of our baptism. This is what Schilder also fought for. He was not satisfied

---

19. Ibid., 141.
20. Ibid., 136, 137.
21. Faber, "American Secession Theologians," 40.
22. Ibid., 41.

with the inner testimony of the Spirit and considered it to
be a subjectivism which was incapable of true assurance.
But the objective promise, given in baptism, was solid and
sure.[23]

However, in 1947 Schilder did repudiate the whole idea of
a subjective covenantal grace, probably after his discussions
with Hoeksema. Faber thinks this may very well have been
the reason, and that the rejection of a general covenantal
grace was a concession to Hoeksema in the interests of
reaching agreement with the PRC.[24] While Faber rejects the
more radical notions of Heyns, Faber regrets that Schilder
made this concession to Hoeksema and considers the
rejection of a general covenantal grace to be the one mistake
of Schilder's theology.[25]

Dr. Schilder came to this country in early 1939 to make
the first face-to-face contact with the PRC. It was not as if the
PRC were unaware of Dr. Schilder prior to this. The editor
of the *Standard Bearer* had kept people informed of developments in the Netherlands and the controversy that was going
on over such questions as common grace, the covenant of
grace, and baptism. As early as 1935 Hoeksema had called
attention to some articles in *De Reformatie* (The Reformation)
in which Schilder had observed that some American
Reformed theologians had called Hoeksema un-Reformed.
Hoeksema accused Schilder of backbiting and slander in an
article entitled "Attentie, Prof. Dr. K. Schilder!" (Attention,
Prof. Dr. K. Schilder!)[26]

But, although the relationship got off to a rocky start,
things soon improved. As can easily be imagined, Hoeksema
was particularly interested in the common grace issue and

---

23. Heyns, *Manual of Reformed Doctrine*, 138, 144.
24. Faber, "American Secession Theologians," 47, 48.
25. Ibid.
26. Herman Hoeksema, "Attentie, Prof. Dr. K. Schilder!" *SB* 11 (September 1,
1935): 484, 485.

Schilder's position on this thorny subject.[27] He was pleased when it became apparent that Schilder repudiated common grace in the sense in which it had been taught in the CRC.[28]

It was with obvious eagerness, therefore, that Hoeksema anticipated Schilder's proposed visit to this country. Although Schilder's purpose in coming was not, in the first place, to visit Hoeksema and the PRC, this did in fact become the main event of the trip when the CRC closed its doors to Schilder, on the grounds that he was under suspicion in the GKN, with which denomination the CRC had sister-church relations.[29]

A notice soon appeared in the *Standard Bearer* that Dr. Schilder was scheduled to give a lecture in First Protestant Reformed Church on the subject of common grace,[30] and

---

27. Herman Hoeksema, *"Dr. Schilder's Standpunt Inzake de Gemeene Gratie"* (Dr. Schilder's Position on Common Grace) *SB* 12 (March 1, 1936): 246–48, in which Hoeksema informs his readers that Dr. Schilder had expressed some reservations and doubts about common grace. See also: *"Schilder over de Algemeene Genade"* (Schilder on Common Grace) 12 (April 1, 1936): 293–95 and 12 (April 15, 1936): 317–19; "Een Vergissing?" (An Error?) 12 (May 15, 1936): 364, 365; "Misverstand" (Misunderstanding), 12 (June 15, 1936): 412; "Dr. Schilder en Dr. A. Kuyper Sr.," 12 (June 15, 1936): 412, 413; "Loochening der Gemeene Gratie in Nederland" (Denial of Common Grace in the Netherlands) 12 (June 1, 1936): 391–95; and "Bespreking der 'Algemeene Genade' in Nederland" (Declarations on "Common Grace" in the Netherlands), 12 (September 1, 1936): 484–87 and 12 (September 15, 1936): 508–11. Many more articles were written, because Hoeksema considered the controversy in the Netherlands to be of such great importance that the people in the PRC, especially, should know about it and about the issues involved.

28. Herman Hoeksema, "Dr. Schilder over de Gemeene Gratie" (Dr. Schilder on Common Grace), *SB* 14 (November 1, 1937): 59–62. Hoeksema called attention to the fact that Schilder did not want a common grace, but did want a common mandate which men are still obligated to fulfill.

29. Herman Hoeksema, "Dr. Schilder Geboycot?" (Dr. Schilder Boycotted?) *SB*, 15 (November 15, 1938): 76–9. Hoeksema expressed his eagerness to meet Dr. Schilder, especially when Rev. H. J. Kuiper, editor of the *Banner*, the official paper of the CRC, expressed his opinion in an editorial that Dr. Schilder ought not to be welcome in the CRC.

30. The notice said, "Dr. K. Schilder gaat DV Woensdagavond, February 8, spreken over de 'Algemeene Genade' in Eerste Protestantsche Gereformeerde Kerk te Grand Rapids" (Dr. K. Schilder will speak, the Lord willing, February 8 on 'Common Grace' in the First Protestant Reformed Church in Grand Rapids). It is

this lecture was subsequently given. A report was given in the *Standard Bearer* that the lecture was delivered to a packed auditorium (which seated between 1,200 and 1,300 people) in which all available standing room was taken and over 100 were forced to listen over loudspeakers in the basement.[31]

The gist of Schilder's speech, according to the report, was that Schilder believed that although God loves all His work, even that which remains of His work in man, there is no common grace to the reprobate ungodly. One may speak of an offer, but only in the sense of a promise and demand presented to man's consciousness pedagogically; however, this "offer" did not indicate a gracious disposition to all who hear the gospel.[32]

One interesting result of Schilder's visit was a conference held on March 29, 1939, between various ministers from the PRC and CRC at which Hoeksema delivered a paper with the provocative title "Hereeniging der Christelijke Gereformeerde en Protestantsche Gereformeerde Kerken: Is ze Geeischt, Mogelijk, en Wenschelijk?" (Reunion of the Christian Reformed and Protestant Reformed Churches: Is It Demanded, Possible, and Desirable?). The conference was suggested and pressed by Dr. Schilder in the mistaken notion that there were men in the CRC who would look with favor on such a reunion. The conference was a disaster, which even Schilder admitted.[33]

---

not entirely clear who sponsored this speech. In the *Standard Bearer* of November 15, 1938, it is said that the Men's Society of First Protestant Reformed Church was sponsoring a lecture (vol. 15, p. 76). Another announcement says that the lecture was sponsored by the Publication Committee of the *Standard Bearer* (vol. 15, January 15, 1939, p. 171).

31. Herman Hoeksema, "Dr. Schilder's Lecture on Common Grace," *SB* 15 (March 1, 1939): 244–46.

32. Ibid., 244, 245.

33. Articles about this in the *Standard Bearer* by Herman Hoeksema included: "Wat Op de Conferentie Voorviel" (What Happened at the Conference), 15 (May 1, 1939): 353–57 and 15 (May 15, 1939): 375–81; "Over Conferenties en Perspolemiek" (Concerning Conferences and Polemics), 15 (June 1, 1939): 396;

Schilder returned to his own country, and World War II broke out. During the war Schilder was briefly imprisoned by the Nazis for his opposition to them,[34] and, after he was released, was forced to go into hiding to escape further imprisonment and the slow death of a concentration camp. It was during his hiding that the GKN actually deposed him and others who agreed with him.[35] This led to the formation of the Liberated Churches (LC).

Schilder visited this country once more in 1947. The *Standard Bearer* assured him of a welcome because, as the editor explained, it is the policy of the PRC to give a hearing to those who desire it. At the same time, in an important dissent from Schilder's views, the editor of the *Standard Bearer* asked the CRC to open their facilities to Schilder on the ground that "they are much closer to the Liberated Churches than we are."[36]

In spite of serious differences in covenant views, the trip of Schilder served to bring the PRC and the LC more closely together. This is evident from a report of a conference between Schilder and PR ministers. On the one hand, the report was critical of Liberated covenant theology: "We shall also criticize the views of the liberated churches. For

---

and "No Biased Presentation," 15 (June 1, 1939): 397–99. Hoeksema's paper that he read at the conference was first published as a pamphlet in Dutch, then translated into English by Rev. H. Veldman and published as a booklet in 1939 by the Reformed Free Publishing Association in Grand Rapids.

34. Schilder was one of very few ministers who dared publicly to oppose Nazi political philosophy.

35. Herman Hoeksema, "Aangaande Dr. Schilder" (Concerning Dr. Schilder), *SB* 21 (February 15, 1945): 222; "Schilder . . . and Others," *SB* 21 (March 1, 1945): 241; "The Separation in the Netherlands," *SB* 21 (August 1, 1945): 454. The injustice of Schilder's deposition may have drawn Hoeksema and Schilder together in spite of their differences. Schilder had been unjustly deposed by the synod in violation of the principles of Reformed church government; and Schilder's case had been treated and the decisions executed even though Schilder was in hiding and could not come to synod's meetings to defend himself.

36. Herman Hoeksema, "The Coming of Dr. Schilder," *SB* 23 (May 1, 1947): 343.

although we may now say with all emphasis that their view is not entirely Heynsian, especially as far as the late professor's views on the so-called subjective baptism-grace is concerned, and although Professor Schilder constantly stated that our differences are only a matter of terminology, we nevertheless are convinced that there are elements in their covenant views, clearly expressed in their written and published treatises, and now corroborated by the spoken elucidations of Professor Schilder which we whole-heartedly reject."[37]

Still, in spite of these obvious differences, the article goes on to say, "We agree with Prof. Schilder, and also with our editor of the *Standard Bearer* who has stressed this conviction, that we ought to become sister churches, we ought to have ecclesiastical correspondence. Strictly speaking, there is no Reformed Covenant view. That is, there is not one Covenant view, be it Kuyperian, Heynsian, Schilderian or Hoeksemanian which is *confessedly* Reformed. There is for that reason room for friendly debate and exchange of ideas."[38]

Such sister-church relations were not to be. Schilder sowed seeds in the churches which were later to reap a whirlwind, and the differences in the covenant theology of the two churches became more marked.

It was really the adoption of the "Declaration of Principles" by the synod of the PRC in 1951 which brought about the complete estrangement between the PRC and the Liberated. Schilder strongly opposed the "Declaration" because it affirmed that an unconditional and unilateral

---

37. Gerrit Vos, "The Schilder Conference," *SB* 24 (December 1, 1947): 101. Hoeksema had suffered a debilitating stroke and could be at the conference for only short periods of time. He nevertheless presented to the conference a series of propositions concerning the covenant which were considered by the men present. See Herman Hoeksema, "Our Conference with Dr. Schilder," *SB* 24 (December 1, 1947): 101–03.

38. Vos, "The Schilder Conference," 101. By "confessedly" Rev. Vos meant "confessionally."

covenant was the teaching of the confessions, and because the Declaration was made binding in the denomination.[39]

Schilder died in March of 1952, and all contact between the two churches came to an end. But the stage was set for controversy in the PRC.

---

39. Herman Hoeksema, "The Stocking Is Finished," *SB* 28 (January 1, 1952): 148–53. See Appendix H for the full text of this article. See also Herman Hoeksema, "Correction Please," *SB* 28 (January 15, 1952): 180–82. Schilder had written an editorial in the November 17, 1951, issue of *De Reformatie*, the paper of the Liberated Churches, entitled "De Kous Is Af" (The Stocking Is Finished) in which he criticized severely the adoption of the "Declaration of Principles" and informed his readers that contact with the PRC was no longer possible. See also Klaas Schilder, "Extra-Scriptural Binding—A New Danger" (collection of articles originally written 1950–1951 by Schilder in *De Reformatie*. These articles were translated by T. van Laar in *"American Secession Theologians on Covenant and Baptism"* & *"Extra-Scriptural Binding—A New Danger"* (Neerlandia, Alberta, Canada: Inheritance Publications, 1996), 55–167. One can certainly find conflict here between prior statements of the PRC that no particular covenant view was binding in the churches, and the "Declaration of Principles," which did make a particular view binding by appealing to the confessions. I shall examine this question more fully in the next chapter.

CHAPTER 15

The Schism of 1953: Preliminary History

Through the refiner's fire of the controversy over conditions our doctrinal position was brought into sharper focus, and our faith with respect to our Protestant Reformed heritage was confirmed.
    —Homer Hoeksema, *God's Covenant Faithfulness*

Storms on the Horizon

Although the contacts with Dr. Schilder and the LC precipitated the troubles which led to the schism of 1953, there were rumblings of discontent in the PRC, which were harbingers of the storm that was to come.

Already as early as 1948 some dissatisfaction with the role which Rev. Hoeksema played in the churches was evident in unhappiness with the proposed appointment of his son Homer to the seminary.[1] Such dissatisfaction was an expression of a general attitude which prevailed among some towards the leadership role which Rev. Hoeksema had played.

In the first volume of *Concordia*, the editor, Rev. Gerrit Vos, expressed some concern about the fact that the churches were not as spiritually strong as in the early years of their history. This was evident, he wrote, from the poor attendance at the pre-synodical prayer service and the graduation

---

1. *Acts of Synod*, 1948, Arts. 76, pp. 82–85.

exercises of the Theological School.[2] To this editorial
Rev. Andrew Petter, later the most articulate defender of
conditional theology, responded that not only could many
positive features be pointed out in the life of the churches,
but that a warning was in order: "We must not make the
mistake of trying to go back to 1924. That has passed. I am
deeply convinced that if our future depends upon inspiring
in our children the spirit of 1924 or of getting them to see
that history with all its incidents as the pioneers did, then the
cause, our cause, is hopeless."[3]

The growing tension came again to the surface when, in an
editorial appearing in the autumn of 1948, Rev. Hoeksema
criticized the introduction of new catechism materials into
the catechism classes without synodical approval. He did
this under the title "A Tendency towards Individualism."[4]
Rev. Andrew Cammenga, the author of the new catechism
material, responded in an article in which he advised the
churches not to lean so much on Hoeksema.[5]

Some of the growing tension in the churches and the
dissatisfaction with Hoeksema's leadership was due to
an unhappiness with the smallness of the denomination.
Those who wanted to grow saw the immigration from the
Netherlands of many who belonged to the Schilder churches
to be an opportunity to bring these immigrants into the
PRC. The price that had to be paid for this was a certain
compromise of the covenant view held within the PRC, a

---

2. Gerrit Vos, "Impressions," *Concordia* 1, no. 9 (June 24, 1944): 2. In fact,
the appearance of this paper, written and published in the western part of the
denomination, was evidence of some unhappiness with the *Standard Bearer*.

3. Andrew Petter, "The Spirit of '24 and of Today," *Concordia* 1, no. 10 (July 7,
1944): 2.

4. Herman Hoeksema, "A Tendency towards Individualism," *SB* 25 (October
15, 1948): 28–30.

5. Andrew Cammenga, "A Reply to Rev. H. Hoeksema," *Concordia* 5, no. 19
(November 25, 1948): 3: "We must not always lean on one and the same staff,
either look in just one direction." Hoeksema briefly responded to this in "Once
More: A Tendency toward Individualism," *SB* 25 (December 1, 1948): 100–03.

covenant view of which Herman Hoeksema was the author and chief defender.[6]

After the split took place, Rev. Hoeksema, looking back, found other factors which contributed to explain the split. He mentioned, for example, the fact that those who left the churches in 1953 had, for the most part, also shown opposition to the establishment of PR schools. He pointed out that many were opposed to "doctrinal" preaching and wanted sermons of a more practical kind. And, in close connection with this objection to the preaching, Hoeksema said that many wanted to emphasize the Bible rather than the confessions. Still more, Hoeksema claimed that many wanted emphasis on the activity of faith, the demands of faith, man's responsibility, and the necessity of conditions for the fulfillment of salvation.

It was clear that trouble was in the offing.

Early Differences
with the Liberated

The discussion between the PRC and the LC had begun a few years prior to Schilder's coming in 1948. Soon after World War II, when communication and exchange of church periodicals between the PRC and the LC once again became possible, the trans-oceanic conversation began. In the October 4, 1945, issue of *Concordia*, a letter from K. Schilder appeared in which he asked for space in that paper to explain what had happened in the Reformed churches in the Netherlands.[7] Gerrit Vos, the editor of *Concordia* at that time, took the opportunity to inform the churches that "It has become crystal clear to me that the Protestant Reformed Churches can have no real interest in the struggle as far as

---

6. Gertrude Hoeksema, "Covenant Faithfulness in Troublous Times," in *God's Covenant Faithfulness*, 35, 36.
7. Klaas Schilder, "Contributed," *Concordia* 2, no. 15 (October 4, 1945): 3, 4.

the heart of the controversy is concerned." The PRC agreed with neither group in the Netherlands. He pointed out, in the same editorial, that the "Kuyper-Hepp group" held to presupposed regeneration, and that the "Schilder-Greydanus group" held to Heyns' view of the covenant and baptism. Vos demonstrated clearly that the latter wanted a general promise in which all *have* salvation, and he pleaded with the brethren in the Netherlands to go along with Hoeksema's view.[8]

About the same time, the editor of the *Standard Bearer* was, somewhat more cautiously, coming to the same conclusion. Hoeksema quoted the editor of the *Banner* to the effect that the LC held to an external grace of the covenant which comes to all children baptized. H. J. Kuiper, the editor, had given Hoeksema the gratuitous advice that Hoeksema could not possibly agree with that position. Hoeksema responded by saying that it was indeed quite likely that he would not agree with the Liberated position on the covenant, but he was sure that Kuiper had misrepresented the Liberated. Nevertheless, Hoeksema charged the LC with holding to the same view as W. Heyns.[9]

This question of whether or not the LC truly held to the Heynsian view became a matter of no little debate.[10] In a series of articles, Hoeksema made these points: (1) that both the GKN (the churches which had deposed Schilder) and the LC wanted a promise to all;[11] (2) that the Liberated view of a general, conditional promise was Heynsian and that the GKN

---

8. Gerrit Vos, "In the Chaos," *Concordia* 2, no. 15 (October 4, 1945): 2, 3.

9. Herman Hoeksema, "The Liberated Churches in the Netherlands," *SB* 22 (October 1, 1945): 6.

10. The Heynsian view, as I noted in the last chapter, was that the covenant was conditional and bilateral, that the promise of the covenant came to all the children who were baptized, that along with that promise came a grace which enabled them to choose for or against the promise, and that the covenant was fully given only to those who fulfilled the conditions of faith and obedience.

11. The GKN because they presupposed that all children baptized were regenerated.

were correct in repudiating that idea; (3) that the LC ought
to tell the church world whether or not they also accepted
Heyns' view of sufficient grace to all the baptized; and
(4) that the Liberated view was a serious departure from the
truth of Scripture.[12]

Very carefully Hoeksema defined his own position over
against that of the LC. He made the following points:

1. The idea of the covenant is neither that of a pact
or agreement, nor that of the promise, nor that of a way
of salvation; but it is the eternal and living fellowship of
friendship between God and His people in Christ, according
to which He is their Sovereign-friend, and they are His
friend-servants.

2. Hoeksema pointed out that by "friendship" he meant
a bond of most intimate fellowship, based on the highest
possible likeness of nature and expressed in personal
distinction.

3. The deepest ground of this covenant relation is the life
of the triune God Himself, of which the covenant of grace is
the highest revelation.

4. That covenant is established with Christ, as Servant of
Jehovah, and with the elect in and through Christ.

5. Historically this covenant is realized in the line of the
continued generations of believers. These generations receive
the sign of the covenant, circumcision in the old, baptism
in the new dispensation, and, in general, are addressed and
treated as the real covenant people of God.

6. Yet, God's election and reprobation cut right through
these generations, and "God is merciful to whom He will be
merciful, and whom He will He hardens."

7. This covenant of God is eternal, and will be realized

---

12. Hoeksema articles in vol. 22 of the *Standard Bearer*: "The Liberated Churches
in the Netherlands," (October 1, 1945): 6; (December 15, 1945): 126–28; (January
1, 1946): 148–50; (January 15, 1946): 175–78; (February 1, 1946): 198, 199;
(March 1, 1946): 245–46; and (March 15, 1946): 268–70.

in its heavenly perfection in the new creation, when the tabernacle of God will be with men.[13]

The Visit of Dr. Schilder

Early in 1947 the thoughts of Dr. Schilder turned more and more towards a visit to America. The PRC officially opened its pulpits and churches to Dr. Schilder at the synod of June 1947. This was done at the advice of the Committee for Correspondence with Foreign Churches.[14] Dr. Schilder made his plans to come in the autumn of 1947 and did not change those plans even though, in the early summer of 1947, Rev. Hoeksema suffered a severe stroke.

The hearty welcome of Dr. Schilder did not mean that all were in agreement with his views on the covenant. In a welcoming editorial, Hoeksema assured Schilder of the love of the PRC for him, but also reminded the readers that Schilder was aware of the fact that "we do not agree with their covenant conception."[15] As if to underscore the point, Hoeksema also, as we have already noted, urged the CRC to open its pulpits to Dr. Schilder on the grounds that the LC were doctrinally closer to the CRC.[16]

During the visit, however, the differences between Dr.

---

13. Ibid., (March 15, 1946): 269.

14. This committee was later to become The Committee for Contact with Other Churches. It is interesting that the committee, composed of Revs. H. Hoeksema, G. M. Ophoff, and J. De Jong, made its recommendation to synod without any grounds. The recommendation itself read: "To advise our consistories to grant Prof. K. Schilder the right to preach the Word of God in our churches during his contemplated visit to our country." Synod itself added a ground, which read: "The Liberated Churches of the Netherlands have the same official standards we have." The recommendation with the added ground was adopted. See, *Acts of Synod, 1947*, Art. 75, p. 54. The ground was a strange one because all the Reformed churches, including the CRC and the GKN, had the same confessional basis as the PRC.

15. Hoeksema, "The Coming of Dr. Schilder," 343. Hoeksema had recovered sufficiently from his stroke to participate in a limited way in the activities surrounding Schilder's visit.

16. Ibid.

Schilder and Rev. Hoeksema over the truth of the covenant were more sharply defined, and it became evident that these differences were substantial.

At a conference held in Sutton, Nebraska, under the sponsorship of the Reformed Church in the United States (RCUS), Schilder spoke plainly of his views.[17] Two conferences were also held in Grand Rapids, and both Dr. Schilder and Rev. Hoeksema were able to present their views.

At the first conference Rev. Hoeksema presented his views in a set of propositions. In addition to the ideas I have spelled out on pages 281–282, Hoeksema rejected the notion of a covenant of works with Adam in Paradise; emphatically asserted that the covenant, both in its establishment and maintenance, is unconditional because of the perfect work of Christ and of the Holy Spirit; and insisted that the covenant is established and maintained only with the elect, who are not a party in the covenant, but who, as the fruit of God's work, stand in the world as the party of the living God.[18]

Dr. Schilder, on the other hand, attempted to minimize the differences in his speech at the conference in Grand Rapids. He spoke of the fact that neither the LC nor the PRC had an official covenant view. When it was said in the course of the conference that, in a certain sense, the administration of the covenant was wider than the elect, Schilder latched on to the idea and spoke of a promise administered to all who were baptized.[19] He repudiated any "idea" of an eternal covenant

---

17. An official conference was scheduled for September 9–11, 1947, at Sutton, but was called off because it appeared as if not many ministers of the PRC were able to attend. An unofficial conference was then held, apparently sponsored by the RCUS, at which Schilder spoke. Ministers from the PRC who were in the area also attended. See Gerrit Vos, "Conferences," *SB* 24 (October 1, 1947): 4.

18. Herman Hoeksema, "Our Conference with Dr. Schilder," 102. See also George Lubbers, "Seven Propositions Submitted by Rev. Hoeksema," *Concordia* 4, no. 17 (October 30, 1947): 3.

19. Schilder was not always clear on what he meant. But apparently at the

and wanted to speak of a covenant only in time.[20] The covenant was maintained in time in the way of promise and demand. The only aspect of the covenant which was of significance was the promise to all baptized children and the demand of obedience, which was temporal. Election and the covenant of grace might never be identified.[21]

Hoeksema answered these assertions of Schilder by making a few additional points by which he meant to confirm what he had said earlier. He stated that the elect children of the covenant are usually regenerated from infancy.[22] He insisted that the phrase "sanctified in Christ," in the first question of the Baptism Form, was meant subjectively and was the only way Scripture used the expression.[23] And he defended the

---

conference reference was made to the fact that all the children of believers were brought up in the sphere of the covenant and received, at least outwardly, all the privileges of such an upbringing, including the sacrament of baptism and Christian nurture in the church, home, and school. Schilder took hold of this and referred to it as a promise of God administered to all.

20. Again Schilder was not clear. It seems, from subsequent discussion, that Schilder did not want any definition of the term "covenant." He apparently expressed his disagreement with the fact that Hoeksema had rejected the *idea* of a covenant as an agreement or pact and had insisted that the covenant was a bond of friendship which expressed the covenant life of God within Himself. Schilder wanted the covenant to be nothing more than the promise which, at baptism, was made to all, and which was accompanied, in time only, with a demand to be obedient. In fact, later in the controversy, Hoeksema wrote extensively against the notion that the covenant was to be identified with the promise.

21. George Lubbers, "Schilder's Reply," *Concordia* 4, no. 17 (October 30, 1947): 3.

22. Schilder could not accept this position, partly because he did not want to speak of election in connection with the covenant, and partly because the covenant was not realized in the hearts of baptized children until they fulfilled the conditions of the covenant, something obviously impossible in a child.

23. The whole question which is asked of parents when they present their child for baptism reads: "Whether you acknowledge, that although our children are conceived and born in sin, and therefore are subject to all miseries, yea, to condemnation itself; yet that they are sanctified in Christ, and therefore, as members of his Church ought to be baptized?" The Liberated could not, of course, accept the interpretation of the expression "sanctified in Christ" as referring to actual sanctification, for that would mean that the elect children are saved already at the time of baptism. The Liberated, therefore, interpret that expression to mean "outward sanctification"; in other words, at the time of baptism all the children baptized are set apart from the world outwardly by virtue of the fact that they

proposition that no distinction could be made between the work of the various persons in the Holy Trinity, but that the triune God was, through our Lord Jesus Christ, the Author of the covenant established through Christ with the elect.[24]

Rev. Vos wrote concerning the conferences held during Schilder's visit, as I pointed out in an earlier reference to a report on one of them (p. 275) that "there are elements in their covenant views . . . which we whole-heartedly reject."[25] He went on to say that ". . . it is also our conviction that even though it were only a matter of difference in terminology, we are of the opinion that their terminology is not correct, not according to Scripture and . . . the form of baptism." But then Vos added that rather strange caveat: "Strictly speaking, there is no Reformed Covenant view . . . There is for that reason room for friendly debate and exchange of ideas."[26]

Schilder's visit had a profound and lasting effect upon the churches. Schilder had had opportunity to visit with almost all the ministers of the PRC, and in these visits he had opportunity to expound his views of the covenant and to discuss with the leaders in the churches the differences between his and Hoeksema's views.

It soon became clear that many in the churches were enamored with Schilder's views and were prepared to defend them over against what had been taught in the PRC. Very shortly after Schilder left these shores, articles began to appear in *Concordia* which questioned certain aspects of

---

are given a place in the church, a Christian home, and the company of believers. Whether they would be inwardly sanctified depends upon their fulfillment of the conditions of the covenant.

24. Again, the reference here might be somewhat obscure, but it is a reference to the relation between the covenant of grace and the so-called *Pactum Salutis*. Hoeksema goes into this whole question in detail in his *Reformed Dogmatics*, 285–336.

25. Gerrit Vos, "The Schilder Conference," 101.

26. Ibid.

Hoeksema's teachings and which began at least a tentative defense of Schilder's position.[27]

What Is Binding in the Churches?

In the years before the split, one question began to dominate: the question of whether or not the views of the covenant taught in the PRC up to the visit of Schilder were actually binding upon the churches. And that question was to contribute directly to the split which occurred in 1953.

Although the issue had been discussed prior to the synod of 1948 in connection with the possibility of sister-church relations between the PRC and LC, the problem came to a head at the synod. The story is rather intriguing.

The Committee for Correspondence with Foreign Churches sent a letter to the Committee for Foreign Correspondence of the LC asking these churches for sister-church relations on the surprising ground that the differences between the PRC and the Liberated were not confessional.[28] The letter was signed by Revs. De Jong, Hoeksema, and Ophoff. This action was duly reported to the synod of 1948. That synod, while not officially condemning the letter, refused to approve it, and sent instead another letter asking merely for steps to be taken towards the establishment of closer relations.[29] The synod

---

27. Andrew Petter, "The Covenant (I)—Introduction," *Concordia* 4, no. 18 (November 13, 1947): 1, 3. This began a long series in *Concordia* on this subject, and Petter was soon joined by others who voiced similar opinions. By the beginning of 1949 Petter was defending a bilateral and conditional covenant in *Concordia*. See "The Covenant (XXXV)—Dr. Schilder," 6, no. 2 (March 3, 1949): 3; "The Covenant (XXXVII)—Dr. Schilder," 6, no. 3 (March 31, 1949): 1; and following issues.

28. *Acts of Synod, 1948*, pp. 38, 39: "Dogmatische verschillen die er mogelijk tusschen U en ons gestaan zijn geen confessioneele verschillen" ("The theological differences which possibly exist between you and us are not confessional differences").

29. *Acts of Synod, 1948*, Art. 51, pp. 53, 54. Later Hoeksema explained how all

apparently had reservations about the question whether the differences were confessional or not, but so did many in the Netherlands. The concern in the Netherlands was intensified by the fact that thousands of immigrants, after World War II, entered the United States and Canada. The question which these immigrants faced was this: To what church ought we to belong in North America? They were prepared to join the PRC and were advised by many leaders in the Netherlands to do this, provided they could maintain their own covenant view within the PRC. And so the question arose whether the covenant view of Hoeksema would be binding on the Liberated who wished to join the PRC.

The importance of this question cannot be overstated. The whole question of whether or not a unilateral and unconditional covenant was binding on the Liberated who intended to join the churches finally came down to the question of whether or not a unilateral and unconditional covenant was *confessional*. If such a view was taught in the confessions, it had to be binding. If it was not taught in the confessions, it could not be made binding, except by a special decision of the synod.

The answers to these questions had been, up to the summer of 1949, ambiguous. But then an event took place which forced a specific and direct answer. It was

---

this came about. He said that the letter was originally composed by Rev. John De Jong, an ardent Schilder follower, and sent to Hoeksema for approval and for his signature. At the time, he was recovering from his stroke in California. Although he was opposed to the letter, he agreed to sign it if Rev. Ophoff would do so. Rev. Ophoff refused, but finally consented under extreme pressure and the letter was sent. But, Hoeksema adds, two things happened: (1) The synod of the Liberated Churches agreed to seek sister-church relations and even open its pulpits to PRC ministers, although the vote was close and several recorded their negative votes; and (2) The members of the Committee for Foreign Correspondence of the Liberated Churches did not write until over a year after the letter from the PR synod was sent. This lapse of time seems to indicate a decided lack of enthusiasm for sister-church relations on the part of the LC. Herman Hoeksema, "The Stocking Is Finished," 148–53.

the unofficial visit of Revs. B. Kok and J. De Jong to the Netherlands in the summer of 1949.[30] These men met with the Committee for Foreign Correspondence of the Liberated Churches, and, though not speaking officially for the PRC, informed the LC that: (1) Hoeksema's doctrine of election was by no means binding in the churches nor held by the majority of people; (2) sympathy for the LC was widespread in the PRC; (3) there was ample room in the PRC for Liberated views of the covenant; (4) because such freedom existed in the PRC, the Liberated immigrants should be free to join these churches.[31]

On the basis of assurances from the Netherlands that some freedom existed in the PRC for Liberated covenant views, two churches of immigrants were organized in Canada, one in Hamilton, Ontario, and one in Chatham, Ontario. The first was organized on April 19, 1949, and the second nearly a year after that, on March 23, 1950. The apparent success of the work among the immigrants prompted the synod of 1949

---

30. For material on this visit see Gertrude Hoeksema, *A Watered Garden: A Brief History of the Protestant Reformed Churches in America* (Grand Rapids: Reformed Free Publishing Association, 1992), 148–52 and Herman Hoeksema, "The Stocking Is Finished," 152. Revs. Kok and De Jong did not go to the Netherlands as official representatives of the churches.

31. This information became public knowledge when Rev. Ophoff obtained a copy of a letter sent to a Canadian immigrant by Professor Holwerda, which letter mentioned these things (see Appendix E). The immigrant had asked Professor Holwerda whether he should join the PRC, and Professor Holwerda answered in the affirmative because of what Revs. Kok and De Jong had said. When the letter was published, a cry of dismay went up from the Schilder supporters, and many accusations were made against Rev. Ophoff for publishing the letter, and against the *Standard Bearer* for printing it. But the fact is that the contents of the letter were never denied. See George M. Ophoff, "Revs. De Jong and Kok in the Netherlands," *SB* 25 (August 1, 1949): 469–73 for the letter itself and Ophoff's comments; and see Gertrude Hoeksema, *A Watered Garden*, 149, 150 for excerpts from the letter. Rev. Ophoff later apologized for publishing the letter before Revs. De Jong and Kok returned from the Netherlands, which would have given the two ministers involved an opportunity to respond to it; but he insisted that the letter would have had to be published sooner or later. George M. Ophoff, "Open Confession to the Brethren Rev. Kok and Rev. De Jong," *SB* 25 (September 15, 1949): 522, 523.

to call a Dutch-speaking missionary to work primarily among the immigrants.[32]

But the question of what was binding in the churches remained. It became an official matter when one of the immigrants in Canada specifically addressed the question to the Mission Committee, and the Mission Committee in turn requested from synod a statement expressing what was binding in the churches, which could be used in mission work in Canada.[33] The Committee of Pre-advice[34] recommended such a document and added that a doctrinal statement that repudiated the idea of a general promise of God in baptism should be included.[35]

Out of this recommendation emerged the "Declaration of Principles," a document which was to cause sharp division within the churches and ultimately lead to a break between the PRC and the supporters of Schilder's covenant view within the PRC. See Appendix F for the text.

The Declaration of Principles

The Declaration of Principles was only provisionally adopted by the synod of 1950. It was referred back to the consistories for study and evaluation.[36] Although the vote was nearly unanimous on the synod of 1950, the document seemed to have caught the Schilder supporters off guard. During the interval between the synods of 1950 and 1951, the forces opposed to the Declaration had time and opportunity to marshal their forces and to inundate the synod of 1951 with objections and protests.

The decision which finally made the Declaration official in

---

32. *Acts of Synod, 1949*, Art. 65, p. 91.
33. *Acts of Synod, 1950*, Arts. 63–67, pp. 54, 55.
34. All the work of synod is divided among committees of pre-advice, which study the material assigned to them and come to the full synod with recommendations. Synod acts on these recommendations.
35. *Acts of Synod, 1950*, Arts. 63–67, pp. 54, 55.
36. Ibid., Arts. 116, 117, pp. 83–90.

the churches came only after prolonged debate, sometimes acrimonious discussion, and various recesses between sessions. It was obvious that the differences were geographical, with the western part of the churches generally voting against the Declaration, and the eastern part voting for it. The final motion to adopt passed by a vote of nine to seven.[37]

The contents of the Declaration laid out the distinctives of PR theology. The document first spelled out the errors of common grace as adopted by the synod of the CRC in 1924, and sets forth the biblical and confessional truths for which the PRC stood over against these errors. In an important second section the Declaration states in clearest language that the PRC hold to the great truths of sovereign election, particular redemption, the particularity and unconditionality of the promise of God in the covenant, and the God-given nature of the gift of faith as the instrument by which salvation is appropriated. Especially on the basis of this second part, the Declaration repudiates a general and conditional promise given at baptism and Kuyper's doctrine of presupposed regeneration. It affirms the particularity of the promise, but adds to that central truth the clear teachings of Scripture, that God fulfills His promise in such a way that He causes His people to do good works, that the wrath of God is upon all who do not repent of sin, and that the preaching comes to all with the command to repent and believe in Christ. All this is concluded with a statement that the PRC believe in the autonomy of the local congregations.

The Declaration is replete with quotations from the confessions, the liturgical Forms, and the Church Order.

---

37. *Acts of Synod, 1951*. The "Declaration" was adopted point by point and the decisions stretch from Art. 218, p. 186, taken at the session of September 26, to Art. 285, p. 196, taken at the concluding session on October 3.

The Binding Character
of the Declaration

There is good reason why so much emphasis is laid on the confessions, both major and minor.[38] The underlying problem which the churches were facing was the question of what is binding in the PRC. That question was not an abstract one, but a question which related directly to the dispute over the binding character of the covenant view held in the PRC. The LC would recommend that immigrants join the PRC only if the PRC had no binding covenant view, for this situation would enable the immigrants to maintain their covenant view while being a part of the PRC. If the PRC had a binding covenant view which differed from that of the Liberated, the immigrants from the LC would not join a PR church, for by joining they would necessarily be bound by the PR covenant view.

The sympathizers of Schilderian theology were well aware of this fact, and thus strove mightily to persuade the churches not to make any statements concerning the covenant, but to assume that nothing binding existed in the PRC. The Declaration defined what was binding.

But this is not the whole story. The Declaration is replete with references to and quotations from the confessions because the PRC did not want to make a "Fourth Confession," a charge laid at the feet of the PRC by the LC.

This is not to say that the PRC could not have drawn up a "Fourth Confession" if it had so desired. The church of Christ

---

38. The "major" confessions are the Heidelberg Catechism, the (Belgic, or Netherland) Confession of Faith, and the Canons of Dordtrecht (Dordt). The minor confessions include the Form for the Administration of Baptism, the Form for the Administration of the Lord's Supper, and the Church Order of Dordrecht. These latter have always been considered confessions because they too contain, especially in their didactic parts, statements which the church believes to be the truth of Scripture. They are minor because their chief purpose is to instruct in, and be used for, the sacraments and the government of the church. Their primary purpose is not to set forth a statement of doctrine.

is always permitted, and in some instances even obligated, to draw up an additional confession.[39] But, strictly speaking, such a confession would rightly have to be submitted to the entire Reformed church world before final adoption. And the PRC was not at this time interested in that procedure.[40] Nor did anyone ever give a thought to the notion that the time was ripe for the addition of another confession.

Furthermore, if the synod of 1950 had thought it propitious to draw up another confession to be added to the three confessions which form the confessional basis of the PRC, it would have gone through a far more elaborate and careful process which would have ensured long and thoughtful deliberation in the churches as a whole. But the synod understood that such a new confession was not necessary. The old confessions would surely do, if only they were understood and rightly applied to the present controversy. The old confessions, in other words, tried and true, would settle the issues that were troubling the churches. But it did need to be spelled out carefully what the confessions taught on the matters that were at issue. Synod set about doing this very thing.

That this was indeed the mind of the synod is evident from especially two considerations. In the first place, the Declaration was drawn up in response to a request from the Mission Committee to express what was binding in the PRC, especially with respect to the doctrine of the covenant.

---

39. The Canons of Dordt, for example, were drawn up as a further explanation of the Heidelberg Catechism and the Confession of Faith on certain doctrines which were attacked by the Arminians.

40. It would have been necessary for such a new confession to be submitted to the entire Reformed church world because the "Three Forms of Unity" that form the confessional basis of the PRC were confessions which belonged to the entire Reformed church world and were not the possession of the PRC only. Although few if any Reformed churches pay any attention to this principle, nevertheless, it would not have been right for the PRC to take something which they held in trust with other denominations, and unilaterally add to it.

After all, an immigrant who wondered whether to join the PRC had originated the question. The obvious answer to the question was: that which is binding in the PRC are the confessions. Nothing else may be considered binding.

But the more specific question then became: What do the confessions teach with regard to the doctrines of the covenant? That question the Declaration set about to answer.

In the second place, the very content of the Declaration demonstrates that it was intended to be nothing else but a statement concerning the teaching of the confessions. That content was composed, first of all, of elaborate and extensive quotations from the confessions, so much so that almost three-fourths of the document consists of such quotations. But, in the second place, Hoeksema had made some significant contributions to an understanding of the biblical doctrine of the covenant. To mention but three: he had pointed out the weakness of the traditional view of the *Pactum Salutis* and had proposed a reformulation of this doctrine much more in keeping with Scripture;[41] he had gone back to the trinitarian life of the triune God to find the source and prototype of the covenant of grace; and he had contributed greatly to the idea of the organic development of the covenant, by which he had explained why all the children born in covenant lines are to be baptized.[42]

But, although these ideas are implicit in some of the formulations of the confessions, they are not explicit, and it can hardly be said that they are directly taught in the confessions. Thus, they were not included in the Declaration. If they had been, it could rightly have been said that they were "extra-confessional."[43]

---

41. I have earlier referred to Hoeksema's treatment of the *Pactum Salutis* in his *Reformed Dogmatics*. I shall be discussing it again a bit later.

42. These ideas I shall also discuss in a later chapter.

43. I do not mean to imply by this statement that in the development of these

The End of Contact

Nevertheless, when the PRC finally adopted the Declaration at the synod of 1951, Schilder considered all relationships with the PRC to be over. He expressed his displeasure with the Declaration in a series of articles in *De Reformatie*, the voice of the LC. And he brought relations to an end with an editorial in the November 17, 1951, issue of that paper entitled "De Kous Is Af" (The Stocking Is Finished).[44] See Appendix G for a translation.

That was the end of any kind of official contact between the PRC and the LC. Peter De Boer, editor at this time of *Concordia*, summed up the history in an important and incisive editorial. De Boer expressed agreement with the Declaration and with Hoeksema's response to Schilder's editorial "De Kous Is Af," which editorial De Boer called Schilder's "farewell to our churches."

De Boer insisted that, because of the fundamental differences in the covenant conceptions of the PRC and the LC, it would have been impossible, in the long run, for the LC to find in the PRC a church home. Nevertheless, De Boer pointed out obvious mistakes that the PRC committed, which led the LC to the notion that it might be possible. Those

---

ideas Hoeksema engaged in illicit activity. The whole development of the truth from the time of Pentecost to the present consists of this sort of activity. The church takes the confessions of the fathers, makes them its own, and develops the truths of them as it continues to study the unsearchable riches of the truth as contained in Holy Writ. Nothing Hoeksema taught was contrary to the confessions. Indeed, all his teachings were confessional in germinal form, and were made explicit by further development.

44. Klaas Schilder, "Extra-Scriptural Binding—A New Danger," 55–167, a translation of Schilder's articles which comment on the "Declaration." For Schilder's article "De Kous Is Af" (The Stocking Is Finished) see Appendix G. For Hoeksema's comments on the editorial, see Appendix H. In this and in subsequent editorials, Hoeksema comments not only on Schilder's editorial, but also on events leading up to the "Declaration," including the letter from the Committee for Correspondence with Foreign Churches, which was rejected by synod (p. 152 of "The Stocking Is Finished") and the visit of Revs. De Jong and Kok to the Netherlands.

mistakes, according to De Boer, were three: 1) Our churches made a mistake when they opened their pulpits to Schilder at the synod of 1947. Lectures? Yes. Preaching? No![45] (2) There was a strong tendency in the PR churches to minimize the differences in the covenant views of the PRC and the LC. De Boer points to Rev. G. M. Ophoff as the only one who clearly saw the differences and understood their importance. (3) The letter of the Committee for Correspondence with Foreign Churches was wrong when it spoke of the differences between the two denominations as being "non-confessional." And, although the synod rightly rejected that letter (even though it had been sent) and substituted another letter, nevertheless the damage was done.[46]

One more comment on the Declaration ought to be made. Although the adoption of the Declaration was not an "extra-scriptural binding" or even an "extra-confessional binding" in the sense of its being some kind of Fourth Confession, the fact is that the Declaration remains a binding document in the churches. Its binding force is that of Article 31 of the Church Order, which states that all decisions of ecclesiastical assemblies are to be considered "settled and binding," unless they are proved to be in conflict with the Word of God or the Three Forms of Unity. This latter has never been done, either within the PRC or from those outside. In fact, it is striking that all the protests brought against the Declaration to the synods of 1951, 1952, and 1953 did not even attempt, for the

---

45. De Boer includes an interesting sidelight to this. He informs his readers that, in Schilder's own mind, he never "preached" in our churches, but only offered "an edifying word." De Boer says that Schilder told this to him (De Boer) and explained the reason for it as being his need to protect his own denomination. In explanation of the technical difference, I add that the Reformed churches have always made a distinction between the official preaching of the Word and an edifying word, as for example that brought by a seminary student who has not been ordained. This makes Schilder's preaching in the churches somewhat ironic. The churches thought he was "preaching"; Schilder considered himself to be offering "an edifying word." Peter De Boer, "It's All Your Fault!" *Concordia* 9, no. 1 (February 14, 1952): 2, 3.

46. Ibid.

most part, to give such proof. And Schilder's own objections against the Declaration did not include arguments that the teachings of the Declaration contradicted Scripture or the Reformed confessions.[47]

The Declaration was greatly needed in the churches, and, even though it precipitated the split which came in 1953, it erected a dam against the flood of Liberated covenant theology.

47. Klaas Schilder, "Extra-Scriptural Binding—A New Danger," 55–167.

CHAPTER 16

The History of the Split

I will never go along with a church that adopts the Heynsian view of
the covenant and of the promise of God . . . If this means a split in our
churches, as some already suggest and as it is rumored in the old country,
I would deplore it, of course. But for the sake of our beautiful Protestant
Reformed conception of the eternal covenant of God I cannot waver . . .
It is always better to be small and strong than to be big and corrupt.
                                    —Herman Hoeksema, *Standard Bearer*

Doctrinal Differences within the PRC

Schilder's covenant view had been seized upon by many
within the PRC, and this view was being openly defended
in *Concordia*. The result was a prolonged debate within the
churches. The issues were discussed in almost every home
in the denomination; they were the topics of many sermons;
and the pages of *Concordia* and the *Standard Bearer* were filled
with the debate. But probably the Declaration, more than
any other writing, crystallized the issues and precipitated the
split.

By surveying the protests that were brought to the synod
of 1951, we can form a good idea of the doctrinal objections
raised against the covenant view which had, until the Schilder
visit, been maintained in the PRC.

Several protests, reminding one of the charge of the synod

of the CRC against Rev. Hoeksema in 1924, said that the Declaration was "one-sided" in its presentation of the truth;[1] that is, the Declaration did not, in the opinion of some, deal adequately with man's responsibility to believe. It overlooked the admonitory character of Scripture, and it failed to deal properly with conversion and sanctification.[2]

Some, in their protests against the Declaration, were concerned that such a narrow definition of doctrine as the Declaration contained would be a barrier to attracting others to the churches. This was a common theme and reflected Schilder's criticism of what he called "extra-biblical binding."[3]

But the deeper doctrinal differences were brought out when these same protests argued for a "Reformed" view of conditions, and protested the condemnation of conditional theology in the Declaration. It was repeatedly asserted that faith is a condition to salvation; and some protests attempted to prove that both Hoeksema and Ophoff had themselves defended a conditional theology in earlier years.[4]

That the opponents of the Declaration were not speaking of conditions in any kind of "Reformed" way became evident from the protests themselves, when they defended a general promise, made to all who were baptized.[5] This general promise, it was said, was realized only in those who fulfilled the condition of faith. This was directly from the mouth of Schilder and his supporters, was a serious departure from the truth of the covenant, and put the whole doctrine of the covenant completely in the context of Arminian theology.

Schilder had refused to apply the doctrine of election to the covenant, because election was contrary to a general

---

1. *Acts of Synod, 1951*, Art. 120, p. 122.
2. Ibid., Art. 120, p. 127.
3. Ibid., Art. 124, p. 151, for example.
4. Ibid., Art. 120, pp.124, 130, 133, 135.
5. Ibid., Art. 124, pp.137, 159.

promise.[6] Some protests reflected that same suspicion of election. One protest, irrelevantly, claimed that election should not be applied to the covenant because the church does not know who the elect are, except insofar as they manifest themselves as believers. And another protest objected to what was perceived as a supralapsarian emphasis in the Declaration, which emphasis was wrong because it made the doctrine of the covenant proceed from election rather than from experience.[7]

These protests against the Declaration made it unmistakably clear that the differences in the churches were important, profound, and unbridgeable.

All these differences were discussed at great length in the church papers, and I can best sum them up by referring to an editorial by Rev. Hoeksema in which, in response to Schilder's editorial "De Kous Is Af," Hoeksema defined the differences between his position and that of Schilder.

The PRC teach that the covenant is a bond of friendship and fellowship; the LC teach that the essence of the covenant is promise and demand. The PRC insist that the covenant is for the elect only; the LC maintain that it is for all born in the covenant line. The PRC teach that the covenant is unconditional; the LC teach that it is conditioned on faith— although, to escape the charge of Arminianism, they insist that God fulfills all the conditions. The PRC speak of "parts" in the covenant, following the language of the Baptism Form;[8] the LC want parties in the covenant, which is in keeping with their view of the covenant as an agreement.[9] The views of Schilder were expressed in the objections which

---

6. A general promise is a promise made to every child baptized, whether elect or reprobate.

7. *Acts of Synod, 1951*, Art. 120, p. 129.

8. The "Baptism Form" reads: "Whereas in all covenants, there are contained two parts . . ."

9. Hoeksema, "The Stocking Is Finished," 150.

PR ministers brought against the Declaration, and by this defense of Schilder's position the battle lines were drawn.

Other Occasions for the Split

Several events were closely connected to the adoption of the Declaration.

The first was the departure of the Hamilton, Ontario, congregation from the PRC. The Declaration, although not yet finally adopted, became the occasion for the unjust deposition of Rev. Herman Veldman by the consistory on the grounds that he refused to refrain from preaching and teaching the PR doctrine of the covenant as outlined in the Declaration; that is, that he refused to preach and teach the doctrine of a conditional and general promise within the covenant as his Liberated members wanted. By this action, later condemned by Classis East of the PRC, the immigrants in Canada clearly showed that they were thoroughly Schilderian in their views.[10]

The other event was the preaching of Rev. Hubert De Wolf. He, along with Revs. Herman Hoeksema and Cornelius Hanko, was pastor of the First Protestant Reformed Church in Grand Rapids, Mich. He was, from the start of the controversy over conditions, a supporter of Dr. Schilder and a proponent of conditional theology. He had, however, kept his views out of the pulpit, until the provisional adoption of the Declaration became the occasion for him to make a public statement of his position. He did this by means of a sermon on the parable of the rich man and Lazarus found in Luke 16:19–31, in which sermon he made the statement concerning the preaching of the gospel: "God promises every one of you that, if you believe, you will be saved."[11]

Although he was referring more generally to the preaching

---

10. For the history of this action, see: Gertrude Hoeksema, *A Watered Garden*, 173, 174.

11. Ibid., 176–83, where the history of this case is described.

of the gospel, he was, with that statement, clearly supporting the Liberated position, which teaches that the promise in the preaching is for every one who hears the gospel. Its realization in the heart of the hearer is dependent upon the fulfillment of the condition of faith.

Whether intentionally or unintentionally, De Wolf demonstrated clearly that Schilder's position of a *general promise* in baptism is essentially the same as the *general offer* of the gospel. Whether God *promises* salvation to all on the condition of faith, or *offers* it to all on the condition of faith, the basic meaning is the same.

The statement brought protests from members of the congregation and put the problem squarely in the hands of the elders. The consistory of First Church found it difficult to deal with the problem, chiefly because the elders reflected in their own ranks the divisions in the congregation.

The congregation was deeply affected. Discussions and debates were constantly carried on over the issues. Divisions and disagreements made difficult the joy of the communion of the saints. Families and friends were driven apart. The worship of God on the Lord's day was seriously affected by the lack of unity.

Because the consistory was unable to come to a resolution of the problem, the case against De Wolf aggravated First Church for almost a year and a half, until it began to fade somewhat into the background, and the hope was even expressed that the whole difficulty could be resolved in such a way that the congregation would remain intact and the differences forgotten.

But then everything changed once more. On September 14, 1952, DeWolf threw caution to the winds and openly affirmed his commitment to conditional theology. It was a preparatory sermon, preached with a view to the administration of the Lord's Supper on the following Lord's day. In the sermon, based on Matthew 18:3, DeWolf made the statement, "Our act of conversion is a prerequisite to enter the kingdom of heaven."

The congregation nearly exploded, and once again the elders had to take up the issues. No longer could differences be forgotten. Something had to be done, and done soon.

And so things began to move swiftly. In February of 1953, the elders subjected DeWolf to an examination of his orthodoxy, as the Church Order requires.[12] Because the men who supported DeWolf were at this time in the majority in the consistory, his examination was approved and he was cleared of all heresy charges.

Some elders, however, not agreeing that the examination proved DeWolf's orthodoxy, protested the decision of the consistory and appealed it to the next meeting of Classis East, in April of the same year. And so the issue came to classis.

Events in Classis East

Classis East, in dealing with the matter, made it its first order of business to appoint a committee of three ministers and two elders to study the whole case and to come to classis with advice. When the committee reported, it became obvious that the committee was split. The three ministers, in a very lengthy report to classis, made an attempt to give to DeWolf's statements an orthodox interpretation. The two elders did not. They prepared a one-page report in which they demonstrated that the statements were contrary to Scripture and the Reformed confessions and had to be condemned. The text of both reports is in Appendix I.

The report of the two elders was given a powerful boost by DeWolf's own repudiation of the majority report on the floor of the classis. The result was the adoption of the minority report. The classis decided that these two statements were heretical and that DeWolf had to apologize publicly for them

---

12. Art. 53 and the Formula of Subscription.

or be subject to the discipline of the church. It was furthermore decided that the elders who agreed with DeWolf's theology had to apologize for their heresy or be disciplined by the consistory.

A committee was appointed by classis to bring its decision to the consistory of First Church and to plead with DeWolf and the elders who supported him to confess their heresy and seek again the truth as it is in Christ.[13]

This committee met with the consistory on June 1, 1953. By a majority vote of the elders the decision of classis was adopted by the consistory. Further action was postponed until June 15, on which night DeWolf was given an apology which the consistory expected him to make. However, instead of doing what the classis and the consistory required of him, he made another apology, one which in no way admitted that his statements were heretical, but rather expressed sorrow for the lack of clarity in the statements and for the misunderstandings that arose because of this lack of clarity.

A meeting of the consistory on June 21 ended in chaos because the elders supporting De Wolf insisted on their right to vote once again on the same question of whether to condemn De Wolf's doctrinal position—even though the consistory had already condemned that position at the meeting of June 1. On the next night, Revs. Hoeksema and Hanko met with the faithful elders from First Church and the consistory of Fourth Protestant Reformed Church (as the Church Order requires) and formally suspended DeWolf and deposed from office the elders who supported him.[14]

---

13. These decisions of Classis East are quoted in an undated letter sent by the consistory to the congregation of First Church very shortly after the split and signed by Revs. H. Hoeksema and C. Hanko and the clerk, Elder G. Stadt. See Minutes of Classis East for 1953 (April 8–10, 14–16; May 19–23, 26–28), Arts. 176–265. Art. 148 contains the decision to appoint a committee to convey the classical decision to First Church. The agenda was not finished until October 6.

14. This history is contained in the letters sent to the congregation by the consistory of First Church, but undated. See Gertrude Hoeksema, *A Watered*

Upon hearing of this, DeWolf's supporters immediately took over the church property, changed the locks, and barred anyone but their supporters from using the premises. The following Sunday the faithful people of First Church met and worshiped in the chapel of Grand Rapids Christian High School.

The end was not yet.

When Classis East met again in October of 1953,[15] two sets of delegates, both claiming to represent First Church, were present: Rev. DeWolf and an elder, and Rev. Hanko and an elder. The classis decided, after hearing the history of what had transpired since its last meeting, that Rev. Hanko and his elder represented the First Protestant Reformed Church, while Rev. DeWolf and his elder did not.[16]

When this decision was taken, a number of ministers and elders, all supporters of DeWolf, rose from their seats and left the classis.

So the split that had begun in First Church now spread through the whole of Classis East.

Events in Classis West

It was not long before Classis West was also split. The matter of DeWolf's deposition had come to Classis West from several consistories. As the Church Order requires, First's consistory had notified all the churches of the suspension of DeWolf. This notification of DeWolf's suspension, for some strange reason, was brought to Classis West at its September meeting. This was strange because the

---

Garden, 193–204, for this and subsequent history. See also Herman Hoeksema, "True Or False" (a pamphlet containing the speech which Rev. Hoeksema gave in Kalamazoo, Mich., and in which he described in detail all that transpired from the time of De Wolf's first heretical sermon to the final split).

15. The normal July meeting was canceled by the meeting of the previous classis, and the October meeting was a continuation of the July meeting.

16. Arts. 301, 309, and 315.

material had no business at Classis West. The notifications of DeWolf's suspension were sent to all the consistories so that no other consistory would, inadvertently, open its pulpit to DeWolf. If those consistories which received the notification had objections to it, the course of action which they should have followed was the procedure of the Church Order: protest to First Church itself, and, if necessary, carry the protest to Classis East and synod.

But Classis West chose to ignore the proper procedure. At its meeting, the actions of both First's consistory and Classis East were condemned without any opportunity for either body to explain and defend itself.[17]

Although most ministers and the majority of the people in the West supported DeWolf, there were also faithful people in that part of the churches. The result was that the tremors of the split in the East rolled like shock waves through the West, and the chasm between the two groups in the East spread to the West.

The split was complete.

When the dust had settled, it became obvious that the split had not only torn the denomination apart, but had resulted in the loss of a majority of members. The *Yearbook* of 1953 lists 24 churches, 29 ministers, 6,063 individuals. The *Yearbook* of 1954 lists 16 churches, 14 ministers, 2,353 members. A very small denomination had become still smaller.

Further Events

It seemed clear from the outset that De Wolf made his first statement in the consciousness that he was approaching the doctrine of the well-meant offer as it had been maintained by the CRC. It seemed as if, already when the statement was first made, De Wolf had in mind some sort of rapprochement

---

17. Minutes of Classis West, September 2, 1953, Arts. 8 and 24.

with those from whom the PRC had come. Subsequent events proved that to be true.

Almost from the beginning of the controversy the defenders of the PRC position had pointed out that Schilder's view of the general and conditional promise bore striking similarities to the well-meant offer of the gospel as defined by the CRC, for the denial of which Rev. Hoeksema had been expelled from that denomination. In fact, one chief concern of the PRC was that, should the position of Schilder ultimately triumph in the churches, such a triumph would be a repudiation of all the PRC had stood for since the beginning of its history.[18]

Those who left the PRC in 1953 had, throughout the controversy, disavowed any intention of bringing the PRC back to the CRC. They had, indeed, insisted that their position was the true PRC position, and the Declaration a caricature and serious modification of the historic beliefs of the church.

Subsequent events proved the truth of the claim that a general and conditional promise was only a slight variation of the well-meant offer of the gospel. Nothing so clearly showed that as a letter which in 1959 Rev. De Wolf addressed to his consistory (the First Orthodox Reformed Church, which met at Calvin College).

The background of the letter was this. A decision had been made by the synod of the De Wolf group to seek contact with the CRC with a view to returning to them. Against this decision the consistory of De Wolf protested. The consistory did not want to return to the CRC and considered it a serious error even to discuss such a return. It addressed a letter to

---

18. Letter from the consistory of First Protestant Reformed Church to its congregation and to those who followed De Wolf in which the doctrinal similarity between the well-meant offer of 1924 and the general promise conditioned by faith of 1953 are compared. The letter has no date, but from an internal reference it is clear that it was written before July 20, 1953.

its synod of 1960 expressing its position, and made that letter public.

In response to that letter from the consistory, De Wolf addressed a letter to them.[19] He stakes out his basic position in an early paragraph when he writes: "That whole matter of common grace, as far as I am concerned, is extra-confessional. It does not concern any truth that is basic to salvation and should never have become a cause for separating brothers and sisters in Jesus Christ."

But it was not sufficient that De Wolf considered common grace to be extra-confessional; he defended "a general goodness or grace of God and a general love of God which goes beyond the elect." Referring to Deuteronomy 10:18, 19 he writes: "I think the Consistory, anyone else for that matter, would find it very difficult to prove that this stranger [referred to in Deut. 10] is exclusively an elect."

Taking on the great truth of predestination, De Wolf writes:

From the point of view of the preaching of the gospel there is no a priori differentiation. When the gospel confronts a man it does not confront him first of all as an elect or a reprobate but as a sinner. He is certainly one or the other according to God's eternal predestination. But what he is does not become apparent before the gospel is preached to him. Mankind, therefore, becomes a *historically* differentiated mankind only after the gospel has been preached and its effect has been revealed in man's response to it. The gospel does not come to a man and say to him first of all, "You are an elect" or "You are a reprobate" but "You are a sinner who is in need of salvation. And here is the Christ standing before you in this word. Believe on Him and you will be saved." Only after he believes does he have the consciousness and assurance of election, and only through faith can he apply to himself what God declares to and concerning the elect.

---

19. Letter from Rev. Hubert De Wolf to his consistory dated December 14, 1959.

In keeping with this position, De Wolf defends the use of the word "offer" and even suggests universal connotations in the mediatorial work of Christ as that which makes the offer serious. In commenting on John 17:9, he writes: "I am not aware of whether or not the Bible says anything about Christ praying for all . . . Notice that the text does not say that Christ does not pray for all but that He does not pray for the world. In the second place, the world here in the text is differentiated from those whom the Father gave Him. The world in this instance is therefore the wicked reprobate world as differentiated from the elect. This has nothing to do with the offer of Christ in the gospel to an undifferentiated world."

Although De Wolf does not say it in so many words, here again he suggests that God's purpose is to save all who hear. De Wolf uses a rather strange expression. He says that God's purpose in the *continued* preaching of the gospel is to harden. His use of the word "continued" would almost suggest, correctly, that hardening is the judicial punishment of God upon those who reject the gospel. But he goes on to say: "But this in no way detracts from the fact that the primary purpose of the gospel as it comes to sinners is not to condemn but to save."

It is not surprising that those who followed De Wolf finally did return to the CRC.

Church Political Issues

Several church political issues arose during the time of the controversy which served to sharpen the understanding of the churches on various aspects of the government of the church of Christ.

The issues were the following. Once again the autonomy of the local congregation vs. the authority of the church federation was debated. This question of the balance between autonomy and denominational authority carried over into a church political challenge of the synod's right to draw up the Declaration. And this same question surfaced in connection with (1) the right of Classis East to advise First Church to suspend De Wolf and depose his supporting elders if he continued to maintain his false doctrines; and (2) the right of a part of the consistory to depose and suspend when De Wolf and his elders were, in fact, disciplined.

When the synods of 1951 and 1952 were flooded with protests against the Declaration, these protests called synod's attention to what many thought were grave and serious church political errors. The most serious had to do with the right of synod to draw up such a document on behalf of the churches, and make such a document binding upon the churches. It was argued that for synod to draw up such a document was hierarchical in the extreme, and was characterized by a rule from "the top down" which effectively destroyed the autonomy of the local congregations.[20]

The argument can hardly be considered to have any force, however, both because of the origin and history of the document, and because of the content and purpose of the document.

The Declaration was drawn up at the request of the Mission Committee, which sought such a document from the synod so that other (especially the Liberated) churches might know what the PRC considered confessional teaching, and therefore binding, concerning particular vs. common grace and concerning God's covenant with His people. It is hard to imagine any legitimate objection to synod acceding to such a request.

In a way, synod went the extra mile when it only provisionally adopted the Declaration and gave all the churches one year to study it and bring the fruits of their

---

20. See *Acts of Synod, 1951*, Art. 120, p. 128, for example.

study to synod. This provision was hardly necessary, but certainly removed any possibility of charges of hierarchy.

That the synod should draw up a document, in which it states forthrightly what the PRC consider to be the truth of the confessions on some points being challenged in the churches, is precisely synod's right. In fact, it may be said that this very work of synod is one of the chief purposes of synodical gatherings. Synods are expressions of the unity of the churches belonging to the federation. That unity is the unity of doctrine. Synod, expressing that unity in its gatherings, determines the doctrine of the federation and the doctrinal basis for the unity of the churches. If this is not synod's business, then one may ask: For what purpose are synods?

It may be argued that the confessions express the basis for unity. And this is true. But the very confessions were under attack by conditional theology, and the synod not only had the right to affirm what the confessions really said on these matters, but synod had the solemn obligation to express the truth of the confessions. To fail in this obligation would have been irresponsible in the extreme. The defense of conditional theology was rooted in a disagreement with the truths of the confessions.[21]

Some attempt was made to defend the position that every congregation had the right to agree or disagree with these decisions of synod and remain in the federation. This position was defended especially in the court case which followed the split. It was refuted in the courtroom and rejected by the

---

21. Presumably, the LC would insist that their covenant conception was also confessional; and, as such, they would, almost certainly, make it binding in their churches. The deposition of Rev. Herman Veldman by the consistory of the Hamilton PRC was, after all, for preaching the PR idea of the covenant. By deposing Rev. Veldman, the elders in Hamilton were clearly saying that they would not tolerate in their churches those who held to the covenant view taught in the PRC.

judge in Chancery Court, and he awarded the property of
First Church to those in First Church who remained faithful
to the PRC.[22]

The defense of this position was a defense of a radical
congregationalism which had rarely if ever been maintained
by any Reformed church since the time of the synod of Dordt
(1618–1619).

However, the same issue of congregationalism had to be
faced at the time of the actual suspension of De Wolf. A brief
history of events will be necessary.[23]

The heretical statements of De Wolf were finally
adjudicated at Classis East in April and May of 1953. As
mentioned earlier, classis decided that the statements of De
Wolf were contrary to Scripture and the confessions, and that
De Wolf had to make apology for them or face suspension. It
was also decided that any elders who supported him should
also be suspended. A committee of classis was appointed to
convey the decision to First Church's consistory and plead
with De Wolf and his elders to submit to that decision.

On a consistory meeting of June 1, 1953, the decision
of the classis was accepted and approved by a majority of
the consistory, and De Wolf was given time to apologize. A
proper apology was never forthcoming, although De Wolf,
without prior knowledge on the part of the consistory, made
a public statement in a worship service.[24] At a meeting on

---

22. State of Michigan Supreme Court, First Protestant Reformed Church of
Grand Rapids, Mich., vs. Hubert De Wolf, et al. and Herman Hoeksema, et al.
vol. 1, pp. 117ff. A discussion of this question of Reformed church polity vs.
congregationalism can be found in Herman Hoeksema, "Autonomy," *SB* 30 (July
15, 1954): 412–15 and 30 (August 1, 1954): 436–45; John A. Heys, "Walking in
Error," *SB* 30 (September 15, 1954): 491, 492, 500; Gerald Vanden Berg, "The
Ministry of the Word" under rubric "Decency and Order," *SB* 31 (November 1,
1954): 68, 69; Herman Hoeksema, "Independentism," *SB* 31 (December 15, 1954):
124, 125; and 31 (January 1, 1955): 148, 149.

23. Found in Gertrude Hoeksema, *A Watered Garden*, 181ff.

24. The consistory had specifically told De Wolf for what he had to apologize.
Instead of following the consistory's decision, De Wolf made his own apology in the

June 22, the chairman ruled that De Wolf and his elders had no right to vote on the satisfactory nature of the "apology," due to the fact that they were already required to apologize and under the condemnation of the consistory until they did apologize. They refused this ruling of the chair, and the meeting ended in chaos.

The following evening the elders who supported the decision of Classis East met and suspended De Wolf and deposed his elders.

Two objections were brought against this action. The first was that classis had no right to advise suspension and deposition; the second was that a segment of the consistory might not depose fellow officebearers.

Both objections are, however, invalid, as a later meeting of Classis East also affirmed. The first objection is invalid because, although no classis has the right to engage in actual discipline,[25] Classis East had not actually engaged in discipline but had only advised it, something which classical assemblies repeatedly do in every discipline case within the churches.

The second objection is also invalid because after June 1, De Wolf and his elders were in a state of guilt and declared worthy of suspension until they apologized for the heresy they had taught. They had no longer any right to function in their office until they apologized, and they certainly had no right to vote on their own case in a consistory meeting. It would seem that elementary principles of justice would indicate that this is indeed the case.[26]

---

worship service of June 21. See the letters from the consistory to the congregation. See also Gertrude Hoeksema, *A Watered Garden*, 182, 183.

25. As had been done in 1924.

26. At the first consistory meeting after classis, De Wolf was confronted with the question whether he would apologize for his heretical statements. He asked for time to consider the matter, which was given him. However, the consistory should have barred him from the pulpit until such a time as he did apologize even though granting him time. It must be remembered that it was not at all certain that the consistory could have mustered sufficient votes to pass such a motion to bar De Wolf from the pulpit. The consistory was about evenly divided, and even a few

Finally, Classis West made a serious church political mistake which precipitated the split in the Western part of the churches.

When the consistory of First Church sent out notices to all the churches of the denomination to inform them that De Wolf had been suspended from office, Classis West took it upon itself to declare this suspension invalid. When the classis did this, the delegates from Doon PRC walked out of the meeting as they had been instructed by their consistory to do, and the split ran its course through that classis as well.

The decision of the classis was wrong on two counts. It decided on a matter of which it had no knowledge. It only knew that De Wolf had been suspended. But the reasons for his suspension, the history leading up to it, and the circumstances surrounding it were not officially reported to the classis. In supporting De Wolf, it was, therefore, judging Classis East and the consistory of First Church without a hearing. This is a violation of the ninth commandment.

If the consistories comprising Classis West truly disagreed with the decisions of Classis East and First Church, they had every right to obtain the decisions, study them, and if they found them contrary to Reformed principles of church government, protest them to the next synod. But to act unilaterally was a hierarchical act of ruling over Classis East which is contrary to Article 84 of the Church Order, which forbids a classis to lord it over any other classis.

Conclusion

The history of the split of 1953 was an extremely traumatic history for the churches. The inability of the churches to

---

who agreed with the decision of classis wanted to give De Wolf every benefit of the doubt and be as lenient as possible.

engage in the work which the church is called to do because of the distractions of doctrinal controversy, the severe decline in the membership of an already small denomination, the pain and suffering in the congregations and in families that necessarily come with a church split make one face the question: Was the controversy worth it? Would it not have been better to permit the Liberated to enter the churches while maintaining their own covenant view? Would it not have saved untold grief to allow room in the confession of the church for a general and conditional promise? Would it not have been preferable to overlook the conditional statements of De Wolf made from the pulpit of First Church?

At first glance, such a course of action might seem to be preferable. But various considerations finally make such a course of action impossible. In the first place, two radically different covenant views cannot exist side by side within one denomination in a peaceful way. The price to be paid for opening the doors to the Liberated was the price of complete sacrifice of the truth of an unconditional covenant established with the elect alone. Neither the Liberated people nor devoted PRC members would have been able to be silent about such crucially important questions; and confrontation would have come sooner or later.

In the second place, the issues did not involve, from a strictly doctrinal viewpoint, irrelevant or peripheral issues. They were, as the adoption of the Declaration showed, confessional matters. The integrity of the PRC as a confessional church was at stake. The question was: Are we going to be faithful to our confessions? To capitulate to Liberated theology would have been a step in the direction of unfaithfulness.

In the third place, the questions which the churches faced were at the very heart of the truth of the gospel because they involved the truths of sovereign and particular grace over against general and conditional grace. This was and remains the battle of the ages. The decisions of the churches in the controversy were a defense of the truths of sovereign and particular grace. No price is too high to pay in the defense of those truths.

CHAPTER 17

*T*he Covenant in God

If you ask me what is the most peculiar treasure of the Protestant Reformed Churches, I would answer without any hesitation: their peculiar view of the covenant. He that has been captivated by this beautiful Reformed truth . . . will go forward and continue to develop the pure Protestant Reformed truth of God's eternal covenant . . . Failure to do this is our death. It is the end of our distinctive existence.

       —Herman Hoeksema, *Standard Bearer*

Early Development

The truth of God's everlasting covenant of grace lies at the very heart of Protestant Reformed theology. It was the key issue in all the debates that led to the split in the PRC in 1953. It was and is the one doctrine which, more than any other, defined PR distinctives and justified the existence of the PRC as a separate denomination.

In a certain sense, the covenant view of the PRC reached maturity through the struggles of 1953 and preceding years. Its sharp definition was, in large measure, due to the need to defend it against error in the heat of ecclesiastical battle. Yet, early in the history of the PRC, really even before the PRC existed as a separate denomination, the broad outlines of the PR view of God's covenant of grace were clearly drawn.

This early development of the central doctrines of the covenant was due in large measure to the work of Rev. Herman Hoeksema. So true is this that to speak of a PR covenant view is all but synonymous with speaking of Hoeksema's covenant view. Especially in the early years of the history of the PRC, Hoeksema, as editor-in-chief of the *Standard Bearer* and as professor of theology in the seminary, developed the doctrine of the covenant as held by the PRC.

This does not mean that the PR doctrine of the covenant is an innovation, a novelty, a completely new thought in the history of the church of our Lord Jesus Christ. It is not that. The view developed by Herman Hoeksema is firmly and deeply rooted in Reformed theology, going back to the Reformation and even beyond.

This claim means two things.

It means, first of all, that the covenant view of the PRC is confessional. As I pointed out in the last chapter, the central truths of the unilateral and unconditional character of the covenant are truths contained in the creeds of the Reformed churches.

But it also means, in the second place, that all the central features of Hoeksema's view and of that of the PRC are to be found in past Reformed writers. Even the idea of the covenant as a bond of friendship and fellowship can be traced back as far as Olevianus, one of the authors of the Heidelberg Catechism. And it reappears in the writings of such men as Cocceius and Bavinck.[1]

Why then do I call this covenant view distinctively PR? Two answers to that question must be given.

First of all, while certainly all the central features of the PR covenant view can be found in other Reformed writings, certain ambiguities were always present in these writings. These ambiguities arose out of the tendency among most in the Reformed tradition to view the covenant, in some

---

1. Johannes Cocceius (1603–1669) was a Dutch theologian whose covenant views were influential in the Netherlands for many centuries. Herman Bavinck (1854–1921) was a Dutch theologian and contemporary of Abraham Kuyper who had considerable influence on Herman Hoeksema's thinking.

measure, as an agreement or pact, and thus, in some sense, bilateral and conditional in character. Even if some theologians suggested that the covenant of grace was a bond of fellowship, the idea of an agreement persisted, even in their own writings.

It is likely that the notion of the covenant as an agreement arose out of the idea of the covenant of works, a covenant supposedly made with Adam in Paradise, bilateral in character and conditional in its execution. So this idea too was subjected to the rigorous scrutiny of Scripture by Rev. Hoeksema. Hoeksema developed the doctrine of the covenant by limiting the idea of the covenant exclusively to a bond of friendship.

Secondly, Hoeksema did offer some important contributions to the development of the doctrine which were, in significant ways, new insights into the truth. Two may be mentioned here. Hoeksema spoke of the so-called *Pactum Salutis* in a way in which it had not been spoken of in previous Reformed thought.[2] And Hoeksema introduced the "organic" idea into the covenant.[3] While the organic emphasis of the covenant was implicit in much of what the Reformed fathers taught, it was made explicit and applied specifically to various aspects of the truth in Hoeksema's development.

Hoeksema came early to his position on the doctrine of the covenant, perhaps even before the beginning of the PRC. He apparently arrived at his views through intense study in the years of his ministry in Fourteenth St. CRC in Holland, and in Eastern Ave. CRC in Grand Rapids.

While he was in seminary, he received instruction in Reformed theology from Professor William Heyns. At that

---

2. I shall point out the differences later in the chapter.

3. I have treated this whole concept in chapter 12 and shall refer to it again in this chapter.

time, Hoeksema did not know what direction Scripture and the confessions led on the doctrine of the covenant; but he did know that the views of Professor Heyns were wrong.[4] Early in his ministry, he developed a revulsion for Heyns' views that never left him. And that revulsion was born out of the Arminianism implicit in Heyns' teachings.

Already during his years as minister at Fourteenth St. in Holland, some of the traditional aspects of covenant theology also troubled Hoeksema.[5] And these troubling aspects of Reformed theology undoubtedly acted as an incentive for him to give the doctrines of the covenant additional attention. By 1923, when he co-authored the book which serves as the watershed of his theology, *Van Zonde en Genade*, his views were in place and the basic questions answered. From the position outlined in that book, he never wavered.

That position, as developed further through the years, remains the position of the PRC. We turn now to a discussion of that covenant view which, developed extensively by Hoeksema, remains the covenant view of the churches.

The Covenant, a Bond of Friendship

The basic and fundamental idea of the covenant in Hoeksema's theology is the covenant as a bond of friendship and fellowship. This idea is quite different from the notion of the covenant which held sway in Reformed thinking for most of the post-Reformation era. Although hints of the covenant as a bond of friendship are to be found in various Reformed thinkers, the dominating thought was of the covenant as a pact or agreement between God and man.

---

4. David J. Engelsma, footnote to his translation of "The Idea of the Covenant of Grace" by Henry Danhof, *Protestant Reformed Theological Journal* 31, no. 1 (November 1997): 17, footnote 7. See also Gertrude Hoeksema, *Therefore Have I Spoken*, 58.

5. Gertrude Hoeksema, *Therefore Have I Spoken*, 96–109, 146.

Henry Danhof had, already before the publication of *Van Zonde en Genade*, spoken of the covenant as a bond of friendship rather than an agreement.[6] But Herman Hoeksema, following Danhof's fundamental thought, developed the idea extensively and gave it a biblical foundation.

In the course of his development of the covenant as a bond of friendship, Hoeksema rejected various other ideas which for a long time had been associated with covenant theology in some branches of the Reformed churches. It is helpful to mention them briefly, for even a brief mention of them will bring Hoeksema's views into sharper focus.

Hoeksema's rejection of the covenant as an agreement between God and man compelled him to reject various other notions of the covenant which were present in the theology of Professor William Heyns,[7] and which were also taken over by Liberated theologians.

Hoeksema rejected the idea that the covenant was limited to the promise of God. Heyns had made it such and had been followed in this by the Liberated. The covenant of grace, it was said, is synonymous with and no more than God's promise, and the promise is an objective bequest to all the children baptized in which God promises to be their God.[8]

---

6. Engelsma, footnote to his translation of "The Idea of the Covenant of Grace," 17, footnote 7. Engelsma points to the "intriguing question" whether Danhof or Hoeksema was the first to suggest the idea of the covenant as a bond of friendship. For an extensive development of Hoeksema's covenant theology, see also Hoeksema, "The Covenant: God's Tabernacle with Men" (Grand Rapids: Evangelism Committee of First Protestant Reformed Church, 1995), 4.

7. See earlier references to Professor Heyns' theology in footnote 41, chapter 4; footnote 6, chapter 11; and footnotes 13–20, chapter 14.

8. See Herman Hoeksema, *Believers and Their Seed*, tr. from the Dutch (*De Geloovigen en Hun Zaad*) by Homer C. Hoeksema (Grand Rapids: Reformed Free Publishing Association, 1971), 20–34. See also Herman Hoeksema, "Our Calling," *The Protestant Reformed Churches: 25th Anniversary 1925–1950* (no city or publisher given, [1950]), 17. The same criticism of the covenant as nothing but an objective promise can be found repeatedly in the writings that appeared in connection with the controversy of 1953. An example is: Herman Hoeksema, "Promise And Prediction," *SB* 28 (March 15, 1952): 269–73.

Hoeksema did not deny that God's promise, spoken of so often in Scripture, is an important part of the covenant; but he insisted that it is not the covenant itself. The covenant is more than that.

In keeping with the idea that the covenant is the promise, Heyns and the Liberated also spoke of the fact that the covenant is a means to an end. They taught, in other words, that the covenant, which consists only in God's promise to all who are baptized, is a temporal means to the full realization of salvation.

Hoeksema claimed, rather, that the covenant is not a means to an end, but the end itself. The covenant as a bond of friendship is established already in this life, but will be finally perfected in the full salvation given to the people of God when the tabernacle of God will be with men.[9]

Still in connection with this same point that the covenant consists only of the promise, the LC maintained that the covenant is only a temporal arrangement. It is a temporal provision, limited in its use to this present time, for temporal purposes only, and thus without any eternal characteristics. This, too, Hoeksema rejected when he insisted that we must understand the covenant to be a bond of friendship which has its prototype in God Himself. The covenant is eternal. God's purpose is to make His people His own covenant people, and that is an eternal determination.[10]

From the dispute over a temporal vs. an eternal covenant arose the dispute over the question whether election can be connected to the covenant. The LC insisted that it cannot. Logically they could come to no other conclusion. If the promise is the covenant, and the promise is made to all the children who are baptized, then God's covenant is with all who are baptized. But the final salvation of each baptized

---

9. Hoeksema, "The Covenant: God's Tabernacle With Men," 1, 4, 15.
10. Ibid., 12.

child depends, not upon the decree of election, but upon the decision of those who are baptized.[11] Over against this view, Hoeksema maintained that the eternal decree of election determined those who belonged to God's covenant people.

The views of Heyns and the LC were rejected. In their place emerged a doctrine of the covenant which is not only fully biblical, but is characterized by a warmth which gladdens the heart of the child of God.

The whole idea of the covenant as a bond of friendship lies at the very heart of Hoeksema's covenant theology. Perhaps the clearest definition of that idea is expressed in these words:

> [God's covenant of grace] is the everlasting relation of friendship between God and His elect people in Jesus Christ our Lord in which He is their Sovereign Friend and blesses them with all spiritual blessings in heavenly places, receiving them by His grace in His family, and they, on their part, are His friend-servants, called and willing to love Him with all their heart and mind and soul and strength, to be to the praise of His glorious virtues antithetically in the midst of the world, and presently praise and glorify Him forever in His eternal tabernacle.[12]

In another place, Hoeksema offers a description of the covenant in these words:

> The idea of the covenant of God is briefly expressed in the term "friendship." In His covenant, God is the Friend-sovereign of man, man is His friend-servant. In His covenant, God reveals Himself to man, and man knows Him; God opens His heart to him, and he tastes that the Lord is good; God takes man into His house, and he dwells with Him, consecrates himself to Him, serves and glorifies Him, and has his whole delight in

---

11. Hoeksema, "Our Calling," 17.
12. Ibid.

the keeping of His precepts. The covenant of God is the very essence of religion.[13]

This idea of the covenant as a bond of friendship Hoeksema based on a solid biblical foundation. He defined the covenant with Adam before the fall in terms of friendship and fellowship.[14] He pointed out that this idea of friendship is expressed in the description of some of the Old Testament saints who "walked with God" and were known as friends of God.[15] He pointed to the tabernacle and temple as Old Testament symbols of the covenant, because in them God dwelt with His people.[16] And he found a powerful argument for the covenant as a bond of friendship in the fact that God Himself defines His covenant with His people in terms of a marriage relationship, which is surely a unity of fellowship.[17]

The New Testament proof for the covenant as a bond of friendship Hoeksema found in Jesus' words in John 17:3, 23 where the Lord equated eternal life with the knowledge of God and union with God through Christ.[18] And the perfect realization of that bond of friendship is in heaven when the tabernacle of God is with men.[19]

The Triune Covenant God

Defining the covenant as a bond of friendship and fellowship, Hoeksema found the highest reality of the covenant within the life of God Himself. Breaking into new

---

13. Hoeksema, "The Covenant: God's Tabernacle With Men," 8. For similar material, see Hoeksema, *Reformed Dogmatics*, 329ff.

14. Hoeksema, "The Covenant: God's Tabernacle with Men" 13, 14.

15. Ibid., 14. The texts cited are Genesis 5:22; 6:8, 13; 9:9; and 18:17ff.; Exodus 33:11; Isaiah 41:8; and James 2:23.

16. Ibid. The texts cited are II Cor. 6:16 and Rev. 21:3; 22:4.

17. Ibid.

18. Ibid., 14, 15.

19. Ibid., 15.

territory, proposing new exegetical insights, often using eloquent language, but always displaying his devotion to God's glory, Hoeksema carried traditional covenant theology to new heights and gave to the Protestant Reformed Churches a heritage that is priceless.

Hoeksema's theological method was, above all, God-centered. That is, he started in his theology with God and ended with God. It is not surprising, therefore, that in his development of the doctrine of the Trinity Hoeksema should introduce the truth of the covenant.

Hoeksema found the prototype of the covenant of grace in God's own trinitarian life which He lives in Himself as Father, Son, and Holy Spirit. This covenant life which God lives in Himself is the rich and blessed life that it is because of the Trinity. God is one in essence—which makes a bond of fellowship the essential character of God Himself as the living God. But God is three in person, for without persons no fellowship is possible.

The chapter on the Holy Trinity in Hoeksema's definitive work, *Reformed Dogmatics*, ends with a paragraph on the covenant.

> And so, as the living God He is the covenant God. For the idea of the covenant is not that of an agreement, pact, or alliance. It is a bond of friendship and living fellowship. Friendship is that bond of fellowship between persons, according to which and by which they enter into one another's life in perfect knowledge and love, so that mind is knit to mind, will to will, heart to heart, and each has no secrets from the other. It presupposes a basis of likeness, of equality: for only like knows like. And on that basis of equality, it requires personal distinction: for without this there is only sameness; there can be no fellowship. And both the equality and the personal distinction are in God. For He is the Triune; the most absolute equality exists between Father, Son, and Holy Spirit. For these Three are one in Essence. And in Him there is the personal distinction between the Three Persons subsisting in

the one Essence. And so the Three Persons of the Holy Trinity completely and perfectly enter into one another's life. Their fellowship is infinitely perfect. They have no secrets from one another. There is no conflict between them. Their relationship is one of perfect harmony: the Father knows and loves the Son in the Spirit; the Son knows and loves the Father in the Spirit; and the Spirit knows and loves the Father through the Son in Himself. The living God is the covenant God. That is the great significance of the truth that God is Triune, and that these three distinct Persons are the one, only, true, and eternal God.[20]

In another place Hoeksema writes:

We [must] proceed from what Scripture teaches us concerning the Being and life of the infinite God Himself. For behind all being and becoming, behind all the relations and connections of the creatures and of them to the Creator, lies the eternal decree of the Most High. Known unto God are all His works from eternity. All that exists is and becomes only according to His eternal will . . . Hence, it is always requisite that we turn from the created things to the decree of God, and that we go back even from the decree to what Scripture teaches us concerning the eternal God Himself. For only from His Being can be explained the being of all things . . . Hence, also the idea and essence of the covenant must be explained from the relation between the Three Persons of the Holy Trinity.

Now the Scriptures teach very clearly that God is in Himself a covenant God. He is a covenant God, not, in the first place, because of any relation wherein He stands to the creature. The creature can participate in and taste His life according to the measure of the creature; but it cannot enrich that life. Thus it

---

20. Hoeksema, *Reformed Dogmatics*, 152. This same truth is expressed in Herman Hoeksema, *Believers and Their Seed*, tr. by Homer C. Hoeksema (Grand Rapids: Reformed Free Publishing Association, 1971). This was first written in the early 1930s, perhaps as early as 1930. Initially it appeared as a brochure and was twice published in the Dutch. The English translation of 1971 was revised for a new edition in 1997 (Grandville, Mich.: Reformed Free Publishing Association). See also Hoeksema, "The Covenant: God's Tabernacle With Men," 15, 16.

is also with the covenant. It is eternally of God. It is eternally perfect in Him. He is the covenant God in Himself. And He is the God of the covenant, not according to a decree or according to an agreement or pact, but according to His very divine Nature and Essence. For God is indeed One in Essence, but He is not lonely in Himself. If nothing else could be said than that God is One, He would not and could not be the living God, Who is in Himself the ever-blessed One. A God that is lonely does not know Himself and love Himself, does not live and is not blessed, is a cold and dead abstraction. But God is One in Being and Three in Persons: Father, Son, and Holy Spirit. And as the Triune God, He is the living God, Who lives the infinitely perfect covenant life in Himself.[21]

Hoeksema then goes on to review briefly the doctrine of the Trinity, and rejects the idea that there are in God "three divine Beings, natures, intellects, wills, wisdoms and powers . . ."[22] For, "if this were the case, it would be conceivable that the covenant could exist in an agreement or pact between these three perfectly equal, distinct divine Persons."[23] There are, however, three persons united in one essence, but distinct from each other according to their personal attributes. "And thus there is an eternal current of divine love-life out of the Father, through the Son, and in the Holy Spirit returning to the Father. Three there are that witness in heaven, the Father, the Son, and the Holy Spirit; and these three are One."[24] Hoeksema continues:

> That divine trinitarian life is the life of the covenant.
> For in the eternal sphere of the divine Essence, the Three Persons of the Holy Trinity live in inseparable, most perfect, and eternally complete communion with one another. It is the life of eternal and perfect knowledge, of a perfect entering into one

---

21. Hoeksema, *Reformed Dogmatics*, 319.
22. Ibid., 320.
23. Ibid.
24. Ibid., 321.

another's life, of a perfect understanding of each other. In the divine economy there are no secrets. The Father never thinks or wills what the Son and the Holy Spirit do not think or will. It is a life of the most perfect love, in which the Three Persons of the Holy Trinity eternally find one another and are eternally united in the most perfect divine harmony in the bond of perfect union. Nowhere is there separation, nowhere disharmony in the divine life of friendship. And therefore God is in Himself most blessed. Therefore He is in Himself the Self-sufficient, Who has no need to be served by men's hands, to Whom no one can add anything, out of Whom and through Whom and unto Whom are all things, and Who has made all things for His own name's sake. And therefore He is also from eternity to eternity the covenant God in Himself, the architect of all covenant life. The life of the divine Trinity is a life of the most intimate communion of friendship.

However, as soon as we present the matter of the covenant in this wise, if the life of the covenant in God is such a life of most perfect friendship, of the most intimate communion, of the deepest knowledge and the most affectionate love, it follows, in the first place, that the idea of the covenant cannot be found in an agreement or pact. In perfect harmony and communion of life, in the perfect, eternal knowing of one another, and in the most perfect love and unity, the idea of an agreement, of the conclusion of a pact, does not fit. In such a relation everything is spirit and life. The covenant idea is given with the life of the Triune God in Himself. It rises in eternal spontaneity from the divine Essence and realizes itself with perfect divine consciousness in the Three Persons. God knows and wills Himself, loves and seeks Himself eternally as the covenant God. The covenant is the bond of God with Himself. It is the eternal life of perfect light.[25]

Thus the doctrine of the Holy Trinity becomes, not the cold and abstract doctrine that it is sometimes presented as being, but a doctrine warm, vibrant with life, a personal

---

25. Ibid.

expression of the truth concerning God made by the people who themselves dwell with Him in covenant fellowship.

Such crucially important doctrines as the relation between the Holy Trinity and the covenant could not and did not go undeveloped in the history of the PRC in the years after Herman Hoeksema completed his earthly labors in 1965.[26] Some development has indeed taken place. Some of the preachers in the PRC have given their attention to and have preached on the work of the Holy Spirit, particularly in His capacity as the Spirit of Christ. It is through His work that God brings His people into His own covenant fellowship through Christ. And covenant fellowship with God through Christ is accomplished by the mystical union between Christ and His people, by which they become one body. In that union with Christ, who is "very God of very God," God's people dwell in fellowship with God.[27]

David Engelsma devoted his Master's thesis to a discussion of the relation between the Trinity and God's covenant. He pointed out that God is, as Father and Son, a family God, living a holy family life. God is Father and Son united in the Holy Spirit. God's own blessed family life which He lives in Himself is revealed in the family life of the covenant of grace in which the triune God is Father, Christ is elder Brother, and the elect are Christ's brothers and sisters.[28] This elect family, one in Christ through the Spirit, is destined to dwell

---

26. In a session of Hoeksema's Dogmatics class, he once informed us that he thought the most crucial area in doctrine which deserved study and development was the area of the role of the Holy Spirit, both in the life of the Trinity and in the covenant life of God and His people.

27. The Heidelberg Catechism speaks of this truth in its discussion of the Lord's Supper when, in answer to the question "What is it then to eat the crucified body, and drink the shed blood of Christ?" the Catechism answers, "It is not only to embrace with a believing heart all the sufferings and death of Christ . . . , but also . . . to become more and more *united to his sacred body, by the Holy Ghost, who dwells both in Christ and in us*" (Q & A 76, emphasis mine).

28. David J. Engelsma, "Trinity and Covenant," Th.M thesis for Calvin Theological Seminary, Grand Rapids, 1994.

with God the Father in eternal bliss in Father's house of many mansions. Both in the being of God and in the covenant of grace, the Holy Spirit is the personal fellowship.

I can only briefly mention here that this has profound implications for family life in a covenant home[29] and for Christian education in covenant schools.[30] It is not an exaggeration to say that covenant theology has shaped the lives of PR people in their marriages, homes, churches, and schools.

The Covenant as Revelation

Basically, the covenant of grace which God establishes with His people is revelation. It is the revelation of the covenant life which God lives in Himself.[31] It is the revelation to God's own people of His infinitely blessed covenant life.[32]

But God reveals His own covenant life to His people, not simply by telling them something of the blessedness that is His as the triune God, but by actually taking them into His own covenant life. As I have explained earlier, God is, in Himself as the triune God, a "family God." Within the Trinity are Father, Son, and Holy Spirit. God's covenant with His people may be compared to a family in which Christ is the "Elder Brother" and all God's people are sons and daughters of God who are destined to dwell with Him in His house

---

29. David J. Engelsma, "As a Father Pitieth His Children" (Grand Rapids: Sunday School of the First Protestant Reformed Church, 1983).

30. David J. Engelsma, *Reformed Education*, reprint of 1st ed. (Grand Rapids: Federation of Protestant Reformed Young People's Societies, 1981). The first edition was compiled and published in 1977 by the Federation of Protestant Reformed School Societies from a 1975 summer course the author gave for teachers in PR Christian Schools under the auspices of the Federation Board.

31. Hoeksema, *Reformed Dogmatics*, 329; Hoeksema, *Believers and Their Seed*, 62, 63.

32. This particularity of God's revelation of His covenant life to His people is one reason why Hoeksema insisted that there was no general revelation, that revelation belonged to the work of the grace of salvation, was not general or common, and was given only to the elect.

of many mansions (II Cor. 6:18; John 14:1–3). But they are God's family in a unique way, for they enter into the very life of the "family God" Himself. They become, as Peter puts it, "partakers of the divine nature" through the fulfillment of God's promises (II Peter 1:4).[33]

This idea of God's covenant can hardly be stressed strongly enough. One must understand it to understand its importance for PR theology of the covenant. God shares His own covenant life as a family God with His elect people who are in themselves sinners and spiritual children of their father the devil.

Perhaps an illustration will help us understand the point. If a happy covenant family wishes to share the joys of its family life with some abandoned, diseased, and starved street child, it will not do for the family simply to tell the waif of the life the family lives. But if they take the little girl into their home, adopt her for one of their children, treat her in every respect as the other children are treated, and make her, with the others, the heir of all the family possessions, then that little orphan will come to know the blessedness of family life by tasting it as it is given her of grace.

So God determines to reveal His own blessed covenant life in the covenant of grace. He has no internal need to reveal Himself and His own blessedness. This revelation of His covenant life will not enrich Him or add to His glory. The determination to reveal Himself is sovereign and free. It is for His own name's sake, to the praise and glory of His own exalted name. Sovereignly and freely, in order to reveal His blessedness in all its glory, God determines to take His people into His own family life so that they live, as it were, within the Trinity and its blessedness.

How much richer and more glorious such a conception of the covenant is than that of a cold and mechanical agreement

---

33. Hoeksema, *Believers and Their Seed*, 62, 63.

or treaty in which are conditions, obligations, stipulations, threats, etc. But a covenant God, making a covenant people by taking them into His covenant life, shows the glory of God's grace to be rich indeed.

God's Covenant with Christ

If Hoeksema had followed a more traditional way of developing the truth of God's covenant, one would expect at this point that he would introduce the covenant which God established with Adam. After all, was not that covenant with Adam the first manifestation of God's covenant?

And yet, Hoeksema did not do this, but turned immediately to God's covenant with Christ. He did that for a very good reason. He was of the conviction that if one did not proceed at this point to Christ, one would have a wrong conception of God's covenant with Adam as well as with His elect people in Christ. One would be tempted to make the covenant with Adam God's first "attempt" to glorify Himself and realize His covenant with men. But that "attempt" would then have failed because of Adam's rebellion. One would then be forced to say that God had to fall back on another plan as a substitute for the failure of the first plan.

But this view would also relegate Christ to "second best." "Christ is not an afterthought of God, so to speak, but in the counsel of God He is the Firstborn. Salvation is no repair work, but the realization of God's eternal covenant, even through the deep way of sin and grace."[34]

God determined eternally to reveal Himself and the blessedness of His own covenant life in the highest possible way; that way was Christ. In Christ are revealed all the riches of God's own infinite blessedness. In Christ, not in Adam, is revealed the hidden treasures of God's covenant with His people.[35]

---

34. Hoeksema, "The Covenant: God's Tabernacle With Men," 17.
35. Hoeksema faces the question whether this is not supralapsarian, and

This approach of Hoeksema led him directly to a discussion of the so-called *Pactum Salutis*, or, as it was sometimes called, the Counsel of Redemption, the Covenant of Redemption, or the Counsel of Peace.[36]

The traditional idea of the *Pactum Salutis* was based on the idea of the covenant as an agreement between persons. It taught that the agreement in this case was between the Father, the first person of the Trinity, and the Son, the second person of the Trinity. Together they determined to save a people through the mediatorial work of the second person. The agreement of the second person to do what had to be done constituted the heart and core of the *Pactum Salutis*.[37]

Although the criticism of the traditional view rests on exegetical grounds, in other words, on the interpretation of various key passages, Hoeksema also points out that this view basically separates the three persons of the Holy Trinity by assigning to each a different role. The wrong of assigning different roles to each person of the Trinity is evident, because the unity of the Godhead requires that the one triune God be Author of all His works.

But Hoeksema finds in the traditional view of the *Pactum Salutis* another and more serious error. The view long held

concluding that it is, he writes: "You can perhaps call this supralapsarianism; and I will not deny it. You may object, perhaps, that our confessions are infralapsarian; and again, I will admit it. But I will add to it immediately that although the supralapsarian conception was not adopted in the confessions, neither was it condemned. And everyone will have to admit that the presentation we offered above is certainly founded on Holy Writ." Hoeksema, *Reformed Dogmatics*, 333. He then proceeds to point out the biblical proof, appealing especially to Colossians 1:14–20.

36. A detailed analysis of the traditional view and a vivid description of his own view is found in, Hoeksema, *Reformed Dogmatics*, 285–336. A rather well-read theologian from the Presbyterian tradition once said to me that this section of Hoeksema's *Dogmatics* was the most difficult to understand. He compared it with using a snow plow to plow through a huge drift of snow. One had to back up repeatedly and forge ahead, hoping to make a few inches of progress with each pass.

37. Ibid., 285–97, where Hoeksema quotes from different theologians in the Dutch Reformed and Presbyterian tradition to give examples of the view of the *Pactum Salutis* which he criticizes.

among Reformed theologians leaves no room for the Holy Spirit in this important and crucial work of the covenant.

Hoeksema, after his critical analysis of the traditional view of the *Pactum Salutis*, develops the biblical position.[38] A full understanding of his position requires that I turn to his three-volume commentary on the Heidelberg Catechism, where is the clearest exposition of this thought.

In connection with his exposition of Lord's Day XX[39] and his discussion of the doctrine of the Holy Spirit, Hoeksema makes a distinction between "the Holy Ghost as such, as the third Person of the Holy Trinity, and that same Spirit as He is become the Spirit of Christ."[40] This distinction is also to be applied to the Son as the second person of the Trinity, and as the Lord Jesus Christ in our flesh.

> Even as the only begotten Son and Jesus Christ are the same Person, so the Holy Ghost and the Spirit of Christ are the same Person.
>
> Again, just as the only begotten Son, the second Person in the Trinity, is the eternal Word, the Logos, through whom all things are made, so the Holy Ghost is the Spirit of all creation, in whom all things are made, giving life to all things.
>
> But, once more, even as the only begotten Son, from before the foundation of the world is ordained to be the Mediator of salvation, the Head of the elect Church, and the Head over all things in the new creation, so the Holy Ghost, in God's eternal good pleasure is promised to Christ, ordained to be the Spirit of sanctification, that he might dwell in the Church and make us partakers of all the benefits of salvation.
>
> And, finally, even as the eternal Son became Jesus Christ, our Lord and Redeemer, in the fullness of time, through His incarnation, His death and resurrection, and His exaltation at the right hand of God, so the Holy Ghost became the Spirit of

---

38. Ibid., 297–336.
39. Herman Hoeksema, *The Triple Knowledge*, vol. 2 (1972), 156–65.
40. Ibid., 156.

Christ after His exaltation, and as such came to dwell in the Church on the day of Pentecost.[41]

The same important distinction is made by Hoeksema in his treatment of Lord's Day IX, a Lord's Day which deals with the Fatherhood of God. After expressing some amazement at the insight of the authors of the Heidelberg Catechism, Hoeksema writes:

> We may distinguish here at once a threefold divine father-hood, viz. the fatherhood of God with relation to our Lord Jesus Christ, His fatherhood as the Creator, with relation to all things, and His fatherhood with relation to His people in Jesus Christ and for His sake . . .
>
> But here we must at once make an important distinction, that, namely, between the eternal fatherhood of the First Person in relation to the Son in the divine nature, and the fatherhood of the triune God in relation to Christ as the Mediator, in His human nature . . .[42]

After referring to a few other older commentaries, including one by Ursinus, one of the authors of the Heidelberg Catechism, he goes on:

> We must, then, make a distinction between the unique fatherhood of the first person of the Holy Trinity with relation to the essential and eternal Son of God, and the fatherhood of God with relation to all creatures. The former is a relation within the economy of the Trinity, the latter a relation of the Triune God to the creature outside of Him. The former is a relation between two persons of the Trinity, the latter is a relation between the Being of God, as subsisting in three persons, and the creature formed by His will and power. The former is an eternal relation, the latter is called into being in time. The former may be called a natural, necessary relation in God, the latter is rooted in God's sovereign counsel and will.

41. Ibid., 156, 157.
42. Ibid., vol. 1, 369, 370.

And for the same reason we must make a distinction between the relation between the Father and the Son within the Holy Trinity, and the relation between the "God and Father of our Lord Jesus Christ," and the Mediator in His human nature.[43]

Although all of this may be somewhat difficult to understand, it nevertheless forms an important part of Hoeksema's doctrine of the *Pactum Salutis*. In brief, Hoeksema points out that the Scriptures distinguish between the eternal Son as the second person of the Holy Trinity, and the eternal Son as He assumed our flesh and blood, lived on this earth, suffered and died, rose again and is exalted at God's right hand, and appears in glory as the Mediator of the covenant of grace.

So crucial is this that Christ's own relation to His Father (in His human nature) cannot be understood apart from it. When Christ calls upon God as His Father, Christ is always speaking of and to the triune God, Father, Son, and Holy Spirit. When Christ hears the words of God: "This is my beloved Son in whom I am well pleased," it is the divine approval of the eternal and triune God on the Mediator of the covenant. When Christ commits His spirit when dying into the hands of His Father, He commits His spirit to the triune God. And when God raises Christ from the dead as the fulfillment of Psalm 2:7,[44] the triune God, through the resurrection, sets Christ upon the holy hill of Zion.[45]

As Hoeksema points out,[46] the same must be said of the

---

43. Ibid., 371, 372.
44. See Acts 13:33.
45. It might be objected that this conception makes the eternal Son in the Trinity His own Father. And that is indeed true. All the works of God are the works of the triune God, through our Lord Jesus Christ, and by the Holy Spirit as the Spirit of Christ. But this explains in some measure how the triune God secures the redemption of His people through His Son in such a way that Christ willingly offers Himself as the sacrifice through which redemption is secured. The willing sacrifice of Christ, the eternal Son of God, is indeed the work of the triune God through the Son.
46. Hoeksema, *The Triple Knowledge*, vol. 2, 156ff.

Holy Spirit and the same distinction must be made. The Holy Spirit is the third person of the Holy Trinity. But at His ascension, the Lord Jesus Christ, the Mediator of the covenant, was given the Holy Spirit as His own to pour out upon the church. That mighty event took place on Pentecost. By the ever-present Spirit of Christ, Christ Himself is with the church unto the end of the age.

It is not surprising that this is the marvelous way in which God works. That God reveals His own covenant life in the covenant of grace which He establishes through Jesus Christ means that God reveals Himself as He is in Himself. He is three in person. And within that Trinity of persons, the first person generates the second; the second is generated by the first; and the third proceeds from the first and second persons, even as the first and second persons breathe out the third person. That inter-trinitarian life is revealed in the triune God begetting the Christ, the eternal Son in our flesh, and in pouring out the Spirit of Christ upon the church as the triune God pours Him out or breathes Him forth through Christ upon the church.

It is this truth which so profoundly emphasizes that God is the sole Author of all salvation and the sole Party in the establishment and maintenance of the covenant.

God, the triune God, saves by His own work, without the work of man. He, as triune God, elects from all eternity. He, the one true God, one in essence and three in person, redeems through the blood of His own Son who becomes like us in all things except for our sin. And He saves His elect people by giving them His Spirit as the Spirit of Christ, through whose work all the blessings of salvation are communicated from Christ to us. God does it all.

The *Pactum Salutis* means, therefore, that the triune God appoints Christ as the Head and Mediator of the covenant.

This, in Hoeksema's thought, has several important implications.

In the first place, preferring to call the *Pactum Salutis* the "counsel of peace,"[47] Hoeksema distinguishes it from the triune covenant life which God lives in Himself, and from the covenant of grace which God establishes with His people in Christ. He defines it as "the eternal decree of God to reveal His own triune covenant life in the highest possible sense of the word in the establishment and realization of a covenant outside of Himself with the creature in the way of sin and grace, of death and redemption, to the glory of His holy name."[48]

In the second place, Hoeksema is concerned about the relation of the *Pactum Salutis* and the fall of our first parents, Adam and Eve, in Paradise. He does not want God's covenant with Christ to be considered as "an afterthought of God" or "repair work" to try to patch up what Adam spoiled by his disobedience.[49] God's one great purpose in His eternal counsel was to glorify Himself through Jesus Christ. To that one eternal purpose all else is subservient. The original creation, as the "stage" on which the great "drama" of salvation in Christ is "enacted," is subordinate to Christ. The fall of our first parents was under the sovereign control of God and came to pass so that God's purpose might be realized, for "the first Adam falls away in order to make room for the second. In this way, certainly, the matter must be presented. The fall of Adam took place according to God's determinate counsel. No Reformed man may doubt that for a moment."[50]

Looking carefully at Colossians 1:14–20, Hoeksema sees the glorious position which Christ occupies in all God's purpose. He is "the image of the invisible God," but also "the firstborn of every creature." It is the Christ, the eternal Son

---

47. Hoeksema, *Reformed Dogmatics*, 330.
48. Ibid.
49. Hoeksema, "The Covenant: God's Tabernacle With Men," 17.
50. Hoeksema, *Believers and Their Seed*, 80.

of God in our flesh, the Mediator of the covenant, of whom these glorious things are said. And He is these things in order that the riches of God's own covenant life may be gloriously revealed in the highest way possible.[51]

And thus, in the third place, the salvation of the elect in Christ is subordinate to God's glory and the revelation of that glory in Christ. God establishes His covenant with Christ, first of all.[52] God does so because Christ is the Servant of Jehovah.

In Hoeksema's covenant theology, the idea of Christ as the Servant of Jehovah occupies a prominent place.[53] As the Servant of Jehovah, Christ is the One with whom God's covenant is established. Hoeksema writes:

> How, then, must we conceive of what is usually called the *pactum salutis* and which I prefer to name the counsel of peace? It will have become plain that this counsel of peace cannot be the same as the covenant life of God Himself. This is indeed the basis for the counsel of peace, but it is not the counsel itself. God's Being and His counsel are to be distinguished. God's Being is what He is in Himself. The counsel of God represents that which with absolute freedom and sovereignty He determines and wills. To be sure, His counsel is always in harmony with His Being, but it cannot, without anything further, be derived from the Being of God immediately. God's counsel is His free and sovereign decree. If, therefore, we can speak of a counsel of peace, this counsel may not be identified with the covenant life in the Triune God Himself. On the other hand, as we have shown, this counsel is not to be identified with

---

51. Hoeksema, *Reformed Dogmatics*, 331–33. For a detailed exegesis of Colossians 1:14–20, see Hoeksema, "Exegesis of Colossians," 1–9.

52. In his pamphlet "The Covenant, God's Tabernacle with Men," Hoeksema writes, "Centrally, therefore, it is with Him that God establishes His everlasting covenant. That this is true is plain from all Scripture. Just read such passages as II Sam. 7; Pss. 2, 34, 89, 110, and several passages in the prophets, and you will be convinced how biblical is this conception" (p. 18).

53. Hoeksema, *Reformed Dogmatics*, 298–304, where the concept as it appears in the prophecy of Isaiah is discussed at length.

the covenant as God establishes it with His Servant and with the elect church in Christ Jesus our Lord. For this is what is usually designated as the covenant of grace, and must be distinguished from the counsel of peace. The covenant of grace is not the counsel of peace itself, but rather the revelation and realization of it. In the covenant of grace Christ appears as man in His human nature, and as man He can have no place in the decree of the Triune God. If, therefore, mention can be made of a counsel of peace, it must lie between the Triune life of God, which is the basis of all covenant relation with men, and the covenant that is established with Christ and His own as the friend-servant of God. In other words, the counsel of peace must be the decree concerning the covenant. Bearing this in mind, and remembering at the same time that the covenant may not be conceived in an infralapsarian sense, as a means to an end, but that it is itself the purpose and end of all things in the works of God *ad extra*, we would define the counsel of peace as *the eternal decree of God to reveal His own Triune covenant life in the highest possible sense of the word in the establishment and realization of a covenant outside of Himself with the creature in the way of sin and grace, of death and redemption, to the glory of His holy name.* In other words, the counsel of peace, which we can also simply call the counsel of the covenant, is the eternal will, the eternal decree of God to reveal Himself as the God Who lives in Himself a perfect covenant life of friendship, and that by receiving a people in His covenant communion and making it partaker in a creaturely way and according to the measure of the creature in His own covenant life, and thus to cause it to taste that the Lord is good.[54]

So the *Pactum Salutis* takes on a meaning quite different from traditional covenantal theology, but opens the door to a beautiful conception of the covenant of grace.

---

54. Ibid., 330.

CHAPTER 18

The Covenant with Man

One more revelation of the wonder of God's grace we expect in the light of the promise [of the covenant]. For the Son of God must be revealed from heaven. Once again God will bring His Firstborn into the world. Then God's covenant shall be perfected. Old things shall pass away, and He will make all things new. Our mortal bodies shall be made like unto the most glorious body of the Son of God, creation shall be delivered from the bondage of corruption to participate in the glorious liberty of the children of God, and all things shall be made conformable to the glory of the risen Lord. The new Jerusalem shall come down from God out of heaven, and the tabernacle of God shall be with men. And He shall walk with them, and they shall see His face, knowing even as they are known, and taste and declare that the Lord is good!

—Herman Hoeksema, "The Covenant: God's Tabernacle With Men"

The Covenant of Works

It is not surprising that Hoeksema, with his view of the covenant as essentially a bond of friendship and fellowship, would come into conflict with the traditional doctrine of the covenant of works.

Using Dr. Charles Hodge as a representative of the traditional view of the covenant of works,[1] Hoeksema finds

---

1. The reference is to Charles Hodge, *Systematic Theology* (New York: Charles Scribner & Co., 1871), 117ff.

three elements in that view: a condition, a promise, and a penalty. Defining the covenant made with Adam as an agreement between God and Adam, Hodge described the covenant of works as an arrangement in which God promised Adam everlasting life on condition of obedience, and threatened him with death if he disobeyed.[2]

According to Hoeksema, therefore, the following can be said to comprise the view, traditionally held, of the covenant of works: (1) it was an agreement between God and Adam as an arrangement made subsequent to Adam's creation; (2) it was a means to an end; in other words, it was a temporary arrangement to attain the end of eternal life; (3) the specific elements were promise, condition, and threat; (4) Adam was placed on probation for a specific period of time, at the end of which, if Adam had kept his part in the agreement, he would have received life in heaven; and (5) the fruit of this obedience would have been given to all Adam's posterity, in other words, to the whole human race.[3]

Such a view quite obviously did not fit with the idea of the covenant as a bond of friendship between the living God and Adam, God's friend-servant. And so, Hoeksema subjected this traditional view to his usual careful, biblical scrutiny, and found it wanting. His objections were the following.

The chief objection is, quite simply, that the concept had no biblical support. While certainly the threat of death for disobedience is clear enough from Genesis 2, the most important feature of the arrangement, namely, the promise of eternal life, is lacking in Scripture. Obviously, if Adam had not disobeyed, he would have continued to live. But such continuous existence is a far cry from everlasting life in heaven. Continuous existence in the world is one thing; life

---

2. Hoeksema, *Reformed Dogmatics*, 215.
3. Ibid., 216.

in heaven with God is quite another.[4] Take away that promise of everlasting life in heaven, and all that is left is the threat of divine retribution for disobedience. A covenant is not a threat.

Another serious objection is the element of the covenant of works which teaches that man can merit with God. If Adam had obeyed during the entire period of his probation, he would have merited eternal life. No other explanation can be attached to the promise of eternal life than that of merit. But the fact of the matter is that it is forever and under all circumstances impossible to merit with God. Obedience is its own reward. To serve God is a privilege. Would a thousand years of faithful service prompt Adam to claim a reward? Would even the "reward" of eternal life have appealed to Adam, who knew perfect bliss in Paradise? Jesus reminds us that even when we do all that is required of us we are still unprofitable servants and have done only what is our duty (Luke 17:10).[5]

The whole conception raises many problems which are incapable of solution. How long would the probationary period have had to last for Adam to merit eternal life in heaven? How can one who is mortal become immortal when Paul himself says: "Flesh and blood *cannot* inherit the

---

4. Ibid., 217.
5. Ibid., 217, 218. In this objection of Hoeksema we find a fundamental characteristic of all his theology. In keeping with the emphasis of the Reformation against the Roman Catholic idea of merit, Hoeksema abhorred any notion of merit. In whatever form it took, under whatever circumstances it was mentioned, and in whatever connection it was introduced, merit with God was, in Hoeksema's judgment, anathema. God is God. Man is less than a speck of dust. He depends every moment for his entire existence upon God. How can a speck of dust merit with the eternal God? The very idea repelled him. In fact, he saw the whole concept of merit as being the crucial issue in the long and never-ending battle between every form of Arminianism and Pelagianism on the one hand, and the truth of sovereign and particular grace on the other hand. Arminianism, in whatever dress, wanted to introduce into salvation the idea of merit. God is somehow put under obligation to man. The truth of Scripture opposes this conception at every turn.

kingdom of God" (I Cor. 15:50). Not only is sinful man incapable of inheriting the kingdom because corruption cannot put on incorruption; but mere man, earthly man, man created for this present world, cannot be transferred to a spiritual realm.

Add to this list the question of how Adam and Eve would have brought forth the human race, and when the children of Adam and Eve would have gone to heaven. And what about the creation? Would that simply have been abandoned?[6]

But there is still more, equally serious. The covenant of works presents God's covenant with Adam as an arrangement added to the relation between God and Adam, and not intrinsic to the relation. Hoeksema insisted that the covenant was not an "accidental relationship, but . . . fundamental and essential."[7]

Finally, the whole conception is unworthy of God, for it presents the matter as if the original intention of God was to glorify His name through the first Paradise and Adam in it. But this intention was frustrated by Adam's fall when he connived with Satan to unseat God from His throne in the universe. And so God's purpose in Christ becomes an alternative plan, another attempt of God to attain His glory, a rescue effort brought about by unexpected events, or, at least, events over which God had no control.[8]

This did not mean that Hoeksema denied a covenant relation between God and Adam prior to the fall. But that covenant relation was not something "incidental" to Adam's creation; instead, it was "a fundamental relationship in which

---

6. Ibid., 219.

7. Ibid.

8. Ibid., 220. Hoeksema sums up these objections by saying in his book *Believers and Their Seed* that the covenant of works "always makes us stand nostalgically with our noses against the fence of Paradise, with the futile wish in our souls that Adam had not fallen" (p. 67, 1971 ed.).

Adam stood to God by virtue of his creation."[9] Nor is it to be understood as an agreement, but rather as a "relation of living fellowship and friendship," which "requires likeness as its basis."[10]

The "likeness" which fellowship "requires" was given to Adam when he was created in the image of God, in true knowledge, righteousness, and holiness. Moreover:

> By virtue of his being created after the image of God, Adam stood in that covenant relation to God and was conscious of that living fellowship and friendship which is essential to that relationship. He knew God and loved Him and was conscious of God's love to him. He enjoyed the favor of God. He received the Word of God, walked with God and talked with Him; and he dwelled in the house of God in paradise the first. And as he stood at the pinnacle of all created things on earth, the whole creation through him was comprehended in that covenant relation of fellowship. In Adam's heart the whole creation was united to the heart of God.[11]

While holding for the most part to the traditional Reformed view of Adam's position in Paradise as prophet, priest, and king, Hoeksema derived the meaning of these concepts from that one dominating covenant relation in which Adam stood to God.

Adam was God's friend-servant: friend, because of the covenant in which God had placed Adam by virtue of his creation; and servant, because within the bonds of friendship, God remained God and Adam remained a creature, created to love the Lord his God in joyful service. He was assigned work, and that work was described in the command to subdue the earth and have dominion over it.[12]

---

9. Hoeksema, *Reformed Dogmatics*, 222.
10. Ibid.
11. Ibid.
12. Ibid.

Adam was officebearer in God's house: prophet, because he spoke the word of God in the entire creation; priest, because he consecrated himself to God in perfect service; and king, because he ruled in God's name in all God's world.

In this way, and in these circumstances, Adam lived in fellowship with God.[13]

The covenant between God and Adam was in essence like the covenant of grace. But it was only a foreshadowing of the covenant of grace as Adam himself was the "figure of him who was to come" (Rom. 5:14). As glorious as that relationship was, it could not compare, except in a dim way, with the glory of the covenant realized in Christ.

That was the significant and crucially important contribution which Hoeksema made to the traditional idea of the covenant with Adam. And, apart from the fact that such a view is eminently biblical,[14] who would dispute that, over against the rather mechanical and coldly formal idea of an agreement between God and Adam in which was promise, condition, and threat, this view pulses with life, vibrancy, and glory? It is the kind of covenant to which one would like to belong. It is the preference of the warmth of family life in contrast to the cold formalities of the treaty table.

The Image of God in Man

In connection with his discussion of the creation of man as covenant-friend of God, Hoeksema also discussed the meaning of man's creation in God's image. It is understandable that this would be so in the light of the fact that Adam's creation in God's image is presupposed in the covenant relation between them.

But the traditional view of the image in which God created

---

13. Ibid., 224, 225.
14. See, for example, Genesis 5:22; 6:8, 13; 9:9; and 18:17ff.; Isaiah 41:8; James 2:23; and Exodus 33:11.

man was not satisfactory to Hoeksema. He concluded
that the traditional distinction was not found either in the
confessions or in Scripture, and that, in fact, it threatened the
doctrine of sovereign grace.

Reformed theologians traditionally distinguished between
the image in a broader and in a narrower sense. In the
narrower sense of the word, the image of God referred only
to three elements: the true knowledge of God, righteousness,
and holiness. But in the wider sense, the image included
rationality, morality, and immortality.[15]

The difficulty with this distinction (other than that it is
not found either in Scripture or in the confessions) is that
it "prepares room for the further philosophy that there are
remnants of the image of God left in fallen man, and that
therefore the natural man cannot be wholly depraved."[16]

When man fell, he remained a rational, moral creature.
If those attributes belong to the image of God in man,
then some remnants of the image of God in man remained
after the fall. It is not a long jump from that position to the
position that man retains such remnants of the image which
enable him to do some good in the sight of God. And thus the
doctrine of total depravity is denied, which denial necessarily
erodes the truth of salvation by grace alone, a grace which
alone can save a hopelessly and helplessly depraved sinner.[17]

Hoeksema, therefore, preferred a distinction between
image in the formal and image in the material sense. The

---

15. Hoeksema, *Reformed Dogmatics,* 206.
16. Ibid., 207.
17. Ibid., 209. It is in this connection that Hoeksema also considered the
traditional view of immortality to be deficient. It had usually been defined in
terms of "life beyond death"; in other words, immortality simply means that man
has existence beyond death—whether that be in heaven or in hell. Hoeksema
pointed out that that was not the meaning of the word "immortality" in Scripture.
It referred, rather, to eternal life in Christ with God, realized perfectly in glory.
The wicked, though existing after death in hell, only enter full and complete death
in the utter banishment from God's presence in hell. But the righteous are given
immortality as a gift of grace in Jesus Christ (Ibid., 208).

first, image in a formal sense, refers to the fact that man was, in his very nature, able to bear the image of God. That is, only a rational and moral creature can bear that image. A tree cannot bear God's image; nor can an animal. Only man can be image-bearer. But the image proper, or the image in the material sense, composed of knowledge, righteousness, and holiness, is the true image, lost because of sin, and regained by the work of Christ.[18]

Thus, in fact, although man retains his rationality and morality after the fall, he loses the image and becomes totally depraved so that he is unable to contribute anything to his salvation, including even the desire to be saved. In fact, his retention of rationality and morality only makes matters worse, because now, still a rational and moral being, but having lost the image of God, he has become an image-bearer of Satan. The wicked are children of their father, the devil. They look like him in that they do his works (John 8:44).

It might not be superfluous to add at this point that this idea of Hoeksema surely reflects the idea presented in the Reformed confessions. Two articles, one in the Canons of Dordt and one in the Confession of Faith, address this issue. The Canons speak of "glimmerings of natural light, whereby [man] retains some knowledge of God, of natural things, and of the differences between good and evil, and discovers some regard for virtue, good order in society, and for maintaining an orderly external deportment."[19] That the Canons did not mean to say that man retains some ability to do good is evident from the remainder of the article, which reads: "But so far is this light of nature from being sufficient to bring him to a saving knowledge of God, and to true conversion, that he is incapable of using it aright even in things natural and civil.

---

18. Ibid., 208, 209.
19. Canons of Dordt, III & IV, 4. This part of the article was quoted by the synod of the CRC in 1924 as proof of man's retention of part of the image, which enabled him to do some good in the sight of God.

Nay further, this light, such as it is, man in various ways renders wholly polluted, and holds it in unrighteousness, by doing which he becomes inexcusable before God."[20]

The Confession of Faith speaks of the fact that man, at the fall, "lost all his excellent gifts, which he had received from God, and only retained a few remains thereof, which, however, are sufficient to leave man without excuse."[21]

By these expressions in the confessions ("glimmerings of natural light" and "remnants of excellent gifts") the fathers referred to the fact that man remained a rational and moral creature. That is the dreadful part of the fall. Man remains a man. But he is now a depraved man, so that he uses the remnants of the excellent gifts with which he had been endowed to sin against God in everything he does. And it is crucial to notice that of these excellent gifts man retains only remnants and glimmerings. Man's present powers of rationality are the tatters of a beautiful fur coat which served as a feast for moths throughout the summer. His remnants of the gifts of natural light are roughly comparable to the light of a candle in comparison to the sun. And these he uses to sin. That is the teaching of the confessions.[22]

Election and Reprobation

One cannot discuss the doctrine of the covenant as developed by Hoeksema without discussing also the doctrine of eternal predestination. Hoeksema himself, after his lengthy discussion of the *Pactum Salutis*, writes: "In the light of this presentation it will be plain that also the counsel of predestination follows logically upon the counsel

---

20. This part of Article 4 was strangely omitted when the synod of 1924, which made common grace official teaching in the church, quoted the first part.

21. Confession of Faith, Article 14, which article was also quoted in support of common grace.

22. Hoeksema, *Reformed Dogmatics*, 209–13.

of peace. It serves the counsel of peace even as the counsel of providence serves the counsel of predestination."[23]

The whole idea of the relation between election and the covenant was a major point of conflict between Schilder and Hoeksema, between the Liberated and the PRC, in the controversies of the late 1940s and early 1950s. The LC did not want to connect election with the covenant in any sense of the word, for these churches could never maintain a general promise to all the children baptized if the membership in the covenant was determined by election and reprobation. One of the chief reasons for the final breach between Schilder and Hoeksema was Hoeksema's insistence on the doctrine of predestination and its application to the doctrine of the covenant.[24] Faber writes, in defense of Schilder, "Moreover, covenant and election are not identical. The number of God's elect is quantitatively not the same as the number of the members of God's covenant."[25] The PRC have emphatically rejected that position.

I need not treat Hoeksema's doctrine of predestination in detail, for he never departed a hair's breadth from the view of the church which had been held from the time of Augustine. He maintained the doctrine as it was taught by Augustine in the fifth century, Gotteschalk in the ninth century, Luther and Calvin at the time of the Reformation, the fathers at the the synod of Dordt, and the orthodox line of theologians in continental and Presbyterian theology since then.

Many specific instances can be cited as examples of Hoeksema's teaching on this subject. The truth of sovereign predestination was woven into the warp and woof of his

---

23. Ibid., 331.
24. In "American Secession Theologians" Dr. Faber devotes a section to a discussion of the relation between election and the covenant in the thinking of Secession theologians and their influence on the thinking of Schilder (pp. 29–35).
25. Ibid., 29.

theology, to such an extent, in fact, that he was often accused of a wrong preoccupation with the doctrine.[26]

There are, however, several areas in which Hoeksema's discussion of this central doctrine is important. In fact, Hoeksema at least made explicit what had been implicit in earlier Reformed theology, and at best developed various aspects of the doctrine in its relation to other truths of Holy Writ.

From a supralapsarian viewpoint, Hoeksema viewed election as "in Christ." God chose to reveal Himself in the highest and best possible way. That way was through His own Son, our Lord Jesus Christ, and the salvation of an elect people in Christ.[27] The election of that people, chosen in Christ before the foundation of the world, is not the election of a mere mass, an arbitrary group of people, but the election of an organic whole which, in Christ, is a perfect unity. It can be compared with a temple[28] in which every saint has his or her place, and in which place he or she contributes to the beauty of the whole. In this temple Jesus Christ is the

---

26. Hoeksema's major works that deal with the subject in a systematic way are: *Reformed Dogmatics*, 159–65, and *The Triple Knowledge*, vol. 2, 189–208. Specific writings dealing just with that subject are: (1) Herman Hoeksema, "The Place of Reprobation in the Preaching of the Gospel" (Grand Rapids: Evangelism Committee of Southwest Protestant Reformed Church, 1993). The text was originally a speech given May 1927 in Dutch and transcribed in Dutch for publication by the Men's Society of the First Protestant Reformed Church, Grand Rapids. Later it was translated into English by Cornelius Hanko, which translation constitutes the current pamphlet. (2) Herman Hoeksema, "Predestination: Revealed, Not Hidden nor Confused" (Grand Rapids: Radio Committee of the First Protestant Reformed Church, 1948). (3) Herman Hoeksema, "Predestination: The Heart of the Gospel" (Grand Rapids: Radio Committee of the First Protestant Reformed Church, 1949). The last two pamphlets were collections of radio sermons that Hoeksema delivered over the Reformed Witness Hour. See also Herman Hoeksema, *God's Eternal Good Pleasure*, ed. and partially revised by Homer C. Hoeksema from a 1940 ed. (Grand Rapids: Reformed Free Publishing Association, 1979). This book contains a series of sermons Hoeksema preached on Romans 9–11.

27. Hoeksema, *Reformed Dogmatics*, 331–36.

28. Ephesians 2:20–22, for example.

Cornerstone. When the building is completed, no stones are left over, nor are there gaps in the building because the material was insufficient to complete it. With Christ, the church is God's bride, God's temple and dwelling place, the object of God's eternal love, His own covenant people, who show forth God's praise.[29]

The doctrine of sovereign reprobation is related to the doctrine of election. Although Hoeksema has been charged with teaching the equal ultimacy of election and reprobation,[30] that is, that election and reprobation are two equally important decrees, Hoeksema did not do this, but made reprobation subordinate to election, as chaff is necessary for the growth and maturation of the wheat.[31] Hoeksema insisted, as the Canons do, that election and reprobation are one decree with two sides to it.[32] The two sides constitute one decree because the one without the other is impossible, and because election is served by reprobation.[33]

This doctrine of sovereign predestination, including both election and reprobation, is "the heart of the gospel,"[34] not only because it is the heart of the contents of the gospel, which is the "good news" that God has sent Christ to save His elect, but also because by the preaching of this gospel the

---

29. See also Hoeksema, *The Triple Knowledge*, vol. 2, 199–208.

30. James Daane, *The Freedom of God: A Study of Election and Pulpit* (Grand Rapids: Wm. B. Eerdmans Publishing Co., 1973), 35, 36, 138, on which pages Daane calls Hoeksema's view "demonic."

31. Hoeksema, "The Place of Reprobation in the Preaching of the Gospel," 9–12.

32. This is the position bitterly attacked by Daane in *The Freedom of God*, 35, 36, 138. But the Canons of Dordt read: "That some receive the gift of faith from God, and others do not receive it proceeds from God's eternal decree . . . according to which decree he graciously softens the hearts of the elect . . . , while he leaves the non-elect in his just judgment to their own wickedness and obduracy" (Canons I, 6).

33. Hoeksema, *Reformed Dogmatics*, 334.

34. See Hoeksema, "Predestination: The Heart of the Gospel."

elect are saved and the reprobate hardened and damned in the way of their impenitence.[35]

Election and the Covenant

Finally, the doctrine of election and reprobation was closely connected to the doctrine of the covenant.

As we noticed in an earlier connection, Dr. Schilder did not want to connect election to the covenant because that would make impossible his contention that the promise of salvation is for all who are baptized.

Hoeksema insisted that the truth of election must be applied to the doctrine of the covenant. In fact, this is an outstanding aspect of Hoeksema's covenant theology, and constitutes a major advance in an understanding of the doctrine.

In the history of the church, theologians always found difficulty connecting the truth of predestination to the covenant of grace. This difficulty arose out of the fact that the covenant was interpreted as an agreement or pact. Those theologians who strongly emphasized eternal predestination, including both election and reprobation, found difficulty in relating God's eternal predestination to a covenant which was an agreement. An agreement does not fit very well with predestination.

If the true nature of a covenant is indeed such an agreement, it follows that the agreement would be in force only if man would consent to enter the agreement, that is, only if man would fulfill the conditions attached to the agreement. Thus the whole covenant rests, in some measure, on man's cooperation, willingness, and obedience.

---

35. Hoeksema, *The Triple Knowledge*, vol. 2, 710, 712. This is only one reference. In his opposition to the gospel as a well-meant offer, Hoeksema was fond of pointing out that Scripture speaks of the gospel, not as an offer, but as "the power of God unto salvation to every one that believeth" (Rom. 1:16); and he gave this title to one of his important books, *Een Kracht Gods Tot Zaligheid, of Genade Geen Aanbod* (A Power of God unto Salvation, or Grace Not an Offer).

If God's covenant with man must be described in terms of an agreement, the agreement remains in force only as long as man continues to maintain the conditions and provisions under which the original covenant was established. Thus man plays a role in the continuation of the covenant as well as in its establishment.

But such a view of the covenant does not square with predestination. The doctrine of predestination is God's eternal decree by which He sovereignly determines who shall be incorporated into His covenant and who shall not. Further, while a view of the covenant which contains conditions always leaves the conditions to man to be fulfilled, the confessions teach that eternal election is itself the fountain of all saving good. This view of election makes conditions impossible, for it rules out any cooperation of man in the work of salvation, and makes the covenant dependent only on God's work.

We can see, therefore, that theologians faced a difficult problem. Because the covenant was viewed as an agreement, it had conditions attached to it. But predestination could not be harmonized with a conditional covenant in any possible way. Hence, it is not surprising that some theologians wanted to separate election entirely from the doctrine of the covenant.

But here the beauty of the biblical concept comes to its own. According to Hoeksema, the covenant, in its essence, is not an agreement at all, but a bond of fellowship and friendship between God and His people in Christ. God is, in Himself, a covenant God. He sovereignly and freely determines to reveal the riches of His own covenant life in Christ, His eternal Son. He does this by choosing unto Himself a people in Christ, who will be incorporated into His own covenant life through Christ, and thus will be God's own covenant people. That people, chosen from eternity, redeemed by the blood of Christ, is sovereignly called into existence by the efficacious call of the gospel. They are preserved by that same gospel throughout all their life in the world. They are, through the wonder of God's grace, brought into the everlasting life of heaven in which God's covenant is realized perfectly when the tabernacle of God is with men.[36] Thus salvation is all of God without any contribution which man must make.

There is a consistency, a harmony, a unifying theme in the treatment of the doctrine of the covenant in its relation to other doctrines of Scripture. The dilemma into which earlier theologians fell disappeared. The unity between God's covenant and the truth of predestination was plain.

This beautiful view of the covenant remains the keystone of the truth of Scripture as maintained by the PRC.[37]

A Particular and Unconditional Promise

We have already noticed that the covenant view taught by W. Heyns at Calvin College and Seminary became the view of the LC. Among other things, this view identified the covenant with the promise of God. When in baptism God promises every baptized child that if that child believes, he will be saved, that is the same as establishing the covenant with that child. Every child is, from that moment on, in the covenant.

However, that covenant is established with every child only in an external sense, just as every child possesses the

---

36. This theme so dominates in Hoeksema's writings that it is impossible to make reference to every instance. I give here some of his major works: *Believers and Their Seed*, 52, 53, 64, 111; "Our Calling," 17; *Reformed Dogmatics*, 331, 334–36. I cite only one reference in the *Standard Bearer* among many: "Our Conference with Dr. Schilder," 102, 103. See also Gertrude Hoeksema, *Therefore Have I Spoken*, 104.

37. David J. Engelsma, "The Covenant of God and the Children of Believers" (South Holland, Ill.: Evangelism Committee of South Holland Protestant Reformed Church, 1990), 15, 16. See also my *God's Everlasting Covenant of Grace* (Grand Rapids: Reformed Free Publishing Association, 1988).

promise in an external sense. That is, as far as his outward life is concerned, the child is within the covenant. Whether that child actually receives the promise subjectively—in other words, internally, within the heart—depends upon his fulfillment of the condition of faith.

The figure of a check was sometimes used. At baptism God gives a check to the baptized child on which is written: "I, God, promise you (baptized child) the sum of eternal life." The check was signed by God. That check is very really the possession of the one who receives it.

But such a child, when come to years of discretion and understanding, can do a number of things with that check. He can, for example, frame it, hang it in a prominent place on the wall of his home, and show others that he possesses a treasure that God has given him, signed by God Himself. Such a one is like the person in the church who boasts of his membership in the church, of the sign of baptism which he carries on his forehead, and of the privileges which are his by virtue of a Christian home and church. But the check does him no good.

Another alternative would be that the child who receives the check would, despising it and considering it worthless, rip it up and throw the pieces in the wastebasket. Such a child would be comparable to a "covenant breaker," who, despising God's covenant, would walk in the ways of sin and the world.

But the demand of God which comes along with the check is this: endorse the check, take it to the bank of heaven, and there cash it. This action would be the same as by faith accepting the promise of God and receiving the promised salvation as one's subjective possession.

Such a promise is general (to all the baptized children) and conditional (dependent upon faith for its realization).

This view of the covenant Hoeksema branded as Arminian. It was Arminian because it left the full realization of the covenant to man's act of faith which he is able to exercise.

Thus faith becomes man's work, and man makes the significant and decisive contribution to his salvation which guarantees him a place in heaven.

It was (and is) argued by those who defend this view of the promise of God that the faith which is required for the promise to be realized is, after all, the gift of God which God works in the hearts of His elect people. It is argued that ascribing faith to God's work guarantees that one escapes the quicksand of Arminianism and remains Reformed.

But such is not the case. One cannot so easily escape the charge of Arminianism.[38] If the promise of the covenant is for all who are baptized, and if the condition for the full realization of the covenant is faith, and if not all are finally brought into that covenant, then faith is man's work.

It was put in a slightly different form during the controversy with the LC. The question was repeatedly put to those who held to a general and conditional promise: Is faith a part of the promise, or a condition to the promise? It cannot be both. If it is a part of the promise, it is no longer a condition to the promise. If it is a condition to the promise, it cannot be a part of the promise—unless faith is a condition to faith. Thus, if the promise of God is that He will give all the blessings of salvation unto His people, then faith, one of those blessings, is also a part of the promise, and cannot be a condition to it. But if faith remains a condition to a promise, then, excluded from the promise, it is excluded from the work of God and can only remain a work of man.[39]

The PRC have maintained from the beginning of their history that God's promise is particular and unconditional.[40]

---

38. Hoeksema, *Reformed Dogmatics*, 697, 698; Hoeksema, *Believers and Their Seed*, 20–22; Hoeksema, *The Triple Knowledge*, vol. 2, 547–51. Because this issue of a general and conditional promise vs. a particular and unconditional promise was at the heart of the controversy with the LC in the late 1940s and early 1950s, it is repeatedly referred to in articles in the *Standard Bearer*.

39. Hoeksema and Hanko, *Ready to Give an Answer*, 179, 182–85.

40. Hoeksema pointed out that a general and conditional promise was much like a well-meant offer of the gospel, the former relating only to baptism within the

God's promise is, from a formal point of view, an oath which God swears by Himself because He can swear by none higher (Heb. 6:16–18). This oath God adds to His counsel so that "by two immutable things, in which it was impossible for God to lie, we might have a strong consolation, who have fled for refuge to lay hold upon the hope set before us" (Heb. 6:18).

As far as its content is concerned, the promise of God is the promise of His covenant which God swears to Abraham and his seed: "For when God made promise to Abraham, because he could swear by no greater, he sware by himself, saying, Surely blessing I will bless thee, and multiplying I will multiply thee" (Heb. 6:13, 14). This promise includes all the blessings of the covenant: in other words, all the blessings of salvation which God gives to His people in Christ.

That promise of salvation God makes only to His elect children and their elect seed. So it was in the case of Abraham; so it is always (Gen. 17:7; Rom. 9:6–13; Gal. 3:14–18, 29). That promise is therefore particular, in other words, to the elect only. It is not a promise which God swears to all the children who are baptized; it is a promise made to believers and their elect seed.[41]

That promise is unconditional in every sense of the word. A general promise has to be conditional. But a particular promise is unconditional. That is, God fulfills His own

---

covenant and the latter referring more broadly to the preaching (*Believers and Their Seed*, 20).

41. The PRC have never denied, as has been alleged, that that particular promise had to be generally proclaimed. That is, the gospel is "good news" exactly because it brings God's promise of salvation. That gospel proclamation of the promise is made widely and generally, but it is the general proclamation of a particular promise. The gospel proclaims that the promise of God is to a particular people: in other words, to believers. And believers are those who have been given the gift of faith, namely, the elect. This is the teaching of the Canons of Dordt, II, 5. See the "Declaration of Principles," in which it is shown beyond doubt that this view of a particular and unconditional promise is the teaching of the Reformed Confessions. The Declaration may be found in Hoeksema and Hanko, *Ready to Give an Answer*, 203–33, and in Gertrude Hoeksema, *A Watered Garden*, 361–72. See also Appendix F, 434–60.

promise. He does so as His own sovereign work. He establishes His covenant; He maintains His covenant. Nothing is left for man to do. God does it all, for salvation is by grace, through faith, and that not of ourselves; it is the gift of God, not of works, lest anyone should boast (Eph. 2:8, 9).

The PRC are aware of the fact that the use of the word "condition" has not always been Arminian. As was shown at the time of the controversy in the early 1950s, many ministers, including the leaders of the denomination, had used the word repeatedly. The word was often used in the past as a way of making God's work of salvation a particular and not a general work. The condition defined the objects of salvation. "If one believes, he will be saved." That is, only believers will be saved. No one else can or ever will inherit salvation.

And, in connection with the use of the term as a limiting clause, a condition also expressed the way in which God saved. When God says in His Word, If you believe, you will be saved, God not only limits salvation to believers, but He also defines faith as the way in which salvation is given. For salvation is by grace, and through faith.

That use of the term was frequent and legitimate.

But gradually the word itself was abandoned. This was done for two reasons. One reason was that the term "condition" is not once found in all the Reformed confessions—except as a term used by the Arminians.[42] The other reason was that the term had taken on so many Arminian connotations that its very use conjured up in the mind of the listener Arminian thoughts.

A good biblical and confessional word may be used by the church even when Arminians corrupt it. This is the case, for example, with the word "world," which the Arminians make

---

42. The word "condition" is found in the Canons of Dordt in sections where the Arminian heresy is condemned. See I, B, 4; II, B, 3; V, B, 1.

refer to every individual head for head—as in John 3:16. Ministers may not permit Arminians to take that word from the vocabulary of Reformed people by giving it an un-Reformed connotation. But when a term, such as "condition," is used neither in Scripture nor in the confessions, then it is better to abandon it to those who use it to introduce into the truth erroneous and unbiblical ideas.

Human Responsibility

The charge has been made against the position of the PRC that it negates human responsibility and reduces man to a stock and a block.[43] In fact, this was the chief charge made against the PR position by the LC. The promise had to be to all who were baptized and the demands of the covenant had to be emphasized because human responsibility had to be preserved. Man is more than an automaton. He is commanded to believe. If he believes, he is saved. If he refuses to believe, he is damned.

This charge of denying human responsibility has been consistently repudiated by the PRC.

The Baptism Form, used for the administration of the sacrament of baptism in the PRC, in its didactic part speaks of "parts" in the covenant.[44] Hoeksema was quick to point out that this could not possibly be changed into "parties," because one can speak of parties only in an agreement. It takes two parties to make an agreement. But the responsibility of those in the covenant is properly called their "part." "God calls us, and we come. God gives the living faith, and we believe. God justifies us, and we stand in righteousness. God sanctifies us, and we love Him with all our heart and mind

---

43. For an example of this, see A. C. De Jong, *The Well-Meant Gospel Offer: The Views of H. Hoeksema and K. Schilder* (Franeker, Netherlands: T. Weaver, 1954), 81.

44. "Whereas in all covenants, there are contained two parts, therefore are we by God through baptism admonished of, and obliged unto new obedience . . ." Form for the Administration of Baptism.

and soul and strength, forsake the world, and crucify our old nature, walking in a new and holy life. God preserves us unto the end, and we persevere and fight the good fight even unto the end. Our part in the covenant is the fruit of God's part."[45]

Thus, all the work of salvation remains God's work, so that He may receive all the glory. Perhaps the PR position is best summed up by the words of Herman Hoeksema in a speech on this very subject:

> Once more I say: that (the doctrine of total depravity) is also denied by the Pelagian, the very superficial, the individualistic, the modernistic Pelagian, that always emphasizes man rather than God. I always say, beloved: Give me God, if I must make a choice. If I must make a choice to lose God or man, give me God. Let me lose man. It's all right to me: no danger there. Give me God! That's Reformed. And that's especially Protestant Reformed! Give me God: there is no salvation in Man![46]

The Covenant with the Creation

A distinctive feature of the doctrine of the covenant as developed and maintained in the PRC is the truth that the covenant of grace is established with the entire creation, which also is, finally, brought into the perfection of God's covenant in heaven.

God's purpose to establish His covenant with the entire creation, though finally realized in Christ, is first revealed in Adam's relation to the first Paradise.

> In paradise God reveals Himself to Adam and speaks to him as a friend with his friend, and Adam knew God in the cool of the

---

45. Hoeksema, "Our Calling," 19.
46. Herman Hoeksema, "Man's Freedom and Responsibility," *SB* 29 (July 1, 1953): 415. This was a transcript of a commencement speech delivered by Hoeksema as rector of the Theological School of the Protestant Reformed Churches.

day. The first creation is concentrated in paradise, the house of God; paradise has its center in the tree of life, that sacrament of God's covenant of friendship; and the whole is concentrated in man, the house-servant of God. The whole earthly creation has its ethical center in the heart of man, and through that heart all creation lies at the heart of God! Adam was the friend of God.[47]

God never intended to realize His full purpose in Adam. Adam's fall into sin, though it remained Adam's horrible rebellion, was also within the eternal determination of God's counsel.[48]

> We see the order of creation, the fall, sin, death, the curse . . .
> Hence, in the first paradise we behold the first, the earthly realization of God's covenant of friendship . . .
> However . . . , [man] violated God's covenant of friendship, and allied himself with the prince of darkness, the enemy of God . . . Return into God's fellowship of friendship has become humanly impossible. The door is closed.
> But what is impossible with man is possible with God. He had provided some better thing for us: the everlasting perfection of His covenant of friendship in Christ . . . The ground is cursed, and the earth will bring forth thorns and thistles. Not only will man eat his bread in the sweat of his face, but he will also eat and drink his own death. And the creature is subjected to vanity, so that all real culture by the fallen lord of creation is become impossible. But upon that stage God reveals His blessed covenant, and in that darkness He causes the light of His promise, the light that shines from the face of the risen Lord, to penetrate, and to fill the heirs of the promise with hope.
> That covenant is revealed to Noah and his seed, as a covenant that embraces the whole creation in its scope. And the bow in the clouds is the sign of the final deliverance for the entire groaning creation . . .[49]

---

47. Hoeksema, "The Covenant: God's Tabernacle With Men," 13, 14.
48. This was originally set down by Danhof and Hoeksema in 1923 in *Van Zonde en Genade*, 40, 91, 142.
49. Ibid., 19–22.

But God's covenant with the creation is realized only through Christ. Adam's relation to all things was only the figure of Christ's relation to all. As Adam was the federal head of the human race and as all fell in Adam, so is Christ the Head of the human race of His elect and all are made alive through Him. As Adam was the servant-king of the creation, so Christ is the Servant-King of all things.

> For Christ is not an afterthought of God, so to speak, but in the counsel of God He is the Firstborn. Salvation is no repair work, but the realization of God's eternal covenant, even through the deep way of sin and grace. Not the first world, but the new creation, of which the risen Lord is the Head, and in which the tabernacle of God shall be with men, is the goal, the purpose of God from eternity. All the rest is means, belongs to the way to that goal. And since all things in the new and heavenly world that is to come are concentrated in the glorified Son of God in the flesh, and all things are created unto Him and for Him, we repeat that, in the eternal good pleasure, the glorified, risen Christ is the firstborn of every creature. In Him God wants to reveal and realize the glory of His everlasting covenant.[50]

Hoeksema found this great truth especially in Colossians 1:15ff. In connection with that passage, he writes:

> Centrally, therefore, it is with [Christ] that God establishes His everlasting covenant. That this is true is plain from all the Scriptures. Just read such passages as II Samuel 7; Psalm 2; 34; 89; 110, and several passages in the prophets, and you will be convinced how biblical is this conception. But the glory of God's covenant of friendship, centered in the risen Lord, must shine forth in a multitude of people, the glorified church. He

---

50. Ibid., 17. Hoeksema was by no means the first in the long line of Reformed theologians to speak of the renewal of all things in the new heavens and the new earth. But Hoeksema, from the viewpoint of his perspective of the covenant as a bond of friendship, could relate this final renewal of all things to the covenant. And, from his supralapsarian viewpoint, he could demonstrate how this final glorification of all things in Christ was the one great purpose of God to which even Adam was subordinate.

must be firstborn among many brethren. Hence, God ordains all the elect, and gives them to Christ. In Him they are chosen. According to His image they must be conformed, in order that the blessed covenant of friendship might be reflected in and established with millions upon millions of sons of God, and thus all might redound to the abundant praise of God.

And what is more, to this glorified Christ and His church all things are given in heaven and on earth. For Christ is the head of heaven and earth. In Him as the head, all things must be gathered together, that the whole creation may be one glorious house of God, embracing every creature, and all things may serve the new man in Christ, that he may serve his God. And unto that end, the final, heavenly realization of God's all embracing covenant, all things in time are strictly subordinated and made subservient, creation and the fall, sin and death, the powers of darkness and the revelation of God's grace in Jesus Christ our Lord. All things must serve the highest realization of God's eternal covenant of friendship.[51]

Who is not moved to adoration of the one true God by this marvelous truth!

---

51. Ibid., 18, 19.

CHAPTER 19

*B*elievers and Their Seed

If one lives out of faith, then he will say: "Lord, I thank Thee that Thou hast counted me worthy to bring forth children for Thy eternal covenant. From Thy grace I desire to receive my children. According to Thy covenant I want to bring them up in the fear of Thy name. For the sake of Thy name and Thy covenant, it is also the desire of my heart that all my children walk in the ways of Thy covenant. But ultimately I desire to serve nothing else than Thy good pleasure. And bowing before Thy divine majesty, I thank Thee when Thou dost save Thy children out of my children and dost receive them in glory."
—Herman Hoeksema, *Believers and Their Seed*

Introduction

The PRC have by no means expressed a new position in the history of the Reformed churches by their doctrine of the covenant in the line of the generations of believers. Already at the time of the Anabaptist controversies in Switzerland, the Reformers stressed the truth that infants had to be baptized because they as well as adults are included in God's covenant of grace. And this truth was consistently maintained in all Reformed and Presbyterian theology.

Furthermore, the PRC are by no means alone in their insistence on the truth that the sovereign decree of God in election and reprobation cuts through covenant lines and the children of believers, so that God's covenant is established only with the elect children of believers and not with all children. Also this position, though denied by some, has been held by an illustrious company of Reformed theologians.[1]

In fact, it is not unique to the PRC to maintain that, as a general rule in God's covenant, the elect children of the covenant are regenerated in infancy. Many in the Reformed tradition who considered the covenant to be an agreement between two parties, God and man, denied this truth because, quite obviously, babies cannot agree to anything.

But others held firmly to the truth that infants also are incorporated into the covenant. In fact, this very truth is imbedded in some of the oldest confessions of the Reformed churches. The Heidelberg Catechism, dating from 1563, emphatically asserts that infants are to be baptized because they, as well as adults, are comprehended in the covenant of grace.[2] And the "Form for the Administration of Baptism" speaks of the children of believers as "sanctified in Christ" and "members of His church." In the prayer of thanksgiving, the church rejoices before God that He has "forgiven us *and our children*, all our sins, through the blood of thy beloved Son Jesus Christ."[3]

Various Questions

But two questions especially troubled the Reformed churches for centuries and are still today subjects for much dispute. They are: Do all the children of believers who are baptized belong to the covenant? And, in closest connection

---

1. See Engelsma, "The Covenant of God and the Children of Believers," 16–19, for examples of these theologians.
2. Lord's Day XXVII, Q & A 74.
3. The emphasis is mine. There has been dispute over the meaning of these words. Some have tried to make them refer to an objective sanctification and an objective forgiveness of sin which is subjectively applied only upon the condition of faith. But this is not the obvious meaning of these expressions, nor is the notion of an objective sanctification ever found in Scripture. Many Reformed theologians held to the position that the reference is indeed to subjective, saving sanctification. See Hoeksema, *Believers and Their Seed*, 50–53.

with that: Knowing that Scripture teaches that not all the children who are baptized are saved, why does the church nevertheless baptize them all?[4]

We must understand this latter question. Any Reformed man would answer it by pointing out that the church baptizes all the children of believers because Scripture commands the church to do this.[5] But the question remains, Why should God command the church to baptize all the children of believing parents when God Himself knows that He does not intend to save them all?

It is to this question that various answers have been given.

Dr. Abraham Kuyper had based the baptism of all the children born in covenant lines on the doctrine of presupposed regeneration. That is, the church and covenant parents baptize all the children because they are to "presuppose" that all these children are in fact regenerated. This view has received sharp criticism by Reformed theologians and has been rejected out of hand as an entirely unsatisfactory ground for baptism.[6]

Others, following W. Heyns and the LC, have answered the question by saying that all the children of believers must be baptized because all, without exception, receive God's promise of salvation. And, because these churches identify the promise of salvation with the covenant, they teach that

---

4. This last question is, of course, the crucial question with those who hold to believers' baptism. Since not all children are saved, the church must wait for a profession of faith before it may legitimately baptize.

5. While we are not primarily concerned here with the question of the biblical grounds for the baptism of infants, this question has repeatedly been addressed by PR theologians. Confer Herman Hoeksema, "The Biblical Ground for the Baptism of Infants" (Grand Rapids: Sunday School of the First Protestant Reformed Church, 1990); Hoeksema, *Believers and Their Seed,* 84–97; Hoeksema, *Reformed Dogmatics,* 680–700; Herman Hanko, *We and Our Children: The Reformed Doctrine of Infant Baptism* (Grand Rapids: Reformed Free Publishing Association, 1981); Engelsma, "The Covenant of God and the Children of Believers."

6. Hoeksema, *Believers and Their Seed,* 46–57. In this book, Hoeksema devotes an entire chapter to a criticism of Kuyper's view.

all the children of believers are included in the covenant, and must, therefore, receive the sign of the covenant. But the promise is always conditional, and unless they fulfill the condition of faith, these children will become covenant breakers.[7]

This view has also been sharply criticized by the PRC, and was, in fact, the major bone of contention in the controversy of the late 1940s and early 1950s which resulted in a split in the PRC. It has been criticized as ignoring the role that election plays in the covenant, and as introducing an Arminian element into the doctrine.

The Organism of the Covenant

Rejecting both the position of Kuyper and the Arminian conception of the LC, Hoeksema broke new ground in his answer to this question by introducing the concept of the "organic" conception of God's covenant.

Hoeksema taught that the church of Jesus Christ, in its historical development and manifestation in the world, must be considered an organism. That is, it must be looked at as one living, unified body in its relation to Christ its life, in which each member has his place, and which grows and develops throughout all time.

In this conception Hoeksema was following a scriptural teaching according to which the nation of Israel is compared to a vine in Psalm 80 and to a vineyard in Isaiah 5. In like manner, the church is compared to the branches of a vine in John 15, of which Jesus is the vine itself, and God the husbandman; or to an olive tree in Romans 11, the natural olive tree being the nation of Israel, from which the branches are cut off, while branches from a wild olive tree, the Gentiles, are grafted in.

---

7. I have described this view in different connections and only mention it here as it becomes the ground for infant baptism.

Especially in these latter figures, it becomes clear that the branches, whether of the vine or the olive tree, are not individuals, but generations, that is, believing parents and their seed, many of whom, becoming with their children branches in their own right, are cut out of the vine in subsequent generations.

Scripture also often uses, to express a similar idea, the figure of wheat, or any other grain. This figure is used in two different ways in Scripture. Sometimes it is used to refer to the entire field in which are wheat and tares (Matt. 13); and sometimes it is used from the viewpoint of a single wheat plant, of which part is wheat and part is chaff (Ps. 1; Matt. 3:12; etc.).

These figures are used by Scripture as helpful illustrations from the creation to depict God's work in His covenant. The covenant line begins with our first parents, who were saved immediately after the fall and who received the promise of Christ as recorded in Genesis 3:15. This covenant line continues throughout the Old Testament in the line of Seth, Enoch, Noah, Shem, Abraham, Isaac, Jacob, Judah, David, Solomon, etc. In the new dispensation, that line is expanded to include in it all the nations of the earth as the church breaks out of the narrow confines of Jewry and the gospel is brought to the nations. Then believers from Jews and Gentiles are the true seed of Abraham (Gal. 3:29). But still, also in the new dispensation, the principle is the covenant in the line of generations.

Nevertheless, as that "tree" or "vine" of the covenant line in its historical manifestation grows throughout history, it is subject to constant pruning. This was true in Abraham's family when Ishmael was cast out, in Isaac's family when God made distinction between Jacob and Esau, and throughout Israel's history, for the true seed of the promise was never every individual born within the nation. And, finally, the branches in the old "olive tree" were all cut out, that branches from a wild olive tree could be grafted in.

Thus, not all the children of believers are saved. Nor did God ever promise the salvation of all children of believers when He promised to be the God of His people and the God of their seed after them. The reason why not every child of believers is saved is, finally, God's eternal decree of election and reprobation, because God loved Jacob, but He hated Esau. Predestination cuts right through covenant lines.

Undoubtedly, Scripture uses these figures of a vine, a stalk of wheat, etc., because they illustrate some important truths concerning God's work in His covenant.

In the first place, the figures show the relation between election and reprobation as this decree of God cuts through covenant lines. The kernels of wheat cannot grow and mature without the straw or chaff. Is the chaff worth anything in itself? No, it is scattered from the threshing floor and carried away by the wind. But it is, nevertheless, useful and necessary for the growing of the wheat. So also reprobation, in God's inscrutable wisdom, serves election, and the reprobate serve the elect.

In the second place, this truth, so forcefully set down in Scripture, serves as the ground for the baptism of all the children born of believers. God deals with His covenant people as an organism. So He dealt with Israel; so He deals with the church. All within the church must be treated the same. All must be baptized; all must be given Christian instruction in the home, the church, and the school. All must come under the preaching.

A farmer does no differently. He fertilizes and irrigates his field of wheat, even though he knows that this treatment of his field will also cause the tares to grow more rapidly. The rain from heaven and the sunshine come down on wheat and tares alike as the preaching comes to all in the church and as baptism is administered to all the children. But, as Matthew 13:24–30, 36–43 and Hebrews 6:7, 8 (almost a commentary on Matthew 13) point out, God's purpose is exactly that the tares may be manifested as tares and the wheat come to maturity as wheat. In this way God accomplishes His sovereign purposes.

In the third place, both the church and parents in the home are obligated to deal with their children according to "the judgment of charity." Calvin already used this expression in connection with his discussion of the presence of hypocrites in the visible church and our attitude towards them as long as they remain hypocrites and do not reveal their true spiritual identity. So also our Reformed fathers spoke of our attitude towards our children. We deal with them all in the same fashion. We consider them true children of God's covenant until such a time as they show the opposite.[8]

This viewpoint towards the children in the line of the covenant has sometimes been rejected as another form of Kuyper's presupposed regeneration. But this is wrong. In the first place, this judgment of love is the only attitude which makes possible the communion of saints within the church of Christ. If the saints go about mutually making decisions concerning which of their fellow members are true believers and which are hypocrites, suspicion and false accusation will destroy the church. The saints will come under the frightening warning of Christ: "Judge not that ye be not judged" (Matt. 7:1).

In the second place, neither the church nor parents may presuppose that all their children are regenerated. They know, from the Word of God, that this is not so, and they do not deceive themselves into thinking the contrary. But they

---

8. Hoeksema, *Believers and Their Seed*, 132–150. This is in a chapter entitled "The Reprobate in the Sphere of the Covenant."

recognize that they are not in a position to pass judgment on the spiritual state of either their children or their fellow saints. They leave this matter with God.

In the third place, it is exactly the awareness of the church and parents that not all the children in the line of the covenant are saved that prompts them to come to their children with the warnings which always accompany the gospel. Both the church and believing parents warn their children with all earnestness that when they walk in sin, they must confess their sins and seek forgiveness in the cross.

These same children must be told, from earliest childhood on, that if they persist in walking in sin and refuse to repent, they show that they are not children of God's covenant, for covenant children walk in the ways of God's covenant. And they must be told that by their continuous unbelief they bring down upon themselves the wrath of God in this life and in the life to come. But these same children must be taught that all who confess their sins and go to Christ for forgiveness are received by God as His covenant people. This instruction is the covenantal responsibility of parents towards their children.

In the fourth place, the entire nation of Israel, and the entire church in the new dispensation are called the people of God, in spite of the presence of wicked and carnal adults and children. The reason for this is clear enough. God looks at Israel and at the church from the viewpoint of His own positive purpose. Israel is His church which He purposes to save. The elect seed of the promise constitute His church which He will save in the end. They will have to be rescued from the evil world to which, by nature, they belong. They will have to be saved from their own sinful flesh. And this will take the agonizing "threshing" of judgment and chastisement.

But the purpose is salvation.

So it is in agriculture as well. A farmer calls his field "a wheat field" a wheat field even though weeds are also to be found in it.

And he calls his crop when harvested a wheat crop even though the greatest part of what grew in the field is destroyed and only the kernels of wheat are brought to the granary. His purpose in all the labor bestowed on the crop is to separate the wheat from the tares and chaff at the proper time, when the harvest is ripe.[9]

One more point in connection with God's organic dealings with men ought to be considered. Baptists, in their defense of believers' baptism, often point to the fact that the baptism of infants necessitates giving the sign of the covenant to many who are not true believers.[10] And the fact that the baptism of infants necessitates the baptism of many who are not elect has always been something of a stumbling block to many who do not understand the Reformed position. In fact, many different views of the covenant and of baptism as a sign of the covenant have been presented as solutions to this problem.

Some consider the fact that many more than the elect are baptized as simply an unavoidable by-product of infant baptism. Because we are unable to distinguish between elect and reprobate among the children born in covenant lines, we must face the fact that, if we are obedient to Scripture when we baptize children, we are going to baptize reprobate as well as elect.

Others look at it more from the viewpoint of the outward "blessings" which all the baptized children receive. All are brought up in covenant homes; all are taught in covenant schools; all come under the influence of the preaching in the

---

9. Ibid., 114–31.

10. See, as an example of this line of argumentation, David Kingdon, *Children of Abraham* (Foxton, England: University Tutorial Press Ltd. published for Carey Publications Ltd., Haywards Heath, Sussex, England, 1978). In his defense of believers baptism, Kingdon employs the "pure church" idea; that is, that the church, as much as possible, ought to be composed of true believers only, and the sacrament of baptism ought to be administered only to such believers. See especially pp. 57–60 for his argument. My book, *We and Our Children,* was written as a response to Kingdon.

church in which they are baptized. While these covenantal blessings are given to all, they are of benefit only to some. And many ask the question, Why does this happen? Is it perhaps true that God seeks the salvation of all who are baptized?

Again, a figure from agriculture will help us here. A farmer may consider it a rather tragic waste of fertilizer and water when the tares suck up these nutrients and grow more rapidly. He may very well consider it a necessary and unavoidable waste because he cannot fertilize the wheat only, nor give water to his crop without giving water also to the weeds. For a farmer such waste may truly be unavoidable.

But God never does anything because it cannot be avoided. God wants all the children born in the line of the covenant to receive the mark of baptism and the covenantal influences which come to a child born within the historical manifestation of the covenant. In all this, God works His purpose sovereignly. He causes all the children to be baptized; He brings the gospel to all; He gives all a Christian education in order that His purpose of election and reprobation may be accomplished. He uses all these blessings as the means of grace whereby the elect are saved. But when these good things come upon the reprobate, they are not grace, but God's way of accomplishing His eternal decree. Sinful man, devoid of grace, rejects the gospel, refuses to heed its commands, spurns the Christ presented in it, and becomes guilty before God. But God sovereignly hardens, and through that sovereign work of God and the unbelief of the wicked whereby they remain accountable for their own sin, God's purpose is accomplished.[11]

In the fifth place, it is within the context of the above considerations that we may answer the question. Do all the baptized belong to the covenant?

---

11. Hoeksema, *Believers and Their Seed*, 132–45.

The answer which the PRC has consistently given to this question is an emphatic No! Only the elect, the true seed of the promise, are within the covenant. The elect are covenant seed. They alone are the heirs of the promises of God.

The question remains: Is it not true that the reprobate and carnal seed of the covenant are, in some sense, within the covenant, at least to the extent that they receive some of the benefits of the covenant, be it but outwardly? Or, to put it a bit differently, do not those born within covenant lines have advantages over those who are born, live, and die in heathendom without ever hearing the gospel?

In answering this question, Hoeksema spoke of a distinction between the covenant proper and "the sphere of the covenant."[12] The former is the covenant itself, into which the elect are brought by sovereign grace so that they become God's covenant people. The latter is that broader sphere in which the covenant is administered. The former, to go back to an earlier figure, consists of the wheat gathered into the granary; the latter is the field where the wheat is grown.

This distinction has been criticized by claiming that it teaches that someone is capable both of being in the covenant and not being in the covenant; of being halfway in the covenant, with one foot in and one out, so to speak.[13] But this surely need not be the case, if the matter is considered rightly. Jesus speaks of the fact that the branches which bear no fruit and which are cut off are, nevertheless, in Him (John 15:2). The tares are in the field where the wheat is grown. But the branches which bear no fruit do not belong to Christ, nor do the tares belong to the wheat.

It is even doubtful whether it is proper to speak of "advantages" which the reprobate possess within the sphere

---

12. Ibid., 134–37.
13. See, for example, Carl A. Schouls, "The Covenant Of Grace," *The Messenger* 45, no. 9 (October 1998): 6–8.

of the covenant. This is as doubtful as it is to speak of the advantages which Chorazin, Bethsaida, and Capernaum possessed as part of the Jewish nation, when it will be more tolerable in the day of judgment for Sodom than for those cities (Matt. 11:20–24). Surely it is not due to God's attitude of favor upon the reprobate that they receive these good things, for Chorazin and Capernaum will be punished worse than Sodom in the judgment day, for the former knew God's wonderful works. But this is nevertheless an outcome of God's own work, for Christ gives thanks to His Father that He "has hid these things from the wise and prudent, and hast revealed them unto babes," and this because, "Even so, Father: for so it seemed good in thy sight" (Matt. 11:25, 26).[14]

One must think in terms of a river like the mighty Mississippi, which runs through the heartland of the United States. The whole river is called by the same name, the Mississippi River. But that river runs in a riverbed, just as God's covenant runs in the "riverbed" of its outward sphere of administration. Into that riverbed pour other rivers, such as the Missouri, the Ohio, and the Tennessee. When these rivers pour into the Mississippi, they lose their own identity and become a part of the Mississippi. They are like new generations which, through the mission work of the church in foreign lands, are brought into the lines of the covenant.

But not all the water in the Mississippi gets to the destination towards which it flows. Some is evaporated because of the sun; some gets caught in eddies and whirlpools; some is pumped out for irrigation. That water, though for a time a part of the river, does not really belong to the river. It is like those born and raised in the sphere of the covenant who are not really of it, and who, in time, manifest themselves as wicked seed. But the true covenant people of God are

---

14. Hoeksema, *Believers and Their Seed*, 134–37.

brought safely to the destination of heaven, where all the elect are forever and ever God's covenant people.

Covenant Issues in 1953

Although controversies concerning the covenant were the background for the split in the PRC in 1953, and although much of the debate before and during the controversy involved issues of the covenant, covenantal issues were not themselves the immediate occasion for the split. The immediate occasion for the split can be found in the two statements which Hubert De Wolf made in his sermons from the pulpit of First Protestant Reformed Church. The first one was: "God promises to every one of you that, if you believe, you will be saved." And the second one was: "Our act of conversion is a prerequisite to entering the kingdom." Neither referred directly to the covenant of grace.

In a way, it is strange that in the history of the split the immediate issue was not even the doctrine which had created uproar in the churches for some six years prior to the split.

In both the *Concordia* and the *Standard Bearer*—the former representing those who promoted the view of the covenant taught in the LC, and the latter, under the editorship of Rev. Hoeksema, promoting the PR view—the lengthy and often acrimonious discussions were almost exclusively about different covenant conceptions. But the split came over two other issues: the preaching of the gospel and the doctrine of conversion.

And yet, the issues were related.

In the first statement which came under attack in First PRC, and which was later condemned by Classis East, De Wolf was speaking of the gospel. He was preaching on Luke 16:27–31, which records the last part of the parable of the rich man and Lazarus, in which the rich man asks Abraham to send Lazarus back to his brethren to testify to them. De Wolf used this passage to develop the concept of the gospel, as it was proper for him to do. And, in dealing with the gospel, he spoke more particularly of the promise of the gospel, something which was not only proper, but important to an understanding of the parable.

But in speaking of the promise of the gospel, De Wolf made the promise of the gospel a general promise which came from God to all who heard the gospel preached: "God promises to every one of you . . ." Hence, De Wolf clearly showed that he was defending a general promise of God, which general promise stood at the very heart of the covenant view of the LC.[15]

Although the LC wanted a general promise in connection with baptism (a promise of God to every baptized child), the sacraments are, after all, added to the preaching and signify and seal with visible signs and seals the promise of God made in the preaching.[16]

In the second place, this general promise became, in De Wolf's sermon, a conditional promise, which was also a key ingredient in the covenant view of the LC. A general promise has to be a conditional promise. The two go together. They are two sides of the same coin.

If God sincerely and in all earnestness promises salvation to all who are baptized or to all who hear the gospel, the question is: Why then are not all who receive the promise actually saved? The only answer that can be given is that He has attached conditions to the promise which have to be fulfilled before those to whom the promise is made will actually receive the inheritance.[17]

The conditional nature of that general promise of the

---

15. The general promise which was taught in the LC was the promise made in baptism, while De Wolf spoke of the promise made in the gospel.

16. Heidelberg Catechism, Lord's Day XXV.

17. If I promise all my children a part of the inheritance and only half receive an inheritance, it can only be because I made reception of the inheritance dependent on certain conditions, and half did not fulfill the conditions.

preaching is found in the part of De Wolf's statement which says: " . . . if you believe." "God promises every one of you that, if you believe, you will be saved." Faith is the condition. Only upon fulfillment of that condition will a man be saved.

Some attempted to defend the statement of De Wolf condemned by classis by claiming that it said nothing more than this: "God promises that if you will believe you will be saved." This is a perfectly legitimate statement and is, in fact, with little difference in the wording, similar to statements in Scripture. The statement in Romans 10:13 is one such example: "For whosoever shall call upon the name of the Lord shall be saved." It is not doing violence to that text to reword it to say: God promises salvation to everyone who believes," as the following verses make clear.

But this is not what De Wolf said, nor is it what he intended to say. The statement in Romans 10 means simply: God promises salvation to believers. And that is true. God promises salvation only to believers, and to none else. But the statement also means that God ordains that faith is the means God uses to save. And because faith is the means, the command to believe accompanies the gospel promise.

When the promise is made to all who are baptized, or to all who hear the gospel on condition of faith, then faith becomes a work which man must perform. No amount of intellectual or rhetorical maneuvering can get around that. The promise which God makes is the promise of salvation. Salvation includes all the blessings merited by Christ. Faith is one of those blessings. When Romans 10:13 speaks of faith as a means, it speaks also of faith as the work of God. That is clear in verses 14 and 15 that follow.[18]

---

18. "How then shall they call on him in whom they have not believed? and how shall they believe in him of whom they have not heard? and how shall they hear without a preacher? And how shall they preach, except they be sent . . . ?" Faith is worked in the hearts of the elect through the preaching of the gospel. Thus the minority report presented to Classis East explained the matter, which report was adopted.

But if the promise is to all who hear the gospel, or who are baptized, it cannot possibly include faith, because faith is not given to all. Hence, the faith which is the condition to the reception of the gospel is the work of man.

Both views taught a general and conditional promise.[19] The second statement was more blatant. It too did not have anything specifically to do with the controversy over the covenant. It was a sermon on the truth of conversion, and its necessity.[20] But in the sermon the rather astounding statement was made: "Our act of conversion is a prerequisite to enter the kingdom."

De Wolf showed no hesitancy in his defense of the term "condition" and in his public commitment to conditional salvation. He was speaking of entering the kingdom of heaven, and he was, correctly, pointing out that entrance into the kingdom is only through conversion. But, without equivocation, he made that conversion "our act." And, to underscore the matter, he made this act of ours a prerequisite to entry into the kingdom. If anything, the term "prerequisite" is a stronger term than "condition," for the term "condition" can conceivably refer to "means," but the term "prerequisite" never can.

---

19. Why De Wolf expressed his basic agreement with the LC in terms of the gospel rather than in terms of baptism is probably a question to which no definite answer can be given. That it was meant to express agreement with the LC is evident from the fact that it was preached very shortly after the provisional adoption of the "Declaration of Principles," when the debate over the Declaration raged in the churches prior to the synod of 1951, which synod was scheduled to make the final decision on the document. The provisional adoption of the Declaration took place in June 1950, and De Wolf's sermon was preached in April 1951. It may be that already at that time De Wolf had his mind set on return to the CRC, for his teaching was partly the teaching of the LC, in that it referred to the promise of God, but partly the teaching of the CRC because De Wolf was talking about God's promise in preaching. De Wolf's desire to return to the CRC was expressed in a letter to his consistory dated December 14, 1959.

20. The sermon was on Matthew 18:3: "Verily I say unto you, Except ye be converted and become as little children, ye shall not enter into the kingdom of heaven."

The assertion was stark and beyond misinterpretation: We must convert ourselves before we can enter the kingdom. De Wolf, quite obviously, made the statement to underscore his insistence on a conditional salvation.

It was said, in defense of De Wolf's statement, that the reference in his assertion was to daily conversion and daily entrance into the kingdom. That is, the reference in Jesus' words is to daily repentance from sin, daily fleeing to the cross, daily seeking salvation in Christ, and thus daily becoming conscious of our place in the kingdom of Christ and the blessedness that belongs to those who are a part of the kingdom.

The decision of Classis East recognized this possible interpretation, but pointed out, correctly, that even in this sense conversion is never our act, but is God's work in us and through us. Again, by making conversion as our act a prerequisite to entry into the kingdom, the statement separates conversion from God's work of salvation, of which conversion is always a part, and gives that work over to man.[21]

De Wolf's statement put an exclamation mark behind the insistence of many to introduce conditions into God's work of salvation and thus detract from the truth of sovereign and particular grace.

Conclusion

The doctrine of God's covenant of grace was a part of the truth as confessed in the PRC almost from the beginning of its history. It marked the PRC as a distinct denomination, making its own contribution to the long and glorious history of the Reformed faith with its emphasis on sovereign and particular grace.

---

21. See decision of Classis East in its meeting of April-May 1953. This decision is quoted in its entirety in an undated letter titled "The Facts in the Case," which the consistory of First Protestant Reformed Church sent to its entire congregation, including those who had left with De Wolf.

The battles of 1924 and subsequent years were battles which made these truths stand out clearly, as they were framed against the background of a common grace of God which extended to all men.

The battles over the truth of God's covenant in the early 1950s were not, in this light, new battles. The issues were basically the same as in 1924. A general and well-meant offer of the gospel or a general promise to all baptized children in the sacrament of baptism are much the same. The latter is only the former applied more narrowly to a sacrament. Both the well-meant offer and the general promise are conditional. Both are dependent for fulfillment on the will of man.

The question was: Will the PRC continue to be Protestant Reformed? That question had to be answered through struggle. God so worked in all those difficult years that the question was answered with a ringing affirmative. And the glory of it was that, through the sometimes soul-wearying way of controversy, the truths of God's everlasting covenant of grace were spelled out with even sharper clarity, for controversy always has the result that the doctrines of the truth of God's Word are developed and seen more clearly in all their glory.

CHAPTER 20

Marriage and Family

Marriage is the union between one man and one woman for life, a union that is based on a communion of nature, on a communion of life, and a communion of love, which is a reflection of the covenant relation between God and His people and of the relation between Christ and His church; a union, moreover, that has its chief purpose in bringing forth the seed of the covenant.

—Herman Hoeksema, *The Triple Knowledge*

Introduction

The doctrine of God's covenant of grace is far from an abstract doctrine devoid of practical benefits for the believing child of God. As a member of God's covenant, he has the blessed assurance of being a friend of God. Nothing in his present world can fill the believer with greater joy in his grief and trouble than to know that he is always God's own friend. This knowledge not only gives him strength to go on when the way of his pilgrimage is difficult; it instills in him great courage in the battle of faith and in the suffering at the hands of the wicked, which is his inevitable lot.

Yet the assurance of his friendship with God does not exhaust by any means the blessings that come directly from the truth of God's covenant. There can be no question about it that the members of the PRC have enjoyed the blessings of stable and solid marriages, of covenant homes in which are unity and peace, and of Reformed schools where the children of the covenant are instructed in all the implications of what it means to live in this world as a covenant friend of God. Nor ought we to omit mention of the faithful attendance at worship services twice on the Lord's day which is characteristic of all PR congregations. God's people faithfully attend worship services, because they find the preaching of the Word biblical, expository, and lively. And for those who are the friends of God, the covenant fellowship between God and His people comes to full expression in the corporate worship of the church. Blessings such as these are of inestimable value to God's people.

These blessings of home, school, and church are directly the fruit of the theology of the covenant in PR churches. God's people in the congregations, instructed in the doctrines of the covenant, seek, by God's grace, to carry out their part of the covenant in their homes and families as well as in the church. And the covenant God of His people blesses those who hold fast to His truth and cherish it in their hearts.

I include a chapter on the doctrine of marriage as it developed in the PRC, partly because the doctrine did indeed develop, and partly because the PRC hold to a *doctrine* of marriage. The PRC in their position on marriage have taken a sharply different stand than the position held by the majority of churches in the Reformed and Presbyterian traditions. The PRC held to the traditional position at the time of their formation and in the early years of their history. But in the course of a few decades, especially because of the exegetical studies of Herman Hoeksema, the PRC changed their views and officially adopted a quite different position.

One can hardly deny that this change in the view of the PRC was brought about by the view of God's covenant which the PRC were teaching. The connection is this. Because God's covenant with His people is unconditional, God maintains His covenant even though His people are often unfaithful.

The covenant bond is not capable of being dissolved. Marriage is an earthly picture of that covenant relation between God and His people. Hence, for marriage to be a true picture of the covenant, the marriage bond itself must be indissoluble. That is the position of the PRC as it developed over the years.

The History of the Doctrine of Marriage

The PRC stand in the tradition of the Reformed churches which trace their history back to the Reformation of the sixteenth century. While the Reformers themselves and the best of the Reformed tradition emphasized strongly the indissoluble nature of the marriage bond, these same Reformers allowed for exceptions.[1] These exceptions which dissolved the marriage were adultery and desertion. It was also believed that the "innocent party," the marriage partner who was not guilty of adultery or desertion, was free to remarry, because the marriage bond was dissolved. The argument here is clear. The Scriptures teach that only one event in a man's life can dissolve the marriage bond, and that is death. But some used the word "death" in a broader sense than physical death only. They spoke of one who committed adultery within a marriage as committing a sin so heinous

---

1. An excellent summary of the history of the doctrine of marriage which goes back to the beginning of the new dispensation church is found in a series of articles written by David J. Engelsma entitled "A History of the Church's Doctrine of Marriage, Divorce, and Remarriage," *Protestant Reformed Theological Journal* 27, no. 1 (November 1993): 4–12; 27, no. 2 (April 1994): 4–20; 28, no. 1 (November 1994): 8–25; and 28, no. 2 (April 1995): 18–36. The article on the doctrine of marriage held in the pre-Reformation church is found in vol. 28, no. 2 (April 1995): 18–36. The article that deals with the history of the doctrine of marriage in the Reformed and Presbyterian traditions is found in vol. 27, no. 2 (April 1994): 4–20. The full series formed a basis for Section 2 of the author's revised and expanded book on marriage entitled *Marriage, the Mystery of Christ and the Church: The Covenant-Bond in Scripture and History* (Grand Rapids: Reformed Free Publishing Association, 1998).

that he or she was in fact "dead" to their spouse. Hence the innocent member in the marriage is free to remarry because it is as if the offending party is dead.

This was the position of the Reformers, and it was generally accepted in both the Reformed and Presbyterian traditions. While some disagreements occasionally surfaced, and while some differences of opinion were expressed, especially concerning the question of desertion as a legitimate ground for divorce, the position of the Reformers was the accepted position. This position was even incorporated into the Westminster Confession of Faith, which is the chief confession of Presbyterian churches worldwide.[2]

In the early history of the CRC, the traditional position on divorce and remarriage was maintained. But in 1956 the CRC seriously compromised this traditional Reformed stand by deciding that "people who are guilty of unbiblical divorce, or who are divorced as the result of their own adultery and having remarried, seek entrance or reentrance into the Church, shall be expected to show their sorrow and genuine repentance during an adequate period of probation."[3] This decision was a fundamental departure from the Reformed tradition because it permitted church membership to people divorced on grounds other than adultery and desertion, and permitted remarriage to divorced people upon repentance, whether they were the guilty or the innocent party. But such a position was contrary to Scripture's doctrine of marriage, and it opened the floodgates to a widespread acceptance of divorced and remarried people who came into the church from outside. It also brought about the sad situation where

---

2. Westminster Confession of Faith, chapter 24 "Of Marriage and Divorce," Arts. 5 and 6. We may be thankful that the generally held doctrine of marriage which prevailed in the Reformed tradition was never made confessional in the creeds subscribed to by the PRC.

3. Quoted by Engelsma, "A History of the Church's Doctrine of Marriage, Divorce, and Remarriage," *Protestant Reformed Theological Journal* 28, no. 2 (April 1995): 29, 30.

divorce on any ground and remarriage of all parties was permitted by members in the church upon sufficient ground of repentance.[4]

In the early years of the history of the PRC the traditional Reformed position was accepted, almost, as it were, without question. The fact that this tradition had a long and illustrious history, coupled with the fact that almost no one in any church questioned the legitimacy of it, led the churches to assume that adultery and desertion opened the way for biblical divorce and possible remarriage of the innocent party.

If one peruses the early minutes of the combined consistories and combined classis of the PRC, one will find an occasional reference to the problem.[5] At the classis meeting of February 1929 an overture appeared on the floor of classis from Fuller Ave. PR Church[6] which asked classis to "appoint a committee to consider and to serve Classis with a well-motivated report on the following matter: If one of the two parties in marriage forsakes the other party and seeks divorce on unscriptural grounds, and obtains this from the worldly court; and the guilty party comes to repentance and confesses the sin committed, and wishes to restore the broken relationship by re-marriage before the worldly court; is then the one who was forsaken duty bound before God to comply with that demand and allow the magistrate to unite them once more in marriage?"

---

4. It must be clearly understood that "repentance" in this context was not intended to mean "forsaking one's sin." One could, for example, commit adultery, forsake and divorce one's God-given wife, marry another, and "repent" of it all while remaining with the second wife and continuing to live with her. The same was true, of course, for a wife who committed adultery and divorced her husband.

5. Combined consistory meetings were held early in the history of the PRC to discuss problems and work of mutual concern in the churches. The last meeting was held in January 1927 when combined consistory meetings were replaced by combined classis meetings, the first meeting of which was held in June 1927 (The term "combined classis" meant the combining of consistories into the one classis).

6. Later known as First Protestant Reformed Church of Grand Rapids, Mich.

One of the three grounds adduced for the overture is an interesting one. Without saying why, the overture says in ground 3: "The matter is not so simple. Nor is there anywhere a definite declaration of Reformed Churches."[7] Although I am guessing, I consider it quite possible that the matter was "not so simple" because it involved the question of the dissolution of marriage by divorce proceedings. If a male member of the church committed adultery, left his wife, and finally divorced her, the marriage was dissolved and existed no longer. In that case, if the guilty party repented and wanted to return to his original wife, he would have to be remarried. But it could be quite different if the divorce did not in fact dissolve the marriage. If the marriage bond was *not* dissolved by the divorce, it would not have to be renewed before the church.[8]

It may be that already in 1929 some questioned whether divorce actually dissolved a marriage. In any case, a committee consisting of Revs. G. M. Ophoff, H. Hoeksema, and Gerrit Vos was appointed to study the overture and return with an answer.[9]

A very strange document appeared on the classis meeting of January 1937. It was a document entitled "Instructions from Fuller Ave." Most of these instructions are of no concern to us here, but one asks classis, "Whether or not the innocent party in a divorce case may marry again." In the minutes of that session of classis no mention whatsoever is made of that request from Fuller Ave. Church, and one is left wondering what happened to it.[10] It seems likely, although

---

7. Minutes of classis of February 1929, Art. 18, Supplement 1.

8. This is not saying anything about what the civil law would require. The civil law recognizes divorce as a dissolution of the marriage bond and would require another marriage if two people, formerly married but divorced, came together again.

9. So far as I have been able to discover from the minutes, this committee never reported, and classis never treated, the overture from Fuller Ave.

10. Minutes of the classis of January 1937. Supplement (with no supplement number given).

once again I am guessing, that the instruction from Fuller Ave. Church in 1937 was prompted by a change in the mind of Herman Hoeksema on the question of divorce and remarriage. In 1933 Hoeksema publicly stated his agreement with the general Reformed tradition, but by 1943 he began to express reservations on the matter and even wrote that he had changed his mind.[11] And in the 1950s his mature and well thought-out position was firmly in place.

Although it took some time, gradually the churches began to adopt the position that Hoeksema had taken, and in various cases which have come to the ecclesiastical assemblies over the years, it has become the official stand of the PRC.

This official stand affirms emphatically that while Scripture permits divorce on the grounds of adultery,[12] such a divorce does not break the marriage bond, which is indissoluble. It is a legal "separation of bed and board" when the sin of one of the marriage partners makes living together impossible. Because the marriage bond is indissoluble, it is not permitted either party to remarry. The guilty party is not permitted to remarry, and if he does, his second marriage constitutes an adulterous relationship and a dreadful sin from which he is able to repent only by leaving his second (or third, or fourth) spouse. But the "innocent party" in the divorce may not remarry either. And in the event he or she does, it is a willful sin of adultery. Repentance from the sin requires forsaking one's new spouse.

---

11. All the material, which it is not necesssary to reproduce here, is found in Engelsma, "A History of the Church's Doctrine of Marriage, Divorce, and Remarriage," *Protestant Reformed Theological Journal* 27, no. 1 (November 1993): 5–12.

The "Instruction from Fuller Ave." came to classis in 1937. In 1943 Hoeksema announced his new conclusions. That there was disagreement over the matter in Fuller Ave.'s congregation, in which Rev. Hoeksema was pastor, is reported on p. 8 of the article referred to in the paragraph above. During this entire period, nothing was said about the "Instruction" by classis, nor did classis (or, after 1940, synod) ever speak to it.

12. Not willful desertion.

This basic position has resulted in what may be called a Protestant Reformed doctrine of marriage. It is our intent in the remainder of this chapter to lay down the main outlines of that doctrine.[13]

The Doctrine of Marriage

Before I begin a discussion of the doctrine of marriage, I should mention that the doctrine was all but forced on the churches by the compelling weight of biblical evidence. The PRC are most reluctant to decide and do anything which runs counter to the Reformed tradition. The great esteem in which tradition is held is due to several factors: (1) a recognition of the unity of the new dispensation church, which unity is a unity of doctrine above all else; (2) a thankful confession of the work of the Spirit of Truth who, as Christ promised, leads and guides Christ's church into the truth; (3) a humble awareness of the organic development of

---

13. The literature outlining and developing the position of the PRC is extensive. I mention here only the chief works, starting with the writings of Herman Hoeksema. "The Unbreakable Bond of Marriage" was originally a speech Hoeksema delivered for the Men's Society of the South Holland, Ill., PR Church. It was published in pamphlet form by the Sunday School of the First Protestant Reformed Church of Grand Rapids. Unfortunately, this pamphlet is no longer being published. The version I have is a reprint from 1969 taken from the first printing of 1957. Another pamphlet by Hoeksema is "Unbiblical Divorce and Remarriage." This was published by the Reformed Free Publishing Association, Grand Rapids. It is undated, but was originally a series of *Standard Bearer* articles that appeared in vols. 32 and 33 (1956 and 1957). Another writing by Hoeksema on the subject appears in *The Triple Knowledge*, vol. 3, 342–77.

Probably no one has written as extensively on the marriage issue as David Engelsma. He wrote two important books on the subject. One is *Marriage, the Mystery of Christ and the Church: The Covenant-Bond in Scripture and History*, which is a revised and expanded version of his *Marriage: The Mystery of Christ and the Church* (Grand Rapids: Reformed Free Publishing Association, 1975). The other book is *Better to Marry: Sex and Marriage in I Corinthians 6 and 7* (Grand Rapids: Reformed Free Publishing Association, 1993). Handy pamphlets by the same author are "Marriage and Divorce" (Grand Rapids: Evangelism Committee of the First Protestant Reformed Church, 1994) and "The Lord's Hatred of Divorce," revised text of a sermon preached 1997 at Hudsonville, Mich., PR Church (Hudsonville: Evangelism Committee of the Hudsonville Protestant Reformed Church, 1998).

FOR THY TRUTH'S SAKE: CHAPTER 20

the truth; that is, the truth of Christ in one generation is developed in connection with and out of the truth of the past.

This veneration of the past is not, however, a hidebound traditionalism which locks up the churches to an idolatrous worship of the past for the past's sake. The PRC recognize that all the confession of the church of the past must be subjected to the scrutiny of Scripture, for Scripture is the only rule of faith and life in the church where Christ is Head. And when the confession of the church of the past is scrutinized in the light of the Word of God and it is found seriously flawed, the church must correct that confession in obedience to Christ Himself.

So it was with the doctrine of marriage. Reading the pertinent literature, especially as it came from the pen of Herman Hoeksema, one gets the distinct impression that the change of mind in him, a change which took place over a number of years, was the result of an agonizing wrestling with tradition in the light of sober exegesis of the Word itself. It was finally only a deep sense of the need to be obedient to Christ that brought about the change. It was not easy. It required a courageous willingness to stand alone for a while until the sheer weight of the testimony of God's Word became overwhelming and the church saw that his view was biblical.

Hoeksema himself, as I intimated above, recognized that his views on marriage and divorce were closely connected to his views on the truth of the covenant. He wrote: "I think that in general Scripture represents marriage as a reflection of God's covenant with His people, that He never breaks. That people can sin in that covenant and thus commit spiritual fornication, but the covenant lies absolutely firm in God, and He never gives His people a certificate of divorce."[14] Very likely, therefore, Hoeksema's views on the

---

14. Quoted in Engelsma, "A History of the Church's Doctrine of Marriage,

unconditional and unbreakable character of the covenant of grace brought him to reconsider his views on divorce and remarriage. He must have realized that the traditional view of divorce and remarriage was out of step with God's gracious covenant, although the latter was the pattern for the former. He reexamined the Bible passages pertinent to the question of divorce and remarriage because of the disparity between his covenant views and his original position on the legitimacy of the remarriage of the innocent party in a divorce.

To turn now to the doctrine of marriage as it is held in the PRC, it is first of all important to understand that marriage is a creation ordinance. It is not an ordinance instituted by God after the fall; it is part of the original creation itself.[15] God instituted marriage when He created Eve from a rib of Adam and brought her to Adam.

This fact has several implications. In the first place, that marriage belongs to the creation ordinance is an implicit condemnation of celibacy in the sense in which the Roman Catholic Church holds to it.[16]

In the second place, marriage *belongs* to the creation ordinance. This fact of marriage necessarily implies that all men everywhere know that monogamy in marriage is God's law for a man and a woman, and every man knows, from the same creation ordinance, that God forbids divorce. Paul makes the point clear that the heathen know the will of God as that is found in the creation ordinance. According to Paul in Romans 1:18ff., the heathen know that God is God and that He must be served. And according to his further development of that theme in chapter 2:14, 15, the knowledge which the heathen have of God includes the

---

Divorce, and Remarriage," *Protestant Reformed Theological Journal* 27, no. 1 (November 1993): 9.

15. Hoeksema, *The Triple Knowledge*, vol. 3, 349, 350.

16. Ibid. The Roman Catholic Church teaches that celibacy is superior to marriage and is to be preferred, because it constitutes a higher level of holiness than marriage. Rome demands celibacy of its clergy.

works of the law which are written in their hearts and according to which their consciences accuse or excuse each other.

From a practical point of view, the knowledge which all men possess of God's will (also concerning marriage) means that the church may not declare that because a divorce and remarriage took place before conversion, no sin is involved, and the remarried couple are permitted to remain together within the church and as members of it.

It is also a part of the doctrine of marriage that, after the fall, God made marriage an earthly picture of the heavenly relationship between Himself and His people in Christ. The Old Testament passages which speak of God's relation to Israel as a marriage relation are too numerous to mention.[17] The key New Testament passages are Ephesians 5:22–33 and I Corinthians 7. As a "communion of nature, a communion of life, and a communion of love," marriage reflects the covenant relation between God and His people in Christ in the same threefold way.

God restores His covenant friends to His own image so that they are partakers of the divine nature (II Peter 1:4). He gives them His own life through Christ so that they enter into the fellowship of the triune life of the covenant God through Jesus Christ. His eternal love for them is shed abroad within their hearts so that they in turn love the Lord their God and so are joined with Him in that love which is the bond of perfection (Col. 3:14).

So in marriage husband and wife, in a fellowship of nature

---

17. One such passage is Hosea 2. Ezekiel 23 speaks of Israel's and Judah's sins as "adulteries," which implies their marriage to God (see also James 4:4). Isaiah 62:4, 5 speaks of Hephzibah, which means "my delight is in her," and Beulah, which means "married." The final perfection of heaven is described as a marriage supper of the Lamb (Rev. 19:9) and the church as "a bride adorned for her husband" (Rev. 21:2).

created by God, become one flesh and are joined in a bond of love.

The implications of this are many. God-fearing men seek God-fearing wives. The deepest bonds of marriage are possible only where husband and wife are one in Christ. The unity of a common nature becomes the unity of a sanctified nature when both are believers. The unity of one flesh becomes the unity of a common purpose to bring forth the covenant seed. And the unity of love is a love rooted in and drawing its power from the love of God.

Let it never be forgotten that unbelievers also are truly married in God's sight. But their marriage, real and indissoluble, is nevertheless a mere shell of what a marriage ought to be. Sin destroys everything. Sin destroys the true and rich nature of the marriage bond. God maintains His own righteous cause, and the wicked are forever responsible for their destruction of marriage.

In Christ the full perfection of marriage is attained. Thus every believing husband and believing wife have the solemn obligation to work hard to make their marriage as near to the reality as they possibly can. If that were done in the church, marital problems would seldom arise.

In the third place, the doctrine of marriage taught in the PRC and held to be scriptural is that the marriage bond is indissoluble. "What God hath joined together, let not man put asunder" (Matt. 19:6). That solemn Word of Christ in His interpretation of God's work of marriage in Paradise is taken seriously in the PRC. One may argue that sin has mitigated Christ's Word somewhat, but Jesus, reaching back to the original creation ordinance, teaches us that the rule in the new dispensation is still the same: "From the beginning it was not so" (Matt. 19:6, 8).

Hence the PR position on divorce and remarriage is that, although Scripture permits divorce on the grounds of adultery, such a divorce is not a dissolution of the marriage

bond. It is a separation of bed and board when, because of
adultery, a husband and wife cannot live together any longer.
Hoeksema writes:

> We must of course discuss the problem of divorce, and the
> closely connected problem of remarriage of divorced parties,
> whether by the innocent party only or by both parties. All
> this . . . is closely connected with the question whether you
> consider the marriage bond as capable of dissolution or as
> a bond for life, that is absolutely indissoluble. Technically,
> according to law, divorce is defended as "a legal dissolution
> of the marriage contract by a court or other body having
> competent authority." This is one definition of what is properly
> called divorce.
>
> It is a divorce *a vinculo matrimonii,* that is, from the bond
> of matrimony. Another definition, however, is what is called
> separate maintenance, the separation of a married woman
> from the bed and board of her husband, *a menso et toro.* Biblical
> divorce I would define as a separation for life of married
> people, that is, a legal separation for life, on the basis of adultery
> or fornication. I put it this way intentionally, in distinction
> from others, who claim that a divorce is the dissolution of the
> marriage tie, so that after the dissolution the bond does no
> longer exist and the married people are and are permitted to
> act as if they were never married. Principally one has to choose
> between these two definitions. And on the basis of Holy Writ
> I am compelled to choose for the former. It is my conviction
> that according to the Word of God, divorce can never mean
> dissolution of the marriage tie. Even if people are legally
> divorced, they are in my opinion according to the Word of God
> still married . . .[18]

It is not my purpose here to argue this position. That has
been done successfully, clearly, and biblically in the works
which I have cited earlier. Here it is my purpose simply to

---

18. Hoeksema, *The Triple Knowledge,* vol. 3, 359. Hoeksema's opinion has now
become the official position of the PRC.

establish the fact that this is the PR doctrine of marriage, divorce, and remarriage.

The marriage bond can be dissolved, but only by death. It is right and good that it should be so. Marriage is an institution for this life only. The angels neither marry nor are given in marriage. When the earthly institution has served its purpose, then the time has come for the heavenly reality to be realized when Christ and His elect bride sit down together for the marriage supper of the Lamb.

Because death dissolves the marriage bond, the widow or widower is free to marry after the death of his or her spouse. The original marriage exists no longer. The way is open for another marriage of the one originally married to another.

Marriage has as its purpose the bringing forth of children. When God instituted marriage, He did so in order that Adam and Eve might be fruitful and multiply and replenish the earth. The human race of God's eternal decree must be brought forth through the institution of marriage.

Sin caused disruption in the marriage relation. Nevertheless, the human race is born according to God's purpose, but God gathers His church from the human race, and marriage within the church has as its purpose the bringing forth of the elect. God saves His church in the line of the generations of believers. Elect believers are given the privilege of bringing forth the church. What a glorious privilege that is! Saints have a part in bringing forth those whom God has chosen from all eternity, those who are so precious in God's sight that He gave His Son to the death of the cross to purchase their redemption. In the Old Testament, believing Israel lived in the consciousness of this high calling to bring forth the seed of the covenant. Every believing mother in Israel wanted a part in that. But the New Testament is no different, for, only when the last elect is born and brought to conversion will Christ come again to take His complete church to Himself in glory.

Covenant parents and covenant children form a covenant family. A family in Scripture is also a picture of God's covenant. That is why Scripture lays so much emphasis on the covenant family both in the Old and New Testaments. In the heavenly family of God's covenant, God is Father and Christ is the Elder Brother. All God's people are brothers and sisters in this spiritual household of faith. And the angels are those glorious servants who serve the elect church day and night in this heavenly family. God and His children live in a heavenly house prepared especially for this heavenly family. As Jesus says, "In my Father's house are many mansions ... I go to prepare a place for you ..." (John 14:1–3).

Covenant parents who live as covenant-conscious people of God strive with all their might to make their homes earthly pictures of that heavenly family, where some day they shall live in Father's house. That is their part in God's covenant.

Even the hope of the saints for the coming of Christ is related to the bringing forth of covenant children. Believing parents eagerly await the coming of Christ. They live in the expectation of that coming. But they know that Christ will not come back until all the church is born (II Pet. 3:9). When the last elect is born and brought to repentance, the coming of Christ can no longer be delayed, not for a second. In the humble awareness that they bring forth the church, covenant parents have children in expectation and longing for Christ's return.

The worldly marriages which come apart at the seams are marriages in which husbands and wives are married for their own selfish interests—to get out of marriage what they can for themselves. When they are "unfulfilled," they cavalierly break the marriage bond because, so they claim, they have a right to be happy.

Believers do not marry first of all for their own enjoyment, but for God's glory. Believing husbands love their wives and cherish them. Believing wives are truly opponents of the feminist movement and know that God has called them to be helps to their husbands. Believing parents live for their children—not to give their children the riches of this world, but to entrust to them the heavenly riches. For this they are willing to undergo every deprivation, every suffering, every denial of self. The spiritual well-being of their children is their one great concern.

Practical Applications

The biblical doctrine of marriage is full of practical applications.

With a firm stand against divorce and the remarriage of those divorced, the church is in a position to sound a clear note in a world gone mad with lust and sex, in which marriage and family are so corrupted that people live worse than animals. This clear note is desperately needed. Let the church sound that note without shame.

With insistence on the fact that married couples stay together, those who have problems in their marriages are called to work them out biblically. God does not permit divorce as an option to a seemingly unhappy marriage. He calls us to strive to bring our marriages into conformity with Scripture.

Furthermore, when remarriage is not an option, the way of reconciliation remains open for those divorced on biblical grounds. Reconciliation is the biblical way. Remarriage shuts the door to such reconciliation. The church must keep the way of reconciliation open if at all possible.

Finally, the biblical doctrine is not necessarily the easy way—if we measure ease by the standards of the flesh. Especially when a believer is married to an unbelieving spouse, the way may be difficult indeed. The wicked spouse may abandon his or her spouse and family for the enticing cup of adultery. He leaves behind pain and loneliness, suffering and poverty. But the Lord has never promised His people ease. To be the Lord's disciples means self-denial, carrying a cross, and always following the Lord.

In the way of faithfulness is joy and peace—even in suffering. In the way of wicked unfaithfulness lie grief and pain, and certain destruction at the end. The believer looks forward to the great wedding feast of the Lamb when the true and heavenly marriage shall be an everlasting reality.

The joy of faithfulness is also a part of the doctrine of marriage.

PART 5:
Concluding Considerations

CHAPTER 21

Concluding Considerations

Introduction

I have concentrated on those doctrines of the Reformed
faith which have been, in a unique way, interwoven with
the history of the PRC. They are the doctrines of particular
grace and God's unconditional covenant of grace. I have
also, in what became the largest section of the book (Part 3),
concentrated on some doctrines which were developed by
the spiritual fathers of the PRC, and which continue to be
developed till the present. But in that section I limited myself
to those doctrines which, in my judgment, were developed in
close connection with the controversies of 1924 and 1953.

I have now come to the last chapter of the book. I have a
certain sense of not having completed my task. If one were
to read all the writings which have come from the pens of PR
people, one would find that other doctrines too have been
discussed, and some have received significant development
in the history of the PR churches. This book would not be
complete unless some mention is made of these.

To give some systematic framework to these doctrines,
I have chosen to follow the six loci of "dogmatics" and to
mention, in connection with each locus, a few doctrines of
importance.

To refresh the minds of our readers, the six loci of

dogmatics are: the doctrine of God (theology), the doctrine of man (anthropology), the doctrine of Christ (Christology), the doctrine of salvation (soteriology), the doctrine of the church (ecclesiology), and the doctrine of the last things (eschatology).[1]

Theology

Turning first of all to the doctrine of God, we must note that Hoeksema made an interesting and significant contribution to the truth of God's attributes.

In most of Reformed theology as it was developed through the ages, the attributes of God were divided into "incommunicable" and "communicable" attributes. That distinction was made to point out that some of God's attributes cannot be "communicated" to man, because they belong to God alone. They are such attributes as omnipotence, eternity, and omniscience. God's "communicable" attributes are those attributes which are "communicated" to man by virtue of the fact that man was created in God's image. The idea was not that these attributes of God are found in man in the same way in which they belong to God. Rather, just as the image of God in man is a creaturely reflection of some of God's perfections, so these attributes of God are found reflected in man in a creaturely way. To these attributes belong such perfections as love, mercy, grace, and truth.

Some Reformed theologians, notably Herman Bavinck, suggested another division than the one between incommunicable and communicable attributes. These men suggested that the attributes were better categorized under the names of God.[2] Hoeksema placed a great deal of

---

1. Most of the material in what follows is found in Herman Hoeksema's two great works on Reformed doctrine: *Reformed Dogmatics* and *The Triple Knowledge*.
2. Hoeksema, *Reformed Dogmatics*, 61–3.

emphasis on the idea of God's names,[3] and emphasized the unity of all God's attributes. Therefore he chose the method which Bavinck had used, but in his own way. He chose to divide all God's attributes under the names "Jehovah" and "Holy One." The name "Jehovah" included God's essential attributes, and the name "Holy One" embraced God's ethical attributes.[4]

Such a division gave Hoeksema an opportunity to show the unity of God's attributes in His own being. This unity of attributes was important in Hoeksema's discussion of grace, especially in the controversy over common grace. If God's attribute of grace is common to all men, the same must be said of all God's attributes, including His love, mercy, longsuffering, benevolence, etc.[5]

Hoeksema placed a great deal of emphasis on God's counsel. I have pointed out before, that in his discussion of God's counsel, Hoeksema was emphatically supralapsarian. But in his discussion of his preference for supralapsarianism instead of the infralapsarian viewpoint of our confessions, Hoeksema pointed out that even the traditional supra-lapsarian approach could be misconstrued and misinterpreted. He was deeply conscious of God's attribute of eternity and did not want to compromise God's eternity in any way, especially by interjecting time into God's counsel.

God is, so he insisted, eternal in Himself. God's counsel is His living will and purpose which He determines in Himself. That counsel is also eternal. Though the counsel has many different decrees, including all that takes place in the history of

---

3. Ibid., 63, 64.
4. Ibid., 61–9. The rest of the chapter deals with the individual attributes of God. God's essential attributes are those historically called incommunicable attributes, and His ethical attributes are the same as God's communicable attributes.
5. Many of the defenders of common grace were quite willing to say that these ethical attributes of God were shown to all men.

heaven, earth, and hell, yet God's counsel is outside of time.[6]

As eternal, that counsel is also unchangeable.[7] God never alters His purpose, never adjusts His plans to meet unexpected events, never makes His counsel contingent on what man may or may not do.

In His counsel God has only one purpose from the beginning, which purpose never changes. That purpose is the glory of His name through His own Son, Jesus Christ, and the salvation of the church in Christ. In His counsel God determines absolutely all that happens in history. All things which God determines to do, including the original creation and the fall of man, are done to accomplish His glory and the salvation of His church.

This emphasis on the immutability of God's counsel also leads one to the conclusion that God is absolutely sovereign in the execution of His counsel. Hoeksema was fond of quoting Isaiah 46:9, 10: "Remember the former things of old: for I am God, and there is none else; I am God, and there is none like me, declaring the end from the beginning, and from ancient times the things that are not yet done, saying, My counsel shall stand, and I will do all my good pleasure."

With his emphasis on the immutability of God's counsel, Hoeksema defined the relation between all the decrees of God in His counsel as being logical, not temporal. We must not introduce time into God's counsel, Hoeksema warned. It is not that God decrees this, then that, and following upon

---

6. When Hoeksema was preaching on God's counsel in the pulpit of First Protestant Reformed Church, Grand Rapids, he would emphasize the eternal character of God's counsel by saying that each decree was eternally before the mind of God. In God's counsel, Cain eternally kills Abel. In God's counsel, Christ eternally sheds His blood on the cross. In God's counsel, the church is God's bride eternally, the object of His eternal love.

7. This immutability or unchangeable character of the counsel played a role in the PR apologetic against common grace. It was shown that common grace holds to a God who loves the wicked in this life, but nevertheless casts them into hell in His wrath. Thus God changes in His attitude towards the wicked from love to hatred.

that yet something else. The whole counsel is perfect, and each decree is related to every other in such a way that the one great master plan of God serves perfectly the glory of His name.[8]

Anthropology

In his treatment of the doctrine of man, Hoeksema emphasized one doctrine which is particularly important.

That doctrine is the doctrine of creation, to which Hoeksema was unwaveringly committed.[9] He insisted that God's work of the creation of all things took place in six days of twenty-four hours. Any other interpretation of Genesis 1 and 2 was a concession to evolutionary theory.

It is interesting that Hoeksema's concern for the doctrine of creation was rooted in his profound respect for Scripture as the infallible Word of God. He was insistent on the point that the effort made on the part of Reformed theologians to interpret the days of Genesis 1 as periods of time was a willingness to set science above the Scriptures: "[The exegesis of Genesis 1 that leads to the period theory] was motivated by the desire to give some satisfaction to so-called science, the science of modern times . . . It is not a product of serious exegesis of Holy Writ. One did not proceed from the certain testimony of Scripture. Rather it is a very weak and defective apologetic attempt to maintain the reasonableness of faith in the light of the facts of science."[10]

---

8. Hoeksema, *Reformed Dogmatics*, 153–65.

9. Ibid., 178–82.

10. Ibid., 178, 179. The whole paragraph is worth reading, also insofar as it sheds light on Hoeksema's theological method. He goes on to say, "Already this very method does not plead for the truth of this theory. Believers in Holy Writ want to maintain its testimony above all. For that reason we cannot go along with their method, which wants to listen first of all to the testimony of science, in order then to distort the testimony of Scripture to bring it in harmony with science. This method is not the method of faith, but that of the wisdom which is from below, which is earthly. Even dogmatics may not dominate exegesis of Scripture: much less modern science. Even though it were true that with an honest explanation of

This adherence to the truth of creation in six days of twenty-four hours has remained the position of the PRC. Not one of the ministers in the PRC, nor one of the school teachers in the PR schools, holds to anything but creation in six twenty-four-hour days. Nor can any agitation for an evolutionary interpretation of creation be found among the membership of the PRC.

In fact, as the pressures of scientific discovery and increased emphasis on evolution were brought to bear on PR thinking, quite the opposite has been true. PR theologians have more fully developed the idea that belief in the doctrine of creation is a matter of faith which receives Scripture's testimony as true; that it is part of God's revelation in Christ; and that, therefore, it cannot be separated from the doctrine of salvation.[11] The doctrine of creation is an object of saving faith.

Christology

I need not linger long on this locus of dogmatics. Hoeksema and the PRC have followed closely the age-old truths enunciated by the Council of Chalcedon (A.D. 451) in the doctrine of Christ.

One area, however, was indeed developed by Hoeksema. This element belongs properly to the doctrine of the covenant, and, in fact, I did already treat it in that connection. I need only mention it here.

In connection with Hoeksema's development of the so-called *Pactum Salutis*, or Covenant of Redemption, and

---

Genesis 1 so-called science cannot receive satisfaction, and although it is certainly true that also we will not be able to solve every problem in this connection, yet we always must proceed from the clear expressions of Holy Writ, and in its light develop a believing conception of the origin of the world."

11. This latter point is important. When I was attending college back in the late 1940s and early 1950s my science teacher assured his class that it made no essential difference to one's faith whether one believed in creation or theistic evolution because neither had anything to do with salvation or our faith in the gospel of salvation in Christ. This erroneous sentiment is repeatedly echoed to the present.

in connection with the truth of Christ as the Head of the covenant, Hoeksema underscored the distinction that Scripture made between the second person of the Holy Trinity, who is the eternal Son of God, and the Lord Jesus Christ, the Mediator and Head of the covenant of grace.

The distinction is, of course, not absolute.[12] Within the Trinity, the eternal Son is the second person, who is begotten of the Father and who, with the Father, breathes forth the Holy Spirit. But God reveals this triune life which He lives in Himself. He reveals Himself in Jesus Christ. In this revelation the triune God is the Father of Jesus Christ, the second person of the Holy Trinity. In His divine person He unites the divine and the human natures. Our Lord Jesus Christ enters the world by being born of the virgin Mary. He suffers and dies on the cross, rises again from the dead, is exalted at the right hand of the triune God, and rules over all so that God's purpose with all things may be accomplished. And so He becomes the Head and Mediator of the covenant. Forever and ever, in all His glory, Christ is the full revelation of the triune God in whom salvation is accomplished.

The triune God brings about conception in the womb of Mary, so that God is Christ's Father. When Christ addresses God as "Father," He speaks as the Mediator to the triune God. When He prays on the cross, He prays to the triune God. When He is raised from the dead, God triune raises Him and exalts Him to the preeminent position in heaven which He now occupies for His church. When we see God in heaven, we shall see Him only in the face of Christ, whom we shall indeed see "face to face" (I Cor. 13:12).

If one should object and say that this makes Christ His own

---

12. The distinction is roughly along the lines of the traditional distinction between the ontological Trinity, which refers to the triune God who is three persons in one essence, and the economical Trinity, which is the revelation of the triune God in Jesus Christ and through the Holy Spirit.

Father in the incarnation, and that Christ prays to Himself, the answer is that this is true. But, although we cannot understand the mystery of God become flesh, it is the clear teaching of Scripture that Christ is not passive in the work of salvation, but eminently active. He *takes on* the flesh of his mother. As the great High Priest, He *makes* His own body an offering for sin. He is not only raised, but, emphatically, He arose from the dead—as an act of His own. All the work of salvation is God's work. But it is also Christ's work. And those two statements mean the same thing. The triune God in Christ works salvation.

The same must be said of the Holy Spirit. The Holy Spirit is the third person of the Trinity. He is fully and equally, with the Father and the Son, God. But as the third person of the Trinity, He was given to Christ as Christ's Spirit (John 7:37–39; Acts 2:33). His Spirit Christ pours out on the church; and by His Spirit in the church Christ Himself dwells with the church in fulfillment of His promise: "Lo, I am with you alway, even unto the end of the world" (Matt. 28:20).

Through Christ, and by means of the Spirit of Christ, the triune God takes His people into His own covenant fellowship.

Soteriology

It is clear to anyone who has read PR literature that the emphasis in PR thinking and preaching is on the great truth of salvation by grace alone, without the works of man. All of salvation is God's work, from beginning to end. Nothing at all is left to man. The salvation of the church, rooted in sovereign election and accomplished in the redemptive work of Jesus Christ, is performed in the hearts of the people of God by the Holy Spirit, who works irresistibly to bring God's chosen and Christ's redeemed to the final glory of heaven.

Two truths must be mentioned in this connection.

In the first place, with respect to the doctrine of regeneration, Hoeksema followed that branch of Reformed theology which emphasized *immediate regeneration*. The doctrine was not new; it was, however, an important part of his theology.[13]

The Reformed churches had been divided on the question. Some had taught that the initial work of God in the heart of the elect sinner (regeneration) is accomplished only by means of the preaching of the gospel.[14] Hoeksema demurred and insisted that the very first work of regeneration is performed by God apart from the preaching of the gospel.[15]

Controversy had raged over this point in the Dutch Reformed churches. A. Kuyper was partly to blame for this. He had taught a doctrine of immediate regeneration which separated regeneration from the preaching in an almost absolute way. He had taught that it was possible for a baby to be regenerated in infancy, but that the seed of regeneration could lie dormant in the heart for years and even decades before it would begin to become manifest in the life of an elect child of God.[16]

Hoeksema had no sympathy for Kuyper's view. Hoeksema distinguished between various aspects of the work of regeneration. He spoke, first of all, of that very first work of God in the heart of the elect sinner by which the sinner was given the spiritual power to hear the Word of God preached. It was a work similar to creation. As the Word of God which

---

13. Hoeksema, *Reformed Dogmatics*, 452–64. See also 635–55.

14. This is mediate regeneration. "Mediate" here has the meaning of "by means of." Regeneration takes place by means of preaching.

15. That is, regeneration is "immediate." "Immediate" here has the connotation of "without means," that is, without the means of the preaching of the gospel.

16. Kuyper had really taught this in connection with his doctrine of presupposed regeneration. Kuyper said that all the children born of believing parents must be presupposed to be regenerated. The trouble was that some of these children walked in sin when they became older. Kuyper said that this was to be explained by the fact that the seed of regeneration could lie dormant. Thus Kuyper's view is sometimes called "presupposed and dormant regeneration." Jelle Faber, "The Confessional History of the Canadian Reformed Churches," *Clarion* 48, no. 4 (February 19, 1999): 82.

called the creation into existence was the immediate calling of God, so that same Word of God created the new man in Christ. How can a deaf sinner hear the preaching unless he is first given ears to hear? How can he see the mysteries of the kingdom unless he is given eyes to see? How can he believe the gospel except faith be first planted in his heart? A corpse cannot hear or see. A dead sinner cannot hear or see. A man totally depraved cannot believe.

Once the dead sinner is called to life, God causes His gospel to be preached to him—just as a newborn babe must have milk to sustain its life. That preaching is made effective through the operation of the Holy Spirit. And preaching feeds the new man in Christ and causes him to grow.

If one would argue that a newborn babe cannot hear the preaching or understand it, Hoeksema reminded his audiences that a newborn babe is subjected to many spiritual influences which are a part of the preaching: the sacrament of baptism, the whole "atmosphere" of the worship services, the spiritual deportment of a covenant home, the influences of a covenant mother caring for her child, all of which God can use for the growth of the new man in Christ which is created through regeneration.[17]

One more truth in the area of the doctrine of salvation must be mentioned. This is the truth concerning the doctrine of faith. Hoeksema was not original in his development of the doctrine of faith, but he did emphasize very strongly two points which badly needed emphasis throughout the theological struggles in which he was involved.

Faith is, in its essential nature, the bond that unites the believer to Christ.[18] As I said, the idea that faith is most

---

17. Modern psychology has insisted that a newborn babe can recognize its mother's voice within a few hours of birth. Is it not possible that a newborn babe in Christ recognizes the voice of its heavenly Father earlier in life than we would suspect?

18. Hoeksema, *Reformed Dogmatics*, 479–492. But for a detailed discussion of this aspect of faith, see Hoeksema, *The Triple Knowledge*, vol. 1, 303–08.

fundamentally the bond of union between Christ and His people is deeply rooted in Reformed theology. It is found in the Heidelberg Catechism (1563), where Ursinus and Olevianus, the authors of the Catechism, speak of faith as the means whereby we are *engrafted* into Christ.[19]

Faith is not, first of all, believing. But it is, first of all, the living "connection" between Christ and His people.[20] The figure of "grafting" which is used in the Heidelberg Catechism is particularly appropriate because: (1) it is a figure which Paul uses in Romans 11:16–24, and it is, therefore, biblical; and, (2) because it so clearly illustrates the point. It not only points us to the fact that the elect child of God receives all his life from Christ his Savior, but the figure can be carried a bit farther. A peach branch may be grafted to an apple tree. The peach branch derives its entire life from the apple tree, but it continues to bear peaches and not apples. So the elect sinner is grafted into Christ and derives all his life from Christ, but he remains an individual saint who bears his own fruit of good works, though only by the power of the life of Christ.[21]

Because faith is the bond that unites the believer to Christ, the church as a whole is, through faith, the body of Christ. Christ and His elect church are one body, so much so that Paul can even say in Ephesians 5:30 that we are "members of his body, of his flesh, and of his bones."

---

19. Lord's Day VII, Q & A 20.

20. In my own days in catechism classes, my pastor (who was also my father) would illustrate this point by various figures. One such figure was of a reservoir connected to the house by pipes through which water passed. So Christ is the "reservoir" of salvation because of His perfect work on the cross. Salvation in Christ comes to us through the "pipeline" of faith. Another figure was that of an electric wire which connects a light bulb to the power plant. The light can shine only when the connection is made and the electricity can flow. So Christ's life becomes ours through the "electric wire" of faith.

21. Our Lord teaches this in John 15:1–7, where Jesus speaks of the branches of the vine which are in Him and which bear fruit as one vine. The power to bear fruit is in Christ: "As the branch cannot bear fruit of itself, except it abide in the vine; no more can ye, except ye abide in me" (vs. 4).

This idea of faith as a bond lies behind the truth that faith is the gift of God. The union which is formed between Christ and His people by which they become one body with Him is not a union created by man; it is God's work entirely. This bond is established between the living Christ, in whom are all the blessings of salvation, and the dead sinner in whom is not a spark of spiritual life. Man cannot establish that bond of union.

This faith is given already at the moment of regeneration. All salvation comes to the child of God from Christ through faith. Every aspect of faith, even conscious believing in Christ, is but the outworking of that bond that makes Christ and His people one. So, once again, the emphasis on faith as God's work is properly maintained.

As that faith comes to consciousness in the life of the child of God, it always remains the bond of union with Christ, for faith is the power by which the regenerated and believing child of God reaches out to lay hold on Christ, consciously embraces Christ as the one source of all his blessedness, and enters fully into union with Christ his Savior. But that conscious believing in Christ is also God's work, as the Canons of Dordt so emphatically put it (III & IV, Art. 14).[22]

Faith itself is a part of the salvation Christ gives freely to His people. Faith is one of the blessings of salvation earned on the cross. Christ works faith in the hearts of the elect by the Holy Spirit. Because Christ wills to give that salvation to His people so that they are conscious of it, enjoy it in all its riches, and seek it in Christ, Christ also gives faith, by means

---

22. The article reads: "Faith is therefore to be considered as the gift of God, not on account of its being offered by God to man, to be accepted or rejected at his pleasure; but because it is in reality conferred, breathed, and infused into him; or even because God bestows the power or ability to believe, and then expects that man should by the exercise of his own free will, consent to the terms of salvation, and actually believe in Christ; but because he who works in man both to will and to do, and indeed all things in all, produces both *the will to believe, and the act of believing also*" (emphasis mine).

of which gift the believer looks only to Christ for every blessing in this life and in the life to come.

Ecclesiology

In his treatment of the doctrine of the church, Hoeksema followed the line of the Reformed faith from the time of the Reformation. I can call attention, however, to one aspect of this doctrine of the church which was stressed in Hoeksema's theology and which had a great impact on the life of the PRC. I refer to the doctrine of the determinative character of the official preaching of the gospel.[23]

Only a few aspects of this doctrine need to be mentioned.

In the first place, Hoeksema emphasized that preaching could be done only by a called and ordained preacher. A called and ordained preacher was one called by Christ's church, and, through the church, by Christ Himself. Not everyone may preach. An unordained clergy has no sanction in Scripture. A preacher is an official ambassador of Christ and receives his official credentials from Christ through the church. Thus preaching is always carried on in the church and by the church through an ordained ministry.

Secondly, when a preacher preaches, Christ Himself speaks. He speaks objectively through the spoken Word of the preacher, and He speaks subjectively by the operation of His Spirit in the hearts of His elect, so that Christ's sheep hear the voice of the Good Shepherd—to use the figure Christ Himself uses in John 10.

Thirdly, this preaching is the central and decisive means whereby God works faith in the hearts of His people. That

---

23. Hoeksema devoted an entire chapter to this subject in his locus on ecclesiology (Hoeksema, *Reformed Dogmatics*, 635–655). But important aspects of this truth can also be found in many other writings. I refer not only to the polemical pamphlets which were written in the early history of the PR churches and were defenses of the gospel over against the error of the well-meant offer, but also to *The Triple Knowledge*, vol. 2, 434–42, 693–712, and to Herman Hoeksema, *God's Eternal Good Pleasure*, 177–207.

implies, negatively, that there are no other ways by which faith is worked in this decisive manner. One cannot sit home, read his Bible, meditate on Scripture, and expect to receive the faith brought through the preaching. Faith, if it is to grow, requires the official preaching of the Word by the church through its ordained ministry. Thus this preaching is indispensable for salvation.[24]

Fourthly, as the fruit of the preaching, God uses other means as well to strengthen and enrich the faith of His people. They are the means of Bible study, prayer, meditation on Scripture, the reading of books on Scripture, discussions among the saints, covenant instruction of the youth, etc. But preaching is first, central, decisive, and absolutely necessary.

Finally, Hoeksema insisted on the fact that the preaching of the gospel is a twofold power by which God accomplishes His purpose. It is the power of God unto salvation to all who believe, but it is also a hardening power by which God accomplishes His purpose in the reprobate. God's Word never returns to Him void (Isa. 55:8–11). God sent Isaiah to preach to Judah to "Make the heart of this people fat" (6:9, 10). Our Lord quotes this very prophecy to explain His reason for teaching in parables (Matt. 13:10–17; Mark 4:11, 12). Paul speaks of the triumph of the gospel both in them that are saved and in them that perish (II Cor. 2:14–17).

Understanding the force of these texts (and others), Hoeksema saw that they were completely contrary to the idea of the preaching as a well-meant offer by which God expresses His love for and desire to save all men. It is God's sovereign power by which God accomplishes His purpose.[25]

---

24. This emphasis Hoeksema derived especially from Romans 10:14, 15. He found in this passage the teaching that the child of God hears Christ Himself only through the preaching of one who is sent.

25. These ideas are especially developed in the two books he wrote in opposition to the well-meant offer: *Een Kracht Gods tot Zaligheid* (A Power of God unto Salvation), and *Het Evangelie* (The Gospel).

This emphasis on preaching has had profound effects on the life of the PRC. I must mention a few of these effects.

First of all, preaching has been considered crucially important in the life of the church. This emphasis on preaching begins in the seminary where much of the curriculum is devoted to teaching students to preach. The role of subjects dedicated to this end is impressive: two semesters of hermeneutics; two semesters of homiletics; seven semesters of exegesis; ten sermons preached and critiqued in practice preaching sessions; one semester of intern work in a congregation under the tutelage of an experienced minister; and preaching in the congregations to gain experience and expertise in the actual situation of the worship services.

Secondly, ministers devote most of their time during the week to the preparation of sermons. They are not caught up in community work, in outreach programs in the inner city, in conferences and meetings of all sorts which take them from their studies, in political involvement in the public square, in psychological analysis of various social ills, etc. They work on sermons to preach. They do so because preaching is the God-ordained means of salvation.

Thirdly, that emphasis on the crucial importance of preaching carries over into the worship services. The emphasis is not on liturgy—whether traditional or contemporary; the emphasis is on preaching. Following the lead of the Reformers of the sixteenth century, the pulpit is in the center with an open Bible on the top of it, and the preaching takes up about two-thirds of the worship service. That preaching is expository, doctrinal, antithetical, but also applied to the life and calling of the saints.

Fourthly, that same emphasis on preaching comes to expression in all the work of the minister. He devotes himself to catechetical instruction of the children and youth of the covenant. Much time is spent in preparation for catechism, and in catechism classes, for preaching must embrace the command of Christ: "Feed my lambs" (John 21:15). And his pastoral work is also preaching, as the ordained minister brings God's Word from house to house.

Finally, the PRC take seriously the command of Christ to go into all the world and *preach the gospel*. Missionary work occupies much time, much work, much of the resources, and much of the energy of the churches. But the PRC insist that preaching is the means that God uses to gather His church, and that preaching is the sole calling of the missionary. The missionaries must *preach*.

Eschatology

Although many doctrines of Scripture are being discussed in the church today, certainly the doctrine of the last things (eschatology) is high on the church's agenda. The historic Reformed position of amillennialism is under fierce attack— by both premillennialists and postmillennialists. The former is the older of the two; the latter, the more recent.[26]

Although, when Hoeksema was doing his writing, the postmillennial position was not the threat to the church that it is today, he nevertheless laid the groundwork for the amil position and defined the parameters of the battle. He accomplished this task in his important work on the book of Revelation, *Behold, He Cometh*.[27] Although many

---

26. In the early years of his ministry, Herman Hoeksema was involved in the question of premillennialism in the CRC when a certain H. Bultema defended premillennial doctrine. Bultema's views are incorporated in his book *Maranatha: Eene Studie over de Onvervulde Profetie* (Maranatha: A Study of Unfulfilled Prophecy) (Grand Rapids: Eerdmans-Sevensma Co., [1917]). Bultema was condemned for denying the kingship of Christ over the church. See Gertrude Hoeksema, *Therefore Have I Spoken*, 92–4.

Postmillennialists would argue that their view is also very old, but although a mild form of postmillennialism goes back to the Puritans, Postmillennial Reconstructionism is a new and novel idea.

27. The present book, available from the Reformed Free Publishing Association in Grandville, Mich., has an interesting history. As pastor of First Protestant

commentaries had been written earlier on this difficult last book of the Bible, Hoeksema's book was one of only two or three to present a sensible, coherent, and biblically sound explanation of the visions of John, the seer of Patmos.[28]

Because the book is a sound explanation of Revelation, it is also an effective weapon in the battle against premillennial and postmillennial errors. Especially because the church today is called to live in the end of the ages when the coming of Christ is near, Hoeksema's eschatology is a precious part of the heritage of the PRC. It puts in the hands of the believer a useful and potent weapon in the battle for the faith in these last days. It gives encouragement to the faithful and keeps before God's saints the need to pray without ceasing, "Come, Lord Jesus; yea, come quickly."

Conclusion

We have come to the end of our journey through the doctrinal history of the PRC.

The church of Christ has survived throughout the two millennia between Pentecost and today, and it is now the beginning of a new millennium. It seems increasingly clear that the Lord will not tarry another millennium, but that the history of Christ's church will soon come to an end with the return of our Lord upon the clouds of heaven. Will the PRC

Reformed Church in Grand Rapids, Hoeksema preached a lengthy series of sermons on the book of Revelation. To help the people understand the difficult material, he prepared his outlines carefully and had them printed and distributed to the congregation prior to the worship service. These outlines were collected and many sets were bound in hard cover. Later, Hoeksema used his exegesis for a series of articles in the *Standard Bearer* on Revelation. These articles were then edited and partially revised by Homer C. Hoeksema for the book *Behold, He Cometh! An Exposition of the Book of Revelation* (Grand Rapids: Reformed Free Publishing Association, 1969).

28. One may disagree with some of the details of Hoeksema's explanation of certain elements of the individual visions. But no one can deny that Hoeksema's explanation appeals to our sanctified common sense; that it is in complete agreement with the rest of Scripture, including Scripture's eschatological passages; and that it is a strong defense of the historic amil position.

still be in existence when the Lord returns? Or, if through the bitter persecution of Antichrist the institute of the church is destroyed, will those who were members of the PRC until the end be found among those who remain faithful in the terrible persecution that shall come before the end?

The answer to this question must be in the affirmative, if, by the grace of God, the members of the PRC remember their heritage. Two reasons can be cited as proof.

The faith which serves as the core of the body of doctrine held to be biblical by the PRC is the same faith which has been believed throughout the entire new dispensation. As I have been at some pains to point out, the most basic truth of all the faith of the church is the truth that God is absolutely sovereign in all His works, and especially in His work of salvation through Jesus Christ. The truth of Ephesians 2:8 is the golden thread that runs through the whole of Scripture: "By grace are ye saved through faith; and that not of yourselves: it is the gift of God." That faith has sustained the church and been its confession in every century of the two millennia which have preceded us. That faith has been the one great truth which put steel in the spine of the defenders of the faith, the Reformers, and the martyrs for the cause of Christ. That truth has been the confession of young and old, rich and poor, preachers and saints in the pew, kings and beggars—of all who have known that their salvation is the gift of God's great grace to wicked and unworthy sinners. If it has been that kind of truth which could give help and strength in life's darkest hours, it will also be a truth which sustains the saints in yet darker days. That truth of God's absolute sovereignty, as the central truth of Reformed theology, will sustain them to the end.

The PRC is only one small branch of the mighty tree of the New Testament church. Yet it has made its own unique contribution to the rich and glorious knowledge of God in Christ, whom to know is life eternal. It is not an idle claim that the church's knowledge of the truth has been enriched by PR theology. It is not pride which leads the PRC to believe that God has used them to make more of the unsearchable treasures of God's Word a part of the confession of the saints. The churches may be confident of this as they gather to give thanks to God on their seventy-fifth anniversary. The churches may be thankful for this as they acknowledge together their own salvation by grace through faith.

If this book, by the mercy of a faithful God, serves to inspire in us that confidence and move us to such thankfulness, we and the generations to come will give praise and glory unto Him to whom alone belongs all glory, now and forever.

Appendix A

Act of Secession (*Acta van Afscheiding*) of 1834 of the Reformed Congregation in Ulrum, the Netherlands, which separated itself thereby from the state church (Nederduitsch Hervormde Kerk)

We the undersigned, Overseers and members of the Reformed Congregation of Jesus Christ at Ulrum, having observed for a considerable time the corruption in the Netherlands Reformed Church, as well in the mutilation or denial of the doctrine of our fathers, based on God's Word, as in the degeneration of the administration of the Holy Sacraments, according to the regulation of Christ in His Word, and in the almost complete neglect of ecclesiastical discipline; all of which matters are, according to our Reformed confession Article 29, distinguishing marks of the true Church; having received through God's grace a Pastor and Teacher who set forth to us according to the Word of God the pure doctrine of our fathers and who applied the same both in particular and in general; the congregation was thereby more and more awakened to direct its steps in confession and walk according to the rule of faith and of God's holy Word: Galatians 6:16, Philippians 3:16; and also to renounce the service of God according to human commandments, because God's Word tells us that this is in vain, Matthew 15:9; and at the same time to make us watchful for the profaning of the signs and seals of God's eternal covenant of grace; through this the congregation lived in rest and peace; but that rest and peace was disturbed by the highly unjust and ungodly suspension of our commonly loved and esteemed Pastor as a consequence of his public testimony against false doctrine and against defiled public religious services; quietly and calmly has the congregation with their Pastor and Teacher conducted itself to this point; various very fair proposals were made, both by our Pastor and Teacher and by the rest of the Overseers of the congregation; repeatedly investigation and judgment on the ground of and according to God's Word was requested, but all in vain. Classical, Provincial, and Synodical Ecclesiastical Boards have refused this most just request, and on the contrary have demanded repentance and regret without pointing out any offense from God's holy Word, as well as unlimited subjection to Synodical regulations and prescriptions, without demonstrating that those are in all things based on God's Word; thereby this Netherlands Ecclesiastical Board has now made itself equivalent to the Popish Church rejected by our fathers; because not only is the previously mentioned corruption observed, but in addition God's Word is rejected or invalidated by ecclesiastical laws and decisions, Matt. 15:4, 23:4, Mark 7:7, 8, and they are persecuted who will live godly in Christ Jesus, according to His own prescriptions, recorded in His Word, and the consciences of men are bound; finally on the authority of the Provincial Ecclesiastical Board the preaching of the Word of God by a publicly acknowledged minister in our midst, the Rev. H.P. Scholte, Reformed Pastor at Doveren and Genderen, in the land of Heusden and Altena, Province of North Brabant, was forbidden, and the mutual assemblies of the believers, which were held with open doors, were punished by fines;—taking all of this together, it has now become more than plain, that the Netherlands Reformed Church is not the True, but the false Church, according to God's Word and Article 29 of our confession; for which reason the undersigned hereby declare: that they in accordance with the office of all believers, Article 28, separate themselves from those who are not of the Church, and therefore will have no more fellowship with the Netherlands Reformed Church, until it returns to the true service of the Lord; and declare at the same time their willingness to exercise fellowship with all true Reformed members, and to unite themselves with every gathering founded on God's infallible Word, in whatever place God has also united the same, testifying hereby that in all things we hold to God's holy Word and to our old forms of unity, in all things founded on that Word, namely, the Confession of faith, the Heidelberg Catechism, and the Canons of the Synod of Dordrecht, held in the year 1618 and 1619; to order our public religious services according to the ancient ecclesiastical liturgy; and with respect to divine service and church government, for the present to hold to the church order instituted by the aforementioned Synod of Dordrecht.

Finally, we hereby declare that we continue to acknowledge our unjustly suspended Pastor.

Ulrum, the 13th of October, 1834.

(signed)   J.J. Beukema, Elder
K.J. Barkema, Elder
K.A. van der Laan, Deacon
D.P. Ritsema, Deacon
Geert K. Bos, Deacon

[and on 14th October, 1834, signed by 67 members of the congregation on behalf of some 268]

$\mathcal{A}$ppendix B

Three Points of Common Grace as formulated by the 1924 Synod of the Christian Reformed Church

NOTE: Since the original Three Points were in Dutch, as published in the CRC *Acta der Synode van de Christelijke Gereformeerde Kerk [CRC] 1924*, Article 132, pp. 145–46, the English translation has been taken from *The Protestant Reformed Churches in America: Their Origin, Early History and Doctrine* by Herman Hoeksema (Grand Rapids: First Protestant Reformed Church of Grand Rapids, [1936]). In writing his own English translation of the points, Hoeksema translated it twice in his book, each with a slightly different translation. The one used in *For Thy Truth's Sake* is from pages 84–85 of the Hoeksema volume. The Scripture proofs following each point below were published in the 1924 *Acta der Synode* on pp. 126, 127, 129, and 132.

First Point:

Regarding the first point, touching the favorable attitude of God toward mankind in general and not only toward the elect, synod declares that according to Scripture and the Confession it is established, that besides the saving grace of God shown only to the elect unto eternal life, there is also a certain favor or grace of God which He shows to His creatures in general. This is evident from the Scripture passages that were quoted and from the Canons of Dordt, II, 5 and III, IV, 8, 9, where the general offer of the gospel is set forth; while it also is evident from the citations made from Reformed writers belonging to the most flourishing period of Reformed theology that our fathers from of old maintained this view.

Scripture passages cited for the first point were: Ps. 145:9; Matt. 5:44, 45; Luke 6:35, 36; Acts 14:16, 17; I Tim. 4:10; Rom. 2:4; Ezek. 33:11; and Ezek. 18:23.

Second Point:

Regarding the second point touching the restraint of sin in the life of the individual man and of society in general, synod declares that according to Scripture and the Confession there is such a restraint of sin. This is evident from the Scripture passages that were quoted and from the Netherland Confession, Arts. 13 and 36, which teach that God by a general operation of His Spirit, without renewing the heart, restrains the unbridled manifestation of sin, so that life in human society remains possible; which the citations from Reformed authors of the most flourishing period of Reformed theology prove, moreover, that our fathers from of old maintained this view.

Scripture passages cited for the second point were Gen. 6:3; Ps. 81:11, 12; Acts 7:42; Rom. 1:24, 26, 28; and II Thess. 2:6, 7.

Third Point:

Regarding the third point, touching the performance of so-called civic righteousness by the unregenerate, synod declares that according to Scripture and the Confession, the unregenerate, though incapable of doing any spiritual good (Canons of Dordt, III, IV, 3) are able to perform such civic good. This is evident from the Scripture passages that were quoted and from the Canons of Dordt, III, IV, 4, and from the Netherland Confession, Art. 36, which teach that God without renewing the heart, exercises such an influence upon man that he is enabled to do civic good; while it is, moreover, evident from the citations made from Reformed writers of the most flourishing period of Reformed theology that our fathers from of old maintained this view.

Scripture passages cited for the third point were II Kings 10:29, 30; II Kings 12:2; II Kings 14:3; II Chron. 25:2; Luke 6:33; and Rom. 2:14.

$\mathcal{A}$ppendix C

Act of Agreement (signed March 6, 1925, by the Combined Consistories of Eastern Ave., Hope, and First Kalamazoo churches)

"Whereas the Synod of 1924, assembled in Kalamazoo, Mich., adopted three points of doctrine which, according to our most sacred conviction, are in direct conflict with our Reformed Confessions and principles;

"2. Whereas by the actions of Classis Grand Rapids East and Classis Grand Rapids West, we are denied the right to discuss and interpret said three points of doctrine of said Synod;

"3. Whereas, by the actions of said Classes, the pastors, elders and deacons of First Kalamazoo, Hope and Eastern Ave., together with their congregations are actually expelled from the fellowship of the Christian Reformed Churches;

"4. Whereas it follows necessarily from the action of said Classes, that said office-bearers and their congregations cannot simply submit themselves to the action of said Classes until such time as Synod shall have considered their appeal, which they made in a legal way to Synod, but were forced by circumstances to continue to function in their respective offices as pastors, elders and deacons of their respective congregations;

"5. Whereas they are informed and know positively, that hundreds of our people outside of our own congregations share our convictions and with us cannot acquiesce in the actions of Classes and Synod, neither from a doctrinal nor from a Church-political viewpoint.

"6. Whereas the above mentioned matters concern us as appealing churches in common, and demand our co-operation and united action;

"Therefore, be it resolved by the Combined Consistories

of First Kalamazoo, Hope and Eastern Avenue, assembled March 6, 1925 in the Eastern Avenue Church:

"a. That we adopt as our common basis the Three Forms of Unity and the Church Order of the Reformed Churches;

"b. That at the same time we stand on the basis of our appeal and intend to address our appeal to the Synod of 1926;

"c. That we unite as Consistories for the following purposes: (1) To unitedly bring our appeal from the actions of Classes Grand Rapids East and West to the Synod of 1926; (2) To decide on such matters as have reference to the interests of our congregations in common; (3) To decide in all matters that pertain to the furnishing of information and advice to others, outside of our own congregations.

"d. That whatever shall be decided by said Combined Consistories by a majority-vote, shall be considered firm and binding."

With regard to the method of voting it was decided, with a view to the considerable difference in the number of members of the different Consistories, that in case of friction the majority-vote of the members present plus the majority of at least two separate Consistories would be necessary to reach a decision.

$\mathcal{A}$ppendix D

Conclusions of Utrecht

(English translation of the Dutch "Conclusies van Utrecht" published at the direction of the Synod of Utrecht of the Reformed Church in the Netherlands (GKN) held in 1905 in Utrecht, the Netherlands. This English translation was approved by the 1942 Synod of the Christian Reformed Church [in North America] and published in the CRC's *Acts of Synod 1942*, Supplement XVII, pp. 352–354.)

I. INFRA- OR SUPRALAPSARIANISM

In regard to the first point, infra- or supralapsarianism, Synod declares:

> that our Confessional Standards admittedly follow the infralapsarian presentation in respect to the doctrine of election, but that it is evident both from the wording of Chapter I, Article 7, of the Canons of Dort, and from the deliberation of the Synod of Dort, that this is in no wise intended to exclude or condemn the supralapsarian presentation;

> that it is hence not permitted to present the supralapsarian view as the doctrine of the Reformed Churches in the Netherlands, but neither, to molest anyone who personally holds the supralapsarian view, inasmuch as the Synod of Dort has made no pronouncement upon this disputed point.

Furthermore, Synod adds the warning that such profound doctrines, which are far beyond the understanding of the common people, should be discussed as little as possible in the pulpit, and that one should adhere in the preaching of the Word and in catechetical instruction to the presentation offered in our Confessional Standards.

II. ETERNAL JUSTIFICATION

In regard to the second point, eternal justification, Synod declares:

> that the term itself does not occur in our Confessional Standards but that it is not for this reason to be disapproved, any more than we would be justified in disapproving the term Covenant of Works and similar terms which have been adopted through theological usage;

> that it is incorrect to say that our Confessional Standards know only of a justification by and through faith, since both God's Word (Rom. 4:25) and our Confession (Art. XX) speak explicitly of an objective justification sealed by the resurrection of Christ, which in point of time precedes the subjective justification;

> that, moreover, as far as the matter itself is concerned, all our Churches sincerely believe and confess that Christ from eternity in the Counsel of Peace undertook to be the Surety of His people; taking their guilt upon Himself as also that afterward He by His suffering and death on Calvary actually paid the ransom for us, reconciling us to God while we were yet enemies; but that on the basis of God's Word and in harmony with our Confession it must be maintained with equal firmness that we personally become partakers of this benefit only by a sincere faith.

Wherefore Synod earnestly warns against any view that would do violence either to Christ's eternal suretyship for His elect, or to the requirement of a sincere faith to be justified before God in the tribunal of conscience.

III. IMMEDIATE REGENERATION

In regard to the third point, immediate regeneration, Synod declares:

> that this term may be used in a good sense, insofar as our Churches have, over against the Lutheran and Roman Catholic Churches, always professed that regeneration is not effected

through the Word or the Sacraments as such, but through the Almighty and regenerating operation of the Holy Spirit;

that this regenerating operation of the Holy Spirit, however, should not be in such a way divorced from the preaching of the Word as if these two were separate from each other. For though the Confession teaches that we should have no doubt concerning the salvation of our children dying in infancy despite the fact that they have not heard the preaching of the Gospel, and though our Confessional Standards nowhere express themselves about the manner in which such regeneration takes place in these and other children, it is, on the other hand, no less certain that the Gospel is a power of God unto salvation to everyone that believeth, and that in the case of adults the regenerating operation of the Holy Spirit accompanies the preaching of the Gospel.

Even though Synod does not dispute that God is able also apart from the preaching of the Word—as, for instance, in the pagan world—to regenerate those whom He will, yet Synod judges that on the basis of the Word of God we are not able to make any declaration in respect to the question whether this actually occurs, and that, therefore, we should adhere to the rule which the revealed Word offers us, and should leave the hidden things to the Lord our God.

IV. PRESUMPTIVE REGENERATION

And finally, in regard to the fourth point, presumptive regeneration, Synod declares:

that according to the Confession of our Churches the seed of the covenant, by virtue of the promise of God, must be held to be regenerated and sanctified in Christ, until upon growing up they should manifest the contrary in their way of life or in doctrine;

that it is, however, less correct to say that baptism is administered to the children of believers on the ground of their presumed regeneration, since the ground of baptism is found in the command and the promise of God;

that, furthermore, the judgment of charity with which the Church regards the seed of the covenant as regenerated, does not at all imply that each child is actually born again, seeing that God's Word teaches that they are not all Israel that are of Israel, and of Isaac it is said: in him shall thy seed be called (Rom. 9:6, 7), so that it is imperative in the preaching constantly to urge earnest self-examination, since only he that believeth and is baptized shall be saved.

Moreover, Synod in agreement with our Confession maintains that "the sacraments are not empty or meaningless signs, so as to deceive us, but visible signs and seals of an inward and invisible thing, by means of which God works in us by the power of the Holy Spirit" (Article XXXIII), and that more particularly baptism is called "the washing of regeneration" and "the washing away of sins" because God would "assure us by this divine pledge and sign that we are spiritually cleansed from our sins as really as we are outwardly washed with water"; wherefore our Church in the prayer after baptism "thanks and praises God that He has forgiven us and our children all our sins, through the blood of His beloved Son Jesus Christ, and received us through His Holy Spirit as members of His only begotten Son, and so adopted us to be His children, and sealed and confirmed the same unto us by holy baptism"; so that our Confessional Standards clearly teach that the sacrament of baptism signifies and seals the washing away of our sins by the blood and the Spirit of Jesus Christ, that is, the justification and the renewal by the Holy Spirit as benefits which God has bestowed upon our seed.

Synod is of the opinion that the representation that every elect child is on that account already in fact regenerated even before baptism, can be proved neither on scriptural nor on confessional grounds, seeing that God fulfills His promise sovereignly in His own time, whether before, during, or after baptism. It is hence imperative to be circumspect in one's utterances on this matter, so as not to desire to be wise beyond that which God has revealed.

$\mathcal{A}$ppendix E

Translation of the Letter
by Professor Benne Holwerda
Sent in 1949 to a
Mr. Koster of Chatham, Ont., Canada

"I received your letter yesterday, and a direct reply per airmail is in order. Day before yesterday we held a meeting with Rev. Kok and Rev. De Jong, the purpose being mutual discourse. We had a wholly openhearted exchange of thoughts. They said this: Indeed, we have much to be grateful for to Rev. Hoeksema. But his conception regarding election, etc., is not church doctrine. No one is bound by it. Some are emitting a totally different sound. Their opinion was that most (of the Prot. Ref.) do not think as Rev. Hoeksema and Rev. Ophoff. And sympathy for the Liberated was great also in the matter of their doctrine of the covenant. They do accentuate differently in America, considering their history, but for the conception of the Liberated there is ample room. And from other quarters I heard that Liberated in the Chr. Ref. churches run into difficulty, if they hold their position.

"They, that is, Rev. Kok and Rev. De Jong, also reported what is being done in their churches for handling the spiritual care of the Liberated. I must honestly say that thereby much of my fear has been removed. I still consider the method of the Amersfoort decision [synod of Amersfoortt, 1948] regarding correspondence with the Protestant Reformed Churches unfortunate. But now I see the thing thus: First, the Prot. Ref. church is the true church, be it that the lay (of conception) regarding election, etc., is somewhat different, considering their wholly different history. However, I am not entirely agreed. Second, the Protestant Reformed Church proves to be the true church also herein that she truly seeks the immigrants from Holland and consciously allows all room for their conception. In this situation I believe that joining the Prot. Ref. church is calling. And let them then as Liberated preserve their contact with Holland by all means, and also spread our literature. Our Liberated would be doing a fruitful work, if they labored in the Prot. Ref. churches to remove misunderstanding and to deepen insight. Rev. Kok said. We can still learn much from each other. The communication that Rev. Hoeksema, who first was skeptical of the immigrants, 'paid them a visit, and returned enthusiastic, struck me as remarkable; and another must have said, 'Those are strong men, who know what it is all about. You could make them all ministers, just like that.' If Rev. Hoeksema's conception' was binding, I would say, Never join. Now I believe, however, that accession is calling; and then so that the Liberated also help to disseminate the dogmatical wealth of Holland in the Prot. Ref. Churches."

$\mathcal{A}$ppendix F

Declaration of Principles
of the
Protestant Reformed Churches
(taken from the Church Order of the PRC, 1999 edition)

A Brief Exposition of the Confessions
regarding Certain Points of Doctrine
As Maintained by the
Protestant Reformed Churches

Adopted by the
Synod of 1951

Preamble

DECLARATION OF PRINCIPLES, *to be used only by the*
Mission Committee and the missionaries for the organization of
prospective churches on the basis of Scripture and the confessions as
these have always been maintained in the Protestant Reformed Churches
and as these are now further explained in regard to certain principles.

The Protestant Reformed Churches stand on the basis of
Scripture as the infallible Word of God and of the Three Forms
of Unity. Moreover, they accept the liturgical forms used in the
public worship of our churches, such as:

Form for the Administration of Baptism, Form for the
Administration of the Lord's Supper, Form of Excommunication,
Form of Readmitting Excommunicated Persons, Form of
Ordination of the Ministers of God's Word, Form of Ordination
of Elders and Deacons, Form for the Installation of Professors
of Theology, Form of Ordination of Missionaries, Form for the
Confirmation of Marriage before the Church, and the Formula
of Subscription.

On the basis of this Word of God and these confessions:

I. They repudiate the errors of the Three Points adopted by the
Synod of the Christian Reformed Church of Kalamazoo, 1924,
which maintain:

A. That there is a grace of God to all men, including the reprobate, manifest in the common gifts to all men.
B. That the preaching of the gospel is a gracious offer of salvation on the part of God to all that externally hear the gospel.
C. That the natural man through the influence of common grace can do good in this world.
D. Over against this they maintain:
   1. That the grace of God is always particular, i.e., only for the elect, never for the reprobate.
   2. That the preaching of the gospel is not a gracious offer of salvation on the part of God to all men, nor a conditional offer to all that are born in the historical dispensation of the covenant, that is, to all that are baptized, but an oath of God that He will infallibly lead all the elect unto salvation and eternal glory through faith.
   3. That the unregenerate man is totally incapable of doing any good, wholly depraved, and therefore can only sin. For proof we refer to **Canons I, A, 6–8:**

> Art. 6. That some receive the gift of faith from God and others do not receive it proceeds from God's eternal decree, "For known unto God are all his works from the beginning of the world" (Acts 15:18). "Who worketh all things after the counsel of his will" (Eph. 1:11). According to which decree he graciously softens the hearts of the elect, however obstinate, and inclines them to believe, while he leaves the non-elect in this judgment to their own wickedness and obduracy. And herein is especially displayed the profound, the merciful, and at the same time the righteous discrimination between men equally involved in ruin; or that decree of election and reprobation, revealed in the Word of God, which though men of perverse, impure, and unstable minds wrest to their own destruction, yet to holy and pious souls affords unspeakable consolation.

Art. 7. Election is the unchangeable purpose of God whereby, before the foundation of the world, he hath out of mere grace, according to the sovereign good pleasure of his own will, chosen from the whole human race, which had fallen through their own fault, from their primitive state of rectitude, into sin and destruction, a certain number of persons to redemption in Christ, whom he from eternity appointed the Mediator and Head of the elect, and the foundation of salvation.

This elect number, though by nature neither better nor more deserving than others, but with them involved in one common misery, God hath decreed to give to Christ, to be saved by him, and effectually to call and draw them to his communion by his Word and Spirit, to bestow upon them true faith, justification, and sanctification, and having powerfully preserved them in the fellowship of his Son, finally to glorify them for the demonstration of his mercy and for the praise of his glorious grace; as it is written, "According as he hath chosen us in him, before the foundation of the world, that we should be holy, and without blame before him in love; having predestinated us unto the adoption of children by Jesus Christ to himself, according to the good pleasure of his will, to the praise of the glory of his grace, wherein he hath made us accepted in the beloved" (Eph. 1:4, 5, 6). And elsewhere: "Whom he did predestinate, them he also called, and whom he called, them he also justified, and whom he justified, them he also glorified" (Rom. 8:30).

Art. 8. There are not various decrees of election, but one and the same decree respecting all those who shall be saved, both under the Old and New Testament: since the Scripture declares the good pleasure, purpose, and counsel of the divine will to be one, according to which he hath chosen us from eternity, both to grace and glory, to salvation and the way of salvation, which he hath ordained that we should walk therein.

Canons II, A, 5:

> Art. 5. Moreover, the promise of the gospel is that whosoever believeth in Christ crucified shall not perish, but have everlasting life. This promise, together with the command to repent and believe, ought to be declared and published to all nations, and to all persons promiscuously and without distinction to whom God out of his good pleasure sends the gospel.

The **Canons in II, A, 5** speak of the preaching of the promise. It presents the promise, not as general, but as particular, i.e., as for believers, and, therefore, for the elect. This preaching of the particular promise is promiscuous to all that hear the gospel, with the command, not a condition, to repent and believe.

Canons II, B, 6:

> Art. 6. Who use the difference between meriting and appropriating to the end that they may instill into the minds of the imprudent and inexperienced this teaching that God, as far as he is concerned, has been minded of applying to all equally the benefits gained by the death of Christ; but that while some obtain the pardon of sin and eternal life, and others do not, this difference depends on their own free will, which joins itself to the grace that is offered without exception, and that it is not dependent on the special gift of mercy, which powerfully works in them, that they rather than others should appropriate unto themselves this grace. For these, while they feign that they present this distinction in a sound sense, seek to instill into the people the destructive poison of the Pelagian errors.

For further proof we refer to the **Heidelberg Catechism III, 8 and XXXIII, 91**:

> Q. 8. Are we then so corrupt that we are wholly incapable of doing any good, and inclined to all wickedness?
> Indeed we are; except we are regenerated by the Spirit of God.
>
> Q. 91. But what are good works?
> Only those which proceed from a true faith, are performed according to the law of God, and to his glory; and not such as are founded on our imaginations, or the institutions of men.

And also from the **Belgic Confession, Art. XIV**:

> Art. XIV. We believe that God created man out of the dust of the earth, and made and formed him after his own image and likeness, good, righteous, and holy, capable in all things to will, agreeably to the will of God. But being in honor, he understood it not, neither knew his excellency, but willfully subjected himself to sin, and consequently to death and the curse, giving ear to the words of the devil. For the commandment of life, which he had received, he transgressed; and by sin separated himself from God, who was his true life, having corrupted his whole nature; whereby he made himself liable to corporal and spiritual death. And being thus become wicked, perverse, and corrupt in all his ways, he hath lost all his excellent gifts, which he had received from God, and only retained a few remains thereof, which, however, are sufficient to leave man without excuse; for all the light which is in us is changed into darkness, as the Scriptures teach us, saying: The light shineth in darkness, and the darkness comprehendeth it not: where St. John calleth men darkness. Therefore we reject all that is taught repugnant to this, concerning the free will of

man, since man is but a slave to sin, and has nothing of himself, unless it is given from heaven. For who may presume to boast that he of himself can do any good, since Christ saith, No man can come to me, except the Father, which hath sent me, draw him? Who will glory in his own will who understands that to be carnally minded is enmity against God? Who can speak of his knowledge, since the natural man receiveth not the things of the Spirit of God? In short, who dare suggest any thought, since he knows that we are not sufficient of ourselves to think anything as of ourselves, but that our sufficiency is of God? And therefore what the apostle saith ought justly to be held sure and firm, that God worketh in us both to will and to do of his good pleasure. For there is no will nor understanding conformable to the divine will and understanding but what Christ hath wrought in man; which he teaches us when he saith, Without me ye can do nothing.

Once more we refer to **Canons III / IV, A, 1–4:**

> Art. 1. Man was originally formed after the image of God. His understanding was adorned with a true and saving knowledge of his Creator and of spiritual things; his heart and will were upright; all his affections pure; and the whole man was holy; but revolting from God by the instigation of the devil, and abusing the freedom of his own will, he forfeited these excellent gifts; and on the contrary entailed on himself blindness of mind, horrible darkness, vanity, and perverseness of judgment, became wicked, rebellious, and obdurate in heart and will, and impure in his affections.

> Art. 2. Man after the fall begat children in his own likeness. A corrupt stock produced a corrupt offspring. Hence all the posterity of Adam, Christ only excepted, have derived corruption from their original parent, not by imitation, as the Pelagians

of old asserted, but by the propagation of a vicious nature.

Art. 3. Therefore all men are conceived in sin, and by nature children of wrath, incapable of saving good, prone to evil, dead in sin, and in bondage thereto; and, without the regenerating grace of the Holy Spirit, they are neither able nor willing to return to God, to reform the depravity of their nature, nor to dispose themselves to reformation.

Art. 4. There remain, however, in man since the fall the glimmerings of natural light, whereby he retains some knowledge of God, of natural things, and of the differences between good and evil, and discovers some regard to virtue, good order in society, and for maintaining an orderly external deportment. But so far is this light of nature from being sufficient to bring him to a saving knowledge of God, and to true conversion, that he is incapable of using it aright even in things natural and civil. Nay further, this light, such as it is, man in various ways renders wholly polluted, and holds it in unrighteousness, by doing which he becomes inexcusable before God.

II. They teach on the basis of the same confessions:
   A. That election, which is the unconditional and unchangeable decree of God to redeem in Christ a certain number of persons, is the sole cause and fountain of all our salvation, whence flow all the gifts of grace, including faith. This is the plain teaching of our confessions in the **Canons of Dordrecht**, I, A, 6, 7. See above [I-D-3].
   And in the **Heidelberg Catechism XXI, 54**, we read:

> Q. 54. What believest thou concerning the "holy catholic church" of Christ?
> That the Son of God, from the beginning to the end of the world, gathers, defends, and preserves to himself by his Spirit and Word, out of the whole human race, a church chosen to everlasting life,

agreeing in true faith; and that I am and forever shall remain a living member thereof.

This is also evident from the doctrinal part of the **Form for the Administration of Baptism**, where we read:

> For when we are baptized in the name of the Father, God the Father witnesseth and sealeth unto us that he doth make an eternal covenant of grace with us, and adopts us for his children and heirs, and therefore will provide us with every good thing, and avert all evil or turn it to our profit. And when we are baptized in the name of the Son, the Son sealeth unto us that he doth wash us in his blood from all our sins, incorporating us into the fellowship of his death and resurrection, so that we are freed from all our sins, and accounted righteous before God. In like manner, when we are baptized in the name of the Holy Ghost, the Holy Ghost assures us, by this holy sacrament, that he will dwell in us, and sanctify us to be members of Christ, applying unto us that which we have in Christ, namely, the washing away of our sins, and the daily renewing of our lives, till we shall finally be presented without spot or wrinkle among the assembly of the elect in life eternal.

B. That Christ died only for the elect and that the saving efficacy of the death of Christ extends to them only. This is evident from the **Canons, II, A, 8:**

> **Art. 8.** For this was the sovereign counsel and most gracious will and purpose of God the Father, that the quickening and saving efficacy of the most precious death of his Son should extend to all the elect, for bestowing upon them alone the gift of justifying faith, thereby to bring them infallibly to salvation: that is, it was the will of God that Christ, by the blood of the cross, whereby he confirmed the new covenant, should effectually redeem out of every people, tribe, nation, and language, all

those, and those only, who were from eternity chosen to salvation and given to him by the Father; that he should confer upon them faith, which together with all the other saving gifts of the Holy Spirit he purchased for them by his death; should purge them from all sin, both original and actual, whether committed before or after believing; and having faithfully preserved them even to the end, should at last bring them free from every spot and blemish to the enjoyment of glory in his own presence forever.

This article very clearly teaches:

1. That all the covenant blessings are for the elect alone.
2. That God's promise is unconditionally for them only: for God cannot promise what was not objectively merited by Christ.
3. That the promise of God bestows the objective right of salvation not upon all the children that are born under the historical dispensation of the covenant, that is, not upon all that are baptized, but only upon the spiritual seed.

This is also evident from other parts of our confessions, as, for instance: **Heidelberg Catechism XXV, 65, 66:**

> Q. 65. Since then we are made partakers of Christ and all his benefits by faith only, whence doth this faith proceed?
> From the Holy Ghost, who works faith in our hearts by the preaching of the gospel, and confirms it by the use of the sacraments.

> Q. 66. What are the sacraments?
> The sacraments are holy visible signs and seals, appointed of God for this end, that by the use thereof he may the more fully declare and seal to us the promise of the gospel, viz., that he grants us freely the remission of sin and life eternal, for the

sake of that one sacrifice of Christ accomplished on the cross.

If we compare with these statements from the **Heidelberger** what was taught concerning the saving efficacy of the death of Christ in **Canons II, A, 8**, it is evident that the promise of the gospel which is sealed by the sacraments concerns only the believers, that is, the elect.

This is also evident from **Heidelberg Catechism XXVII, 74**:

> Q. 74. Are infants also to be baptized?
>
> Yes: for since they, as well as the adult, are included in the covenant and church of God; and since redemption from sin by the blood of Christ, and the Holy Ghost, the author of faith, is promised to them no less than to the adult; they must therefore by baptism, as a sign of the covenant, be also admitted into the Christian church; and be distinguished from the children of unbelievers as was done in the old covenant or testament by circumcision, instead of which baptism is instituted in the new covenant.

That in this question and answer of the Heidelberger not all the children that are baptized, but only the spiritual children, that is, the elect, are meant is evident. For:

a. Little infants surely cannot fulfill any conditions. And if the promise of God is for them, the promise is infallible and unconditional, and therefore only for the elect.

b. According to **Canons II, A, 8**, which we quoted above [II-B], the saving efficacy of the death of Christ is for the elect alone.

c. According to **this answer of the Heidelberg Catechism**, the Holy Ghost, the author of faith, is promised to the little children no less than to the adult. And God surely fulfills His promise. Hence, that promise is surely only for the elect.

The same is taught in the **Belgic Confession, Articles XXXIII-XXXV**. In Article XXXIII we read:

> **Art. XXXIII.** We believe that our gracious God, on account of our weakness and infirmities, hath ordained the sacraments for us, thereby to seal unto us his promises, and to be pledges of the good will and grace of God toward us, and also to nourish and strengthen our faith; which he hath joined to the Word of the gospel, the better to present to our senses both that which he signifies to us by his Word, and that which he works inwardly in our hearts, thereby assuring and confirming in us the salvation which he imparts to us. For they are visible signs and seals of an inward and invisible thing, by means whereof God worketh in us by the power of the Holy Ghost. Therefore the signs are not in vain or insignificant, so as to deceive us. For Jesus Christ is the true object presented by them, without whom they would be of no moment.

And from **Article XXXIV**, which speaks of holy baptism, we quote:

> **Art. XXXIV.** We believe and confess that Jesus Christ, who is the end of the law, hath made an end, by the shedding of his blood, of all other sheddings of blood which men could or would make as a propitiation or satisfaction for sin: and that he, having abolished circumcision, which was done with blood, hath instituted the sacrament of baptism instead thereof; by which we are received into the church of God, and separated from all other people and strange religions, that we may wholly belong to him whose ensign and banner we bear, and which serves as a testimony to us that he will forever be

our gracious God and Father. Therefore he has commanded all those who are his to be baptized with pure water, "in the name of the Father, and of the Son, and of the Holy Ghost"; thereby signifying to us that as water washeth away the filth of the body when poured upon it, and is seen on the body of the baptized when sprinkled upon him, so doth the blood of Christ, by the power of the Holy Ghost, internally sprinkle the soul, cleanse it from its sins, and regenerate us from children of wrath unto children of God. Not that this is effected by the external water, but by the sprinkling of the precious blood of the Son of God, who is our Red Sea, through which we must pass to escape the tyranny of Pharaoh, that is, the devil, and to enter into the spiritual land of Canaan. Therefore the ministers, on their part, administer the sacrament and that which is visible, but our Lord giveth that which is signified by the sacrament, namely, the gifts and invisible grace; washing, cleansing, and purging our souls of all filth and unrighteousness; renewing our hearts, and filling them with all comfort; giving unto us a true assurance of his fatherly goodness; putting on us the new man, and putting off the old man with all his deeds.

Article XXXIV speaks of holy baptism. That all this, washing and cleansing and purging our souls of all filth and unrighteousness, the renewal of our hearts, is only the fruit of the saving efficacy of the death of Christ and therefore is only for the elect is very evident. The same is true of what we read in the same article concerning the baptism of infants:

> Art. XXXIV. And indeed Christ shed his blood no less for the washing of the children of the faithful, than for adult persons; and therefore they ought to receive the sign and sacrament of that which Christ hath done for them; as the Lord commanded in

the law, that they should be made partakers of the sacrament of Christ's suffering and death, shortly after they were born, by offering for them a lamb, which was a sacrament of Jesus Christ. Moreover, what circumcision was to the Jews, that baptism is to our children. And for this reason Paul calls baptism the circumcision of Christ.

If, according to **Article 8 of the Second Head of Doctrine, A, in the Canons,** the saving efficacy of the death of Christ extends only to the elect, it follows that **when in this article of the Belgic Confession** it is stated that "Christ shed his blood no less for the washing of the children of the faithful than for the adult persons," also here the reference is only to the elect children.

Moreover, that the promise of the gospel which God signifies and seals in the sacraments is not for all is also abundantly evident from **Article XXXV of the same Belgic Confession,** which speaks of the holy supper of our Lord Jesus Christ. For there we read:

> Art. XXXV. We believe and confess that our Savior Jesus Christ did ordain and institute the sacrament of the holy supper to nourish and support those whom he hath already regenerated and incorporated into his family, which is his church.

In the same article we read:

> Further, though the sacraments are connected with the thing signified, nevertheless both are not received by all men: the ungodly indeed receives the sacrament to his condemnation, but he doth not receive the truth of the sacrament. As Judas and Simon the sorcerer both indeed received the sacrament, but not Christ who was signified by it, of whom believers only are made partakers.

It follows from this that both the sacraments, as well as the preaching of the gospel, are a savor of death unto death for the reprobate, as well as a savor of life unto life for the elect. Hence, the promise of God, preached by the gospel, signified and sealed in both the sacraments, is not for all but for the elect only.

And that the election of God, and consequently the efficacy of the death of Christ and the promise of the gospel, is not conditional is abundantly evident from the following articles of *the Canons*.

Canons I, A, 10:

> **Art. 10.** The good pleasure of God is the sole cause of this gracious election; which doth not consist herein, that out of all possible qualities and actions of men God has chosen some as a condition of salvation; but that he was pleased out of the common mass of sinners to adopt some certain persons as a peculiar people to himself, as it is written, "For the children being not yet born neither having done any good or evil," etc., it was said (namely to Rebekah): "the elder shall serve the younger; as it is written, Jacob have I loved, but Esau have I hated" (Rom. 9:11, 12, 13). "And as many as were ordained to eternal life believed" (Acts 13:48).

In **Canons I, B, 2,** the errors are repudiated of those who teach:

> **Art. 2.** That there are various kinds of election of God unto eternal life: the one general and indefinite, the other particular and definite; and that the latter in turn is either incomplete, revocable, non-decisive and conditional, or complete, irrevocable, decisive, and absolute. . . .

And in the same chapter of **Canons I, B, 3,** the errors are repudiated of those who teach:

> **Art. 3.** That the good pleasure and purpose of God, of which Scripture makes mention in the doctrine of election, does not consist in this, that

God chose certain persons rather than others, but in this that he chose out of all possible conditions (among which are also the works of the law), or out of the whole order of things, the act of faith, which from its very nature is undeserving, as well as its incomplete obedience, as a condition of salvation, and that he would graciously consider this in itself as a complete obedience and count it worthy of the reward of eternal life. . . .

Again, in the same chapter of **Canons I, B, 5,** the errors are rejected of those who teach that:

Art. 5. . . . faith, the obedience of faith, holiness, godliness, and perseverance are not fruits of the unchangeable election unto glory, but are conditions which, being required beforehand, were foreseen as being met by those who will be fully elected, and are causes without which the unchangeable election to glory does not occur.

Finally, we refer to the statement of the **Baptism Form:**

And although our young children do not understand these things, we may not therefore exclude them from baptism, for as they are without their knowledge partakers of the condemnation in Adam, so are they again received unto grace in Christ. . . .

That here none other than the elect children of the covenant are meant and that they are unconditionally, without their knowledge, received unto grace in Christ, in the same way as they are under the condemnation of Adam, is very evident.

C. That faith is not a prerequisite or condition unto salvation, but a gift of God, and a God-given instrument whereby we appropriate the salvation in Christ. This is plainly taught in the following parts of our confessions:

Heidelberg Catechism VII, 20:

> Q. 20. Are all men then, as they perished in
> Adam, saved by Christ?
> No; only those who are ingrafted into him, and
> receive all his benefits, by a true faith.

Belgic Confession, Article XXII:

> Art. XXII. We believe that, to attain the true
> knowledge of this great mystery, the Holy
> Ghost kindleth in our hearts an upright faith,
> which embraces Jesus Christ with all his merits,
> appropriates him, and seeks nothing more besides
> him. For it must needs follow, either that all
> things which are requisite to our salvation are
> not in Jesus Christ, or if all things are in him, that
> then those who possess Jesus Christ through faith
> have complete salvation in him. Therefore, for
> any to assert that Christ is not sufficient, but that
> something more is required besides him, would be
> too gross a blasphemy: for hence it would follow
> that Christ was but half a Savior. Therefore we justly
> say with Paul, that we are justified by faith alone,
> or by faith without works. However, to speak more
> clearly, we do not mean that faith itself justifies
> us, for it is only an instrument with which we
> embrace Christ our Righteousness. But Jesus Christ,
> imputing to us all his merits, and so many holy
> works which he has done for us and in our stead, is
> our Righteousness. And faith is an instrument that
> keeps us in communion with him in all his benefits,
> which, when become ours, are more than sufficient
> to acquit us of our sins.

Confer also **Belgic Confession, Articles XXXIII-XXXV**,
quoted above [earlier].

In **Canons III / IV, A, 10, 14** we read:

Art. 10. But that others who are called by the gospel obey the call, and are converted, is not to be ascribed to the proper exercise of free will, whereby one distinguishes himself above others equally furnished with grace sufficient for faith and conversions, as the proud heresy of Pelagius maintains; but it must be wholly ascribed to God, who as he has chosen his own from eternity in Christ, so he confers upon them faith and repentance, rescues them from the power of darkness, and translates them into the kingdom of his own Son, that they may show forth the praises of him who hath called them out of darkness into his marvelous light; and may glory not in themselves, but in the Lord, according to the testimony of the apostles in various places.

Again, in the same chapter of **Canons, Article 14**, we read:

Art. 14. Faith is therefore to be considered as the gift of God, not on account of its being offered by God to man, to be accepted or rejected at his pleasure; but because it is in reality conferred, breathed, and infused into him; or even because God bestows the power or ability to believe, and then expects that man should by the exercise of his own free will consent to the terms of salvation, and actually believe in Christ; but because he who works in man both to will and to do, and indeed all things in all, produces both the will to believe, and the act of believing also.

III. Seeing then that this is the clear teaching of our confession,
  A. We repudiate:
    1. The teaching:
      a. That the promise of the covenant is conditional and for all that are baptized.
      b. That we may presuppose that all the children that

are baptized are regenerated, for we know on the basis of Scripture, as well as in the light of all history and experience, that the contrary is true. For proof we refer to **Canons I, A, 6–8** [quoted earlier in I-D-3]; and the doctrinal part of the **Baptismal Form**:

The principal parts of the doctrine of holy baptism are these three:

First. That we with our children are conceived and born in sin, and therefore are children of wrath, in so much that we cannot enter into the kingdom of God except we are born again. This, the dipping in, or sprinkling with water teaches us, whereby the impurity of our souls is signified, and we admonished to loathe and humble ourselves before God, and seek for our purification and salvation without ourselves.

Secondly. Holy baptism witnesseth and sealeth unto us the washing away of our sins through Jesus Christ. Therefore we are baptized in the name of the Father, and of the Son, and of the Holy Ghost. For when we are baptized in the name of the Father, God the Father witnesseth and sealeth unto us the washing away of our sins through Jesus Christ. Therefore we are baptized in the name of the Father, and of the Son, and of the Holy Ghost. For when we are baptized in the name of the Father, God the Father witnesseth and sealeth unto us that he doth make an eternal covenant of grace with us, and adopts us for his children and heirs, and therefore will provide us with every good thing, and avert all evil or turn it to our profit. And when we are baptized in the name of the Son, the Son sealeth unto us that he doth wash us in his blood from all our sins, incorporating us into the fellowship of his death and resurrection, so that we are freed from all our sins, and accounted righteous before God. In like manner, when we are baptized in the name of the Holy Ghost, the Holy Ghost assures us, by this holy sacrament, that he will dwell in us, and sanctify us to be members of Christ, applying unto us that which we have in Christ, namely, the washing away of our sins, and the daily renewing of our lives, till we shall finally be presented without spot or wrinkle among the assembly of the elect in life eternal.

Thirdly. Whereas in all covenants there are contained two parts: therefore are we by God through baptism admonished of and obliged unto new obedience, namely, that we cleave to this one God, Father, Son, and Holy Ghost; that we trust in him, and love him with all our hearts, with all our souls, with all our mind, and with all our strength; that we forsake the world, crucify our old nature, and walk in a new and holy life.

And if we sometimes through weakness fall into sin, we must not therefore despair of God's mercy, nor continue in sin, since baptism is a seal and undoubted testimony that we have an eternal covenant of grace with God.

The Thanksgiving after baptism:

Almighty God and merciful Father, we thank and praise thee that thou hast forgiven us and our children all our sins, through the blood of thy beloved Son Jesus Christ, and received us through thy Holy Spirit as members of thine only begotten Son, and adopted us to be thy children, and sealed and confirmed the same unto us by holy baptism; we beseech thee, through the same Son of thy love, that thou wilt be pleased always to govern these baptized children by thy Holy Spirit, that they may be piously and religiously educated, increase and grow up in the Lord Jesus Christ, that they then may acknowledge thy fatherly goodness and mercy, which thou hast shown to them and us, and live in all righteousness, under our only Teacher, King, and High Priest, Jesus Christ; and manfully fight against and overcome sin, the devil, and his whole dominion, to the end that they may eternally praise and magnify thee, and thy Son Jesus Christ, together with the Holy Ghost, the one only true God. Amen.

The prayer refers only to the elect; we cannot presuppose that it is for all.

2. The teaching that the promise of the covenant is an objective bequest on the part of God, giving to every baptized child the right to Christ and all the blessings of salvation.

B. And we maintain:
1. That God surely and infallibly fulfills His promise to the elect.
2. The sure promise of God which He realizes in us as rational and moral creatures not only makes it impossible that we should not bring forth fruits of thankfulness but also confronts us with the obligation of love, to walk in a new and holy life, and constantly to watch unto prayer.

All those who are not thus disposed, who do not repent but walk in sin, are the objects of His just wrath and excluded from the kingdom of heaven.

That the preaching comes to all; and that God seriously commands to faith and repentance; and that to all those who come and believe He promises life and peace.

Grounds:
   a. The **Baptism Form, part 3.**
   b. The **Form for the Lord's Supper, under "thirdly"**:

All those, then, who are thus disposed, God will certainly receive in mercy, and count them worthy partakers of the table of his Son Jesus Christ. On the contrary, those who do not feel this testimony in their hearts eat and drink judgment to themselves.

Therefore, we also, according to the command of Christ and the apostle Paul, admonish all those who are defiled with the following sins to keep themselves from the table of the Lord, and declare to them that they have no part in the kingdom of Christ; such as all idolaters, all those who invoke deceased saints, angels, or other creatures; all those who worship images; all enchanters, diviners, charmers, and those who confide in such enchantments; all despisers of God, and of his Word, and of the holy sacraments; all blasphemers; all those who are given to raise discord, sects, and mutiny in church or state; all perjured persons; all those who are disobedient to their parents and superiors; all murderers, contentious persons, and those who live in hatred and envy against their neighbors; all adulterers, whoremongers, drunkards, thieves, usurers, robbers, gamesters, covetous, and all who lead offensive lives.

All these, while they continue in such sins, shall abstain from this meat (which Christ hath ordained only for the faithful), lest their judgment and condemnation be made the heavier.

c. The **Heidelberg Catechism** XXIV, 64; XXXI, 84; XLV, 116:

Q. 64. But doth not this doctrine make men careless and profane?

By no means: for it is impossible that those who are implanted into Christ by a true faith should not bring forth fruits of thankfulness.

Q. 84. How is the kingdom of heaven opened and shut by the preaching of the holy gospel?

Thus: when according to the command of Christ it is declared and publicly testified to all and every believer, that, whenever they receive the promise of the gospel by a true faith, all their sins are really forgiven them of God, for the sake of Christ's merits; and on the contrary, when it is declared

and testified to all unbelievers, and such as do not
sincerely repent, that they stand exposed to the
wrath of God and eternal condemnation so long as
they are unconverted: according to which testimony
of the gospel God will judge them, both in this, and
in the life to come.

Q. 116. Why is prayer necessary for Christians?
Because it is the chief part of thankfulness which
God requires of us: and also because God will give
his grace and Holy Spirit to those only who with
sincere desires continually ask them of him, and are
thankful for them.

Canons III / IV, A, 12, 16, 17:

Art. 12. And this is the regeneration so highly
celebrated in Scripture, and denominated a new
creation: a resurrection from the dead, a making
alive, which God works in us without our aid. But
this is in no wise effected merely by the external
preaching of the gospel, by moral suasion, or
such a mode of operation that, after God has
performed his part, it still remains in the power
of man to be regenerated or not, to be converted
or to continue unconverted; but it is evidently a
supernatural work, most powerful, and at the same
time most delightful, astonishing, mysterious, and
ineffable; not inferior in efficacy to creation, or
the resurrection from the dead, as the Scripture
inspired by the author of this work declares; so
that all in whose heart God works in this marvelous
manner are certainly, infallibly, and effectually
regenerated, and do actually believe. Whereupon
the will thus renewed is not only actuated and influenced by God, but in consequence of this influence becomes itself active. Wherefore also, man is
himself rightly said to believe and repent, by virtue
of that grace received.

Art. 16. But as man by the fall did not cease to be a creature endowed with understanding and will, nor did sin, which pervaded the whole race of mankind, deprive him of the human nature, but brought upon him depravity and spiritual death; so also this grace of regeneration does not treat men as senseless stocks and blocks, nor takes away their will and its properties, neither does violence thereto; but spiritually quickens, heals, corrects, and at the same time sweetly and powerfully bends it; that where carnal rebellion and resistance formerly prevailed, a ready and sincere spiritual obedience begins to reign; in which the true and spiritual restoration and freedom of our will consist. Wherefore unless the admirable author of every good work wrought in us, man could have no hope of recovering from his fall by his own free will, by the abuse of which, in a state of innocence, he plunged himself into ruin.

Art. 17. As the almighty operation of God, whereby he prolongs and supports this our natural life, does not exclude, but requires the use of means, by which God of his infinite mercy and goodness hath chosen to exert his influence, so also the before-mentioned supernatural operation of God, by which we are regenerated, in no wise excludes or subverts the use of the gospel, which the most wise God has ordained to be the seed of regeneration, and food of the soul. Wherefore, as the apostles, and teachers who succeeded them, piously instructed the people concerning this grace of God, to his glory, and the abasement of all pride, and in the meantime, however, neglected not to keep them by the sacred precepts of the gospel in the exercise of the Word, sacraments, and discipline; so even to this day, be it far from either instructors or instructed to presume to tempt God in the church by separating what he of his good pleasure hath most intimately joined together. For grace is conferred by means of admonitions; and the more readily we perform our duty, the more eminent usually is this blessing of God working in us, and the more directly is his work advanced; to whom alone all the glory both of means and of their saving fruit and efficacy is forever due. Amen.

Canons III / IV, B, 9:

Art. 9. Who teach: that grace and free will are partial causes, which together work the beginning of conversion, and that grace, in order of working, does not precede the working of the will; that is, that God does not efficiently help the will of man unto conversion until the will of man moves and determines to do this. For the ancient church has long ago condemned this doctrine of the Pelagians, according to the words of the apostle: "So then it is not of him that willeth, nor of him that runneth, but of God that hath mercy" (Rom. 9:16). Likewise: "For who maketh thee to differ? and what hast thou that thou didst not receive?" (I Cor. 4:7). And: "For it is God who worketh in you both to will and to work, for his good pleasure" (Phil. 2:13).

Canons V, A, 14:

Art. 14. And as it hath pleased God, by the preaching of the gospel, to begin this work of grace in us, so he preserves, continues, and perfects it by the hearing and reading of his Word, by meditation thereon, and by the exhortations, threatenings, and promises thereof, as well as by the use of the sacraments.

Belgic Confession, Article XXIV:

Art. XXIV. We believe that this true faith, being wrought in man by the hearing of the Word of God and the operation of the Holy Ghost, doth regenerate and make him a new man, causing him to live a new life, and freeing him from the bondage of sin. Therefore it is so far from being true that this justifying faith makes men remiss in a pious and holy life, that, on the contrary, without it they would never do anything out of love to God, but only out of self-love or fear of damnation. Therefore it is impossible that this holy faith can be unfruitful in man: for we do not speak of a vain faith, but of such a faith which is called in Scripture a faith that worketh by love, which excites man to the practice of those works which God has commanded in his Word.

Which works, as they proceed from the good root of faith, are good and acceptable in the sight of God, forasmuch as they are all sanctified by His grace: howbeit they are of no account towards our justification. For it is by faith in Christ that we are justified, even before we do good works; otherwise they could not be good works, any more than the fruit of a tree can be good before the tree itself is good.

Therefore we do good works, but not to merit by them (for what can we merit?), nay, we are beholden to God for the good works we do, and not he to us, since it is he that worketh in us both to will and to do of his good pleasure. Let us therefore attend to what is written: When ye shall have done all those things which are commanded you, say, we are unprofitable servants; we have done that which was our duty to do. In the meantime, we do not deny that God rewards our good works, but it is through his grace that he crowns his gifts.

Moreover, though we do good works, we do not found our salvation upon them; for we do no work but what is polluted by our flesh, and also punishable; and although we could perform such works, still the remembrance of one sin is sufficient to make God reject them. Thus then we would always be in doubt, tossed to and fro without any certainty, and our poor consciences continually vexed, if they relied not on the merits of the suffering and death of our Savior.

3. That the ground of infant baptism is the command of God and the fact that according to Scripture He established His covenant in the line of continued generations.

IV. Besides, the Protestant Reformed Churches: Believe and maintain the autonomy of the local church. For proof we refer to the **Belgic Confession, Article XXXI**:

> **Art. XXXI.** We believe that the ministers of God's Word, and the elders and deacons, ought to be chosen to their respective offices by a lawful election by the church, with calling upon the name of the Lord, and in that order which the Word of God teacheth. Therefore everyone must take heed not to intrude himself by indecent means, but is bound to wait till it shall please God to call him; that he may have testimony of his calling, and be certain and assured that it is of the Lord. As for the ministers of God's Word, they have equally the same power and authority wheresoever they are, as they are all ministers of Christ, the only universal Bishop, and the only Head of the church. Moreover, that this holy ordinance of God may not be violated or slighted, we say that every one ought to esteem the ministers of God's Word, and the elders of the church, very highly for their work's sake, and be at peace with them without murmuring, strife, or contention, as much as possible.

Church Order, Article 36:

> **Art. 36.** The classis has the same jurisdiction over the consistory as the particular synod has over the classis and the general synod over the particular.

Only the consistory has authority over the local congregation. **Church Order, Article 84:**

> **Art. 84.** No church shall in any way lord it over other churches, no minister over other ministers, no elder or deacon over other elders or deacons.

The **Form for the Installation of Elders and Deacons** [in "Concerning the Deacons" section]:

> " . . . called of God's church, and consequently of God himself. . . ."

Appendix G

The Stocking Is Finished (by Schilder)

(Translation by Theodore Plantinga of "De Kous Is Af," an article by Klaas Schilder that originally appeared in the magazine *De Reformatie* of November 17, 1951, pp. 61–63, as found in Appendix II of *Schilder's Struggle for the Unity of the Church* by Rudolf Van Reest. Two paragraphs near the end of the original Dutch article have been omitted in this translation. Used with permission of Inheritance Publications, Neerlandia, Alberta, Canada.)

From the United States and Canada I have received reports, some public and some private, that compel me to write this article. Those reports have to do with the Protestant Reformed Churches. What has happened there in recent weeks leads me to make the following statements.

(i) I have never regretted what I wrote about the Protestant Reformed Churches in the past, or what I have done and pleaded for, and I still believe I was doing the right thing then.

(ii) But now that they have changed course over there, contrary to all fraternal advice and theological argumentation, I accept the consequences of their change of course, and I do not regard it as responsible to keep silent any longer. What remains to be said is this: The stocking is finished, and so we must call it a day (*we zetten er een streep onder*) and say goodbye—with a feeling of regret, but in full awareness of what we are doing.

As for statement (i), readers of *The Reformation* know that for years, beginning long before the liberation took place, I have said: "Let's make sure we don't forget about those Protestant Reformed Churches, and do what you can to set right what was done wrong in relation to them." I believed then—and still believe today—that the Christian Reformed Church in North America, following poor leadership and incited by some preposterous argumentation (à Mastricht!) here and there at its Synod of Kalamazoo (1924), perpetrated an abominable injustice toward—to mention only one name—one of her most capable ministers and theologians, Rev.

Herman Hoeksema. You will recall that the battle had to do with so-called common grace. Now, as for all the things that Hoeksema wrote about this matter, there is no person who will subscribe to all of it, from A to Z. But the ammunition which the Synod used against him did not hit its target at all; the Synod was too rash. The upshot was that he was suspended anyway, and then came all the rest of it. The result was a situation of miserable misunderstanding, like the one that celebrated its orgiastic triumph in the Netherlands in 1944.

When I made my first visit to the United States in 1939, the damage that had been done already made a deep impression upon me. And when there was a conference of ministers at which Hoeksema appeared fully prepared for the battle whereas the others had virtually nothing to say in response to him, with some of them even taking refuge behind a newspaper, without making any attempt to understand him (now that was a conference [samenspreking] based on a one-sided written preparation!), I understood that this injustice would never be made right. I also understood that Hoeksema is of concern to us in the Netherlands, for we should not allow ourselves to become accountable in relation to the injustice done to him by the Christian Reformed Church, with which we were in correspondence. Naturally, part of the Free University was angry (you should come and see today what they have made of common grace over there), but that didn't matter. I am convinced that to some extent, the wrath of the Free University as it rained down upon us in 1944 was also a consequence of the dark cloud that has hung there since my trip to the United States. I know enough about the correspondence that was carried on behind my back. The Protestant Reformed Churches may remember it, or perhaps forget it; it doesn't matter to me, for I have never taken pride in saying that we here in the Netherlands have taken upon ourselves *some of the scorn aimed at them.* That was not something of merit on our part; it was simply the consequence of the propagation of certain misunderstandings in which some Free University people dared to engage.

Now, I believed then—and I still believe it today—that it was our task first of all to keep the number of churches in God's wide world as small as possible, at least within regional bounds. It is necessary to recognize some geographical church boundaries; as for other church boundaries, they must be eliminated or prevented from arising *insofar as it is within our power*. We expected that the *stream* of immigrants, whom we were sorry to see departing from our churches as they moved especially to Canada, would not be part of our church federation in the Netherlands, and this indeed turned out to be the case (although for a long time the churches in Indonesia did remain part of our federation here, and still are today). Instead those immigrants would organize themselves within a geographically based federation in their new "fatherland." When they were crossing the ocean, I thought that if it was at all possible, we should keep them and the Protestant Reformed Churches, toward which we had some obligations in virtue of past history, from *needlessly* increasing the number of institutes. Taking account of the fact that the Protestant Reformed Churches were special to us from a *historical* point of view (as having been isolated unjustly by the Christian Reformed Church, and then having rightly liberated themselves), we sought help for our immigrants at the right time (at first they were overwhelmed with friendliness on the part of people with which they could better not establish ties); and we were happy that at first the help we sought was given. We were *also* happy about this for the sake of the Protestant Reformed Churches themselves. Whoever is sensible and obedient does not take a self-satisfied delight *(binnenvetters-pleizier)* in being needlessly isolated. Such isolation must *always* be the fault of the *others*, e.g. of people who refuse, permanently, to give a clear answer to clear and necessary questions.

When colleague Hoeksema and I were involved together in an extensive and patient final conference and he himself proposed to bring our theological discussions to an end, declaring (after hearing my reply), "That is Reformed," I went back to the Netherlands a cheerful man. I thought to myself, "Well then, there are still people who respect the divine command not to take pleasure in expanding the number of 'denominations.'"

I do not regret all that I did in those days. I will say again, this *had* to happen, and that *was permissible*—in those circumstances.

As to statement (ii), the spirits are still not at rest. To my considerable amazement, colleague Hoeksema, who knows from his own painful experience what misery can result from foolish bindings, did not step into the breach when the inclination also arose in his own circles to begin "binding" again. He helped to draw up a "Declaration" and recommended it to the church—a "Declaration" which I dealt with at great length (you will soon be able to buy what I have written about this matter in the form of a separate publication) arguing that it is not necessary, that it does not represent a good interpretation of the Confessions, and that, insofar as it proposes to sharpen or clarify the Confessions through new formulations, it labors under certain delusions which, if the "Declaration" is once accepted, will create a little church with a narrow basis. The basis would be so narrow that, note well, because of what has *"ecclesiastical validity"* for this small group (I can already hear the jeers from the Dutch synodocracy in The Hague!), this small church would have to start "dealing with" people, people who simply want to affirm what our revered fathers affirmed before us and placed in the preface to the Statenvertaling's New Testament.

And it has come to pass. The Declaration has been definitively accepted. The able theologian Hoeksema allowed himself to become entangled in a system in which contra-Kalamazoo manipulations (rather than anti-Kalamazoo achievements) could be produced—and those manipulations became unavoidable. Alas, we are already hearing about discipline exercised against people who dared to continue speaking the language of the Statenvertaling and have not a drop of Arminian blood in their veins. I do not propose to pass judgment on all the possible stories of which the ins and outs are not known to us here in the Netherlands. I am passing judgment only on the consequences of accepting the Declaration.

I will not even make a judgment regarding the correctness of the following letter that was received by our office:

Grand Rapids
10-23-'51

Gentlemen:

For some time there has been a rupture in church life here in Grand Rapids between brothers of the same household, who ought to be one because they stand on the same basis, namely, Scripture and the confessions. The rupture came about because in the church in which there had not yet been any acts of unscriptural censure or suspension, the church to which we felt the closest affinity, there were certain phenomena of ecclesiastical dissolution and binding which were making it extremely difficult for some of us, and impossible for others of us, to join ourselves to this church, and so we waited for an official decision from the Synod. There were others, however, who regarded it as their calling to let their reformational voice be heard in the churches in order to force them into a crisis in which it would become apparent which way they were going—whether back to the Word, or farther along the downward path.

It is now clear to all of us who have constituted ourselves as the Orthodox Reformed Church that it would be sinful to live in the federation of the Protestant Reformed Churches, given that its Synod of 1951 has officially accepted the Declaration of Principles and has excluded, by public announcement, all those who could not agree with the content of that declaration, regarding them as mutineers and heretics. That this is in fact what happened is evident from the censuring of brothers H. R. De Bolster and H. De Raad. These brothers had objections to the Declaration of Principles and demonstrated on scriptural grounds what was false about this Declaration. But the consistory decided that the protest was in conflict with the Protestant Reformed truth and also that these brothers were not to speak up in the congregation regarding this matter. Naturally, these brothers refused to obey the command of the consistory because they would then no longer be able to exercise the office which Christ has given us. Next came censure because of agitation. One of the grounds for this decision was that the covenant idea which they propounded really contained the notion of a universal atonement and a denial of the total depravity of man and the vicarious suffering of Christ.

For these reasons, those who were unable to agree with the Declaration of Principles liberated themselves from the Protestant Reformed Church and joined with others who did not regard it as justifiable to join with these churches, and together they lawfully continued the church of our Lord Jesus Christ in America, which church came to be called the Orthodox Reformed Church.

Will you be so kind as to place this in the next issue of *The Reformation?* Thanking you in advance for taking the trouble to be of assistance, we remain yours, with cordial fraternal greetings. In the name of the consistory.

J. LAND
706 Alexander SE
Grand Rapids (Mich.), USA

We reckon with the possibility that there were some factors at work in these events which were not known to us here and are not included in this discussion. This could well be the case in good faith—we are accusing no one.

Neither is it necessary to sift through the details of this letter. *The Standard Bearer* should not regard our publication of this letter—under the qualifications mentioned above—as an unfriendly deed.

We have enough in *this* fact, that if *I* were to live in Grand Rapids, *I* would also refuse to accept the Declaration of Principles. I would also refuse to remain silent. *In the name of this order*—an order which I call disorder and which I abhor—I would also have to be censured. The die is cast, and the Evil One has again managed to spoil something beautiful. Yet another little church has been established, and it was not necessary, not necessary, not necessary. For I know what the Arminian position is, and I also know that one can set the entire Declaration aside without falling into Arminianism. On the contrary, in order to hang on to sound, fundamental Reformed ideas, we affirm that the promise of God is not prediction and is not realized without involving our responsibility. And faith is never a condition in the Arminian sense, any more than the condition of which the preface to the Statenvertaling speaks is an Arminian notion.

And so, the stocking is finished. All there is left for us to do is to continue to prophesy. We will ask, but we will not beg. We will help, but we will not haggle. We do not wish to take upon ourselves the blame for establishing yet another church—number such-and-such. However, when we reject a foolish binding, we will not regard the consequences of such *obedience* as the sin spoken of in Articles 79 and 80 of the Church Order. We will say: "Keep your heads high, for God is the Leader of history." The one who is isolating *himself* this time—for the first time, alas, in his beautiful life—is our friend Hoeksema. And so we say farewell to him—not as a good friend

but as "angel" of the receiving church, the church that receives immigrants with arms that are both gentle and carefully controlled in their embrace. K.S.

Postscript. Perhaps there are some readers who are now thinking, "The title of this article is not quite correct. This is not a matter of a stocking being finished; rather, the unfinished parts are just lying there." But I maintain that the title *is* a good one. The article is not about other people or about the possibility of cooperation with them but about *our task*. We were responsible. If we had done nothing (insofar as the possibility of action rests with us) in terms of seeking affiliation with *what was already there* ecclesiastically, then we would have been guilty right from the outset. But our people and churches *have* sought contact and *have* made it clear in good time what our position is and what views we do *not* hold, and we *have* patiently looked over the whole Declaration on this side of the ocean, and if after all of this the people in the United States— even while we were discussing steps toward a correspondence relationship!—succumbed to the temptation of requiring more in the church federation than is good, then *our* stocking is finished. We should not talk about the matter any more but simply go our way. . . .

To make people responsible to press them to make a decision— that is much more often the knitting the church must do. —K.S.

$\mathcal{A}$ppendix H

The Stocking Is Finished (by Hoeksema)

(Text of article "The Stocking Is Finished"
by Herman Hoeksema in the
Standard Bearer of January 1, 1952,
in reply to "De Kous Is Af," by Klaas Schilder
in the November 17, 1951, issue of *De Reformatie*)

Under, the caption "De Kous Is Af" (The Stocking is Finished),
Dr. Schilder published an article in *De Reformatie* of Nov. 17, 1951,
on which he certainly must expect a reply in the *Standard Bearer*,
and which I certainly cannot afford to pass up without comment.

The main thrust of the article, as I understand it, is that the
relationship between the Gereformeerde Kerken (Art. 31) in the
Netherlands and our churches is finally and definitely severed,
and that, on their part, at least, no further attempts will be made
at correspondence. And the blame for this situation is placed, of
course, entirely on us, the Protestant Reformed Churches. As
the reader will expect, the immediate occasion for the writing
of this article by Dr. Schilder is the passing of the Declaration of
Principles by our last Synod.

I will not take the trouble to quote and to translate the entire
article. This is not necessary, and it would take too much space
in our paper: But we will reflect on a few items, and at the same
time review the history of our correspondence with the Liberated
Churches in the Netherlands. And the readers may judge where
the blame lies. Dr. Schilder writes that the stocking is finished. But
I would say that the knitting of the stocking was a complete failure,
and that the failure must be blamed not on our churches, but 'on
the churches in the Netherlands. Instead of knitting a stocking, we
tangled up the whole business.' And the best that can be done is
to unravel that tangle and start from the beginning, that is, if the
Liberated Churches in the Netherlands still desire correspondence
with us. And in spite of the history we made in the last couple of
years, I still think that a certain form of correspondence between

our churches, is desirable, and that not only for us,—in fact, not in the first place for us,—but also, and in the first place, for the Liberated Churches in the Netherlands. For although Dr. Schilder writes that I have entangled myself in a network,—I suppose he means: of confused doctrines; and again, I suppose he refers to the Declaration of Principles,—I maintain, and I am ready to prove it, that we as Prot. Ref. Churches maintain the purest form of Reformed truth, and that moreover that purest form of Reformed truth, as principally expressed in our Confessions, is declared in the Declaration of Principles.

Dr. Schilder writes that he has clearly shown that the Declaration was not necessary, that it is not the correct interpretation of the Confessions, and that it is based on misunderstanding. And he writes also that before long he will publish what he has written, about the Declaration in pamphlet or book form, so that everyone may buy it. I promise him that I will pay attention to that pamphlet or book, whatever it is. And he can expect my answer. I would be willing to give him, some advice in regard to its contents, but I suppose that would be too late.

As to the rest of the article, I will begin my reflections by referring to the paragraph in which Dr. Schilder writes about the conferences we had when the brother was here in 1947 in Grand Rapids, Michigan. He writes (and I translate): "And when after a very broad and patient final conference colleague Hoeksema himself made a motion to put a period after the theological discussions, declaring (after we were heard, also in rebuttal): that is reformed, then we returned cheerfully to the Netherlands. We thought: good, there are still people that have a feeling for the divine prohibition, to help with pleasure to extend the number of denominations."

And now Dr. Schilder writes about that conference, it is well that we obtain a complete picture of the discussions that were carried on in those meetings. The first of these conferences was held on Oct. 16. The second lasted three days, from Nov. 4 to Nov. 6. At the first of these conferences I was able to be present only part of the time, due to, my sickness. The second conference I attended from the beginning to end.

Now in those conferences I presented thirteen very definite propositions on the subject of the covenant and the promise. And these propositions I will now quote. Here they follow.

I. The idea of the covenant is not:
   a. The promise.
   b. A contract.
   c. The way of salvation;
   d. An alliance between two parties against a third.

II. But it is the communion of friendship between God and His people in Christ Jesus.
   a. The highest revelation of God's own life as the Triune God. God is one in Being and three in Persons.
   b. Proof:
      1) Scripture speaks of an eternal covenant.
      2) The tabernacle and temple are the dwelling place of God with men.
      3) Abraham is called the friend of God.
      4) Enoch and Noah walked with God.
      5) Texts as Ps. 25:14, II Cor. 6:16-18, etc.
      6) The end of all things is: the tabernacle of God with men. Rev. 21:3.
      7) The center of this communion of friendship between God and His people is the incarnation.

III. This was the idea of the covenant in paradise. No covenant of works.

IV. God alone establishes His covenant and maintains it. He does this on the basis of the merits of Christ and through the grace of the Holy Spirit. Unconditional.

V. The fruit of the establishment of God's covenant with us is that we love the Lord our God with all our heart, with all our soul, with all out mind, with all our powers, forsake the world, crucify our old nature, and walk in a new and holy life.

VI. The promise of the covenant God realizes only in the elect even as it is meant for them alone. Rom. 9:6-8, 15; Heb. 6:16-18.

VII. The dispensation of the covenant runs in the line of the generations of believers.
   a. In that line the promise is administered by the church to all

without distinction. All are baptized; instructed in the way of the covenant, come under the preaching, and are subject to the discipline of the church. All therefore confront, the responsibility to love the Lord their God, to forsake the world, etc.

    b. The reprobate, however, violate the covenant of God, as Esau, and thereby aggravate their judgment.

    c. The elect, however, in whom God realizes His promise are saved and by grace come to stand in the world as of the party of the living God.

VIII. The elect children of the covenant are usually regenerated from infancy:

    a. The promise of God is fulfilled in them.

    b. God places them from infancy in the sphere of the preaching.

    c. Experience plainly teaches this.

IX.   The meaning of "sanctified in Christ" in the first question of the baptism form is subjective:

    a. That is the only meaning of the phrase in the Bible.

    b. It stands over against "conceived and born in sin".

    c. This interpretation is historically correct.

X.   No separation can be made in the first part of the Baptism Form between the work of the Father and the Son; on the one hand, and that of the Spirit, on the other.

    a. The Father seals unto us that He establishes an eternal covenant of grace with us.

    b. The Son that He washes us in His blood from all our sins.

    c. The Holy Spirit assures us that He will apply unto us that which we have in Christ.

    d. All this is applicable only to the elect.

XI.   The thanksgiving in the Form also has in view only the elect.

    a. The forgiveness of sin.

    b. Membership in Christ.

    c. Adoption unto children.

XII. Children of the promise in Rom. 9 means the elect seed of the covenant.

XIII. What is usually called the covenant of redemption or the counsel of peace has no ground in Scripture, but is the covenant between Triune God and Christ as the Mediator, or the Servant of Jehovah.

Although it was far beyond my power at the time, yet I managed to discuss these propositions for approximately four hours in both conferences.

And now I will quote what I wrote in the *Standard Bearer* concerning these propositions, and especially concerning the reply by Dr. Schilder at the time. About the first conference, that of Oct. 16, I wrote as follows:

"In the afternoon Dr. Schilder replied to these propositions, but my strength was still too limited to attend the afternoon session.

"According to reports, however, he seems to have emphasized that our differences were not a question of churches but of theologians. For the rest it was largely a matter of terminology and emphasis."

On the second conference, that of Nov. 4 to 6, I wrote as follows:

"The first day of this conference Dr. Schilder spoke. He elaborated on his view of the covenant, especially emphasizing the covenant as a historical institution. He explained his idea of the parties in the covenant, elaborated especially on his conception of the conditions in the covenant, on the relation between promise and demand, and rejected the view of the late Prof. Heyns in as far as he proposes a subjective covenant grace for all the children of the covenant. Dr. Schilder spoke freely, and I am sorry that he did not briefly summarize his view in the form of definite propositions."

And again, in the same conference, I proposed my second set of propositions, propositions 8 and 13 above. And concerning this I wrote as follows.

"The afternoon of the same day, that is, the 5th of November and the forenoon of the next day was occupied by Dr. Schilder's reply to those propositions.

"On the whole, we had very interesting and instructive meetings.

"The differences between the Liberated Churches and us, as

they were brought out in the discussion, concerned especially the following points:

> "1. First of all, the definition of the covenant. According to us the idea of the covenant is essentially that of friendship and fellowship between God and His people in Christ; the Liberated Churches, although they do not define the covenant, nevertheless lay all emphasis on promise and demand.

> "2. In our view the promise of the covenant is for the elect only; according to the Liberated Churches the promise is for all that are born in the covenant line, although this must not be understood in the Arminian sense, since also they emphasize the truth that God Himself must fulfill all the conditions of the covenant.

> "3. The Liberated Churches speak of parties in the covenant, although they admit that in the real sense man cannot be a party over against God; we prefer to speak with the Baptism Form of parts rather than of parties.

Now Dr. Schilder, in the paragraph which I quoted and translated above, once more states that at the close of his reply I must have said: "That is Reformed." I have called his attention to this error before, and now I will repeat it emphatically, and hope that Dr. Schilder will take note of it that I did not say, "That is Reformed," but that I said, "He is Reformed." (The difference is plain to all that can read. If I said, "That is Reformed," I would have subscribed emphatically to all that friend Schilder said at the conference, and that meant that I would have subscribed to the Heynsian idea of the covenant, which in my conviction is far from Reformed. But we must remember, in the first place, that we had a very friendly discussion with Dr. Schilder, although we agreed to differ. In the second place, we were undoubtedly all somewhat under the influence of Schilder's charming personality, and in his entire talk he emphasized repeatedly that our differences were no differences of principle, but rather of terminology. Besides, at the time I received the impression that Dr. Schilder himself did not entirely agree with the Liberated view of the covenant. I cannot definitely state why I received that impression, and I am sorry that

Dr. Schilder did not leave something black on white in the form of definite propositions which we could criticize today. I remember that during the conference one of our ministers approached me and said, "When you speak, we all know what you mean; but when Schilder speaks, I don't know what exactly he is driving at." I remember, too, the sharp remark which the Rev. G. Vos made during that same conference, virtually accusing Dr. Schilder of Arminianism. And certainly, the Rev. Ophoff was not satisfied, and wanted to ask Dr. Schilder some very pointed questions, for which, however, he was too late, because the meeting had adjourned when he came in. And therefore, friend Schilder must never write again that I said at the end of his reply: "That is Reformed." For I never did. But I do remember that I said, "He is Reformed," understanding that statement in a general sense, and certainly not in the specific sense in which we as Protestant Reformed Churches, since 1924, are Reformed. That I do not regard the Liberated conception of the covenant Reformed, Dr. Schilder knows, very well. And he was aware of that even before he came to this country in 1947. For immediately after the war, as soon as we could have correspondence together, I wrote friend Schilder a long letter, stating in unambiguous terms what I thought of his stand, and asking him how it were possible that he could so have changed that he now adopted the Heynsian view of the covenant, and that, in a speech at the conference at the Hague, where the *Acte der Vrijmaking* was signed, he could make a plea for union with the Christelijke Gereformeerde Kerken, which before the war, he always considered as walking in the way of disobedience.

Now in the main those thirteen propositions which I defended at our conferences certainly represented the doctrine as had always been maintained in our Protestant Reformed Churches, especially over against Heynsianism. How then could Dr. Schilder when he returned to the Netherlands, advise his people everywhere, when they immigrated to this country or to Canada to join the Protestant Ref. Churches? Surely, we desired correspondence. But correspondence does not necessarily mean an organic union. The differences between us were rather fundamental, although Dr. Schilder called them differences in terminology. Of this we were not convinced. But, as I said, Dr. Schilder advised his people to join the Protestant Reformed Churches when they came to America, although we stood in no relation as sister churches as yet, and therefore could not receive attestations from them, or they from us. The result was that when we labored in Canada among the immigrants, we did not at once organize them into Prot. Ref. Churches, but first thoroughly instructed them, so that they knew the differences in doctrine between their churches and ours. Only when they were sufficiently indoctrinated and understood our position, and agreed with our truth, did we organize them into churches in our communion. And, even after those churches were organized, like Hamilton and Chatham, we did not receive membership papers from any Reformed Churches of the Netherlands, and did not receive prospective members into the communion of our churches until they had first been instructed in regard to the truth as taught in our Prot. Ref. Churches. Naturally, this caused trouble. For evidently in the Old Country the people had received the impression that when they came to America, they would be received without question and without condition as members of the Protestant Reformed Churches. That they labored under such an impression certainly was not our fault, but was the fault of Dr. Schilder, who, according to reports, had advised all the people of the Liberated Churches to join the Prot. Ref. Churches in America. But once more the differences in regard to the doctrine of the covenant and of the promise were too great and too fundamental to permit members from the Liberated Churches into our communion. Hence, we demanded that they promise to submit to our instruction, and in the meantime not to agitate against our doctrine. This was honest and fair to all concerned. We did not excommunicate any brethren and sisters in our Lord Jesus Christ and bar them from the table of communion. But we wanted to preserve the Reformed truth in its purest form, the truth as we have always maintained it in our Prot. Ref. Churches. The result is, first, the sad history of Hamilton, and now the even worse history of Chatham. Certainly, that the stocking was not knitted and properly finished was not our fault.

Nor was it our fault that the stocking of correspondence was not properly knitted officially, but became one entangled mess. Let me relate the history.

In the early part of 1948 (I forget the date) the Comm. of Correspondence of the Prot. Ref.. Churches addressed a letter to the deputies for correspondence of the Liberated Churches in the Netherlands, suggesting correspondence between the two churches. This letter was originally composed by the Rev. J. de Jong. I received that letter in California, where I was still recuperating from my attack of thrombosis. I did not agree with the contents of the letter, but I signed it on condition that the Rev. G. M. Ophoff, the third party of the committee, would also be willing to sign it. The latter, however, at first was not willing at all, because he too did not agree with the contents of the letter. But under repeated pressure he signed his name to the document, and so it was sent to the deputies for correspondence in the Old Country. However, when the work of the committee for correspondence was reported at the Synod of 1948, the latter condemned that letter, and decided to rewrite it and to send a different letter to the same deputies for correspondence in the Netherlands, and to their Synod that was to be held at Amersfoort the same summer. I write this because not the letter from the deputies of correspondence, but the letter from the Synod of our churches is therefore the only official document which the Synod of Amersfoort could consider. In that letter of our Synod we did not ask for complete correspondence, but we asked that the matter concerning correspondence would be thoroughly discussed before correspondence was finally established.

The Synod of the Reformed Churches (Art. 31) convened that same year at Amersfoort, acted upon our request, and decided: 1) To empower the deputies for correspondence with foreign churches to get into contact with the Prot. Ref. Churches, in order to prepare the relation of correspondence between these churches. 2) That the deputies for correspondence with foreign churches would have to serve the following synod with advice. And 3) that in the meantime, the ministers of the Protestant Reformed Churches may be admitted to the pulpits of the Reformed Church (Art. 31) of the Netherlands, to speak an edifying word. Several delegates of the Synod voted against this proposal of the committee of pre-advice, and at least 7 or 8 of them requested that their negative vote be recorded in the minutes. Among the latter were such well-known figures as the Rev D. van Dijk, Prof. Holwerda, and the Rev. van Raalte of Neede. To my mind, it certainly was not very wise of the Synod to open the pulpits of the Reformed Churches (Art. 31) of the Netherlands for our ministers before the relation of complete correspondence was established.

But what happened further? For more than a year we never heard anything from the deputies for correspondence with foreign churches of the Netherlands. In fact, officially we did not hear of them until November, 1949. That was a mistake. Those deputies should have sought contact with our Committee of Correspondence as soon as possible, so that at least we could report something officially to our Synod of 1949. But, as I said, we never heard of them. That the Synod opened their pulpits for our ministers was the first wrong stitch in the stocking. That the deputies for foreign correspondence did not get into contact with our Committee for Correspondence was the second wrong stitch. And the whole thing became one entangled mess when in the meantime, in August 1949, the letter written by Prof. Holwerda to the immigrants in Canada was brought to our attention.

That letter revealed: 1) That instead of transacting ecclesiastical business in an ecclesiastical way, and therefore, instead of contacting officially our Committee of Correspondence, the Committee for Foreign Correspondence in the Netherlands decided to transact the business of the churches unofficially by meeting behind the back of the Committee for Correspondence of our churches with the Revs. de Jong and Kok. 2) That the fears of those that had objections against correspondence with our churches, such as van Dijk, van Raalte, Holwerda, and others, were mysteriously allayed. 3) That the impression was created that no definite interpretation of the Confessions was maintained and binding in the Prot. Ref. Churches. 4) That the impression was made that there was ample room for the covenant view of the Liberated in our Prot. Ref. Churches, and that therefore the immigrants could make free propaganda for the Liberated view in our churches. 5) That only on that basis the immigrants were advised to join the Protestant Reformed Churches, but at the same time that, if the conception of such men as the Revs. Hoeksema and Ophoff were maintained in the Prot. Ref. Churches, they should never join.

This was not knitting a stocking, surely not the stocking of ecclesiastical correspondence, but was working on a hopeless and tangled mess.

On our part, in the light of all this history, and especially in the light of our experience with the Liberated in Canada, the Mission Committee felt the need of a definite statement which might be used by them and by our missionaries as the basis for the organization of our churches. That need was filled by the Declaration. And that Declaration was passed by our last Synod.

Let not Dr. Schilder therefore say that the stocking is finished. It must be entirely unravelled, until we come to the first false stitch, and then start kniting anew.

To one more item I must needs call the attention of our readers. In the same article Dr. Schilder publishes a letter of a certain J. Land, who lives at 706 Alexander St., Grand Rapids, Michigan. In this letter Mr. Land blames our Consistory for censuring the brethern H. R. de Bolster and H. de Raad.

Personally I am very sorry that this matter concerning the censure of de Bolster and de Raad was given publication without first consulting our Consistory. For this publication savors of the sin of condemning any man rashly or unheard, the sin against the ninth commandment. And Dr. Schilder especially should know better than that. I am sorry that this matter is published, not because the action of our Consistory cannot stand the light, but because the brethren de Bolster and de Raad certainly sinned grievously and became the proper objects of censure. I am very sorry that this matter must be published, because personally I was rather attached to these young students and did everything I could for them.

Besides, I never had any trouble with them in class, and they always behaved very well.

Then all of a sudden I heard from the Rev. Hanko that they had sent a protest against the Declaration to the Consistory. I stood aghast. For to me personally, or in school, they had never objected to the doctrine that I taught, nor to the contents of the Declaration. And they had plenty opportunity to acquaint themselves with the Declaration, because in my young people's catechism class I devoted a whole year to the discussion of that document. But they never attended. Now, mark you, in the abstract they had the perfect right to protest against the Declaration at our Synod, for they were members of our church. Nevertheless, I considered it rather impudent for two young men that were after all only visitors for three months at a time in our country, to put their nose into the official business of our churches. I called them to my home, and talked to them personally. They asked me whether I would not explain the Declaration once more in our classroom in school in the presence of all the students. I answered them that I would not take time for that in school, but that I would meet with all the students in the presence of the Rev. Ophoff and Hanko in my home, and then offer a free discussion on the subject. This meeting was held. I expounded to them the truth as it always had been maintained in our churches, and they had nothing to say. Nevertheless, they insisted on their protest.

In the meantime, of course, the Consistory treated the matter. And also the Consistory did not object to their protesting against the Declaration of Principles. For they too considered that it was their perfect right. But they did object to the Liberated doctrine which they defended in their protest openly. Mr. J. Land states in his letter that the brethren de Bolster and de Raad proved the truth of their protest on Scriptural grounds. Nothing could be farther from the truth. Yet even so, the Consistory did not censure them because they harbored Liberated doctrines, but they demanded of them the promise that they would not make agitation in the congregation for their views. And this they refused.

At a meeting of our Consistory at which I was personally present and presided, the two brethren appeared. I once more entered carefully into the contents of their protest, and proved to them that it certainly was not Reformed truth. And again the two brethren had nothing to say, and did not defend themselves with one word. But when I asked them again whether they would promise not to agitate for their views in the congregation, they refused once more. And what is worse, they both stated personally that if the Consistory would censure them for this, they would make propaganda for the Liberated view in all our churches. In other words, they would try to create a schism in the Prot. Ref. Churches. Then they were censured, not on the basis of their doctrine or of their views, but because they meant to agitate for the Liberated views not only in our church but also in all the other churches of the Prot. Ref. communion. Thereupon they separated from our churches. In other words, these two brethren broke their solemn oath before God and the churches that in case of misdemeanor they would submit themselves to the government of the church and to church discipline. They could, of course, have appealed their case to the Classis. And the Classis certainly would have done justice to them. They could have appealed to the Synod. But instead of taking that proper ecclesiastical way they acted as revolutionaries and rebels and broke their vow. Once more I talked to them. They approached me, and told me that they were sorry that they had separated and would like to confess their sin. I informed them that that would certainly be possible, but that seeing that their sin was public before the whole congregation (for they had already assembled in a separate group on the sabbath) they would also have to make public confession. After that I never saw them again.

Such is the case of the two Henks. And once more I state here that I am very sorry that I was compelled to reveal this case because of the letter in the *Reformatie*.

In conclusion, I want to emphasize once more that the stocking is not finished. And if Dr. Schilder feels that because of the stand of our churches as revealed in the Declaration of Principles he does not want to unravel the tangle and start knitting anew, it suits me. Nevertheless, I want to state in that case that I am disappointed in him, and for the rest say: "Vale, Amice Schilder."—H.H.

$\mathcal{A}$ppendix I

Report of the Committee of Pre-advice in Re Protests of the Revs. H. Hoeksema and G. M. Ophoff against the Consistory of First Church [Minority Report Follows Majority]

[Majority Report]

Classis East of the Protestant Reformed Churches convened on May 19, 1953

Esteemed brethren in the Lord:

Your committee, undersigned, after receiving your charge to study the protests of the Rev. H.H. and G.M.O. against the First Church has performed its duty and herewith submits to you for your consideration the fruits of its labors. Your committee assures you, that it has labored diligently, devoted many hours of study and thought to the questions at hand, and that it has met several times during the past month. Although we will not say that the last word has been said about this question, we are nevertheless convinced that the judgment expressed herein and the advice given should be adopted by Classis and that the protestants be answered accordingly. It is our ardent hope and firm trust and constant prayer that in the way herein set forth the Reformed truth may be confessed, confidence and joy may be restored in our churches to the glory of God's Name.

The Duty of Your Committee

The duty of your committee is formulated for us in Art. 148 of the Minutes of the former sessions of this Classis, held on April 8–16, and reads as follows: "Moved to place the matter of First Church in the hands of a committee to report at the next meeting, to begin on May 19, and to come with well-grounded advice."

From the foregoing Article of the minutes it is evident, that your committee is expected to read, study, evaluate and render judgment of the issue presented by the protestants and, after thorough discussion and understanding of the issue, to render judgment. Thus guidance will be given to Classis in its decision of the matters of these protests.

The Documents Placed in our Hand

Your committee had the following documents to consider in this study for giving pre-advice.

From Classis we received the following documents.

1. The two separate protests of the Revs. H. Hoeksema and G. M. Ophoff.

2. The various protests to the Consistory by the protestants as well as the letters of correspondence to the Consistory by Rev. DeWolf, under the heading "Protests", and "Answers" to questions in the examination.

3. A transcript of all the Minutes having to do with this entire case from April 1951 till April 1953.

Your committee has also received all the supplementary material for study from the Clerk of First Church so as to be able to interpret the decisions as given in the Transcript of Minutes. Besides, your committee has read the sermon outlines of Rev. DeWolf of the sermons in question in these protests.

Note: Your committee realizes that this material in the "outlines" is no evidence of how the statements were given, but that the outlines do serve to show the exegesis and the dogmatic construction of Rev. DeWolf as expressed in these sermons.

From these documents we will only quote or make reference as far as is necessary to substantiate our report and findings. We will limit ourselves to the actual body of the protests in our advice.

The Method of Treating These Protests

In our study of these protests of the two protestants, we find, that both protests deal with the same alleged grievances against the Consistory of First Church in re its decisions to approve of the "Answers" given by Rev. DeWolf in the examination given him according to the Formula of Subscription.

The question, therefore, arose how to formally treat these protests. It was decided that:

1. Although both protests deal with the same matters, and although the arguments employed in each protest are also in good

part identical, nevertheless each protest be treated separately, and that, too, on the basis of their separate merits and demerits. This does not imply a separate report of each, for we have "sandwiched" our study of each of these protests in one report.

2. Your committee has also given study to each sermon by itself, both as to the doctrinal and church political aspects.

3. In our study and report on each sermon we pass through the following steps of investigation:

a. Ascertaining the matter against which the protest is directed whether doctrinal or church political.

b. Ascertain the *interpretation* given by the protestants in matters doctrinal and the *proof given* in matters church political.

c. The evaluation of the protests, the argumentation, premises and conclusions of the protestants, as well as of the alleged "heresy" in the "statements" in question.

d. The advice of the committee to Classis together with certain recommendations.

Note: Since these two sermons were preached at least 17 months apart and each sermon has its own peculiar history and background, your committee offers its advice on each case separately, both as to the doctrinal and the church political questions.

We now turn to the task at hand proper. We submit the following:

I. The protest of the protestants as they deal with the Consistory's action anent the sermon delivered April 15, 1951. The following calls for our consideration:

A. The statement in question *as such*

1. It seems quite evident, that the protestants do not agree as to the exact version of the statement. According to protestant Hoeksema the statement alleged to be heresy is "God promises every one of you that, if you believe, you shall be saved," while according to protestant Ophoff the statement is "God promises to save you all, if you believe."

2. Nor is the version given in the official Minutes of the Consistory again exactly identical with that of either protestant. Here we read "God promises to all of you salvation, if you believe."

See Transcript of Minutes, page 7, Art. 22. See also the protests of H. H. and G.M.O. for their versions.

Although your committee can not express any judgments on this point your committee nevertheless judges that there is an element of confusion as to the exact statement.

However, since these versions do not necessarily differ essentially we will say no more about this matter of version, except that your committee proceeds on the assumption that the version of H. Hoeksema is correct in view of earlier letters written to the Consistory shortly after April 15, 1951. Furthermore this version is not contested by Rev. DeWolf.

B. This "Statement" as interpreted by the protestant

1. In general: It is the contention of protestant Hoeksema, that the Consistory of First Church erred fundamentally and principally in their decision of February 16, 1953. On this meeting by a 9-8 vote they decided as follows:

> "To declare the answers of Rev. DeWolf to the examination to be satisfactory" . . . "and that the doctrine set forth in the "Answers" of Rev. DeWolf to be the true doctrine of the Scriptures and Confessions." Compare Transcript of Minutes, Art. 7 of Jan. 19, and Art. 5 and 6 of Feb. 16, 1953.

Against this decision the Rev. Hoeksema protests as follows:

1. That the Consistory has approved by so doing of the heresy taught publicly by Rev. DeWolf that "God promises every one of you, that if you believe you shall be saved," and "that our act of conversion is a prerequisite to enter into the Kingdom of God."

2. That by this approval, the Consistory has:

a. Forsaken and denied the Protestant Reformed truth, and approved the First Point of 1924 in its worst form.

b. Principally cast out protestant Hoeksema.

c. Necessitated itself to censure the protestant, for not being willing to subscribe to this teaching, and to suspend him from office.

Such is the stand of Rev. Hoeksema and in this stand the Rev. Ophoff concurs in his protest.

2. The statement in question is according to both protestants

Arminian in the real sense of the term, it is heresy worthy of deposition from office.

We shall have to judge whether this is true. Hence, we shall let the protestants speak for themselves.

a. Protestant Ophoff has the following interpretation of this statement. He sums it up in saying, "God promises every one of you, reprobate and elect alike, that if you believe, He will save you." That this promise means "In My (God's) love for you, I promise, pledge, swear by myself, am everlastingly and lovingly resolved, to save every one of you, elect and reprobate alike, if you believe."

Hence, according to protestant Ophoff, Rev. DeWolf's heresy is that of general atonement, free-willism etc. *Forsooth*, a grave error.

b. Protestant Hoeksema gives us his analysis of this statement rather in detail. His conclusion is the same as that of protestant Ophoff. Rev. Hoeksema's analysis of the statement is as follows:

1/ It is *God* that promises. The Rev. DeWolf did not say, "I preach to every one of you that, if you believe, you shall be saved." This might pass, even though it would not be the whole truth. But it is God that promises salvation to everyone in the audience.

2/ God promises. God's promise is always an oath. Moreover, He always fulfills His promises. Still more, He promises salvation only in His grace and everlasting love. The statement is tantamount to saying: "I swear with an oath that I love every one of you, that I am gracious to you all in the preaching of the Gospel, and on my part, am willing and longing to save you all." This is the First Point of 1924 of Kalamazoo accentuated. It is worse than 1924.

3/ God promises every one of you. Who are every one of you? All in the audience, of course, strangers as well as members, righteous and wicked, believers and unbelievers, elect and reprobate. Again, the Rev. DeWolf did not say, "to every one of you I preach the Gospel," but to every one of you, "God promises salvation." This is worse than a general, well-meant offer of salvation.

4 / But perhaps you say: "there was a conditional clause attached to this promise: if you believe; hence, after all, he preached that the promise is only for believers." This I deny. I say once again; if Rev. DeWolf said "I preach to every one of you that if you believe, you shall be saved: he would have preached truth. Or if he had said: God promises to every one of you that believes eternal life he would have preached truth. But he preached something radically different. He did not preach as we always maintained, and as I defended in my pamphlet "Calvin, Berkhof and H. J. Kuiper" and from which the Rev. DeWolf erroneously quotes to sustain his own heresy, the truth of a general preaching of a particular promise, but he preached that God promises to every one head for head and soul for soul, salvation if they believe. What does this mean? This:

a- God, on His part, is willing to save every one. It is He that promises to all. The promise is as general as possible.

b- But whether the promise is to be realized depends on an act on the part of man. God is willing, if man is willing."

We will quote no more. The delegates can find the remainder of this quotation in Rev. Hoeksema's protest.

C. The committee's evaluation of this statement:

1. Introductory observations.

a. It is the task of the committee to judge what the statement in question actually says. It is in our case rather one of *bare analysis* than of *exegesis*.

b. The reason?

1 / Because we do not have a copy of the context in which the statement occurred. This we do have when we exegete a passage from Holy Writ. We have there no statements by themselves. Your committee has read the outline of this sermon, but did not read the statement in question. So this helps us nothing. Hence, we have nothing but the statement. And that throws us back on mere analysis.

2 / Your committee recognizes the fact, that we must distinguish between the statement as such and any explanation of the statement. Were that not so we would need no explanation. We would simply say: there is the statement; read it! In this case we will have an explanation based on bare analysis.

c. This fact of the distinction between the statement and the analysis has in it the consequence, that in approaching this statement your committee had to proceed on the assumption, that the analysis of the protestants was not to be identified with the statement and, therefore, need not *necessarily* be the proper meaning of the statement.

Note: We would have the delegates of Classis remember too, that the Consistory of First Church ruled out everything else but this statement, and that there is not record in the Minutes nor in the archives that they have ever taken any document such as the sermon outline to check their findings.

2. Taking the foregoing into consideration your committee herein sets forth its judgment in this matter:

a. That, in the judgment of the committee, the statement "God promises every one of you that, if you believe, you shall be saved" is indeed open for the analysis and subsequent interpretation of the protestants as this was, more particularly set forth in the protest of Rev. Hoeksema. And, if understood as thus interpreted the statement surely is heresy; a heresy which your committee despises with all their hearts, as do the protestants. And, we may add, a heresy which also the Rev. DeWolf assures us he rejects with all of his heart. Repeatedly he has assured the Consistory of this in various letters, and repeatedly he affirmed the same in the answers in the examination.

b. That, in the judgment of your committee, this statement need not necessarily have all the evil implications as given by the analysis of protestant Hoeksema. We submit that this statement can also simply mean: God's assurance of salvation and ultimate triumph to elect-believing saints. It can have this meaning if taken all by itself and when placed in the proper setting on a Protestant Reformed pulpit. Attend to the following:

1 / The phrase "every one of you" need not necessarily mean "every one in the audience," elect and reprobate alike, the church viewed as a "mixed gathering," but that as we have always maintained that the church is addressed according to the election of grace, called saints in Christ, so this statement "every one of you" means: Every one in the Lord Jesus Christ. The church is

then not a group of *geachte toehoorders*, but she is the living church viewed as she is the body of Christ. In the beginning of each service we address the church as "Beloved in our Lord Jesus Christ," and then we do not mean this in the sense of the "church in the church," but we address the tree according to its good nature in Christ. We caution, however, that it should be quite evident throughout the sermon too that such is the meaning of the minister when he addresses the congregation as "every one of you"; that he is addressing her in the *distributive sense* and not in the collective sense.

2 / That the clause "if you believe" need not necessarily mean that to believe is merely an act of man, which he performs in his own native strength and free-will. As is admitted by protestant Hoeksema it can properly mean simply: it is only for believers. It limits salvation. The phrase is then in a conditional *sentence*, expressing *in what way and by what means* salvation as a conscious reality, forgiveness of sin etc, is received and how the elect apply (*Zueigen*) the same to themselves. It underscores then, that "I cannot receive and apply the same to myself in any other way than by faith only." Thus interpreted (analyzed) the clause agrees very well with the language of the Scriptures, Confessions, Question 84, Heidelberg Catechism and of Reformed Theologians from Calvin down.

3 / That the clause "*God promises* every one of you" then is exactly what it says.

a- God *promises*. God's promise is the oathbound word of assurance of his immutable purpose to apply all the blessings of salvation to the hearts of the individual believer. God does not merely promise this to the whole of the church without due regard for each saint. What he says to Abraham on Moriah (Hebrews 6:16–18) he says to each saint, every struggling believer.

b- *God* promises. Not the preacher promises. He faithfully brings this word of promise as expressed in the Scriptures and, as the Ambassador of Christ, he preaches what *God promises*. No preacher can say I promise you. He must needs say: God promises you all things, believing church, His love, grace, mercy, and peace revealed on the Cross and rooted in sovereign election.

Then God does not merely promise something to the church, but in the preaching where the bread of life is broken, God promises to every believing saint what he needs, the gift of faith, forgiveness of sins, hope of glory, and life everlasting. But to underscore the need of active trust he says: if you believe.

        c- It makes no difference to the committee, *in this analysis*, how Rev. DeWolf now says he meant the statement, we are only interested to show that the statement need not have the "heretical implications" attributed to it by the protestants Hoeksema and Ophoff.

We believe, that we have demonstrated conclusively, that this statement allows for a different interpretation than the one given by the protestants.

Before we pass on to our Advice to Classis we would call attention to the *usus loquendi* (current usage) of the term *promise* in the Confessions. In the Confessions the term promise often has the meaning of the word that is spoken to the church in the Name of the King. It then is a term addressed to believers and not merely concerning them. It speaks to them in the second person and not merely about them in the third person. Confer 69, 71 of the Heidelberg Catechism, Canons III, IV, 8. Promise thus approaches the meaning of "admonition and assurance." This is God's admonition and assurance brought by the preacher.

D. Your committee advises that Classis express:

        1. That it is an axiom of justice, that a man is innocent until proven guilty, and that a statement is not necessarily heretical until proven so. The burden of such proof is for the protestants. Rev. DeWolf's statement stands as non-heretical unless and until it is proven to be heretical, and to be the only possible analysis and interpretation.

        2. That the protestants, Hoeksema and Ophoff have not shown that the statement in question is *necessarily heretical*, that is, implying God's loving intention to save all men, provided they are willing to believe, since the statement can have the implications as stated above under I, C, 2 by your committee.

        3. That at the same time it remains true, that the protestants have conclusively demonstrated the very actual possible heresy that

can be implied in the statement; a statement which rather naturally lends itself to the interpretation of a general promise which we all reject.

4. That, therefore, this statement, if used, should be employed only in such a way that there is no possibility of doubt, that is, that the meaning of the statement in question is indeed a Reformed one. Whether the statement as made by DeWolf would meet the above requirement your committee is not able to judge.

5. That there is sufficient reason in this case to sound the warning of our Fathers of Dort as given in the "Conclusion" of the Canons. "Finally, this Synod exhorts all their brethren in the gospel of Christ to conduct themselves piously and religiously in the handling of this doctrine, both in the universities and in the churches; to direct it as well in discourse as in writing, to the glory of the Divine Name, to holiness of life, and to the consolation of afflicted souls; to regulate by the Scriptures according to the analogy of faith, not only their *sentiments*, but also their *language*; and to abstain from all those phrases which exceed the limits necessary to be observed in ascertaining the genuine sense of the Holy Scriptures; and may furnish insolent sophists with a just pretext for violently assailing, or even vilifying, the doctrine of the Reformed Churches."

II. We now turn to the protest of the protestants as directed against the sermon delivered September 15, 1952. We call attention to the following:

A. The Scripture text and the version of the statement in question.

1. The text in question is Matthew 18:1–4, and it reads as follows: "At the same time came the disciples to Jesus, saying, who is the greatest in the Kingdom of heaven, And Jesus called a little child unto Him, and set him in the midst of them, and he said, Verily I say unto thee, except ye be converted and become as little children, ye shall not enter into the Kingdom of heaven. Whosoever therefore shall humble himself as this little child the same is the greatest in the kingdom of heaven."

Note: The Holland Staten Vertaling translates the Greek

"*strapheete*" by "*gij u verandert*," while the Revised Version translates it "ye turn." We shall have more to say on this point later in this report.

2. The version of the allegedly made statement of Rev. DeWolf in this sermon.

a. It should be noticed that in neither of the protests do we have a literal quotation from the sermon proper. When we say protests we have in mind the copies of the protests to Classis. All we have is a statement of the protestants *in their version* as to what the heretical statement is. This makes it very hard for your committee to judge of this statement in question.

b. Here follow some quotations of the statement in question from the protest to Classis as well as from their letters of protest to the Consistory.

1 / From the pen of Rev. H. Hoeksema. In his first protests to the Consistory we quote the following: "It exclusively emphasized in the body of the sermon, conversion as the work of man." In the same missive to the Consistory Rev. Hoeksema writes, "Now I want you to understand, that I do not fall over the term "prerequisite" as such. But I do want to protest against the context of the sermon in which the word is used. The Rev. DeWolf in that part of the sermon exclusively emphasized conversion as the work of man. And, in that sense, it is not conversion that is the prerequisite, but regeneration, which is absolutely and sovereignly the work of God alone. Thus the Rev. Hoeksema wrote in the first missive.

2 / In a later missive the Rev. Hoeksema changed the wording. He makes distinction between the *work* of conversion and the *act* of conversion. This is a distinction not made by him when he initiated his protest against the sermon. The Rev. Hoeksema changes the *version* of the statement in question. We quote, "In the sermon of last Sunday evening, he literally preached that our *act* of conversion is a condition or prerequisite to enter into the kingdom of God. This is neither Scripture nor the Confessions. There never was a word of explanation about the truth of conversion, that, from the beginning of conversion to our *act* of conversion it is the work of God, (we underscore) that the entrance into the kingdom is not

our act of conversion but God's work of regeneration . . . " Here the Rev. Hoeksema introduces the distinction of *act* of conversion over against the *work* of regeneration.

3 / Again in a later letter the Rev. Hoeksema writes: "The fundamental error of the Rev. DeWolf's sermon is, as I have said before, that he separated man's act of conversion from God's work of conversion, in order to make man's act of conversion a prerequisite to enter the kingdom." Notice again the distinction of God's work and the believer's act.

What must we say of this changing of the version of the statement by protestant Hoeksema? Evidently the first version was incorrect when he presented the Rev. DeWolf as making the work of conversion a prerequisite to enter the kingdom. The later version is evidently correct.

1. Because thus it is "in substance" quoted by the Rev. Ophoff in a letter addressed to the Consistory in protest against this sermon. Writes the Rev. Ophoff, "Rev. DeWolf made in substance the following statements: Except a man humble himself and become as a little child he shall never enter the kingdom of heaven. Whether we call this act of man's humbling himself the way in which he enters the kingdom or the condition on which he enters the kingdom makes little difference: It—namely, a man's becoming as a little child through his humbling himself—is a prerequisite to entering the kingdom." Here, according to Rev. Ophoff, the Rev. DeWolf was speaking of the act of conversion and not of the work of conversion.

2. When we turn to the sermon outline of Rev. DeWolf we read the following under II, B, 3.

3. Meaning—"Except . . ."

a. Call it a condition or a way—makes little difference— evident that it is a prerequisite for entering into the kingdom.

b. . . .

c. Why?

1 / Because no one can enter into the Kingdom in any other way than as a child.

2 / Due to the nature of the Kingdom—it is a K. in which there is no room for anyone who seeks himself—own honor and glory—only room for the glory of God in Christ . . .

Since it is also stated in the sermon of Rev. DeWolf that he has in mind the daily entering, it must refer to the *act* of conversion. Writes he in II, B, 2, b. "Implies that the question for us is always first that of entering—

1 / There is an entering in the final sense.

2 / But also a continual entering, a principle of life— always entering in all our life—as conscious activity. To this the Lord refers in Luke 13:23ff "Strive to enter in." (we underscore).

We therefore except the version of the statement that DeWolf was speaking of the *act* of conversion, the "conscious activity" as he puts it.

B. Our task in giving advice in regard to the protest against this sermon is, at bottom, one of exegesis, and then of determining the validity of the Theological-Confessional construction.

1. In the case of this sermon we are not merely dealing with the meaning of a statement, but rather of the *exegesis of a text* together with the statement that "our act of conversion is prerequisite to enter the kingdom of heaven." Our task here is not one of simple analysis, but it is one of exegesis.

2. Your committee judges that each premise must be proven from the text and the exegesis of the same. That implies that we cannot accept the simple deductive syllogistic reasoning in which the major and minor premises are assumed to be true rather than proven to be true.

A simple sample we have in the following:

1. John is a good farmer.
2. Good farmers are good citizens.
3. John is a good citizen.

But suppose that John is not a farmer, but an office worker. Then the major premise is not pure. Then the whole syllogism fails. The same would happen to the syllogism if the minor premise were not true. In either case the conclusion would be false.

Applied to the case at hand this means: That we cannot simply reason as follows:

1. The use of the term "prerequisite" as such is Arminian.
2. Rev. DeWolf employed the term.
3. Ergo: Rev. DeWolf is Arminian as his usage of the term.

The first matter that must be proven is that the term *as such* is Arminian, but that is not possible, according to your committee, for the simple reason that the term "prerequisite" simply is a formal term when taken by itself. The question is not whether the term is employed, but rather in what thought structure it is employed. And therefore we must proceed exegetically.

We must seek to see whether Rev. DeWolf could on good exegetical grounds preach on this text as he did, and whether "the act of man is the prerequisite to enter into the Kingdom," can stand.

Such is our task as committee. And on the basis of this investigation we must judge of the protests in question.

C. Our evaluation of the protests

1. Our evaluation of the protest of Rev. Ophoff

a. His basic reasoning

1 / The term "prerequisite" puts a sinner outside of the Kingdom of God . . . In this sphere the sinner cannot convert himself. This term therefore cannot be applied to continual conversion for the carnal Christian is in the Kingdom. To insist that this is true makes one an Arminian.

2 / Hence, we cannot speak of conversion in the sense that Christians need daily conversion as a "prerequisite" to enter into the Kingdom.

b. Your committee calls attention to the fact, that Rev. Ophoff here begs the question on three points:

1 / On the possible meaning of "Kingdom" in the text and not in general.

2 / On the possible usage of the term "prerequisite" when taken in connection with the exegesis of the text. Dogmatics may not rule exegesis.

3 / On the exegetical implication of "entering into the Kingdom."

2. The protest of Rev. H. Hoeksema.

a. Here we have the same reasoning as above in the protest of Rev. Ophoff.

b. That in this protest too it is forgotten that the statement of Rev. DeWolf was made in a sermon on Matthew 18:1–4 and not on Colossians 1:13. The Rev. DeWolf was not preaching on the latter text but on the former. And that makes a great deal of difference, in the judgment of your committee.

c. In the judgment of your committee it makes quite a good deal of difference whether one is preaching on being "translated into the Kingdom" or whether one "enters into the Kingdom." The former is a passive notion, the latter may be very active in idea. And yet the two are not mutually exclusive if the former is passive and the latter is active. It simply means that the one is God's work upon us and in us, and the latter is our activity of faith by virtue of this work of God.

d. This distinction is also given in the Canons of Dort. We refer to III, IV, A, Articles 11, 12, 14. Here the work of God is confessed in our conversion in which work of God man does not cooperate one iota. But our Fathers here also speak of the act of believing by virtue of this work. And it is Reformed to hold that we convert ourselves by faith. The order in Theology is "faith and conversion". We quote the latter part of Article 14 where we read "But because He works in man both to will and to do, and indeed all things in all, produces both the will to believe, and the act of believing also." Your committee judges that this act of believing is wrought in us by the Holy Spirit through the precepts of the Gospel in the exercise of the Word. And that this "act of believing" is entering into the Kingdom-life, and in that sense we often speak, according to Scripture of entering into the Kingdom, when we simply mean: walking according to the Spirit of life in Christ. We refer to such a portion of Scripture as Matthew 5:17–48. To forget this is to limit the various aspects in which the Scriptures confront us with the Kingdom of heaven. For it must not be forgotten that the term "Kingdom of Heaven" cannot simply be given in one statement. And in each case the term must be carefully seen in its scope and viewpoint. Thus we read:

1. Simply the Kingdom.
2. The Kingdom of God.
3. The Kingdom of Christ.
4. The Kingdom of *heaven*.
5. The Kingdom of *light*.

Our Fathers interpret the meaning of the Kingdom also from the subjective standpoint of our consciously entering into it in their interpretation of the second petition in Lord's Day 48, Q. 123. Here the believer prays, standing in the Kingdom, that God may so rule us by His Word and Spirit that we submit ourselves more and more unto God's dominion and gracious rule. This submitting of ourselves to God is our actively becoming like little children and thus entering into the Kingdom joys, peace, tranquility of the Holy Spirit. It is our walking by the Spirit even as we live by the Spirit. Galatians 5:25–26.

3. That the exegesis on the basis of taking *"strapheete"* as middle voice, rendering it "ye turn" is based on good Greek grammar, and necessitates taking the "Kingdom" to mean: the Kingdom life, joys etc. It is the Kingdom blessings in Christ Jesus according to eternal election. We have the firstfruits of the Kingdom now, we are in the Kingdom, but we must daily enter *into* the life of the Kingdom, and joy of the Lord.

Note: In the judgment of your committee the following should in this connection be borne in mind:

1. That the exegesis which renders "strapheete" middle voice, and not passive voice, translating it "be turned" instead of "converted" referring this to the act of faith (for faith precedes repentance) has never been considered unreformed. In the Staten Vertaling it is thus meant as is evident from the Kantteekening. We read: "3. Gr. *keert; dat is, afkeert, namelijk, van dezen hoogmoed en eergierigheid."*

2. That the compound verb *"eis-eltheete eis"* should not be read and interpreted as if it were the simple verb *"eltheete eis."* Obviously to *enter the Kingdom* is not the same as to *enter into the Kingdom.*

a. If the text read *"eltheete eis teen basileian"* it would mean that we are outside the Kingdom and now have come into it. This is regeneration. This is the meaning of Colossians 1:13.

b. But the text reads *"eiseltheete eis teen basilei an".* This means that a man is in the Kingdom. The "first part" of the Covenant is our portion. But in the "second part" wherein our obligation to a new obedience is set forth we are told, admonitioned to "enter *into* the Kingdom." That is quite different. And this is the sense of the construction of the double preposition *eis* in the Greek. Comp. Matt. 5:20; 7:13, 21; 18:8; 19:17; 25:21; Rom. 5:12; Heb. 10:5. Besides this is confirmed by the *usus loquendi* of the compound construction of the verb in Classical Greek. In Liddel and Scott, Greek Lexicon, we read on page 408 "II. As Attic law term, to come into court (of the accuser) to bring on the charge: also G. Acc. (with accusative) to enter upon the charge."

c. Because the term "Kingdom of heaven" is a concept, that does not have such a fixed dogmatic denotation, which can simply be employed in a dogmatic way, to determine meaning in each text where the term occurs. In each text the occasion in which the Kingdom is spoken of, the context, and the place in the sentence must be carefully and painstakingly considered.

d. That, in the judgment of your committee, the term "prerequisite" is limited to its proper place in the above exegesis. It does not mean that we perform a work in our native strength to *enter* the Kingdom. In this work of God whereby we are translated into the kingdom we are wholly passive. But the text in the judgment of your committee speaks of our entering into the Kingdom. And the text teaches that we must have the *act* of *humbling ourselves* to thus enter into the Kingdom, that is, for the conscious tasting of being lifted up by God and set in a broad place. Then the act of humbling is prerequisite to the wonderful experience of being lifted up. That we are told to humble ourselves is not then the command of the law: *do this and thou shalt live*, as stated in Romans 10:5, but it is the precept of the Gospel whereby we are called, admonished, and exhorted unto the new obedience, unto the performance of our "part" in the Covenant. Such a presentation of the *precepts of the Gospel* wholly concurs with the *Ordo Salutis* of Reformed Theology. Compare Canons III, IV, Articles 16–17.

e. That, your committee judges that it should not be overlooked, that the Rev. DeWolf is not too insistent on the term "condition." This he states in the "Answers" and also in the sermon on Matthew 18:1–4. He is willing to call it a "way" of entering too when speaking of "our turning". Besides, it should be noted, that it is not altogether factual to assert, as does protestant Hoeksema, that "it is an afterthought of the Rev. DeWolf that he spoke to the regenerated and spoke not of the initial entering into the Kingdom. So above under II, A, 2, the Rev. DeWolf quotes Luke 13:24–28 to prove his point of continual entering. Whether the point thus is well taken is not the question; the point is that Rev. DeWolf did not have the initial entering the Kingdom in mind when he made that reference in the sermon.

"Implies the question for us is always first that of entering—

1 / There is an entering in the final sense.

2 / But also a continual entering, a principle of life— always entering in all our life—as *conscious activity*. To this the Lord refers in Luke 13:23ff 'Strive to enter in.'" (we underscore).

f. That your committee judges that in the examination before the Consistory neither the Consistory nor Rev. DeWolf sufficiently kept this matter of meaning of "entering into the Kingdom" in mind.

1 / The examination went out from the presupposition that Rev. DeWolf had taught that our *entering* the Kingdom was contingent upon man's conversion; nowhere in the entire examination is there room allowed for the distinction your committee observed above between "entering the Kingdom", and "entering *into* the Kingdom." This latter is what the Rev. DeWolf had in mind in the examination.

2 / And still the Rev. DeWolf did not clearly see this distinction. Hence, in the rather long answer on pages 22, 23 the Rev. DeWolf is struggling with the dilemma of *being in the Kingdom and not being in the Kingdom.* Had he clearly seen and maintained the distinction suggested by your committee he would have not been pinned between the horns of the just stated dilemma. Your committee does not believe that this is due to Pelagian-Arminian heresy but due to not succeeding to have the proper Theological construction of the text in question. He did not want the simple construction *that in the Kingdom is in the Kingdom,* for the text seemed to teach something *more* (not different). But Rev. DeWolf could not lay his finger on it and, so to speak "pin point" it. Hence, his confusion and his attempt to solve it with the well-known figure used by Karl Barth. But since Rev. DeWolf does not share the Barthian Theology, his borrowing the figure is of little moment. Others besides Rev. DeWolf have been influenced by Barthian terminology without adopting Barth's conception of the "Wholly Other" etc. Our point is that this is confusion rather than heresy.

D. We advise Classis to express on this doctrinal issue:

1. That the protestants have pointed out a very serious heresy

in the proposition, "Our act of conversion is a prerequisite *to enter* the Kingdom"; a heresy which *is* rank Arminian and Pelagianism, against which Augustine, Calvin and the Fathers of Dort fought and which they condemned. And where this heresy is preached it cannot be tolerated on a Protestant Reformed pulpit. This would indeed be worse than the First Point of 1924.

2. That it appears from the documentary evidence as well as from the repeated assertion of Rev. DeWolf that the issue is not our act of conversion *"to enter"* the Kingdom, but our act of conversion "to enter into" the Kingdom of heaven. This latter is then the new obedience unto which we are obliged in our "part" in the Covenant of Grace.

3. That, therefore, the matter between the protestants and Rev. DeWolf is not one of "heresy" but *lack of clarity* on the part of Rev. DeWolf and *misunderstanding* on the part of the protestants.

a. Rev. DeWolf lacked clarity on the question of the meaning of entering into the Kingdom *by regeneration.* This gave the impression of Arminianism.

b. Rev. DeWolf lacked clarity on the matter of entering *into* the kingdom as a conscious activity. This brought Rev. DeWolf within the dilemma of saying that the believer is *in* the Kingdom and yet *not in* the Kingdom, which is an impossible position to maintain or even demonstrate in plain English. And so Rev. DeWolf took refuge to what "he really meant". But the trouble is that Rev. DeWolf did not say in language clear and concise just what he meant. The Theological conception was not clear to him. This same lack of conciseness is evidenced in the sermon.

c. The protestants *misunderstood* the matter.

1 / They themselves do not state the difference between "entering the Kingdom" and "entering into the Kingdom." They understood by entering "regeneration" in the narrow sense. And "prerequisite" simply became the "prerequisite" of the Arminians.

2 / Operating with these premises to the bitter end the protestants simply came to the crossroads where they say: Either DeWolf retracts his statement or he must be suspended. The tragedy is that this "either-or" position rests on a misunderstanding of the real issue in question.

4. That the Consistory consequently became involved in the

same dilemma of DeWolf, on the one hand, (those supporting him) and in the misunderstanding by others on the other hand. That there was great wrestling of the spirits was the inevitable result. The entire Consistory thus pursued a course lacking proper and desired unanimity, resulting in a lack of parliamentary procedure.

E. We advise Classis to express on the church political question touching parliamentary procedure as follows;

1. That the protestants are correct in insisting that the Consistory might not make the decision recorded in the Minutes, Art. 7, January 19, 1953 and Articles 5 and 6 of the meeting of February 16, 1953 without having first rescinded the decision of October 22, 1952 Article 8 and of October 27, 1952 Article 22. (See page 7 of Minutes and also page 13), for such is the evident application of Article 31 D.K.O which embodies the principle that nothing be decided by arbitrary caprice or fancy. However, this is equally true of the decision recorded on page 3, Article 17, March 24, 1952 where the Consistory without rescinding its decision to express that the statement in (first sermon) was not a "concise" expression of the truth of God's Word, made the decision that the statement "is contrary to the Scriptures and the Confessions." (See report of Yonker-Ophoff Committee, I, C, April 28, 1952)

2. That the Consistory rectify these matters of parliamentary procedure by duly rescinding both the decision of January 19 and February 16 instant. This will clarify the matter, and that this be done in each case according to its separate merit and demerit as shown earlier in this report.

a. In regard to sermon I:

1 / That the Consistory maintain its stand taken in March 24, 1952 that the statement "God promises every one of you that, if you believe, you shall be saved" is not a *concise* expression of the truth of Scripture and the Confessions. (See Minutes p. 3)

2 / That the Consistory accept the assurance given by Rev. DeWolf "I will avoid *using* the statement in No. 2" (the Lord promises every one of you). That the Consistory do this not on the grounds that "There are those who can interpret that only as a general promise", but on the grounds that the phrase itself allows very well for the interpretation of a general promise, and since our

Fathers of Dort warned against the use of phrases which might cause the Reformed faith to be vilified.

3 / That this decision of the Consistory be duly announced to the Congregation of First Church.

b. In regard to sermon II:

1 / That the Consistory of First Church reconsider the matter of "the act of conversion is a prerequisite to enter into the Kingdom" in the light of the exegetical observation made on the distinction between "entering the Kingdom" and "entering *into* the Kingdom."

2 / That according to the wisdom and grace given them the Consistory judges that it was lack of clarity and misunderstanding on the part of Rev. DeWolf and not an attempt to set forth heretical teaching.

3 / That the decision declaring that the answers of Rev. DeWolf are the doctrine of the Scriptures and Confessions is too sweeping if due regard be given to every statement made, particularly the statements in the long answer on pps. 22–23. That the decision herein referred to be rescinded and that instead they decide that the examination proved:

a- That there was no heresy as expressed in Article 80 D.K.O. but a lack of clarity and some confusion on the issues involved.

b- That it appears that the Rev. DeWolf thus considered is not heretical in his assertion, the act of conversion is prerequisite for entering into the Kingdom as taught by Jesus in Matt. 18:1–4.

4 / That this decision be duly announced to First Church.

Respectfully submitted,
YOUR COMMITTEE
w.s.   R. Veldman
     G. Lubbers
     E. Knott

P.S. Two members of the committee, R. Newhouse and P. Lubbers, will present their minority report.

[Minority Report]
Grand Rapids, Michigan
May 18, 1953

To the Classis East of the Protestant Reformed Churches
convening May 19, 1953

Esteemed Brethren:

We, the undersigned, members of the committee appointed
to study the protests of the Rev. Hoeksema and the Rev. Ophoff
against their Consistory in re its action with the Rev. DeWolf
cannot agree with the necessity nor with the contents of the long
document which precedes the advice given by the other members
of our committee. Neither can we sign the advice that they have
drawn up. Instead, as our minority report we present the following:

1. We cannot agree that the Consistory should maintain its
former stand that the statement "God promises every one of you
that if you believe you will be saved" is not a concise statement of
the truth. In our opinion both the statements which the protestants
condemn are literally heretical regardless of what the Rev. DeWolf
meant by them, regardless of how he explains them and regardless
of however much we may rejoice that his examination shows that
he does not believe the heresy implied in them. We take this stand:

a. because the protestants have clearly shown from the
Scriptures and the Confessions that the literal statements are
heretical.

b. and because we believe this is necessary for us to state in
the light of our past experiences and history with the Liberated
Churches who use these Arminian expressions.

2. As far as the making known to the congregation is concerned
we believe:

a. that the statements which the Rev. DeWolf himself made
at his examination should be announced to the congregation.
We have in mind the following: in regard to the expression "God
promises every one of you . . ." this statement found on page 4 of
the examination, "I didn't realize that I shouldn't have used the
word 'promise' there because of the implications which it might
have." And in regard to the expressions, "our converting ourselves

is a prerequisite to entering into the kingdom," this statement found on page 23 of the examination, "I will frankly admit that I said more on the pulpit than what I now realize I said. I didn't realize all the implications."

b. The way in which this is to be announced we leave to the discretion of the Consistory—whether by an announcement that is read or by the Rev. DeWolf himself personally—as Art. 75 of the Church Order also allows.

c. This action we feel is necessary lest a very dangerous precedent be set in our churches that public statements which in their literal form are heretical are explained in private and the unskilled in the congregation who never hear the explanation are left to believe all and any of the implications in the statements. This is all the more so necessary when, as was the case with these two statements of the Rev. DeWolf, there was such an abundance of protest made over against the statements he made.

Wishing you the Lord's blessing and guidance,

w.s. R. Newhouse
       P. Lubbers

General Bibliography

Algra, H. *Het Wonder van de Negentiende Eeuw* (The Wonder of the Nineteenth Century). Kampen, Netherlands: J. H. Kok, 1965.

Bavinck, Herman. *Our Reasonable Faith.* Tr. by Henry Zylstra. Grand Rapids: Wm. B. Eerdmans Publishing Co., 1956.

Berkhouwer, G. C. *Sin.* Tr. by Philip C. Holtrop. Grand Rapids: Wm. B. Eerdmans Publishing Co., 1971.

Boer, Harry R. "Ralph Janssen After Fifty Years." *Reformed Journal* 22 (December 1972):17–33.

_____. "The Janssen Case: Aftermath." *Reformed Journal* 23 (November 1973): 21–4.

_____. "Viewpoint in Religion." *Grand Rapids Press* (April 25, 1987): D4.

Bratt, James D. *Dutch Calvinism in Modern America: A History of a Conservative Subculture.* Grand Rapids: Wm. B. Eerdmans Publishing Co., 1984.

Breen, Quirinus. "My Reflections on Prof. Ralph Janssen and on the Janssen Case of 1922" [undated typewritten sheets]. In Quirinus Breen file, Archives, Hekman Library of Calvin College and Calvin Theological Seminary, Grand Rapids.

Bultema, H. *Maranatha: Eene Studie over de Onvervulde Profetie* (Maranatha: A Study of Unfulfilled Prophecy). Grand Rapids: Eerdmans-Sevensma Co., [1917].

Calvin, John. *Calvin: Institutes of the Christian Religion.* 2 vols. Tr. by Ford Lewis Battles and ed. by John T. McNeill in vols. 20 and 21 of the Library of Christian Classics. Philadelphia: The Westminster Press, 1960.

_____. *Calvin's Calvinism: Treatises on "The Eternal Predestination of God" and "The Secret Providence of God."* Grand Rapids: Reformed Free Publishing Association, [1987].

Cammenga, Andrew. "A Reply to Rev. H. Hoeksema." *Concordia* 5, no. 19 (November 25, 1948): 3.

Christian Reformed Church. *Acts of Synod of the Christian Reformed Church* for years 1926, 1942, 1966–1968, and 1991. Grand Rapids: Office of the Stated Clerk. (Note: Early *Acts* were in Dutch under the title *Acta der Synode van der Christelijke Gereformeerde Kerk.*)

Church Order of the Protestant Reformed Churches and Constitutions of Standing Synodical Committees, Rules and Regulations, Formulas, By-laws. Revised and updated. n.p.: Synod of the Protestant Reformed Churches in America, 1999.

Clark, Gordon H. *God's Hammer: The Bible and Its Critics.* Jefferson, Md.: The Trinity Foundation, 1982.

Daane, James. *The Freedom Of God: A Study of Election and Pulpit.* Grand Rapids: Wm. B. Eerdmans Publishing Co., 1973.

Danhof, Henry. "God Is God" *SB* 1, no. 1 (October 1924): 4–7.

_____. "De Idee von het Gendadeverbond" (The Idea of the Covenant of Grace). Grand Rapids: Van Noord Publishing Company, 1920.

Danhof, Henry and Herman Hoeksema. *Langs Zuivere Banen* (Along Straight Paths). n.p.: by the authors, n.d.

Danhof, Henry and Herman Hoeksema. *Niet Doopersch maar Gereformeerd* (Not Anabaptist but Reformed). n.p: by the authors, n.d.

Danhof, Henry and Herman Hoeksema. *Om Recht en Waarheid: Een Woord Van Toelichting* (Concerning Right and Truth: A Word of Explanation). n.p.: by the authors, [1924].

Danhof, Henry and Herman Hoeksema. *Van Zonde en Genade* (Concerning Sin and Grace). n.p.: by the authors, [1923].

De Boer, Peter. "It's All Your Fault!" *Concordia* 9, no. 1 (February 14, 1952): 2–3.

De Jong, A. C. *The Well-Meant Gospel Offer: The Views of H. Hoeksema and K. Schilder.* Franeker, Netherlands: T. Weaver, 1954.

De Jong, Peter Y. *The Covenant Idea in New England Theology: 1620–1847.* Grand Rapids: Wm. B. Eerdmans Publishing Company, 1945.

Engelsma, David J. "As a Father Pitieth His Children." Grand Rapids: Sunday School of the First Protestant Reformed Church, 1983.

_____. *Better To Marry: Sex and Marriage in I Corinthians 6 and 7.* Grand Rapids: Reformed Free Publishing Association, 1993.

_____. "The Covenant of God and the Children of Believers." South Holland, Ill.: Evangelism Committee of South Holland Protestant Reformed Church, 1990.

_____. "Creation and Science . . . and Common Grace." *SB* 67 (February 15, 1991): 221–23; 67 (March 1, 1991): 245–47.

_____. "A History of the Church's Doctrine of Marriage, Divorce, and Remarriage." *Protestant Reformed Theological Journal* 27, no. 1 (November 1993): 4–12; 27, no. 2 (April 1994): 4–20; 28, no. 1 (November 1994): 8–25; and 28, no. 2 (April 1995): 18–36.

_____. *Hyper-Calvinism and the Call of the Gospel: An Examination of the "Well-Meant Offer" of the Gospel.* Revised 2nd ed. Grand Rapids: Reformed Free Publishing Association, 1994.

_____. "The Lord's Hatred of Divorce." Hudsonville: Evangelism Committee, Hudsonville Protestant Reformed Church, 1998.

_____. "Marriage and Divorce." Grand Rapids: Evangelism Committee of the First Protestant Reformed Church, Grand Rapids, 1994.

_____. *Marriage, the Mystery of Christ and the Church: The Covenant-Bond in Scripture and History.* Grandville, Mich.: Reformed Free Publishing Association, 1998.

_____. *Reformed Education.* Grand Rapids: Federation of Protestant Reformed Young People's Societies, 1981.

_____. "Trinity and Covenant." Th.M. thesis for Calvin Theological Seminary, Grand Rapids, 1994.

Faber, Jelle and Klaas Schilder. *"American Secession Theologians on Covenant and Baptism" and "Extra-Scriptural Binding—A New Danger."* Tr. by T. van Laar. Neerlandia, Alberta, Canada: Inheritance Publications, 1996.

_____. "The Confessional History of the Canadian Reformed Churches." *Clarion* 48 no. 4 (February 19, 1999): 82.

_____. "Klaas Schilder's Life and Work," in *Always Obedient: Essays on the Teachings of Dr. Klaas Schilder*, ed. by J. Geertsema. Phillipsburg, N.J.: P and R Publishing, 1995, 1–17.

Frame, John M. *Cornelius Van Til: An Analysis of His Thought.* Phillipsburg, N.J.: P and R Publishing, 1995.

Francken, Aegidius. *Kern der Christelijke Leer* (Kernel of Christian Doctrine). Groningen, Netherlands: R. Boerma, 1894.

Geertsema, J., ed. *Always Obedient: Essays on the Teachings of Dr. Klaas Schilder.* Phillipsburg, N.J.: P and R Publishing, 1995.

Gritters, Barry. "Renewing the Battle." *SB* 69 (April 1, 1993):

308–10; 69 (May 1, 1993): 351–53; 69 (May 15, 1993): 379–81; 69 (August 1993): 446–48; 69 (September 1, 1993): 465–68; 70 (December 15, 1993): 139–41.

Hanko, Herman. "The Christian and the Film Arts." Grand Rapids: Evangelism Committee of the First Protestant Reformed Church, n.d.

_____. "The Confessions in the Life of the Church." *SB* 58 (July 1, 1982): 416–19.

_____. *God's Everlasting Covenant of Grace.* Grand Rapids: Reformed Free Publishing Association, 1988.

_____. "The History of the Free Offer." Syllabus. Grandville, Mich.: Theological School of the Protestant Reformed Churches, 1989.

_____. *Ready to Give an Answer: A Catechism of Reformed Distinctives,* with Herman Hoeksema as co-author. Grandville, Mich.: Reformed Free Publishing Association, 1997.

_____. "A Study of the Relation between the Views of Prof. R. Janssen and Common Grace." Master of Theology thesis for Calvin Theological Seminary, Grand Rapids, 1988.

_____. *We and Our Children: The Reformed Doctrine of Infant Baptism.* Grand Rapids: Reformed Free Publishing Association, 1981.

Heslam, Peter S. *Creating a Christian Worldview: Abraham Kuyper's Lectures on Calvinism.* Grand Rapids: Wm. B. Eerdmans Publishing Co., 1998.

Heyns, William. *Manual of Reformed Doctrine.* Grand Rapids: Wm. B. Eerdmans Publishing Co., 1926.

Heys, John A. "A Walking in Error." *SB* 30 (September 15, 1954): 491-92.

Hodge, Charles. *Systematic Theology.* 3 vols. New York: Charles Scribner and Co., 1871.

Hoeksema, Gertrude, ed. *God's Covenant Faithfulness: The 50th Anniversary of the Protestant Reformed Churches in America.* Grand Rapids: Reformed Free Publishing Association, 1975.

_____. *Therefore Have I Spoken: A Biography of Herman Hoeksema.* Grand Rapids: Reformed Free Publishing Association, 1969.

_____. *A Watered Garden: A Brief History of the Protestant Reformed Churches in America.* Grand Rapids: Reformed Free Publishing Association, 1992.

Hoeksema, Herman. See separate "Bibliography of Works by Herman Hoeksema" that follows this bibliography.

Hoeksema, Homer C. *The Doctrine of Scripture.* Grand Rapids: Reformed Free Publishing Association, 1990.

Janssen, Ralph. "De Crisis in de Christelijke Gereformeerde Kerk in Amerika" (The Crisis in the Christian Reformed Church in America). Grand Rapids: n.p., 1922.

_____. "De Synodale Conclusies" (The Synodical Conclusions). Grand Rapids: n.p., 1923.

_____. "Het Synodale Vonnis in Zijne Voorgeschiedenis Kerkrechtelijk Beoordeeld" (The Synodical Verdict in Its Previous History Church Politically Judged). Grand Rapids: n.p., 1922.

_____. "Voortzetting van den Strijd" (Continuation of the Controversy). Grand Rapids: n.p., 1922.

Kingdon, David. *Children of Abraham.* Foxton, England: University Tutorial Press Ltd. Published for Carey Publications Ltd., Haywards Heath, Sussex, England, 1978.

Klooster, Fred H. *The Incomprehensibility of God in the Orthodox Presbyterian Conflict.* Thesis for University of Amsterdam. Franeker, Netherlands: T. Wever, 1951.

Kromminga, D. H. *The Christian Reformed Tradition.* Grand Rapids: Wm. B. Eerdmans Publishing Co., 1943.

Kuyper, Abraham. *Abraham Kuyper: A Centennial Reader,* ed. by James D. Bratt. Grand Rapids: Wm. B. Eerdmans Publishing Co., 1998.

_____. *Dat De Genade Particulier Is* (That Grace Is Particular) in book series Uit Het Woord (Out of the Word). Amsterdam: J. H. Kruyt, 1884.

_____. *De Gemeene Gratie* (Common Grace). 3 vols. Amsterdam: Höveker and Wormser, 1902.

Lindsay, T. M. *The Reformation.* Edinburgh: T. and T. Clark, 1882.

Lubbers, George C. "Schilder's Reply." *Concordia* 4, no. 17 (October 30, 1947): 3.

_____. "Seven Propositions Submitted by Rev. Hoeksema." *Concordia* 4, no. 17 (October 30, 1947): 3.

Lucas, Henry S., ed. *Dutch Immigrant Memoirs and Related Writings.* Revised ed. Grand Rapids, Wm. B. Eerdmans Publishing Co., 1997.

Marsden, George M. *Understanding Fundamentalism and Evangelicalism*. Grand Rapids: Wm. B. Eerdmans Publishing Co., 1991.

Masselink, William. *General Revelation and Common Grace*. Grand Rapids: Wm. B. Eerdmans Publishing Co., 1953.

Michigan Supreme Court. Appeal from Superior Court of Grand Rapids, Mich., in Chancery in the matter of First Protestant Reformed Church of Grand Rapids, Mich. (plaintiff) vs. Hubert De Wolf, et al. (defendants and appellants) and Herman Hoeksema, et al. (cross-defendants and appellees). Record on Appeal, 1953. Grand Rapids: American Brief and Record Company, 1953, vol. 1: 117–154 and vol. 2: 461–682.

Miersma, Thomas. "Scripture Interprets Scripture: Spiritually." *SB* 63 (November 1, 1986): 60–2.

Minutes, Classis East, Protestant Reformed Churches, for meetings of June 1, 1932; April 8–10 and 14–16, 1953; and May 19–23 and 26–28, 1953.

Minutes, Classis West, Protestant Reformed Churches, for meeting of September 2, 1953.

Minutes, Combined Classis, Protestant Reformed Churches, for meetings of February 1927, June 1927, February 1928, February 1929, June 1929, February 1930, June 1930, and January 1937.

Minutes, Combined Consistories, Protestant Reformed Churches, for meetings of November 3, 1926, and January 1927.

Murray, John. *Redemption—Accomplished and Applied*. Grand Rapids: Wm. B. Eerdmans Publishing Co., 1955.

Oostendorp, Lubbertus. *H.P. Scholte, Leader of the Secession of 1834 and Founder of Pella*. Thesis, Amsterdam. Franeker, Netherlands: T. Wever, 1964.

Ophoff, George M. "May a Classis Depose a Consistory? or, The Plain Truth about the Institution of Christ's Church." *SB* 4 (January 15, 1928): 179–87; 4 (February 15, 1928): 225–32; 4 (March 1, 1928): 250–51; 4 (March 15, 1928): 273–80; 4 (April 1, 1928): 299–305; 4 (April 15, 1928): 327–32.

_____. "Open Confession to the Brethren Rev. Kok and Rev. De Jong." *SB* 25 (September 15, 1949): 522–23.

_____. "Revs. De Jong and Kok in the Netherlands." *SB* 25 (August 1, 1949): 469–73.

_____. "Calvin College, or Jerusalem and Athens." *SB* 10 (October 15, 1933): 43–48.

Petter, Andrew. Series of articles on "The Covenant" in *Concordia*, as listed below:

"I—Introduction." 4, no. 18 (November 13, 1947): 1.

"IV—Wrong Approaches." 4, no. 21 (December 25, 1947): 3.

"XV—Solving the Problem." 5, no. 12 (August 19, 1948): 1

"XXXV—Dr. Schilder." 6, no. 2 (March 3, 1949): 3.

"XXXVII—Dr. Schilder." 6, no. 3 (March 31, 1949): 1.

_____. "Is Christian Drama Possible?" *SB* 18 (October 1, 1941): 19–22.

_____. "The Spirit of '24 and of Today." *Concordia* 1, no. 10 (July 7, 1944): 2.

Piersma, Albert. "Wereldsche Vereenigingen, Critiek en Repliek." *SB* 7 (July 15, 1931): 470. Start of discussions on union membership that continued in *SB* for many years.

Protestant Reformed Churches. *Acts of Synod of the Protestant Reformed Churches in America* for years 1941, 1944, 1946–1951, 1957–1962, and 1964. Published by Synod of the Protestant Reformed Churches in America, Office of the Stated Clerk.

The Protestant Reformed Churches: Twenty-Fifth Anniversary 1925–1950. No city or publisher indicated, [1950].

The Psalter, with Doctrinal Standards, Liturgy, Church Order, and Added Choral Section. Rev. ed. Grand Rapids: William B. Eerdmans Publishing Co., 1998. Includes Form for the Administration of Baptism pp. 86–90 and Form for the Administration of the Lord's Supper, pp. 91–6.

Ridderbos, Herman. *Paul: An Outline of His Theology.* Tr. by John Richard De Witt. Grand Rapids: Wm. B. Eerdmans Publishing Co., 1975.

Schaff, Philip. *History of the Christian Church*, vol. 1. Grand Rapids: Wm. B. Eerdmans Publishing Co., 1956.

Schilder, Klaas. "Contributed." *Concordia* 2, no. 15 (October 4, 1945): 3–4.

_____. "The Stocking Is Finished," tr. from the article "De Kous Is Af" in *De Reformatie* of November 17, 1951, by Theodore Plantinga. Appendix II in *Schilder's Struggle for the Unity of the Church* by Rudolph Van Reest, tr. by Theodore Plantinga. Neerlandia, Alberta, Canada: Inheritance Publications, c. 1990, 433–440.

Schouls, Carl A. "The Covenant Of Grace." *The Messenger* 45, no. 9 (October 1998): 6–8.

Smilde, E. *Een Eeuw van Strijd over Verbond en Doop* (A Century of Struggle over the Covenant and Baptism). Kampen, Netherlands: J. H. Kok, 1946.

Spykman, Gordon J. "The Van Raalte Sermons." *Reformed Review* 30, no. 2 (Winter 1977): 100.

Stob, George. "The Christian Reformed Church and Her Schools." Th.D. dissertation for Princeton Theological Seminary, Princeton, N.J., 1955.

Stob, Henry. "Observations on the Concept of the Antithesis" in *Perspectives on the Christian Reformed Church: Studies in Its History, Theology and Ecumenicity*, ed. Peter De Klerk and Richard R. De Ridder. Festschrift for John Henry Kromminga. Grand Rapids: Baker Book House, 1983, pp. 241–58.

Strauss, S. A., "Schilder on the Covenant" in *Always Obedient: Essays on the Teachings of Klaas Schilder*, ed. by Jacob Geertsema. Phillipsburg, N.J.: P and R Publishing Co., 1995, pp. 19–33.

Synod of the Protestant Reformed Churches in America, Mission Committee. *Three Forms of Unity,* including Confession of Faith (Belgic), pp. 24–36; Heidelberg Catechism, pp. 3–22; and Canons of Dordrecht, pp. 38–55. n.p.: Synod of the PRC, 1991.

Terry, Milton S. *Biblical Hermeneutics.* Grand Rapids: Zondervan Publishing House, 1976.

van Baalen, Jan Karel. *De Loochening der Germeene Gratie: Gereformeerd of Doopersch?* (The Denial of Common Grace: Reformed or Anabaptist?) Grand Rapids: Eerdmans-Sevensma Co., 1922.

_____. *Nieuwigheid en Dwaling* (Novelty and Error). Grand Rapids: Eerdmans-Sevensma Co., 1923.

Vanden Berg, Gerald. "The Ministry of the Word." *SB* 31 (November 1, 1954): 67–9.

Van Dooren, G. . . . *And We Escaped*. Tr. from the Dutch. Burlington, Canada: Golden Jubilee Committee, [Canadian Reformed Churches], 1986.

Van Eyck, Wm. O. *Landmarks of the Reformed Fathers*. Grand Rapids: The Reformed Press, 1922.

_____. *The Union of 1850: A Collection of Papers by the Late Wm. O. Van Eyck, Esq. on the Union of the Classis of Holland with the Reformed Church in America, in June, 1850*. Selected and ed. by Permanent Committee on History and Research, General Synod of the Reformed Church in America. Grand Rapids: Wm. B. Eerdmans Publishing Co., 1950.

Van Til, Cornelius. *Common Grace*. Philadelphia: Presbyterian and Reformed Publishing Co., 1947.

Van Til, Henry R. *The Calvinist Concept of Culture*. Grand Rapids: Baker Book House, 1959.

Veldman, Richard. "The Movie" (pamphlet). Grand Rapids: Sunday School of the First Protestant Reformed Church of Grand Rapids, 1956.

Verduin, Leonard. *Honor Your Mother: Christian Reformed Church Roots in the 1834 Separation*. Grand Rapids: CRC Publications, 1988.

Vergunst, Arie. "The Sincere Offer of Christ and the Covenant Benefits in the Gospel." *Banner of Truth* 63 (September 1997): 230.

Vos, Gerrit. "Repliek" in "Wereldsche Vereenigingen, Critiek en Repliek." *SB* 7 (July 15, 1931): 470–74.

_____. "Conferences" *SB* 24 (October 1, 1947): 4–6.

_____. "Impressions." *Concordia* 1, no. 9 (June 21, 1944): 2

_____. "In the Chaos." *Concordia* 2, no. 15 (October 4, 1945): 2–3.

_____. "The Schilder Conference." *SB* 24 (December 1, 1947): 101–03.

Warfield, Benjamin B. *The Inspiration and Authority of the Bible*. Philadelphia: Presbyterian and Reformed Publishing Co., 1948.

_____. *Selected Shorter Writings of Benjamin B. Warfield*. Vol. 2. ed. by John E. Meeter. Nutley, N.J.: Presbyterian and Reformed Publishing Co., 1973.

Westminster Confession of Faith. Reproduced in *The Confession of Faith; the Larger and Shorter Catechisms, with Scripture Proofs at Large: together with the Sum of Saving Knowledge, etc.* Glasgow: Free Presbyterian Publications, 1976.

Wood, A. Skevington. *Captive to the Word.* Grand Rapids: Wm. B. Eerdmans Publishing Co., 1969.

Wormser. *Infant Baptism Seen in Its Relation to Life on the Level of the Individual, Church, [and] Society.* No city or publisher indicated, 1853.

Zwaanstra, Henry. *Reformed Thought and Experience in a New World: A Study of the Christian Reformed Church and Its American Environment, 1890–1918.* Kampen, Netherlands: J. H. Kok, 1973.

Bibliography of Works Cited

"Aanganade Dr. Schilder" (Concerning Dr. Schilder). *SB* 21 (February 15, 1945): 222.

"The Antithesis in Paradise." *SB* 1, no. 1 (October 1924): 7–9.

"Antithesis, Synthesis, and Dualism." *SB* 4 (May 1, 1928): 353–57.

"Appeals to Common Grace." *SB* 18 (October 1, 1941): 4–6.

"Attentie, Prof. Dr. K. Schilder!" (Attention, Prof. Dr. K. Schilder!) *SB* 11 (September 1, 1935): 484, 485.

"Autonomy." *SB* 30 (July 15, 1954): 412–15; 30 (August 1, 1954): 436–45.

Behold, He Cometh! An Exposition of the Book of Revelation. Grand Rapids: Reformed Free Publishing Association, 1969.

Believers and Their Seed. Tr. from the Dutch *De Geloovigen en Hun Zaad* by Homer C. Hoeksema. Grand Rapids, Mich.: Reformed Free Publishing Association, 1971.

"Bespreking der 'Algemeene Genade' in Nederland" (Decisions on 'Common Grace' in the Netherlands). *SB* 12 (September 1, 1936): 484–87; 12 (September 15, 1936): 508–11.

"Bibles and Bible Reading." *SB* 11 (October 15, 1934): 28; 11 (November 1, 1934): 52–3.

"The Biblical Ground for the Baptism of Infants." Grand Rapids: Sunday School of the First Protestant Reformed Church, 1990.

Calvin, Berkhof, and H. J. Kuiper: A Comparison. Grand Rapids: Reformed Free Publishing Association, 1930.

"A Catechism on the History of the Origin of the Protestant Reformed Churches." *SB* 6 (September 1, 1930): 536–39; 7 (December 1, 1930): 111–14; 8 (July 1, 1932): 450–53.

The Clark-VanTil Controversy. Hobbs, N.M.: The Trinity Foundation, 1995.

"The Coming of Dr. Schilder." *SB* 23 (May 1, 1947): 343.

"Common Grace." *SB* vol. 19, nos. 5–10, 12, 13, 15, 17, 19, and 22; vol. 20 nos. 1 and 2 (December 1, 1942, through October 15, 1943).

"A Compromise on Movies." *SB* 3 (April 15, 1927): 318–21.

"Correction Please." *SB* 28 (January 15, 1952): 180–82.

"The Covenant: God's Tabernacle with Men." Grand Rapids: Evangelism Committee of First Protestant Reformed Church, Grand Rapids, Mich., 1995.

"Dr. Martin Luther on the Stage." *SB* 4 (February 1, 1928): 197–99.

"Dr. Schilder en Dr. A. Kuyper Sr." (Dr. Schilder and Dr. A. Kuyper, Sr.). *SB* 12 (June 15, 1936): 412, 413.

"Dr. Schilder Geboycot?" (Dr. Schilder Boycotted?) *SB* 15 (November 15, 1938): 76–9.

"Dr. Schilder over de Gemeene Gratie" (Dr. Schilder on Common Grace). *SB* 14 (November 1, 1937): 59–62.

"Dr. Schilder's Lecture on Common Grace." *SB* 15 (March 1, 1939): 244–46.

"Dr. Schilder's Standpunt Inzake de Gemeene Gratie" (Dr. Schilder's Position on Common Grace). *SB* 12 (March 1, 1936): 246–48.

"Dr. Ubbink's Proeve Eener Nieuwe Belijdenis" (Dr. Ubbink's Example of a New Confession). See "Nieuwe Belijdenis Aangaande Schrift en Kerk."

"Essentials of Reformed Doctrine: A Guide in Catechetical Instruction." Grand Rapids, n.p., 1927.

Het Evangelie: Of De Jongste Aanval Op De Waarheid der Sovereine Genade (The Gospel: or The Latest Attack on the Truth of Sovereign Grace). Grand Rapids: Mission Committee of the [Synod of] the Protestant Reformed Churches, 1933.

"Exegesis of Colossians." Syllabus, revised. Grandville, Mich.: Theological School of the Protestant Reformed Churches, 1997.

"The Fallen King." *Banner* 53 (October 31, 1918): 789.

God's Eternal Good Pleasure. Ed. by Homer C. Hoeksema from 1940 ed. Grand Rapids: Reformed Free Publishing Association, 1979.

"God's Handwriting in Nature." *SB* 5 (September 15, 1929): 572–74.

"Hereeniging der Christelijke Gereformeerde en Protestantsche Gereformeerde Kerken: Is Ze Geeischt, Mogelijk, en Wenschelijk" (Reunion of the Christian Reformed and Protestant Reformed Churches: Is It Demanded, Possible, and Desirable?) (No city or publisher given, [1939].

"History of Dogma." Syllabus. Grandville, Mich.: Theological School of the Protestant Reformed Churches, 1982.

"Independentism." *SB* 31 (December 15, 1954): 124, 125; 31 (January 1, 1995): 148, 149.

"Independentism Gehaald?" (Independentism Proposed?) *SB* 13 (March 15, 1937): 268, 269.

"Kastanjes Uit 't Vuur Gehaald?" (Chestnuts Pulled from the Fire?) *SB* 13 (March 15, 1937): 268, 269.

Een Kracht Gods Tot Zaligheid, of Genade Geen Aanbod (A Power of God unto Salvation, or Grace Not an Offer). Grand Rapids: Reformed Free Publishing Association, 1932. (Tr. in syllabus form entitled "A Power of God unto Salvation, or Grace Not an Offer." Grand Rapids: Theological School of the Protestant Reformed Churches, 1996.)

"De Kwestie 'Leergeschillen' op de Synode der Gereformeerde Kerken in Nederland" (The Question of Differences in Doctrine on the Synod of Reformed Churches in the Netherlands). *SB* 13 (October 15, 1936): 35–9; 13 (November 1, 1936): 52–6.

Langs Zuivere Banen (Along Straight Paths), with Henry Danhof as co-author. Kalamazoo: by the authors, n.d.

"The Liberated Churches in the Netherlands." *SB* 22 (October 1, 1945): 5, 6; 22 (December 1, 1945): 100–02; 22 (December 15, 1945): 126–28; 22 (January 1, 1946): 148–50; 22 (January 15, 1946): 175–78; 22 (February 1, 1946): 198, 199; 22 (March 1, 1946): 245, 246; 22 (March 15, 1946): 268–70.

"De Loochening der Gemeene Gratie in Nederland" (The Denial of Common Grace in the Netherlands). *SB* 12 (June 1, 1936): 391–95.

"Man's Freedom and Responsibility." *SB* 29 (July 1, 1953): 412–17.

"Misverstand" (Misunderstanding). *SB* 12 (June 15, 1936): 412.

Niet Doopersch maar Gereformeerd (Not Anabaptist but Reformed), with Henry Danhof as co-author. Grand Rapids: by the authors, n.d.

"De Nieuwe Belijdenis Aangaande Schrift en Kerk" (The New Confession concerning Scripture and the Church), also titled, at times, "Dr. Ubbink's Proeve Eener Nieuwe Belijdenis." *SB* 8 (February 1, 1932) through 8 (September 15, 1932), skipping issue nos. 17, 22, and 23. Articles start p. 4 of each issue.

"No Biased Presentation." *SB* 15 (June 1, 1939): 397–99.

"Notes on the Church Controversy in the Netherlands," prepared for a post-confession class, mimeographed. Unpublished, n.d.

"Een Nuchtere Blik" (A Sober Glance). *SB* 13 (December 1, 1936): 100, 101.

Om Recht En Waarheid: Een Woord Van Toelichting (Concerning Right and Truth: A Word of Explanation), with Henry Danhof as co-author. n.p.: by the authors, [1924].

"On Card Playing." *SB* 10 (May 1, 1934): 342–43; 10 (June 1, 1934): 388–89; 10 (June 15, 1934): 412, 413.

"Once More: A Tendency toward Individualism." *SB* 25 (December 1, 1948): 100–03.

"Our Calling," in *The Protestant Reformed Churches: 25ᵗʰ Anniversary 1925–1950*. No city or publisher given, [1950]. pp. 13, 15, 17, 19, 21, and 23.

"Our Conference with Dr. Schilder." *SB* 24 (December 1, 1947): 101–03.

"Our Doctrine." *Banner* 53–56 (October 31, 1918, through January 6, 1921).

"Over Conferenties en Perspolemiek" (Concerning Conferences and Polemics). *SB* 15 (June 1, 1939): 396.

"The Place of Reprobation in the Preaching of the Gospel." Grandville, Mich.: Evangelism Committee of Southwest Protestant Reformed Church, 1993.

"Predestination: Revealed, Not Hidden nor Confused." Radio sermons printed in booklet. Grand Rapids: Radio Committee of the First Protestant Reformed Church, 1948.

"Predestination: the Heart of the Gospel." Radio sermons printed in booklet. Grand Rapids: Radio Committee of the First Protestant Reformed Church, 1949.

"Professoren op de Synode" (Professors at Synod). *SB* 13 (January 15, 1937): 173, 174.

"Promise and Prediction." *SB* 28 (March 15, 1952): 269–73.

The Protestant Reformed Churches in America: Their Origin, Early History and Doctrine. Grand Rapids: First Protestant Reformed Church of Grand Rapids, [1936].

Ready to Give an Answer: A Catechism of Reformed Distinctives, with Herman Hanko as co-author. Grandville, Mich.: Reformed Free Publishing Association, 1997.

Reformed Dogmatics. Grand Rapids: Reformed Free Publishing Association, 1966.

"The Reunion of the Christian Reformed and Protestant Reformed Churches: Is It Demanded, Possible, Desirable?" by Herman Hoeksema. Tr. by H. Veldman. Grand Rapids: Reformed Free Publishing Association, [1939].

"Schilder . . . and Others." *SB* 21 (March 1, 1945): 241.

"Schilder over de Algemeene Genade" (Schilder on Common Grace). *SB* 12 (April 1, 1936): 293–95; 12 (April 15, 1936): 317–19.

"The Separation in the Netherlands." *SB* 21 (August 1, 1945): 454.

"Sketches on the Theory of Doctrine: Dr. Abraham Kuyper and Common Grace." *SB* 6 (April 1, 1930): 303–05.

"Stemmen over de Synode in Nederland" (Opinions about the Synod in the Netherlands). *SB* 13 (December 15, 1936): 128, 129.

"The Stocking Is Finished." *SB* 28 (January 1, 1952): 148–53.

"A Tendency towards Individualism." *SB* 25 (October 15, 1948): 28–30.

"The Text of a Complaint: A Critique about the 'Clark Case.'" Syllabus. Grandville, Mich.: Theological School of the Protestant Reformed Churches, n.d. [original text from 1944–1946].

A Triple Breach in the Foundation of the Reformed Truth: A Critical Treatise on the "Three Points" Adopted by the Synod of the Christian Reformed Churches in 1924. Grandville, Mich.: Evangelism Committee of Southwest Protestant Reformed Church, 1992.

The Triple Knowledge: An Exposition of the Heidelberg Catechism. 3 vols. Grand Rapids: Reformed Free Publishing Association, 1972.

"True or False." Speech concerning the 1953 controversy given by Herman Hoeksema in Kalamazoo, Mich. [publication data not available].

"Unbiblical Divorce and Remarriage." Grand Rapids: Reformed Free Publishing Association, [from articles 1956–1957].

"The Unbreakable Bond of Marriage." Grand Rapids: Sunday School of the First Protestant Reformed Church, Grand Rapids, 1969.

"De Union-Kwestie onder Ons" (The Union Question among Us). *SB* 6 (May 1, 1930): 349–51; 6 (May 15, 1930): 371–74; 6 (June 1, 1930): 399–402; 6 (July 1, 1930): 455; 6 (August 15, 1930): 515–17.

Van Zonde en Genade (Concerning Sin and Grace), with Henry
   Danhof as co-author. No place or publisher indicated, [1923].
"Een Vergissing?" (An Error?) *SB* 12 (May 15, 1936): 364, 365.
"Wat Op de Conferentie Voorviel" (What Happened at the
   Conference?). *SB* 15 (May 1, 1939): 353–57; 15 (May 15, 1939):
   375–81.
"Wrath Revealed from Heaven: Rom. 1: 18ff." *SB* 2 (September 1,
   1926): 412–15.

Scripture Index

$\mathcal{S}$ubject Index

baptism (*continued*)
See also Form for the Administration of Baptism
of believers, 369–74
believers and, 11–12
covenant and, 369–76
general promise and, 298
Heidelberg Catechism on, 365
Helenius De Cock's position on, 13
Hendrik De Cock's views on, 12
of infants of believers, 364–68
Kuyper's position on, 15–16, 366
LC view of, 354–56
Reformed theology and, 265–367
Schilder's views on, 266–67
Scholte's views on, 11–12
Secessionists and, 10–11
Baptists, 372
Bavinck, Herman, 69, 69 n. 3, 143, 145, 233, 317, 317 n. 1, 402
Belgic confession. *See* Confession of Faith (Belgic)
Berkhof, Louis, 32 n. 22
Boston, Thomas, 8
Breen, Quirinus, 92 n. 55, 180 n. 19
Brummelkamp, A., 7, 9 n. 11, 11 n. 13, 29, 43
Bultema, H., 104 n. 9, 416 n. 26

C
Calvin, John, 7, 7 n. 5, 91 n. 53, 221
Calvin College, 34, 76
Calvinism, 84, 200 n. 4
Cammenga, Andrew, 278
Canons of Dordtrecht, 18, 65 n. 28, 219, 232, 291 n. 38, 292 n. 39
card playing, doctrine of antithesis and, 196

catechetical instruction of youth, 226, 415
censure, of protestants, 100–103
Chalcedon, Council of, 405
Christ, doctrine of, 406–8
Christian Reformed Church (CRC)
adoption of Kuyperian common grace by, 77
adoption of Three Points, 68–78
Arminianism and, 95
early commitment to sovereign grace by, 29–30
early doctrinal condition of, 35
founding of, 21–23, 26–30
position on divorce and remarriage, 385–86
synod of 1922, 41–42, 44
synod of 1924 on common grace, 54–57
church government, 118
Church Order, Article 31, 101–2, 102 n. 5, 113
congregational autonomy and, 103–6
exercise of keys of kingdom, 62–63, 111
hierarchism, 108, 118, 309, 313
judicatory power of broader assemblies, 112–15
reformed, 100
right of classis to depose officebearers and, 106–11
synods, power of, 112, 310
church of Jesus Christ, 104–6. *See also* ecclesiology
Christ as head of, 4, 104–6
corporate responsibility and federal headship in, 240–44
crucial role of, in salvation, 119

covenant, doctrine of (*continued*)
  promise of God and, 354–59
  RCA and, 23
  Reformed view of, traditional
    agreement or pact, 267, 318–19, 326
    bilateral, 265, 267, 318
    covenant of works in Adam, 318, 340–44
    federal covenant theology, 240–44
  reprobation and, 348–52
  as revelation, 329–31
  Schilder's refusal to apply election to, 298–99
  Schilder's teachings of, 265–68
  schism of 1953 over, 263
  Scholte's views on, 12
  Secessionists and, 10–11, 265
Covenant of Redemption, 332, 406
covenant parents, 396
CRC. *See* Christian Reformed Church (CRC)
creation, doctrine of, 93–94, 170–71, 405–6
  covenant and, 360–63
  as miracle, 170–71
  as organic, 236–38
  revelation and, 155–56
  Scripture and, 148–50
cultural mandate, 74, 91, 96, 195–96, 254

D

Danhof, B. J., 111–12, 233
Danhof, Henry, 52, 103, 320
  CRC synod of 1924 and, 54–57, 54 n. 10
  Kuyperian common grace and, 75 n. 16

opposition to common grace, 41–42
  view of church history, 47–48
De Boer, Peter, 294, 295 n. 45
Declaration of Principles
  adoption of, 275–77, 289–90
  binding character of, 291–93, 295–96
  condemnation of conditional theology, 298
  protests against, 297–99
De Cock, Helenius, 30 n. 17
  influence of, 29–30
  views of, 13–14
De Cock, Hendrik, 4, 6, 7, 7 n. 6, 9 n. 11
  early followers of, 21
  nature of covenant and, 12
  Pietism of, 11
  views on baptism, 11–12
decretive will, 205
De Hervormde Kerk, 6, 6 n. 3
deism, 139 n. 9
De Jong, John, 282 n. 14, 286–88, 286 n. 29, 288 n. 30, 288 n. 31, 294 n. 44
Dekker, Harold, 83 n. 40
depravity, total, 31, 53, 92
desertion of spouse. *See* Marriage
De Wolf, Hubert, 300–302
  commitment to conditional theology, 300–302
  letter from, to his consistory, suggesting return to CRC, 306–7, 379 n. 19
  position on conditional promise, 305–9
  position on well-meant offer of the gospel, 305–9

De Wolf, Hubert (*continued*)
  statements of, leading to 1953
    controversy, 376–80
  suspension of, 311–12
discipline, by churches and church
  councils, 106–11, 110
divorce. *See* marriage, doctrine of;
  marriage, indissolubleness of
Docetism, 165 n. 14
Doleantie, 14–15, 14 n. 22, 16–17
Doon, Iowa, PRC, 313
Dordtrecht, Canons of, 18, 65 n.
  28, 219, 232, 291 n. 38, 292
Dordtrecht, Church Order of,
  Article 31, 101–2, 102 n. 5, 113
Dordtrecht (Dordt), synod of
  1618–1619, 6, 48, 232
dramatic productions, doctrine of
  antithesis and, 193–94
dualism, 130–31, 148. *See also* two-
  track theology
  antithesis and, 183–84
Dutch immigrants, to U.S., 20–
  22
  after World War II, 287
  doctrinal knowledge of, 27–29
  in early seventeenth century,
    20–21
  followers of Kuyper in *Doleantie,*
    34
  from Secession of 1834
    (*Afscheiding*), 6–7, 21–22, 34
dynamic equivalence in translating
  Scripture, 162–63

E

Eastern Ave. CRC, 51, 54
  censuring of protestants, 59–61,
    100–103
ecclesiology, 413–16

elect, the, 93
  children of, 364–65
  death of Christ and, 82–83
election, doctrine of, 25, 53. *See also*
  predestination; reprobation.
  antithesis and, 185–86
  doctrine of covenant and, 348–
    54, 352–54
  doctrine of sovereign
    reprobation and, 351
  Schilder's refusal to apply to
    covenant, 298–99
empirical proof, 225 n. 39
Engelsma, David J., 328–29, 384 n.
  1, 389 n. 13
Enlightenment, 177, 177 n. 3
Erskine, Ebenezer, 8
Erskine, Ralph, 8
eschatology, as locus of dogmatics,
  174, 416–17
Eternal Predestination of God, The
  (*Consensus Genevensis*), 91 n. 53,
  207 n. 11
evolution, 145, 146 n. 12, 148, 148
  n. 18, 153, 163, 170–71, 226,
  405–6
exegesis, defined, 162 n. 6

F

faith
  defined, 223–24
  doctrine of, 410–13
fall, the, 33, 56, 73, 89, 92, 93, 146,
  148, 151, 186, 217, 254, 337,
  343, 346–48, 361
federal covenant theology, 240
federations of churches, 106, 308–9
First PR Church, Grand Rapids, 50
  n. 5, 386 n. 6

Form for the Administration of
Baptism, 12, 13, 13 n. 20, 285,
291 n. 38, 359–60, 359 n. 44,
360, 365
Form for the Administration of the
Lord's Supper, 291 n. 38
Formula of Subscription, 182 n. 22,
302 n. 12
Fourteenth St. CRC, Holland,
Mich., 50 n. 5
Frame, John M., 205–6, 205 n. 9
Francken, Aegidius, 9, 9 n. 10
on covenant, 10 n. 12
free offer. *See* well-meant offer of
the gospel
Free Reformed Churches, 17 n. 31
free will, 85, 232, 243–44, 412 n. 22

G

gemeene gratie. See common grace,
Kuyperian
general grace (*algemeene genade* of
the Secessionists), 95, 262, 264
general promise, 277–280, 298–99,
299 n. 6
De Wolf's position on, and well-
meant offer of the gospel,
305–8
general revelation. *See* revelation
Gereformeerde Kerk in Nederland
(GKN), 17
Gezelle-Meerburg, G. F., 7 n. 4
gifts of God to mankind, 69
common grace and, 79–83
GKN. *See* Gereformeerde Kerk in
Nederland (GKN)
good works. *See* salvation, good
works and
gospel, preaching of, and PRC,
85–91

gospel offer. *See* well-meant offer of
the gospel
grace, PR definitions of, 69, 80
Groen, Johannes, 33 n. 26, 77, 147

H

Hanko, Cornelius, 300, 303
headship of Adam and Christ. *See*
federal covenant theology
Heidelberg Catechism, 16, 65 n. 28,
219, 290 n. 38, 328 n. 27, 333,
334, 365, 411
hermeneutics, 415
defined, 162 n. 6
Heyns, William, 51, 84 n. 41, 203,
318–19
on baptism, 366–67
on doctrine of covenant and
promise of God, 268–71, 280–
81, 280 n. 10, 354–56
higher criticism of Scripture, 104
n. 9, 163, 166–67, 168, 174–75,
225 n. 39
Janssen's use of, 37–42
history, church. *See* church, history
of
Hodge, Charles, 340–41, 340 n. 1
Hoeksema, Herman
charge of rationalism against, 84
n. 41, 200–203, 207–11
condemnation of Janssen's views,
43–44
contributions of, to doctrine of
covenant, 318–19
CRC synod of 1924 and, 54–57
denial of well-meant offer, 207
deposition of, by CRC classis,
117, 119–20
differences between Schilder
and, 299–300

incomprehensibility of God, 203–5,
204 n. 7, 208–11
independentism, 22, 113, 278, 278
n. 4, 278 n. 5, 311 n. 22
infallibility, proof of Scripture's,
169–70
infant baptism. *See* baptism, of infants of believers
infralapsarianism, 97, 248, 248 n.
33
inspiration, in the writing of Scripture, 170–71
common grace and, 168
doctrine of Scripture and,
164–65
human element and, 167–68
seen as miracle, 166, 170–71
Institutes of the Christian Religion (by
John Calvin), 7

J

Janssen, Ralph, 104 n. 9, 145, 168
application of common grace to
biblical studies of, 38–41
CRC controversy over views of,
37–42
denial of miracles by, 128–29
higher critical views condemned
by 1922 synod of CRC, 41,
129
infallibility of Scripture and,
159
jongeren movement, 36

K

Kalamazoo, First CRC of, 52, 54,
107
knowledge, extent of man's, 210
Kok, B., 114 n. 25, 287–88, 288 n.
30, 288 n. 31, 294 n. 44
Kuiper, H. J., 272 n. 29, 280

Kuyper, Abraham, 14–15, 144, 221
on the antithesis, 176–78
on atonement for the elect only,
15
on baptism, 15–16, 366
Dutch immigrant followers of
Doleantie of, 34
Hoeksema's attack on common
grace views of, 91–92
Hoeksema's critique of common
grace position of, 35–37
Neo-Calvinsim of, 31–32
objections to well-meant offer
of, 15
on organic unity, 232–33
position on common grace and,
15–16, 30–31, 31 n. 20, 43–44,
72–77
regeneration and, 16, 409

L

labor unions, 181–82, 186–93
doctrine of antithesis and,
186–93
Later Reformation, 8, 8 n. 8, 11
latitudinarian party, 36
LC. *See* Liberated Churches (LC)
Liberated Churches (LC), 18, 274.
See also Schilder, Klaas.
on baptism, 356, 366–67
beginning of, 274
differences between PRC and,
279–82, 299–300
immigrants from LC become PR
congregations in Canada, 288
view of covenant, 354–56
liturgy, 118. *See also* specific forms
logic, 211–14, 216
Luther, Martin, 6, 102, 102 n. 6,
217 n. 30, 218–19

M

man, as organism, 238–44

marriage, doctrine of, 382–84, 384 n. 1
  children and, 395–96
  covenant parents and, 396
  as creation ordinance, 391–93
  desertion of spouse, 384
  as earthly picture of heavenly relationship, 392–95
  history of, 384–89
  Hoeksema's change of view on, 390–91
  indissolubleness of, 393–95
  practical applications of, 397–98
  remarriage and, 387

Marrow Men, 8, 71 n. 6

Masselink, W., 143

ministers. *See* clergy

miracles
  Hoeksema's doctrine of, 129–39
  inspiration of Scripture and, 166–67, 170–71
  interpretations of, 132–34
  Janssen controversy and, 38, 40–41, 128–29
  particular grace and, 134–35
  providence and, 129–31
  as signs, 135–39

modernism, 7, 14

moral law, 146–47

movie attendance, doctrine of antithesis and, 193–94

N

natural light, mentioned in Canons III and IV, Art. 4, 94, 144 n. 9, 146, 146 n. 13, 147, 152, 347–48

Neo-Calvinism, 31–32

Nicea, Council of, and Nicene Creed, 5, 219

O

Olevianus, Caspar, 16, 317, 411

Ophoff, George M., 61–62, 103, 217 n. 31, 295, 387

organic
  Augustine's idea of concept, 231, 240
  characteristics of, 233–36
  Christ and His church as, 244–48
  covenant and covenant children as, 367–76
  creation as, 236–38
  development of sin as, 251–58
  man as, 238–44
  meanings of term, 230–31
  Scripture as, 171–73

Orthodox Presbyterian Church, 203, 204

P

Pactum Salutis, 285 n. 24, 293, 318, 332–39, 332 n. 37, 348, 406

paradox, doctrine of, 202, 207, 208
  rationalism and, 207, 211–14

particular grace. *See also* sovereign grace
  as central doctrine of PRC, 67
  in church history, 47–48
  as heart of Hoeksema's work, 51
  miracles and, 134–39
  objections to Hoeksema's view of, 52

Pelagianism, 5, 48, 86, 231 n. 3, 232 n. 4, 240, 244, 342 n. 5, 360

Petter, Andrew, 266 n. 3, 278, 286 n. 27

Pietism, 11, 31–32, 34

PRC. *See* Protestant Reformed Churches (PRC)

well-meant offer of the gospel
(*continued*)
  among Secessionists, 8–9
  Clark-Van Til controversy on,
    203–7
  common grace and, 70–72,
    83–91
  defined, 8 n. 7, 70
  De Wolf's position on, and
    conditional promise,
    305–8
  Helenius De Cock's position on,
    13–14
  Hoeksema's denial of, 207
  Kuyper's objections to, 15
  PRC and, 88–89
  rationalism and, 201–2
  RCA and, 23–25

Westminster Confession of Faith,
  164 n. 10, 385
will of God, 202–3
  decretive, 205
  hidden, 202
  preceptive, 205
  revealed, 202–3
  secret, 202
will of God's command, 90, 90 n.
  52, 202
will of God's decree, 90, 90 n. 52,
  202
works, covenant of, 16, 155 n. 33,
  267, 283, 318, 340–43, 343 n. 8
world-flight, 32
worldliness, 36, 57, 75 n. 16, 92, 96,
  181, 181 n. 21, 193–94
  antithesis and, 193–96

About the Author

Professor Herman Hanko holds an A.B. degree from Calvin College and a Th.M. degree from Calvin Seminary, Grand Rapids, Michigan. He received an M.Div. from the Theological School of the Protestant Reformed Churches in Grand Rapids, which is now located in Grandville, Michigan.

In 1955 the author was ordained as a minister of the gospel in the Protestant Reformed Churches. He served ten years in the pastoral ministry, first at Hope Protestant Reformed Church, Grand Rapids, then at Doon Protestant Reformed Church, Doon, Iowa. While at Doon, he accepted a call to teach at the Theological School of the PRC, where for thirty-three years he was professor of New Testament and church history.

In addition to his work at the seminary, Professor Hanko preached and lectured on behalf of the churches, both in the United States and abroad, and he continues to do this in retirement.

Over the years Professor Hanko has written countless articles for the *Standard Bearer* magazine and the *Protestant Reformed Theological Journal*. He has written syllabi for his seminary classes and authored the following:

Books
Far above Rubies: Today's Virtuous Woman (editor)
God's Everlasting Covenant of Grace
The Mysteries of the Kingdom: An Exposition of the Parables
Portraits of Faithful Saints
Ready to Give an Answer: A Catechism of Reformed Distinctives (co-author)
We and Our Children: The Reformed Doctrine of Infant Baptism

Pamphlets

"The Battle for the Bible"
"Biblical Ecumenicity"
"The Building of a Home"
"The Christian and the Film Arts"
"The Christian and the Social Gospel"
"Creation: Fact or Fiction"
"Ought the Church to Pray for Revival?"
"Phoebe: An Example for the Christian Woman"
"What It Means to Be Reformed"